"Rules against violence, bullying, child abuse, and sexual assault too often fail to improve safety while escalating the numbers of individuals incarcerated, separated from their families, schools, and chances for learning and starting anew. Restorative justice methods make inroads but remain marginal or even coopted by dominant and punitive approaches, but the authors of this book demonstrate how prevention strategies and rigorous efforts to strengthen relationships and communities can better protect individuals and communities from violence and other harms. Drawing lessons from settings as diverse as a nuclear power plant meltdown, auto industry cheating on emissions, and a sports stadium riot, to foster care crises and campus sexual assault and harassment, this book shows the elements in lasting solutions that draw on knowledge and build capacities of those most affected and the concentric circles of communities, professionals, and flexible systems focused on fixing problems rather than stigmatizing individuals."

Martha Minow, A.B., Ed.M., J.D.
Author, *Between Vengeance and Forgiveness*
300th Anniversary University Professor, Harvard University

"This groundbreaking collection from the leading theorists of responsive regulation and restorative justice offers an insightful investigation of alternatives to the prevailing punitive authoritarian approach to human services and regulation. Contributors offer impressive evidence of the benefit of an empowerment relational approach to human services as well as the ability of ordinary citizens to, in turn, demand state and market accountability – whether on behalf of nursing home residents, farmworkers, or child-welfare involved African American mothers. The book places restorative justice and responsive regulation in dialogue and examines critically overlapping goals as well as divergence. It is a must-read not only for human service providers and policy makers, but for all who seek justice and who believe in the capacity of communities to create social change."

Donna Coker, B.S.W., M.S.W., J.D.
Professor of Law
University of Miami Law School

RESTORATIVE AND RESPONSIVE HUMAN SERVICES

In *Restorative and Responsive Human Services*, Gale Burford, John Braithwaite and Valerie Braithwaite bring together a distinguished collection providing rich lessons on how regulation in human services can proceed in empowering ways that heal and are respectful of human relationships and legal obligations. The human services are in trouble: combining restorative justice with responsive regulation might redeem them, renewing their well-intended principles. Families provide glue that connects complex systems. What are the challenges in scaling up relational practices that put families and primary groups at the core of health, education and other social services?

This collection has a distinctive focus on the relational complexity of restorative practices. How do they enable more responsive ways of grappling with complexity than hierarchical and prescriptive human services? Lessons from responsive business regulation inform a reimagining of the human services to advance wellbeing and reduce domination. Readers are challenged to re-examine the perverse incentives and contradictions buried in policies and practices. How do they undermine the capacities of families and communities to solve problems on their own terms?

This book will interest those who harbor concerns about the creep of domination into the lives of vulnerable citizens. It will help policy makers and researchers to re-focus human services to fundamental outcomes at the foundation of sustainable democracies.

Gale Burford is Emeritus Professor of Social Work, University of Vermont, and currently a visiting scholar of restorative justice at Vermont Law School. Until his retirement from University of Vermont in 2014, he was Director of the University-State Child Welfare Training Partnership and Principal Investigator for the Vermont Community Justice Consortium. Gale first came to university teaching and research in 1981 at Memorial University of Newfoundland with experience as a foster and group home parent, caseworker and social work practitioner, trainer, supervisor, manager and senior administrator in services for children, young people and their families. He has taught, carried out research and program evaluation activities and consulted with programs internationally mainly on social work in statutory settings including child protection, youth justice and corrections. His best known research focuses on the use of family engagement and restorative approaches at the intersection of child protection and interpersonal violence.

John Braithwaite is a professor at RegNet (the School of Regulation and Global Governance) at the Australian National University. Since 2004 he has led a comparative project called Peacebuilding Compared (see johnbraithwaite.com). He also works on business regulation and the crime problem. His best known research is on the ideas of responsive regulation and restorative justice. Braithwaite has been active in the peace movement, the politics of development, the social movement for restorative justice, the labor movement and the consumer movement, around these and other ideas for 50 years in Australia and internationally.

Valerie Braithwaite is an interdisciplinary scholar and professor of regulatory studies in RegNet (School of Regulation and Global Governance), Australian National University. With a disciplinary background in psychology, her work focuses on how relationships of hope, trust and distrust ebb and flow between regulators and regulatees with often unexpected outcomes for society. Her work encompasses a diverse range of fields including human services. On behalf of the Australian Government, Braithwaite has conducted reviews of regulation in higher education and vocational education. Her most recent report "All Eyes on Quality" addresses how regulation can build learning communities and incentivize high performance and innovation.

RESTORATIVE AND RESPONSIVE HUMAN SERVICES

Edited by Gale Burford, John Braithwaite and Valerie Braithwaite

Routledge
Taylor & Francis Group

NEW YORK AND LONDON

First published 2019
by Routledge
52 Vanderbilt Avenue, New York, NY 10017

and by Routledge
2 Park Square, Milton Park, Abingdon, Oxon, OX14 4RN

Routledge is an imprint of the Taylor & Francis Group, an informa business

© 2019 Taylor & Francis

Library of Congress Cataloging-in-Publication Data
Names: Burford, Gale, author. | Braithwaite, John, author. | Braithwaite, V. A. (Valerie A.), 1951– author.
Title: Restorative and responsive human services / Gale Burford, John Braithwaite & Valarie Braithwaite.
Description: Abingdon, Oxon ; New York, NY : Routledge, 2019.
Identifiers: LCCN 2018049171 (print) | LCCN 2018051173 (ebook) | ISBN 9780429398704 (Ebook) | ISBN 9781138387119 (hardback) | ISBN 9780367026165 (pbk.)
Subjects: LCSH: Restorative justice. | Human services.
Classification: LCC HV8688 (ebook) | LCC HV8688 .B87 2019 (print) | DDC 361.2—dc23
LC record available at https://lccn.loc.gov/2018049171

ISBN: 978-1-138-38711-9 (hbk)
ISBN: 978-0-367-02616-5 (pbk)
ISBN: 978-0-429-39870-4 (ebk)

DOI: 10.4324/9780429398704

To Kathleen (Kathy) Burford

From Gale, John and Val

From Gale: Thank you for years of love, support and for being the "village" behind such efforts as this book.

From Val and John: Thank you, Kathy, for all your help and allowing Gale to visit us in Australia. Val insists that John apologize for his lapses in supervision with Gale and we both sincerely hope the soccer ball did no permanent damage.

And to Gale and Kathy's grandchildren and great-grandchildren, and to Val and John's grandchildren, two of whom were born in the final run to finishing this volume, providing joyful distraction for John and Val from Gale's all-hours-of-the-night emails.

CONTENTS

List of Figures   *xi*
List of Tables   *xii*
Contributing Authors   *xiii*
Preface   *xv*
by Gale Burford

1 Introduction: Restorative and Responsive Human Services   1
   Gale Burford, John Braithwaite and Valerie Braithwaite

2 Broadening the Applications of Responsive Regulation   20
   John Braithwaite, Valerie Braithwaite and Gale Burford

3 Families and Schools That Are Restorative and Responsive   38
   Valerie Braithwaite

4 Burning Cars, Burning Hearts and the Essence of Responsiveness 56
   Brenda Morrison and Tania Arvanitidis

5 Familiness and Responsiveness of Human Services: The Approach of
   Relational Sociology   74
   Elisabetta Carrà

6 Families and Farmworkers: Social Justice in Responsive and
   Restorative Practices   91
   Paul Adams

7 Children's Hopes and Converging Family and State Networks
  of Regulation   100
  Joan Pennell, Kara Allen-Eckard, Marianne Latz, and Cameron Tomlinson

8 Black Mothers, Prison, and Foster Care: Rethinking Restorative Justice   116
  Dorothy E. Roberts

9 Responding Restoratively to Student Misconduct and Professional
  Regulation: The Case of Dalhousie Dentistry   127
  Jennifer J. Llewellyn

10 Restorative Justice and Responsive Regulation in Higher Education:
  The Complex Web of Campus Sexual Assault Policy in the United States
  and a Restorative Alternative   143
  David R. Karp

11 Responsive Alternatives to the Criminal Legal System in Cases of Intimate
  Partner Violence   165
  Leigh Goodmark

12 Responsive and Inclusive Health Governance Through the Lens of Recovery
  Capital: A Case Study Based on Gambling Treatment   179
  David Best and Amy Musgrove

13 Why Do We Exclude the Community in "Community Safety"?   195
  Robin J. Wilson and Kathryn J. Fox

14 Learning from the Human Services: How to Build Better Restorative Justice
  and Responsive Regulation   210
  John Braithwaite, Gale Burford and Valerie Braithwaite

Index   *235*

FIGURES

2.1	The Regulatory Pyramid	24
2.2	Swiss Cheese Model of Risk Prevention	26
2.3	Regulation for Harm Minimization	27
2.4	Regulatory Assumptions and Approaches	29
2.5	Enforcement Pyramid and Strengths-based Pyramid	32
5.1	Graph of the alleged familiness of Education FGCs	82
5.2	The responsive regulatory pyramids of familiness and defamilization	84
10.1	The Regulatory System for Campus Sexual Assault	146
10.2	Braithwaite's Sanctioning Pyramid Adapted for Campus Sexual Assault Regulation	151
10.3	Whole Campus Restorative Justice Approach to Campus Sexual Assault	153
12.1	Conceptual framework of a recovery-oriented system of care	182
12.2	The Regulatory Diamond	186
12.3	Regulatory processes and responsive regulation	190

TABLES

5.1	Alleged familiness of Education FGC	83
7.1	CCPT Survey	107
7.2	Service Provider Survey	108
7.3	Service Provider Survey	109
10.1	Rates of Campus Sexual and Gender-Based Victimization (University of Texas)	144
10.2	Distinguishing Regulatory Formalism and Responsive Regulation for Campus Sexual Assault	159

CONTRIBUTING AUTHORS

Paul Adams, Professor Emeritus of Social Work, University of Hawaii at Manoa, Honolulu, Hawai'i, USA

Kara Allen-Eckard, Center for Family and Community Engagement, Center for Family and Community Engagement, North Carolina State University, Raleigh, North Carolina, USA

Tania Arvanitidis, PhD student, School of Criminology, Simon Fraser University, Burnaby, British Columbia, Canada

David Best, Professor of Criminology, Centre for Regional Economic and Social Research, Sheffield Hallam University, Sheffield, United Kingdom

Elisabetta Carrà, Associate Professor, Family Studies and Research, University Centre, Catholic University of Milan, Milano, Italy

Kathryn J. Fox, Associate Dean, College of Arts & Sciences, Professor of Sociology, Director, UVM Liberal Arts in Prison Program (LAPP), Department of Sociology, University of Vermont, Burlington, Vermont, USA

Leigh Goodmark, Professor and Director of Gender Violence Clinic, Maryland Carey School of Law, Baltimore, Maryland, USA

David R. Karp, Professor of Sociology, Director of the Project on Restorative Justice, Skidmore College, Saratoga Springs, New York, USA

Marianne Latz, Center for Family and Community Engagement, North Carolina State University, Raleigh, North Carolina, USA

Jennifer J. Llewellyn, Professor of Law, Yogis & Keddy Chair in Human Rights Law, Schulich School of Law, Director of Restorative Approach International Learning Community, Commissioner for Restorative Public Inquiry into the Nova Scotia Home for Colored Children, Dalhousie University, Halifax, Nova Scotia, Canada

Brenda Morrison, Director of Centre for Restorative Justice and Assistant Professor, School of Criminology, Simon Fraser University, Burnaby, British Columbia, Canada

Amy Musgrove, Principal Lecturer, Deputy Head of Criminology, Department of Law and Criminology, Sheffield Hallam University, Sheffield, United Kingdom

Joan Pennell, Professor Emerita, Department of Social Work, and Founding Director, Center for Family and Community Engagement, North Carolina State University, Raleigh, North Carolina, USA

Dorothy E. Roberts, George A. Weiss University Professor of Law & Sociology, Raymond Pace & Sadie Tanner Mossell Alexander Professor of Civil Rights, Professor of Africana Studies, University of Pennsylvania, Philadelphia, Pennsylvania, USA

Cameron Tomlinson, Center for Family and Community Engagement, North Carolina State University, Raleigh, North Carolina, USA

Robin J. Wilson, Assistant Clinical Professor (Adjunct) of Psychiatry and Behavioural Neurosciences, McMaster University, Hamilton, Ontario, Canada, and Psychologist, Wilson Psychology Services LLC, Sarasota, Florida, USA

PREFACE

Long in the making, this volume consists mainly of chapters that build from papers presented by their primary authors at the *Restorative Justice, Responsive Regulation and Complex Problems* conference held at the University of Vermont in June 2014. I say build as we gave authors encouragement to reflect on conversations that came out of their presentations and on their work since. Given that all the authors are established scholars and researchers, we didn't want to miss the potential for their ongoing work to help the volume take shape. And in one case we extended the invitation to authors who were not at the conference but whose research opens up an important and relevant vista in the human services (Best and Musgrove, Chapter 12 this volume).

Of course, the marriage of restorative justice and responsive regulation has a much longer research and relational trajectory than just this volume with roots in the work and generosity of John and Valerie Braithwaite.

It is now 30 years since John and Valerie Braithwaite started working on Restorative Justice and Responsive Regulation of care for the aged (see Braithwaite, Makkai, & Braithwaite, *Regulating Aged Care*, 2007) and over 15 years since John's book *Restorative Justice and Responsive Regulation* (2002) was published. Restorative justice and responsive regulation represent vibrant traditions of scholarship and practice (see special issue of *Regulation & Governance*, Volume 7, 2013) but they have continued to travel on mainly separate tracks and tend to be understood as matters best suited to criminal justice, when they are understood at all.

This volume benefits from the generous support of many people over a considerable period of time. Some brief context is offered. My colleague Dr. Joan Pennell and I were introduced to John Braithwaite in the early 1990s while we were involved with ground work that led to the *Family Group Decision Making Project* in the Canadian Province of Newfoundland and Labrador. John's generosity, originality, productivity, ebullience and substance as a scholar were already widely known and, like so many others, we benefitted instantly from the introduction. Soon after, we were introduced to Valerie's long and deep pool of scholarship connecting corporate and human service regulation, her work on the centrality of hope and motivation in behavior change, and in child and family welfare, all of which is since evident in both our own scholarly records.

Happily, one thing led to another. As the Canadian project was winding down, informal discussions amongst a group consisting mainly of North American social workers who had contributed to my and Joe Hudson's edited volume *Family Group Conferencing: New Directions in Community-Centered Child and Family Practice* (2000) continued to be stimulated by John and Val's work. At the same time our work was finding its way, thanks to them, into their large and interdisciplinary networks of connections internationally. And we dug further into their scholarship spanning disciplines we yearned to see connected in North America. This was especially so for me with many re-readings of John's chapter "Democracy, Community and Problem Solving" (2000). That was two years prior to the publication of his book *Restorative Justice and Responsive Regulation* (2002) which more or less the same group of us snapped up rather quickly, intrigued in particular with the idea of *responsive regulation*. The phrase awakened interest in discussions that had either grown pretty stale in the disciplines in which we toiled or were fraught with conflict. The other *R*-word (regulation) was for the most part lumped in with compliance, a topic many people think only authoritarians would relish talking about, except maybe for those in the human services who had long-examined theory and practice strategies for working with the "involuntary client". But those conversations too often sit alongside separation-focused and bifurcating discussions invoking talk of "perpetrators", "oppressors" and other totalizing and stigmatizing labels that perpetuate continuing constructions of them as alien beings; "others" who must be individualized, studied, managed and regulated separately from their relations as members of communities and families, often with considerable impacts on their capacities to take up roles as students, employees and even as citizens. Years of dominance, as would be described so well by scholars who later unearthed the nuanced impacts of "crime logic" (Coker, 2016), the carceral "dance" of criminal justice (Kim, 2014), and the "creep" of the ethos of commodification into all aspects of social and political life (Drahos, 2017) would track back to authoritarianism by any other name, that dominated and fueled the systematic buildup of un-responsive regulatory systems. Systems, as is seen from several chapters in this volume, that have shown immunity to challenge from the very persons, families, communities and cultures most affected.

Those informal discussions led to Paul Adams taking up the challenge of guest editing a special issue of the *Journal of Sociology and Social Welfare* (Volume 31, 1, 2004) that sought to extend RJ and RR by reconceptualizing, mainly within the discipline of social work, the relation between care and control, two themes discussed in that issue that have historically contributed to theoretical, practice and research divides within that discipline (Burford & Adams, 2004). That volume skyrocketed into scholarly obscurity with few citations, few reviews and little other response, with notable exceptions from a small handful of international scholars. It served mainly to stimulate further conversations among a somewhat expanded international and multi-disciplinary group.

The idea of holding a themed, international conference took shape and was held at the University of Vermont. Hosted by a wide range of partners and contributors the title *Restorative Justice, Responsive Regulation and Complex Problems* was the source of some amusement and suspicion, especially the responsive regulation part, but aroused considerable curiosity and interest partly in its rather wordy defiance of contemporary preferences for pithy short titles for conferences. The conference attracted local, national and international scholars, practitioners, state policy and administration leaders and a smattering of legislators. Feedback from the conference praised the high quality of speakers, many of whom appear in this volume.

Much has happened since then that impacts on this volume. I mention only two. One occurred during the process of preparing the proposal for submission of this volume to Routledge resulting in our dropping *complex problems* from the title and bringing a focus on the human services front and center.

We reasoned that complexity theory remains in its early stages especially in the social sciences where relatively few scholars have stepped outside their disciplinary and research-funded silos and substantively tackled it. The stratified disciplinary and academic structures, echo chambers, as it were, have long frustrated efforts to try on creative solutions and to refine, reconfigure and respond over time. To use a metaphor from John's work, there is still too much emphasis on bricks-and-mortar and not enough on building tents that can be taken down and moved, or adjusted, in the face of failing strategies, emerging trends and learning. Instead, we decided to ask our authors to include some comment on the history of failure to address complexity in their area of writing. I owe a thanks to Chris Koliba at the University of Vermont for his presentations on complexity theory in my classes over a number of years before I retired from teaching. Conversations with him helped, along with John and Valerie's usual thoughtfulness, to bring me around to accepting that the complexity theme was too much to tackle head-on for this volume. The human services focus opened the terrain beyond conceiving of restorative justice within criminal justice parameters and helped deepen discussions of regulation as a complex relational concern about injustice and involves everyone.

The second significant shift came with an invited visit courtesy of the School of Regulation and Global Governance (RegNet) and the Crawford School of Public Policy at Australian National University (ANU) College of Asia & the Pacific for me to spend January and February of 2017 in residence. RegNet (pronounced "reg" as in the first part of the word *regulation*) was established by John and Valerie Braithwaite in 2000. RegNet is the most fully realized example of interdisciplinary research and inquiry being carried out in a fresh and enthusiastic spirit of collegiality that I have experienced in my now 50+ year career.

As if spending time with John and Valerie and their colleagues in the stimulating environment of RegNet, and the network of people that constitute Canberra as a Restorative City weren't enough, the visit happily corresponded with the publication by ANU Press of a volume called *Regulatory Theory: Foundations and Applications* (2017) edited by Peter Drahos, a founding member of RegNet, who has since moved on to the European University Institute as Professor of Law. That volume has done more to shape my thinking, including further challenging some of my own disciplinary orthodoxy, than anything since first reading John's 2002 publication. I am grateful to RegNet and the Crawford school and trust that my good fortune is passed along to readers in a way that will stimulate and deepen their appreciation of regulatory theory.

Such is the originality and impact of John and Valerie's work, along with their RegNet colleagues, that I must say my name appears as first editor on this volume with them only at their insistence. True, I have worked to be a catalyst and connector but that merely speaks to recognizing good ideas and fine people when I see them. I took the liberty of writing this preface to thank John and Valerie, but also to spare them the page-after-page embarrassment of reading their own ideas, even their own words (that appear on the page in most of my own writing these days), in chapters that bear my name, and from having to constantly speak about themselves in the third person! Let me be clear, I am quite happy to join them in this work and integrate it into my own but the conference and this volume have always been about inviting others to deepen the conversations about justice, regulation, and the hopes for careful exploration of the relevance of this work in areas where it is most needed.

The Preface serves one other purpose. To thank the authors of the chapters whose ongoing conversations and relationships with me throughout this journey have continued to challenge and deepen my learning; but also for taking up the challenge of grappling with the *R*-word and taking us to new places. Thanks to Ellen Boyne, Kate Taylor, Autumn Spaulding and Emma Harder at Routledge. Ellen's encouragement and support paved the way from the very beginning and Kate's, Autumn's and Emma's timely and supportive responses and guidance have made it a smooth ride. Great team. Thanks to Kathy Burford, again, for expert editing and to Diane Richer (Vermont), Yan Zhang and Jacinta Mulders (Canberra) for formatting and research assistance, Rick and Elizabeth for cover consultation and encouragement and to a certain DIY-in-residence person in Australia who seems to know how to do everything but prefers to remain anonymous. And to the wonderful people at RegNet especially Mary Ivec, John and Valerie and others who went out of their way to ensure that my time there was comfortable and positive.

by Gale Burford

References

Adams, P., & Chandler, S. M. (2004). Responsive regulation in child welfare: Systematic challenges to mainstreaming the family group conference. *Journal of Sociology and Social Welfare, 31*(1), 93–116.

Braithwaite, J. (2000). Democracy, community and problem solving. In G. Burford & J. Hudson (Eds.), *Family group conferencing: New directions in community-centered child and family practice* (pp. 31–39). New York: Aldine de Gruyter.

Braithwaite, J. (2002). *Restorative justice and responsive regulation.* Oxford, UK: Oxford University Press.

Braithwaite, J., Makkai, T., & Braithwaite, V. (2007). *Regulating aged care: Ritualism and the new pyramid.* Cheltenham, UK: Edward Elgar.

Burford, G., & Adams, P. (2004). Restorative justice, responsive regulation and social work. *Journal of Sociology and Social Welfare, 31*(1), 7–26.

Burford, G., & Hudson, J. (Eds.). (2000). *Family group conferencing: New directions in community-centered child & family practice.* New York: Aldine de Gruyter.

Coker, D. (2016, December). Crime logic, campus sexual assault, and restorative justice. *Texas Tech Law Review,* 146–210.

Drahos, P. (Ed.) (2017). *Regulatory theory: Foundations and applications.* Canberra: ANU Press, The Australian National University.

Kim, M. (2014). The mainstreaming of the criminalization critique: Reflections on VAWA 20 years later. *CUNY Law Journal.* VAWA @ 20. Online publication.

Parker, C. (Guest Editor) (2013). Special Issue: Twenty years of responsive regulation: An appreciation and appraisal. *Regulation & Governance, 7*(1).

1

INTRODUCTION

Restorative and Responsive Human Services

Gale Burford, John Braithwaite and Valerie Braithwaite

The overall goal of this book is to advance the understanding and fit of restorative justice and responsive regulation, its achievements and limits, evidence and trajectories with particular focus on the ways their theories and applications serve as a bridge between disciplines and between formal and informal human services. We take up restorative justice as justice that heals the harms that derive from injustice and regulation as what we do when obligations are not being honored. Many of the chapters in this collection show that this makes restorative justice a relational form of justice. As will be discussed in greater detail, responsive regulation builds from a framework of empowerment and aims to engage actors in cooperating with the development of the details of how their obligations will be met even when their compliance could be required. Restorative justice coupled with responsive regulatory strategies help chart practical pathways for moving from healing to problem solving and contributes to the development of theory and research relevant to tackling complex social problems.

While there are many wonderful collections on restorative justice this one has quite a distinctive focus. First, it is about exploring the ways that the nuance of restorative and relational theory enables more responsive ways of grappling with complexity than do hierarchical and prescriptive intervention approaches to the human services. We will draw upon lessons from responsive business regulation to apply them to redesigning human services delivery to advance well-being, reduce domination and to respond more quickly in ways that are supportive and responsive to evolving circumstances.

Second, we examine the potential for restorative and responsive-relational theory, along with the empirical evidence and related strategies and competencies, to contribute to the broader project of developing and maintaining robust, resilient and responsive human services as a key pillar of a healthy civil society. This requires deepening our understanding of the complex interplay of markets and human or social capital that underwrite capitalism, democracy and justice that flourish together. In this view, the system of social welfare services is understood to play an important role in regulating what Drahos calls capitalism's three large-scale processes of destructive change that currently confront regulatory networks and institutions everywhere: eco-processes collapse, techno-processes collapse and financial processes collapse (2017, p. 761). We reiterate the prediction that both the scale and intensity of relationships between and among regulators and those being regulated will increase (Parker & Braithwaite,

DOI: 10.4324/9780429398704-1

2003; Drahos, 2017; Levi-Faur, 2011) and this presents, even necessitates, opportunities to re-think the aims and design of the human services as sites for advancing justice. When organized for coherence and responsiveness around the principles of equity and integrity, with account taken of emergent needs and risks, welfare services are good for business over time; not for business driven by maximum profit with no regard for its impacts on people, but for businesses that thrive in republican expressions of democracy (Braithwaite, 2002, 2008, 2013, 2017a; Hodges & Steinholtz, 2017). This means taking words like *regulation* and *welfare* back from their pejorative meanings, revisiting their underlying principles and aligning them as crucial elements of social and economic justice (V. Braithwaite, 2017).

Restorative Justice, Responsive Regulation and Republican Democracy

In the face of increasing evidence that despotic, authoritarian or simply invisible powerful hands control matters in everyday life for most citizens, the marriage of restorative justice and responsive regulation aims to encourage both the sense of possibility and responsibility. Both are vital components of innovative, purposeful and meaningful responses to complex human services challenges. But the hard questions remain about when, how, with whom and in what contexts to punish and when to persuade, when to enforce and when to support and how best to offer these processes so they invigorate mutual aid and self-help and regulatory capacities in affected social networks like groups, families and communities in the long run.

We take injustice to include harms that derive from crime, but we extend its scope to include experiences of relational, historical and structural injustice that may or may not involve legal constructions of wrongdoing. Restorative justice and responsive regulation offer a path forward for the timely sorting out of injustice in all spheres of human relations. This includes injustices seeded in structural imbalances of power and privilege that are so well known to regenerate and manifest themselves in the laws, policies and practices in human services, often cloaked in the best of intentions of the helping hand, but also often seen as politically driven tactics of repression and punishment. Restorative and responsive regulation is offered as a relational approach to program and service delivery and to engaging with the programs and providers themselves in holding to principled courses of action. This means accounting for the competent and ethical delivery of services by engaging in thoughtful problem analysis and enlisting stakeholders in partnerships while simultaneously remaining alert to the "creep" of excessive intrusion into the lives of citizens.

Such approaches sit within republican theory (Pettit, 1997; Braithwaite & Pettit, 1993) in which liberty is conceived to be freedom as non-domination. It is understood that any public protection or provision of security, including with the human services, involves some coercion. Lovitt and Pettit (2009) elaborate three ideas central to this notion of freedom. First, a free person is conceptualized as one who does not live under the arbitrary will or domination of others. By extension, a free state is one that promotes the freedom of its citizens without itself coming to dominate them. The third involves the obligations of citizenship; good citizenship requires vigilant commitment to preserving the state in its distinctive role as an "undominating protector against domination" (Lovitt & Pettit, 2009, p. 11).

The chapters of this book recurrently affirm the insight that human services without domination cannot be delivered without regulation of human services dominations, for example without regulation of abuse and neglect in aged care, without indigenous rights enforcement against child protection services that fail to honor the legislative principle of 'restoration' (the presumption in favor of restoring indigenous children to indigenous extended families, even if it is to grandparents rather than parents) (Behrendt, 2017).

Restorative justice and responsive regulation both seek to be forward-thinking, that is, moving to problem solving and to planning for the future. Both hold in common the view that punishment, when it is seen as excessive, unfairly administered, or is seen as a bluff, typically fails in its goals and often provokes defiance and a rippling loss of trust in the system of regulation. Quite often even backlash. They also hold in common that when people have access to safe, timely, fair and trustworthy means of having their grievances, including their experiences of persecution, or even questions about the way they are being treated, heard and understood, that the likelihood of conflict escalation and the associated costs are reduced. Then hopes of harmonious relations and reduced threat of continued strife are increased. We expect this to hold true in most areas of the human services including heath, education, social services and justice settings and encounters.

Despite its rapid increase in popularity and infusion into many areas of human services and human relations, restorative justice continues to be mainly understood as having value in criminal justice matters where the restorative justice practitioner brings all parties to an offense (the offender, law-enforcement agents and victims) together to discuss how each has been impacted, what can be done to repair or heal the effect of the harm and what needs to be done to keep further harms from occurring. The usual criminal justice conceptualizations and applications of restorative justice tend to either be fixed around diversion from legal processes or get offered wholly separately as voluntary post-legal healing opportunities. Law tends to be positioned at the center of these programs. As we enter into other areas, where the role of law and of the state is decentered to form regulatory partnerships that are hybrid, state-private, pluralistic and involve a range of formal and informal actors and stakeholders, the need for interdisciplinary research cooperation and fresh thinking about complexity is inescapable.

In its criminal law applications, a small number of disciplines and state agencies organized around crime, its reduction and its vast system of detection, prosecution, sentencing, incarceration and re-entry contribute to narrowing the spread and full realization of restorative justice. For example, scholars like Hanan (2018) argue that some restorative justice applications fail to offer genuine alternatives to the criminal court system by imposing criminal justice assumptions such as the requirement that a wrong-doer must admit to their wrongful behavior beforehand. Untested, assumptions rooted in the logic of criminal justice like this one may prefigure the process and perhaps mask outcomes that stakeholders prefer while hijacking the possibility that people may want to define their situation as a conflict for which they share responsibility.

Thus, in widening the scope to injustice, we refer to sites where the experiences of coercion and exclusion at the interpersonal level may or may not rise or best be dealt with as criminal matters can still rapidly escalate in harms to individuals and relationships, flare up through social and other media mechanisms and leave people relationally and economically, if not also physically, disadvantaged or harmed. Several chapters in this volume focus on examples of what Lejano and Funderberg (2016) might refer to as relational or "regulatory hotspots", or even "weak" spots that render vulnerable people and resources particularly exposed to exploitation and oppression. These include examples such as interpersonal violence, bullying, riotous behavior, organized labor, family and child safety, sexual behavior and assault in public institutions, community regulation and reintegration of sex offenders, and the impact of racialized decision processes associated with mass incarceration and the use of foster care with African-American families and gendered violence. But these could well be extended out into areas such as medical errors, unfair procedures in workplaces and schools and lopsided decision-making processes that range from environmental hazards and protections to personal choices about biological reproduction and health and the gendered use of power and control in relationships across a spectrum of relational and institutional settings (Gil & Bakker, 2006).

These examples all give testimony to the need to value pluralistic, multi-dimensional and interdisciplinary approaches to the study of social problems and recognition that it is in human encounters when people need help, including with self-regulation, that they are highly vulnerable to exploitation and manipulation by people and forces beyond their awareness and control. This necessitates careful and responsive examination of the multiplicity of influences including the excessive reach of market, state and professional powers that interact with complex rules and regulations that impact people's lives, and so often conflict with each other, but also from the persons in their own families and communities. We describe the ethical basis of the regulatory state in terms of its formal, juridical, deontological underpinnings. In contrast to this stands the alternative ethical concept of care, which is inherently relational, contextual and preferentially attentive to the needs of the vulnerable.

Restorative Justice: Praxis, Process, Social Movement and Law

Many advocates, including the present authors, have argued that restorative justice as a social movement has only partially succeeded in dissuading the entrenched power of the legal profession from resisting restorative reform. This is a major constraint to full realization of restorative justice in the human services. It is one of the reasons why the Vermont Law School, a nationally recognized top environmental law school, has taken up offering graduate and certificate programs in restorative justice: to take upstream the study and practice of law in its role to safeguard holistic principles that protect freedoms of people wanting to play active roles in solving their own problems and increasing their engagement in civil society.

Restorative justice is not simply a way of reforming the criminal justice system; it is a way of transforming the entire legal system, our family lives, our conduct in the workplace and our practice of politics. Its vision is of a holistic change in the way we do justice in the world. Yet, justice reform efforts mostly draw on internal traditions of reform within western traditions (Braithwaite, 2017b; Braithwaite & Zhang, 2017; van Ness & Strong, 2015; Zehr, 1990) and this is seen as a continued source of threat to indigenous and other sources of cultural and relational problem solving and conflict resolution (Blagg, 2017; Warren, 2016). Closer examination of the host historical, legal, policy and cultural contexts of both regulation and restorative justice is, as we will see, in need of careful and nuanced study from interdisciplinary and multi-cultural perspectives.

Access to restorative processes remains largely on the margins. This despite restorative justice having a presence in many corners of human activity and having inched its way into most spheres of conflict resolution, mediation, healing, victim aid, human resources and personnel work, human rights commissions and inquiries into historical wrongdoing across the human services and human relations spectrum. It is offered at the discretion of providers, a discretion mostly not exercised, as part of pilot projects, an add-on or alternative to taking matters to court. Its development is seen in fits and starts. A leader or a group takes up the work, falters when champions leave, funding ends, program mandates change. This is true of restorative justice in schools, a major domain of implementation. Yet, its rise in popularity is fueled in large measure by a heightened passion of people who want to do the "right thing", give people a "say" and find antidotes to the widespread perception that democracy has been hollowed out with poll-driven alarmist predictions of what inevitability is going to happen next. Organized around strengths and best hopes, one of the biggest challenges to the spread of restorative justice is the manipulation of public fear and anxiety that cyclically drives state and state-sponsored actors to justify assertions of control (Burford, 2018). "There is no other way" became a tag-line for neoliberal austerity and political trashing of "welfare" programs and further stigmatizing people in need of services as feckless and undeserving (Featherstone, White, & Morris, 2014; Morris & Burford, 2017).

Through a legal lens, restorative justice, like other forms of justice, can be understood as a mechanism for the maintenance or administration of conflicting claims and halting escalations of retaliation. Instead of relying strictly on legal protocols and rules, RJ works through cooperative behavior, dialog, negotiation and other processes such as mediation to arrive at agreements about the assignment of rewards and punishments. In a fully realized system of restorative and responsive human services, actors across systems from police, health, education, social services, child protection, management and administration would be armed, so to speak, with the regulatory enforcement and support tools of persuasion, negotiation, de-escalation, even coaxing (Braithwaite, 2010; Grabosky & Braithwaite, 1986; Wood, 2018) and other skills of the regulatory craft (Ivec, 2013; Morrison and Arvanitidis, Chapter 4 this volume); and would cooperate across systems in their use (Braithwaite & Harris, 2009; Cherney & Cherney, 2018; Featherstone et al., 2014; Featherstone et al., 2018; Grabosky, 1995; Harris, 2011; Ivec et al., 2015; Pennell, 2004; Pennell, Shapiro, & Spigner, 2011) as will be discussed more under the topic of responsive regulation.

Attending to Relational-Restorative Contexts

As is seen in several of the chapters in this volume, especially those addressing matters in the USA, where some of the world's most successful and creative expressions of human service innovation and experimentation can be found, there is also the enduring threat to democratic institutions that emanate from disproportionate treatment and outcomes by race, gender and inequality of wealth. These inequalities are well documented and traceable directly to the legal foundations of citizenship and privilege in the birth of the nation (Meacham, 2018; Saito, 2010). Mechanisms that hold inequality in place are understood to derive from complex interplay of law (Berman, 2006, 1983), narratives of exceptionalism and essentialism (Chase, 2018), religion (Morone, 2004; Wilson-Hartgrove, 2018; Van Molle, 2017), jurisdictional or interest-group centric constructions and interpretations of law and international law (Roberts, 2017; Saito, 2010), and even from what Chimamanda Ngozi Adichie (2009) calls 'The Danger of the Single Story'. They are reinforced largely through sanctioned decision processes and informal processes of relational influence.

The need to check bias in decision making is well researched (Sloman & Fernbach, 2018; Mercier & Sperber, 2017; Plaster, 2010; Tavris & Aronson, 2007) and important to this volume, but our scope goes beyond investigating and checking bias to further include the need for ongoing dialog including scrutiny of how comfortably the commitments to republican democracy fit with the on-the-ground outcomes and progress associated with social justice and human rights, and in how to make them work more closely in harmony. Done badly, restorative justice processes, like other regulatory interventions, are far from immune to capture or corruption (Strang, 2002; Braithwaite, 2002). Done well, restorative justice holds people to high standards for ethical and legal behavior and the practice of respect. Restorative justice itself, like all justice practices and policies, is seen to flourish in contexts where there is ongoing commitment to inclusive, relational and pluralistic decision making, including the principles of tripartism, the crucial role of "third-parties" addressed in detail in Chapter 2, subsidiarity, the preference for handling matters at the most local level, rather than stepping them up to a central authority, and forbearance, the practice of self-restraint, respect for the dignity of others and refraining from the exercise of power in order to encourage enlistment of self-regulation and cooperation.

We appreciate that in extending restorative justice and responsive regulation beyond the domains where they are most well understood as alternatives to criminal and civil law proceedings, or post-legal intervention healing, that we are leaving the door open rather wide to cover anything from a perceived slight, "put down" or misstep in decorum or ritual that causes discomfort all the way to heinous crimes repeated over generations against a group. We do value the 'restorative practices continuum' developed by the International Institute for Restorative Practices (IIRP, n.d.) that covers everything from heading off a budding conflict in a hallway conversation at school to formal proceedings or inquiries carried out under the auspices of a statutory authority or beyond. And we value fertile hybrids between restorative justice and other traditions, even as our focus is mainly with what McCold (2000) first attempted to characterize as fully restorative processes. In this he included processes such as community and family conferencing, peacebuilding circles and other processes that emphasize the use of face-to-face group meetings that bring together voluntary members of the affected relational network and go beyond technical and transactional settlements (Braithwaite, 1989, 2002; Llewellyn, 2011; Zehr, 1990).

In each, we see the need for considerable investment of time in relationship building. The undervaluing of time and human labor does not square well with the needs of the human services for building trust that is so essential to reciprocity, security and relational healing whether that is at the level of engagement with human services or in the governance of these services. The transactional commodification of time as labor that underwrites the investment in relationships bumps against the needs of responsive and relational human services. We prioritize processes that tie to wider social movements in which positive behaviors are supported and reinforced over time, but also processes in which people can integrate their healing, recovery, hopes and aspirations into citizenship, purposeful and meaningful activities, that is, into roles in which they feel they have a say and experience competence.

Which brings us to another important theme. John and Valerie have studied processes of shame, stigmatization and shame management extensively and we here revisit current understandings around these very sensitive subjects. We think it is a mistake to paper over the study of shame and stigmatization with superficial applications of strengths-based approaches or by underestimating the role of shame in healthy human development. We see unhealthy shame and unhealthy pride as profound dangers to human flourishing, while healthy shame and pride management are also vital. It is vital both that men consider rape as shameful and that men take pride in their contributions as men to families and work groups that affirm and strengthen gendered rights. As is well understood, the process of acknowledging past or present domination and agreeing to transcend it is almost by definition laden with shame for some or all of people involved. It exposes one to the risk of humiliation and even cruelty. Yet, this letting go and presenting one's self as vulnerable in the moment is also understood as the very path that can naturally lead to open expressions of pain and struggle, relief and release, to apology and forgiveness. It underwrites building relational, family, peer and mentoring connections and associations that transcend restorative meetings. As will be seen in chapters in this volume, these extended connections with peers that foster hope and practical opportunities to engage in purposeful and meaningful activities have been demonstrated as crucial to recovery from addictions, reintegration post-separation and in channeling trauma and frustration into narratives of growth and overcoming. We stress voluntary engagement while acknowledging the existence of power and influence in all relationships. What emanates from these processes contributes to building social-emotional intelligence, including building healthy strategies for shame management, and socialization into prosocial contexts of belonging that are characterized by dignity, the possibilities of forgiveness and the experience of having been treated justly.

The Restorative Journey: The Role of Places, Spaces and Stories

Before turning to the subject of regulation, we consider the role of narrative or "origin stories" and the values that lend themselves to more relational understandings of justice and regulation in the jurisdictional contexts in which they are used to guide policy, practice and research.

Oral traditions of indigenous peoples and recorded history show ways that people have ameliorated cycles of violence and revenge. Long rooted in most cultures and long pre-dating the codification of rights and protections in Asia, the Middle East and among most indigenous peoples and cultures of the Pacific, the Americas and Europe, certain enduring principles stand out as the basis of mediation, conflict resolution and relational reconciliation (Braithwaite, 2017b; Braithwaite & Zhang, 2017; Llewellyn & Downie, 2011; Llewellyn & Philpott, 2014; Zehr, 1990). They also sit at the core of most of the world's religions including Christianity, Islam, Buddhism (Braithwaite & Zhang, 2017; Kahn, 2006; Rich, n.d.) where conceptualizations of justice, charity and fairness are linked, and which constitute the bedrock visions for state-citizen relations in most modern conceptualizations of social justice and social welfare (Day, 2008). Broadly speaking, the Golden Rule about treating others as you would have them treat you, or the so-named Platinum relational revision about doing unto others as they would want done to them, sits at the heart of what matters. It is understood as the basis for continuing civility in social arrangements, heading off cycles of retaliatory escalation and holding open the door to possibilities of forgiveness and reconciliation while honoring the importance of kin and kith ties that are cross-cutting in social institutions in many societies from ancient times.

Despite what seems on the surface like compatibility, integrating indigenous and culturally embedded conceptualizations of justice into colonial constitutions and legal systems is fraught with challenges. Legal pluralism and hybridity have many desirable features and allow different traditions to learn from one another (Forsyth et al., 2018). Yet there are dangers that legal transplants from another culture into a colonial legal architecture can fatally threaten the holism or integrity of the lifeworld of that other culture (Blagg, 2017; Moyle & Tauri, 2016). At the same time it can be an error to view the holism or integrity of any culture as static or fully formed; at every point in history every legal culture inevitably adapts and changes in better and worse ways. It is vital for restorative and responsive reformers to be reflective and sensitive on these complex issues, and to apply restorative values of listening to those with views on them in particular contexts. It is a mistake to listen and never learn from non-western traditions of justice; it is a mistake to believe that it is a good thing for western universities to provide scholarships to non-western students to sit at the feet of western law professors, but an appropriation for westerners to sit at the feet of indigenous elders.

Some indigenous justice approaches have been seen as a legitimate way to contest, or provide a counter-weight to the weight of authoritarian creep through the lopsided administration of laws and rules and their disproportionate impact of advantage that the rule- and law-making systems give to people with the most access to institutionalized power. As was argued by some Māori leaders in New Zealand in the lead-up to their 1989 implementation of family group conferences (Children, Young Persons and Their Families Act, 1989; Ministerial Advisory Committee, 1986; Rangihau, 1986) in matters concerning the care and protection of children and youthful offending, it was the historical and continued harms perpetrated by state intervention that they wanted front and center in all considerations of their dealings with the state. This included disruption in their connections to and roles as stewards of natural resources, the forced separation of families from their kin and kith, including the removal of their children and young people and the systematic eradication of their languages all being accomplished through the administration of laws and policies that criminalized behaviors crucial to their survival and fostered shame (Kupumamae, n.d.). The dominant legal decision processes, they argued, were contributing through legally sanctioned decision-making processes to their own genocide. Masked in practices carried out in the name of mercy, charity, protection of children, education and progress were views that regarded them as primitive people whose culture should be regulated out of existence. The "origin story" of restorative justice in NZ, then, attends to far more than individual incidents of harm and focuses also on historical harm and decision-making processes. The family group conference was intended to invigorate contextual-relational understandings and discussions of the complex of ways in which harm and structural advantage occur, and to stand against single or dominant explanations that marginalize less powerful persons or groups. This requires vigilance to the "creep" of dominant and technical changes that can signal stepping away from central principles, especially empowerment. A 2005 international survey of restorative and family engagement practices found over 50 unique names in the USA for restorative practice that revealed more about the marketing of the practices and suggested erosion of principles meant to be driving the practice (Nixon et al., 2005).

We do not intend to place at the feet of restorative justice the responsibility for fixing all the structural inequalities in the world but we do agree that all restorative justice and regulatory responses ought to seek to be transformative by exposing ongoing disadvantage as in the case of gender and racially based violence and control, environmental harms and other complex structurally reproduced disadvantages. Justice that is restorative and responsive, according to this volume, should work to open new spaces for the law and social sciences to complement one another, for disciplines to set aside differences and work together to solve complex problems while supporting insider leadership of locally affected relational networks.

On the subject of complementarity and coordination, Gunningham, Grabosky and Sinclair (1998) pointed out that strategies like restorative justice could not sit in isolation, in silos, apart from other regulatory approaches. They must sit as strategies, combined or sequenced amongst others, avoiding incompatible combinations of strategies, yet embedded with other approaches available that have compatible aims: those of both ensuring that people step up to the plate to meet their obligations but also to restrain the excesses of state and powerful non-state actors from overreach into the lives of citizens. This extends to the role of research on the use of restorative justice that must examine the fit of restorative innovations within a continuum of restorative options and be understood within hybrid approaches to governance. This requires exploration of how restorative values and practices resonate with existing and emerging values and systems rather than being plugged in as set pieces to existing institutional forms. Responsiveness can in this way be seen as principled hybridity with restorative justice that responsively checks and balances restorative justice principles. Understanding restorative justice in such ways helps us understand what restorative justice informed decision processes and systems might look like across institutional, disciplinary settings and environmental contexts. Hence, our interest is in more fully restorative practices driven by values and principles associated with the democratization of decision processes emphasizing pluralism, inclusion and unfettered access in working to achieve just processes and outcomes and to expand freedom (Llewellyn, 2011).

Responsive Regulation

Why indeed, to paraphrase Peter Drahos (2017) should a book, in this instance aimed mainly at people who toil in the human services, be devoted to understanding regulation? Drahos (2017) said of regulation that lawyers have long since turned it into a dull topic mainly concerned with authoritative rules issued by the state and how these rules get delegated into practice (xxvii). On the other hand, few words, especially in the USA, trigger off reactions as strong as "well-regulated militia" (US Constitution, 2nd Amendment). Frankly, it's a pretty confusing picture in the US where deregulation efforts beginning in earnest in the early 1980s resulted in an increase of regulations by more groups instead of fewer (Levi-Faur & Jordana, 2005; Jordana, Levi-Faur, & Marin, 2011; Braithwaite, 2006), although some might say that the deregulation movement has been more about gaming regulations by people with the most power than about reducing the number of regulations. To top it off, the system of rulemaking at the federal level in the US has become so "ossified" as to invite circumvention through presidential policy making that leaves the public and members of Congress in the dark about what is happening (Kovacs, 2017). Little wonder that confidence in this body is strained (NPR/PBS, 2018).

Regulation in the human services is even more confusing where it seems that many advocates of less government intrusion into people's lives advocate very specific controls such as drug testing to qualify for certain services and policing of women's exercise of reproductive rights. Evidence of racialized increases in regulatory intrusion when people attempt to board aircraft, excessive force in policing, incarceration, burgeoning foster care usage, proliferating drug testing, the use of graduated sanctions to withhold health care and social services all point to much greater regulation, scrutiny and use of punishment and exclusion of some groups (Abramowitz, 2018; Metzl & Roberts, 2014; Wu, Cancian, & Wallace, 2014). Untangling regulatory overreach from regulation that is necessary and desirable for security and well-being and are competently and ethically carried out is a theme of this book. From a republican perspective regulatory overreach is regulation that increases the amount of domination in the world; necessary and desirable regulation or deregulation is that which reduces domination. But these conceptualizations of regulation are only a part of why regulation should be on our minds.

Peter Drahos (2017) and Valerie Braithwaite (2017) both eloquently describe how ubiquitous regulation is in our daily lives, much of it informal and much of it beneath our immediate span of awareness. We may say "move along" when the person in front of us stops abruptly to check their cell phone while blocking the exit from the cinema. Or smile at a child's parent when that child is tending to another child's scuffed knee on the playground. Or demand to know "how can this be?" when we hear of a city where residents were not told their water was contaminated by city health officials. Ford (2018) shows how complicated is the relationship between innovation and regulation. On the one hand, regulation should support industriousness, creativity and strengthen self-reliance and self-regulation, but on the other it is hard to imagine life without some consensus about governance and what kind of relationships people prefer to have with each other.

For example, a PEW poll (2012) showed that overall Americans dislike the idea of regulation but when the aims and mechanisms of a particular regulation or a regulatory strategy are spelled out and clearly understood, people are more inclined to support a wide range of regulations and their entrenched views tend to dissipate. The same poll suggests that views of regulation are highly divided along political lines, particularly on certain hot-button topics.

In its responsive-relational use, regulation helps in the development of a less dominating society and in the development of theory, practice and new research propositions and approaches that can help more fully realize what it means for human services to be collaborative, to be offered in partnerships, to engage thoughtfully with complex problems, to avoid blame and retribution and reward success, citizenship and ethical behavior. It does this by re-centering government's role as but one strand in the production of well-being and security. Networked relations hold promise of improving standards relating to security, accountability and well-being while promoting healing and inclusivity in decision making as building blocks of empowerment practice (Braithwaite, 2002). Mimi Kim (n.d.) pointed out that "The first responders to a violent situation are usually friends, family, community members, and clergy. . . . Why aren't we doing more to equip them with the knowledge and the skills to be able to intervene effectively?" We go further in this volume to ask why aren't the members of these social networks, the informal relations, front and center in all human service considerations?

We take up this challenge as one of incorporating the ethic of "responsiveness" into all work in the human services. Quoting Selznick (1992, p. 336), Hong and You (2018) centered the notion of responsiveness as a cornerstone for maintaining "institutional integrity while taking into account new problems, new forces in the environment, new demands, and expectations" (p. 6). "Responsiveness in this context becomes a democratic ideal—responding to peoples' problems, environments, demands: 'responsiveness begins with outreach and empowerment . . . The vitality of a social order comes from below, that is, from the necessities of cooperation in everyday life'" (Selznick, 1992, p. 465 as cited in Hong & You, 2018, p. 7).

The responsive principle of tripartism, about which more will be said in Chapter 2, should be quite familiar and even agreeable to many practitioners in the human services who subscribe to contemporary empowerment practices that employ strengths-based strategies and techniques found in motivational interviewing (Miller & Rollnick, 2012), community oriented narrative approaches (Buckley & Decter, 2006), solution focused counseling (de Jong & Berg, 2002), certain family therapies (Denborough, 2001), behavioral health and primary care (SAMHSA-HRSA, n.d.), positive psychology (Snyder & Shane, 2006), social work (Saleeby, 2013) and learned optimism (Seligman, 1998).

Tripartism was originally invoked to highlight the limits of transactional relationships between the state and business (Braithwaite, 2018). With the worst excesses of business-state corruption almost any third party might help in exposing the corruption to the disinfectant of sunlight. The presence of third parties, which most often means a number of them, especially when confronting complex problems, increases the likelihood of cooperation and compliance with obligations to reduce domination. Regulation can too often be captured or corrupted by the power of money and other dominant sources of influence like lobbying. The more complex the regulatory environment and the higher the stakes, the more likely transactional approaches will fail. Engaging other actors who have a stake in the outcomes can offset the power dimensions. Witness the onslaught of power brought to bear on environmental protection concerns to protect financial interests. The amount of money Volkswagen was able to invest in software development to fool the emissions control inspectors was evidently worth the risk of fines it ultimately paid and even the sacrifice of its CEO. The importance of listening to multiple stakeholders and making responsive, that is, deliberative and flexible choices from regulatory strategies was key to the EPA finally eliciting an admission that VW was cheating. A key concept is that of the regulatory pyramid that conceptually arranges the possible strategies starting at the bottom of the pyramid with those that privilege persuasion over coercion, enlist cooperation over threat and encourage self-regulation and learning (see Chapter 2). In the human services, fully restorative justice processes move regulation to the level of inclusion of social networks of influence including family, group and community beyond the use of more transactional, individualized approaches to casework and therapy that are embedded in the very infrastructure of state-centered human services and often in their contracted-out services.

Widening the Circle of Justice Reform: A Human Services Context for Justice that Heals

We decided not to struggle too much with a definition of the human services. Their core concerns with the care and protection of children and the aged, education, health services broadly conceived, public housing, services for the disabled and protective services for the general population (such as ambulance, fire and emergency services) and various forms of social security is a clear enough core. Rather than become preoccupied with defining boundaries beyond that core, we are concerned about the contexts in which they are experienced by the people who need them, the ways they are governed and whether they are "any good". What makes the human services a unique site for the pursuit of justice? Having set out that restorative justice is essentially relational, we are interested in the economics of human capital that underwrites investment in a 'relational state' (Cooke & Muir, 2012). Consistent with the focus on human capital, Gill and Bakker (2006) point to the human services as being mainly about regulation of labor (as compared to market buying and selling) and particularly the investment of time that relationships involve when contrasted with transactional or contractual approaches.

The interplay of markets and human services is an important challenge to take up in re-visioning what virtue- and principle-driven human services would look like if they embraced checks and balances on the excesses of market manipulation and fostered full participation of people as citizens. It is a central conceit, an hypocrisy, that the opiate crisis in the USA and its interconnections with racialized use of incarceration, policies of zero tolerance, mandatory arrest and no-drop polices (Goodmark, Chapter 11 this volume), foster care (see Roberts, Chapter 8 this volume), including the now acknowledged inappropriate use of psychotropic medications with foster children and other interventionist handling of families in child protection (see Pennell et al., Chapter 7 this volume) are at the same time so well understood as products of both the legal and illegal manipulation by pharmaceuticals (Carr, 2018; DHHS, 2015; Dukes, Braithwaite, & Moloney, 2014; Jacobson, 2018; Villanueva, 2018) and damaging lack of regulatory oversight of pharmaceuticals with vulnerable populations (USGAO, 2011).

This is important in realizing the potentials for partnerships across settings where enlisting cooperation amongst actors who have vastly different funding sources and work parameters lacks support. Restorative justice practitioners who have spent time coaxing police officers to restorative city meetings or restorative sessions, let alone entreating them to imagine themselves as "public health interventionists" (Wood, 2018), or convincing medical and mental health personnel who are unable to bill for their time to attend a family's group conference, well understand the different value placed on their time and the underlying values behind the allocation of time as labor.

In this connection, we are mindful of the conceptualizations of the welfare state that took shape in the 20th century and how these positioned the state or government at the center of the protection and promotion of the social and economic well-being of its citizens. In his introduction to Esping-Andersen's *Welfare States in Transition* (1996), Dharam Ghai (1996) pointed out that "despite the progress made by Western welfare states in the centuries-old struggles to achieve social protection and security, social policy is in such a state of flux that advanced welfare states are under siege" (p. vi). Indeed, in the USA the grand accomplishments since the New Deal as laid out by the American Academy of Social Work and Social Welfare (2013) are many, and so are the regulatory challenges.

Comparing business regulation with regulation in the welfare state, Mabbett (2011) says that labor market regulations "reach deep into the heart of the welfare state . . . having pronounced implications for social policy, even while its proponents seek to preserve national welfare state competencies" (p. 14). She points to the strong impact on the welfare state of ideas and institutions exerting what she calls "a race-to-the-bottom dynamics in welfare provision" warning that liberalism's notions of safeguarding domestic stability no longer constrain market integration (2010). Gill and Bakker (2006) argue that in the era of neoliberalism, the welfare state is trampled under the forward march of global capitalism. But we caution that this may over-romanticize past eras. The argument that caring institutions were once governed by enabling professions and are now run over with profit motives needs to be understood alongside the reasons social, civil rights, shelter and anti-violence movements mobilized to call attention to the many abuses in foster and congregate care, hospitals, prisons and families and the ways that these same powers continue to reproduce themselves (see Llewellyn, Chapter 9 this volume; Llewellyn & Morrison, 2018).

These legacies endure. Beyond the "creep" of crime and commodification logic (Coker, 2016; Drahos, 2017) into everyday life, the historical evidence, as Saito (2010) points out, is abundant on the enduring impact of an "insistent and unilateral perspective of 'what's good for America is right for the world'" (as quoted in Higginbotham, 2012, p. 486; see also Roberts, 2017, on international law as western and exclusionary of the marginalized). Speaking of criminal justice reforms, Boyes-Watson (1999) also early on warned of the likely subversion of the very aims of criminal justice reforms when the state's role in restorative justice programming dominates non-state partner interests. Coker (2016) and Kim (2014) have described the "creep" of crime and "carceral" logic, while Heiner and Tyson (2017) and Whalley and Hackett (2017) point to "carceral" feminism, all pointing to authoritarianism by any other name, as interventions dominated by the criminal justice system, but which we argue extend well beyond into "business as usual" in the human services as top-down governance and regulatory formalism. Despite years of commitment to the rhetoric of empowerment, participatory governance, student-centered learning, patient-centered medicine and family- and community-engaged practice, the drift is back to command-and-control. Heiner and Tyson (2017) warn for example that repackaging justice as caring in the guise of gender-responsiveness still looks like carceral-authoritarian control instead of genuinely reducing and undoing domination and the reproduction of injustice.

What is seen by some as the widespread failure of the welfare state can also be understood as at best a widespread failure to regulate capitalism and at worst a deliberate extension of the politics of enslavement and exclusion (Hyslop, 2016; Roberts, 2002, 2012). Few would now dispute that the extremes in wealth accumulation and disparity are the result of the power of money to game laws and to use the legal system in the favor of corporate interests and that welfare state services do not get to the citizens who are most needy (Bywaters et al., 2014; Katznelson, 2006; Piketty & Goldhammer, 2013; Wilkinson & Pickett, 2009). Yet, prosecutors devote more resources to prosecuting welfare fraud than to financial crimes that create the kinds of mass welfare dependency that we saw following the sub-prime mortgage crisis (Friedrichs & Schwartz, 2008). The important focus may be as much or more about ensuring that people are brought up to a "floor" as trying to put a lid on the ceiling.

It is also true that the infrastructure of welfare state services was designed for a very different time and set of circumstances than we presently face (Cottam, 2015). How do we conceive of human services in a time of great social reckoning especially in the USA around our history of race and gender, shifting economic lenses and volatile swings of partisanship that with each swing erase the investments in regulatory protections and innovation of the last regime?

This requires ongoing consideration of context and relational definitions of citizenship and the "floors", that is, the minimum standards for well-being (V. Braithwaite, 2004, 2006, 2009; Gill & Bakker, 2006; Lewellyn, 2011) and framing justice as a central concern across institutions, across disciplines, across sites of delivery of human services, and perhaps most importantly the complex responsive-relational interplay between and among these institutions and the ways they nurture, or undermine hope. Here we are speaking of hope, not of the kind that is passed along from top-down political or poll-driven declarations of promises, but hope of the kind empirically valorized by contributors to Valerie Braithwaite's (2004) special issue on hope; hope that is grounded in the aspirations of the every-day lives of citizens and realizable in the expression of freedom and in meeting of obligations as citizens.

Who Cares? Re-centering Justice in the Human Services

Adams and Nelson (1995), in their pioneering work centering human services in community and family contexts, asked "What would it be like if services were designed to strengthen rather than substitute for the caring capacity of families and communities?" (p. 2). Besides calling out the dangers of the state substituting for, and by extension harming the capacities of families and communities, they also acknowledged that "flexible, responsive, empowerment-oriented services already exist". Citing the ground-breaking work of Lisbeth Schorr (1988), they write that the crucial, most efficacious elements of the services shown to be of greatest worth, including responsiveness, are the very ones sacrificed when programs grow to scale. Typically, the elements that are eroded or simply taken away are those that have to do with processes associated with empowerment, particularly investments in human relationships (Adams & Chandler, 2004). Why would that be so? Who benefits? And to what ends?

As several chapters in this volume make clear, keeping the integrity of relationships with primary social groups and relational networks at the forefront of policy, research and practice has proven to be challenging for a variety of reasons. These include the disempowering impacts that legal, professional and other special interest influences can directly have on the self-help and mutual aid capacities of families and indirectly through the design of funding and reimbursement regulations. Beyond this are the long-standing fears that resurface from time-to-time that associate social group and community work with radical political activism (Andrews & Reisch, 1997, 2002; Reisch & Andrews, 2002; Specht & Courtney, 1995) and the structural challenges the human services are up against in achieving social justice and supporting people to exercise their rights. Individualized, case management and casework-driven processes in the human services have lent themselves to silencing of grievances, distancing of workers from clients and to separating them from allies in their social networks. This book locates the need to support the family, broadly defined, as a cornerstone of civil society (Burford, 2005; J. Braithwaite, 2004).

We take up Ghai's challenge to reimagine the welfare state and its human services as part of wider reforms beyond simply trying to save this or that service from the chopping block or ceding that a service or category of services ought to be offered by the state or privatized. The marriage of restorative justice and responsive regulation is best understood in the wider shifts occurring in governance from a top-down command and control emphasis to a state that de-centers, or perhaps re-centers regulation to better match conditions of high complexity. This involves new partnerships between government and non-government actors in hybrid, pluralistic arrangements, some self-directed, others part of relational networks that are negotiated. This trend, once thought of as a move to greater privatization of services, getting the state out of the business of providing direct services, is now understood in more flexible terms and necessary to sustain reforms (Patashnik, 2008).

The hybridization of governance, as applied in the human services, means that a service might be contracted out but taken back if a provider fails repeatedly to deliver, and returned to the state for reassessment. Reassessment might mean an end to privatization, re-contracting to another business provider or contracting to a charitable provider. The critical thing, according to our analysis, is that contractors can be responsively regulated. Levi-Faur (2011) argues that these relations can be understood as processes of governing capitalism through regulatory relationships that are "constitutive and mutually supportive rather than competitive and substitutive" (p. 3). It is this potential for a "happy marriage" in which "governments shed their responsibilities for service provision and shift more of their energies to regulate the service provision of diverse types of actors, including other state actors (Gilardi, Jordana, & Levi-Faur, 2006; Parker & Braithwaite, 2003; Jordana et al., 2011). This is neither privatization nor nationalization, neoliberalism, nor socialism nor conservatism. This is a way of bringing together broader views of the ways that capitalism is regulated with a more diverse group of scholars with a broader outlook on the political economy of capitalism (p. 13)".

This sits within a republican conception of justice as freedom from domination that opens space for consideration of what it means to work towards justice across institutions beyond criminal justice to explore the possibility of citizen-involved movements that could parallel or take the place of the imposition of the law.

An absence of regulation for relationality is one answer of this volume to why flexibility and empowerment are ground down by growth to scale. More than that, meta-regulation for relationality is needed. Hence, when regulators are asking service providers to provide proof of boxes that are ticked, wise meta-regulators of those regulators ask them why they do not instead give more emphasis to peer review; they ask why regulators do not opt for "conversational regulation" (Black, 2002), why regulators do not demand that service providers convene meetings with stakeholders to decide which failures of service delivery are most in need of continuous improvement, and what might be the action plan to deliver that continuous improvement (as discussed for aged care regulation in Braithwaite et al., 2007).

References

Abramowitz, M. (2018). *Regulating the lives of women: Social welfare policy from colonial times to the present* (3rd ed.). London: Routledge.

Adams, P., & Chandler, S. M. (2004). Responsive regulation in child welfare: Systematic challenges to mainstreaming the family group conference. *Journal of Sociology and Social Welfare, 31*(1), 93–116.

Adams, P., & Nelson, K. (1995). *Reinventing human services: Community- and family-centered practice.* New York: Aldine de Gruyter.

Adichie, Chimamanda Ngozi. (2009). *The danger of the single story. TED talks: Ideas worth spreading.* Retrieved from www.ted.com/talks/chimamanda_adichie_the_danger_of_a_single_story/transcript?language=en.

American Academy of Social Work and Social Welfare. (2013, November). *Grand accomplishments in social work* (Grand Challenges for Social Work Initiative, Working Paper No. 2). Baltimore, MD: Author. Retrieved from http://aaswsw.org/wp-content/uploads/2013/12/FINAL-Grand-Accomplishments-sb-12-9-13-Final.pdf

Andrews, J., & Reisch, M. (1997). The legacy of McCarthyism on social group work: An historical analysis. *Journal of Sociology and Social Welfare, 24*(3), 211–235.

Andrews, J., & Reisch, M. (2002). *The road not taken: A history of radical social work in the United States.* New York: Routledge.

Behrendt, L. (2017). *After the apology.* Retrieved from https://letterboxd.com/film/after-the-apology/.

Berman, H. J. (2006). *Law and revolution II: The impact of the protestant reformations on the Western legal tradition.* Cambridge, MA: The Belknap Press of Harvard University.

Berman, H. J. (1983). *Law and revolution, I: The formation of the Western legal tradition*. Cambridge, MA: Harvard University Press.

Black, J. (2002). Regulatory conversations. *Journal of Law and Society, 29*, 163–196.

Blagg, H. (2017). Doing restorative justice 'otherwise': Decolonising practices in the global south. In I. Aertsen & B. Pali (Eds.), *Critical restorative justice* (pp. 61–78). Oxford, UK: Hart Publishing.

Boyes-Watson, C. (1999). In the belly of the beast? Exploring the dilemmas of state-sponsored restorative justice. *Contemporary Justice Review, 2*(3), 261–281.

Braithwaite, J. (1989). *Crime, shame and reintegration*. Cambridge, UK: Cambridge University Press.

Braithwaite, J. (2002). *Restorative justice and responsive regulation*. New York: Oxford University Press.

Braithwaite, J. (2004). Families and the republic. *The Journal of Sociology and Social Welfare, 31*(1), 199–215.

Braithwaite, J. (2008). *Regulatory capitalism: How it works, ideas for making it better*. Cheltenham, UK: Edward Elgar.

Braithwaite, J. (2006). The regulatory state? In S. A. Binder, R. A. Rhodes, & B. A Rockman (Eds.), *The Oxford handbook of political institutions* (pp. 407–430). Oxford Handbooks Online. doi: 10.1093/oxfordhb/9780199548460.003.0021.

Braithwaite, J. (2010). *The essence of responsive regulation*. Vancouver, BC: University of British Columbia, Fasken Lecture. Retrieved from www.anu.edu.au/fellows/jbraithwaite/documents/Articles/essence_responsive_regulation.pdf.

Braithwaite, J. (2013). Relational republican regulation. *Regulation & Governance, 7*, 124–144.

Braithwaite, J. (2017a). Responsive excellence. In C. Coglianese (Ed.), *Achieving regulatory excellence* (pp. 23–35). Washington, DC: Brookings Institutions Press.

Braithwaite, J. (2017b). Hybrid politics for justice: The silk road of restorative justice II. *Restorative Justice, 5*(1), 7–28. doi: 10.1080/20504721.2017.1294795.

Braithwaite, J. (2018, May 16). *Responsive regulation*. Retrieved from http://johnbraithwaite.com/responsive-regulation/.

Braithwaite, J., Makkai, T., & Braithwaite, V. (2007). *Regulating aged care: Ritualism and the new pyramid*. Cheltenham, UK: Edward Elgar.

Braithwaite, J., & Pettit, P. (1993). *Not just desserts: A republican theory of criminal justice*. Oxford, UK: Oxford University Press.

Braithwaite, J., & Zhang, I. (2017). Persia to China: The silk road of restorative justice I. *Asian Criminology, 12*, 23–38.

Braithwaite, V. (2004). Collective hope: Preface to hope, power and governance. *Annals of the American Academy of Political and Social Science, 592*(1), 6–15.

Braithwaite, V. (2006). *Ten things you need to know about regulation but never wanted to ask* (Occasional Paper #10). Canberra: Regulatory Institutions Network, Australian National University. Retrieved from http://regnet.anu.edu.au/sites/default/files/ publications/attachments/2015–07/10thingswhole.pdf.

Braithwaite, V. (2009). *Defiance in taxation and governance*. Cheltenham, UK/Northampton, MA: Edward Elgar.

Braithwaite, V. (2017). Closing the gap between regulation and the community. In P. Drahos (Ed.), *Regulatory theory* (pp. 25–41). Canberra, AU: ANU Press.

Braithwaite, V., & Harris, N. (2009). Seeking to clarify child protection's regulatory principles. *Communities, Children and Families Australia, 41*(1), 5–21.

Buckley, E., & Decter, P. (2006). From isolation to community: Collaborating with children and families in times of crisis. *International Journal of Narrative Therapy & Community Work, 2*, 3–12. Retrieved from https://dulwich-centre.com.au/from-isolation-to-community.pdf.

Burford, G. (2005). Families: Their role as architects of civil society and social inclusion. *Practice, 17*(2), 79–88.

Burford, G. (2018). Keeping complexity alive: Restorative and responsive approaches to culture change. *The International Journal of Restorative Justice, 1*(3), 356–371.

Bywaters, P., Brady, G., Sparks, T., & Bos, E. (2014). Child welfare inequalities: New evidence, further questions. *Child & Family Social Work, 21*(3), 369–380.

Carr, E. L. (2018). *Drug short*. Retrieved May 14, 2018, from www.netflix.com/title/80118100.

Chase, S. (2018). Narrative inquiry: Toward theoretical and methodological maturity. In N. K. Denzin & Y. S. Lincoln (Eds.), *The SAGE handbook of qualitative research* (5th ed., pp. 544–560). Thousand Oaks, CA: Sage Publications.

Cherney, L., & Cherney, A. (2018). Regulation beyond the state: The role of non-state actors. In L.Y. C. Chang & R. Brewer (Eds.), *Criminal justice and regulation revisited: Essays in honor of Peter Grabosky* (pp. 19–32). London: Routledge.

Children Young Persons and Their Families Act (CYPFA). (1989). *Ministry of children, youth, and families.* Wellington, New Zealand: Published under the authority of the New Zealand Government.

Coker, D. (2016, December). Crime logic, campus sexual assault, and restorative justice. *Texas Tech Law Review*, 146–210.

Cooke, G., & Muir, R. (2012, November). The possibilities and politics of the relational state. In G. Cooke & R. Muir (Eds.), *The relational state: How recognizing the importance of human relationships could revolutionize the role of the state* (pp. 3–19). London, UK: Institute for Public Policy Research. Retrieved from www.ippr.org/files/images/media/files/publication/2012/11/relational-state_Nov2012_9888.pdf?noredirect=1.

Cottam, H. (2015, September). Social services are broken: How we can fix them. Ideas worth spreading. *TED Global London.* Retrieved from www.ted.com/talks/hilary_cottam_social_services_are_broken_how_we_can_fix_them.

Day, P. (2008). *A new history of social welfare* (6th ed.). London, UK: Pearson.

de Jong, P., & Berg, I. K. (2002). *Interviewing for solutions.* Pacific Grove, CA: Brooks Cole Publishers.

Denborough, D. (2001). *Family therapy: Exploring the field's past, present and possible futures.* Adelaide, South Australia: Dulwich Centre Publications.

Department of Health and Human Services, Office of Inspector General. (2015, March). *Second-generation antipsychotic drug use among Medicaid-enrolled children: Quality of care concerns.* Retrieved from https://oig.hhs.gov/oei/reports/oei-07-12-00320.pdf.

Drahos, P. (2017). Regulating capitalism's processes of destruction. In P. Drahos (Ed.), *Regulatory theory: Foundations and applications* (pp. 761–783). Canberra: ANU Press, The Australian National University.

Dukes, G., Braithwaite, J., & Moloney, J. P. (2014). *Pharmaceuticals, corporate crime, and public health.* Cheltenham, UK: Edward Elgar.

Esping-Anderson, G. (1996). After the golden age? Welfare state dilemmas in a global society. In G. Esping-Anderson (Ed.), *Welfare states in transition: National adaptations in global economics* (pp. 1–31). London, UK: Sage Publications.

Featherstone, B., Gupta, A., Morris, K., & White, S. (2018). *Protecting children: A social model.* Bristol, UK: Policy Press.

Featherstone, B., White, S., & Morris, K. (2014). *Re-imagining child protection: Towards humane social work with families.* Bristol, UK: Policy Press.

Ford, C. (2017). *Innovation and the state: Finance, regulation, and justice.* Cambridge, UK: Cambridge University Press.

Ford, C. (2018, March). Innovation as a challenge to regulation. *The Regulatory Review.* Retrieved May 4, 2018, from www.theregreview.org/2018/03/12/ford-innovation-regulation/.

Forsyth, M., Kent, L., Dinnen, S., Wallis, J., & Bose, S. (2018). Hybridity in peacebuilding and development: A critical approach. *Third World Thematics, 2*(4), 407–421. https://doi.org/10.1080/23802014.2017.1448717.

Friedrichs, D. O., & Schwartz, M. D. (2008). Low self-control and high organizational control: The paradoxes of white-collar crime. In E. Goode (Ed.), *Out of control: Assessing the general theory of crime* (pp. 145–159). Stanford, CA: Stanford Social Sciences.

Ghai, D. (1996). Foreward. In G. Esping-Anderson (Ed.), *Welfare states in transition: National adaptations in global economies* (p. vii). London, UK: Sage Publications.

Gilardi, F., Jordana, J., & Levi-Faur, D. (2006). Regulation in the age of globalisation: The diffusion of regulatory agencies across Europe and Latin America. In G. Hodge (Ed.), *Privatisation and market development: Global movements in public policy ideas* (pp. 127–147). Cheltenham, UK: Edward Elgar.

Gill, S., & Bakker, I. (2006). New constitutionalism and the social reproduction of caring institutions. *Theoretical Medicine and Bioethics, 27*, 35–57. Retrieved from https://link.springer.com/article/10.1007/s11017-005-5756-z. doi: 10.1007/s11017-005-5756-z.

Grabosky, P. (1995). Using non-governmental resources to foster regulatory compliance. *Governance, 8*(4), 527–550.

Grabosky, P., & Braithwaite, J. (1986). *Of manners gentle: Enforcement strategies of Australian business regulatory agencies.* Australia: Oxford University Press.

Gunningham, N., Grabosky, P., & Sinclair, D. (1998). *Smart regulation: Designing environmental policy (Oxford socio-legal studies).* Oxford, UK: Oxford University Press.

Hanan, E. M. (2018). Decriminalizing violence: A critique of restorative justice and proposal for diversionary mediation. *New Mexico Law Review, 46*(10), 123–170.

Harris, N. (2011). Does responsive regulation offer an alternative? Questioning the role of assessment in child protection investigations. *British Journal of Social Work, 41*(7), 1383–1403.

Heiner, B., & Tyson, S. (2017). Feminism and the carceral state: Gender-responsive justice, community accountability, and the epistemology of antiviolence. *Feminist Philosophy Quarterly, 3*(1), 1–35. doi: 10.5206/fpq/2016.3.3.

Higginbotham, S. (2012). Meeting the enemy: American exceptionalism and international law. *Contemporary Justice Review, 15*(4), 485–487. doi: 10.1080/10282580.2012.734578.

Hodges, C., & Steinholtz, R. (2017). *Ethical business practice and regulation: A behavioural and values-based approach to compliance and enforcement.* Oxford, UK: Hart Publishing.

Hong, S. H., & You, J. S. (2018). Limits of regulatory responsiveness: Democratic credentials of responsive regulation. doi/abs/10.1111/rego.12193.

Hyslop, I. K. (2016). Social work in the teeth of a gale: A resilient counter-discourse in neoliberal times. *Critical and Radical Social Work, 4*(1), 21–37.

IIRP. (n.d.). *International Institute for Restorative Practices Continuum.* Retrieved from www.iirp.edu/defining-restorative/restorative-practices-continuum.

Ivec, M. (2013). *A necessary engagement: An international review of parent and family engagement in child protection.* Hobart, Tasmania: The Social Action and Research Centre Anglicare Tasmania. Retrieved from http://regnet.anu.edu.au/sites/default/files/publications/attachments/2015-10/Ivec_A%20necessary%20engagement%20-%20An%20international%20review%20of%20parent%20and%20family%20engagement%20in%20child%20protection.pdf.

Ivec, M., & Braithwaite, V. with Wood, C., & Job, J. (2015). *Applications of responsive regulatory theory in Australia and overseas: Update.* Retrieved from http://regnet.anu.edu.au/sites/default/files/publications/attachments/2015-05/Occasional%2520Paper%252023_Ivec_Braithwaite_0.pdf.

Jacobson, K. (2018). *Cartel bank.* Retrieved from www.netflix.com/title/80118100.

Jordana, J., Levi-Faur, D., & Marin, X. F. i. (2011). The global diffusion of regulatory agencies: Channels of transfer and stages of diffusion. *Comparative Political Studies, 44*(10), 1343–1369.

Kahn, M. W. (2006). *The concept of charity in Islam.* J & K Insights. Retrieved from www.jammu-kashmir.com/insights/insight20000330a.html.

Katznelson, I. (2006). *When affirmative action was white: An untold history of racial inequality in twentieth-century America.* New York: W. W. Norton.

Kim, M. (2014). The mainstreaming of the criminalization critique: Reflections on VAWA 20 years later. *CUNY Law Journal.* VAWA @ 20. Online publication.

Kim, M. (n.d.). *Reimagining the movement to end gender violence.* Retrieved from http://mediaforchange.org/reimagine.

Kovacs, K. E. (2017, November 13). Getting back to the basics with agency rulemaking. *The Regulatory Review.* Retrieved from www.theregreview.org/2017/11/13/kovacs-basics-agency-rulemaking/.

Kupumamae: Words from mamae. (n.d.). Retrieved from https://kupumamae.com/2016/07/17/the-great-maori-shame-legacy/.

Lejano, R. P., & Funderburg, R. (2016). Geographies of risk, the regulatory state, and the ethic of care. *Annals of the American Association of Geographers, 106*(5), 1097–1113. doi: 10.1080/24694452.2016.1179565.

Levi-Faur, D. (2011, November). *The odyssey of the welfare state: Episode one: The rescue of the welfare state* (Jerusalem Papers in Regulation & Governance, Working Paper No. 39). Retrieved from http://regulation.huji.ac.il/papers/jp39.pdf.

Levi-Faur, D., & Jordana, J. (2005). The rise of regulatory capitalism: The global diffusion of a new order. *The Annals of the American Academy of Political and Social Science, 598*(1), 200–217.

Llewellyn, J. J. (2011). Restorative justice: Thinking relationally about justice. In J. Downie & J. Llewellyn (Eds.), *Being relational: Reflections on relational theory & health law.* Vancouver: UBC Press.

Llewellyn, J., & Downie, J. (Eds.). (2011). *Being relational: Reflections on relational theory & health law.* Vancouver: UBC Press.

Llewellyn, J. J., & Morrison, B. (2018). Deepening the relational ecology of restorative justice. *The International Journal of Restorative Justice, 1*(3), 343–355.

Llewellyn, J. J., & Philpott, D. (2014). Introduction. In J. J. Llewellyn & D. Philpott (Eds.), *Restorative justice, reconciliation, and peacebuilding* (pp. 1–13). Oxford, UK: Oxford University Press.

Lovitt, F., & Pettit, P. (2009). Neorepublicanism: A normative and institutional research program. *Annual Review of Political Science, 12*, 11–29. Retrieved from https://doi.org/10.1146/annurev.polisci.12.040907.120952.

Mabbett, D. (2010, December). *The rescue of the regulatory state* (Jerusalem Papers in Regulation & Governance. Working Paper Number 28 1–20). Retrieved from http://regulation.huji.ac.il/papers/jp28.pdf.

Mabbett, D. (2011). The rescue of the regulatory state. In D. Levi-Faur (Ed.), *Handbook of the politics of regulation* (pp. 215–226). Cheltenham, UK: Edward Elgar.

McCold, P. (2000). Toward a mid-range theory of restorative criminal justice: A reply to the maximalist model. *Contemporary Justice Review, 3*(4), 357–414. Retrieved from www.researchgate.net/profile/Paul_Mccold/publication/292733753_Toward_a_holistic_vision_of_restorative_juvenile_justice_A_reply_to_the_maximalist_model/links/58deb80f92851c36954572cf/Toward-a-holistic-vision-of-restorative-juvenile-justice-A-reply-to-the-maximalist-model.pdf.

Meacham, J. (2018). *The soul of America: The battle for our better angels.* New York: Random House.

Mercier, H., & Sperber, D. (2017). *The enigma of reason.* Cambridge, MA: Harvard University Press.

Metzl, J. M., & Roberts, D. E. (2014, September). Structural competency meets structural racism: Race, politics, and the structure of medical knowledge. *AMA Journal of Ethics, 16*(9), 674–690.

Miller, W. R., & Rollnick, S. (2012). *Motivational interviewing: Helping people change* (3rd ed.). New York: The Guilford Press.

Ministerial Advisory Committee. (1986). *Puao-te-Atatu: The report of the Ministerial Advisory Committee on a Maori perspective for the Department of Social Welfare.* Wellington, NZ: Department of Social Welfare.

Morone, J. A. (2004). *Hellfire nation: The politics of sin in American history.* New Haven, CT: Yale University Press.

Morris, K., & Burford, G. (2017). Engaging families and managing risk in practice. In M. Connolly (Ed.), *Beyond the risk paradigm: Current debates and new directions in child protection.* London, UK: Palgrave MacMillan.

Moyle, P. J., & Tauri, J. (2016). Māori, family group conferencing and the mystifications of restorative justice. *Victims and Offenders, 11*(1), 87–106.

Nixon, P., Burford, G., & Quinn, A. with Edelbaum, J. (2005, May). *A survey of international practices, policy & research on family group conferencing and related practices.* Englewood, CO: American Humane Association, National Center on Family Group Decision Making. Retrieved from www.academia.edu/891986/A_survey_of_international_practices_policy_and_research_on_family_group_conferencing_and_related_practices?auto=download.

NPR/PBS News Hour/Marist poll. (2018, January). Retrieved from http://maristpoll.marist.edu/nprpbs-newshourmarist-poll-results-january-2018/.

Parker, C., & Braithwaite, J. (2003). Regulation. In P. Cane & M. Tushnet (Eds.), *The Oxford handbook of legal studies* (pp. 119–145). Oxford: Oxford University Press.

Patashnik, E. M. (2008). *Reforms at risk: What happens after major policy changes are enacted?* Princeton, NJ: Princeton University Press.

Pennell, J. (2004). Family group conferencing in child welfare: Responsive and regulatory interfaces. *Journal of Sociology and Social Welfare, 31*(1), 117–135.

Pennell, J., Shapiro, C., & Spigner, C. (2011). *Safety, fairness, stability: Repositioning juvenile justice and child welfare to engage families and communities.* Washington, DC: Center for Juvenile Justice Reform, Georgetown University.

Pettit, P. (1997). *Republicanism: A theory of freedom and government.* Oxford, UK: Oxford University Press.

PEW Research Center. (February 23, 2012). Retrieved from www.people-press.org/2012/02/23/section-2-views-of-government-regulation/.

Piketty, T., & Goldhammer, A. (2013). *Capital in the twenty-first century.* Cambridge, UK: Harvard University Press.

Plaster, R. I. (2010). *Confirmation bias* (Amazon Kindle). Createspace Independent Publishers.

Rangihau, J. (1986). *Puao-Te-Ata-Tu (Daybreak): The report of the ministerial advisory committee on a Maori perspective for the department of social welfare.* Wellington, NZ: Department of Social Welfare.

Reisch, M., & Andrews, J. (2002). *The road not taken: A history of radical social work in the United States.* Routledge.

Rich, T. R. (n.d.). *Judaism 101.* Retrieved from www.jewfaq.org/tzedakah.htm.

Roberts, A. (2017). *Is international law international?* Oxford, UK: Oxford University Press.

Roberts, D. (2002). *Shattered bonds: The color of child welfare.* New York: Basic Civitas Books.

Roberts, D. E. (2012). Prison, foster care, and the systemic punishment of black mothers. *University of California at Los Angeles Law Review, 59*, 1474.

Saito, N. T. (2010). *Meeting the enemy: American exceptionalism and international law.* New York: New York University Press.

Saleeby, D. (2013). *Strengths perspective in social work practice* (6th ed.). New York: Pearson.

SAMHSA-HRSA Center for Integrated Health Solutions. (n.d.). *Integrated models of behavioral health in primary care.* Retrieved May 28, 2018, from www.integration.samhsa.gov/integrated-care-models/behavioral-health-in-primary-care#integrated models of BH in PC.

Schorr, L. (1988). *Within our reach: Breaking the cycle of disadvantage.* New York: Random House.

Seligman, M. E. P. (1998). *Learned optimism.* New York: Pocket Books.

Selznick, P. (1992). *The moral commonwealth: Social theory and the promise of community.* Berkeley, CA: University of California Press.

Sloman, S., & Fernbach, P. (2018). *The knowledge illusion: Why we never think alone.* New York: Random House.

Snyder, C. R., & Shane, J. L. (2006). *Positive psychology. The scientific and practical explorations of human strengths.* Thousand Oaks, CA: Sage.

Specht, H., & Courtney, M. (1995). *Unfaithful angels: How social work has abandoned its mission.* New York: Free Press.

Strang, H. (2002). *Repair or revenge: Victims and restorative justice.* Oxford: Clarendon Press.

Tavris, C., & Aronson, E. (2007). *Mistakes were made (but not by me): Why we justify foolish beliefs, bad decisions and hurtful acts.* Wilmington, MA: Mariner Books.

US Government Accountability Office. (2011, December). *Foster children HHS guidance could help states improve oversight of psychotropic prescriptions.* Retrieved May 14, 2018, from www.gao.gov/products/GAO-12-270T.

Van Molle, L. (2017). Comparing religious perspectives on social reform: An introduction. In L. Van Molle (Ed.), *Charity and social reform: The dynamics of religious reform in Northern Europe, 1780–1920* (pp. 7–38). Leuven, Belgium: Leuven University Press.

van Ness, D., & Strong, K. H. (2015). *Restoring justice: An introduction to restorative justice* (5th ed.). New York: Routledge.

Villanueva, M. (2018). *Drugs funding terrorism.* [online] philstar.com. Retrieved May 14, 2018, from www.philstar.com/opinion/2017/11/01/1754493/drugs-funding-terrorism.

Warren, S. (2016). *Whanganui river and Te Urewera treaty settlements: Innovative developments for the practice of rangatiratanga in resource development.* Wellington, NZ: Victoria University of Wellington. A thesis in fulfillment of the requirements of the degree of Master of New Zealand Studies.

Whalley, E., & Hackett, C. (2017). Carceral feminisms: The abolitionist project and undoing dominant feminisms. *Contemporary Justice Review, 20*(4), 456–473. doi: 10.1080/10282580.2017.1383762.

Wilkinson, R., & Pickett, K. (2009). *The spirit level: Why greater equality makes societies stronger.* London, UK: Bloomsbury Press.

Wilson-Hartgrove, J. (2018). *Reconstructing the gospel: Finding freedom from slaveholder religion.* Downers Grove, CA: InterVarsity Press.

Wood, J. D. (2018). Regulating through enrolment: Emerging conceptions of police as public health interventionists. In L.Y. C. Chang & R. Brewer (Eds.), *Criminal justice and regulation revisited: Essays in honor of Peter Grabosky* (pp. 51–69). Routledge.

Wu, C. F., Cancian, M., & Wallace, G. (2014). The effect of welfare sanctions on TANF exits and employment. *Children and Youth Services Review, 36*, 1–14.

Zehr, H. (1990). *Changing lenses: A new focus for crime and justice.* Scottsdale, PA: Herald Press.

2

BROADENING THE APPLICATIONS OF RESPONSIVE REGULATION

John Braithwaite, Valerie Braithwaite and Gale Burford

Introduction

This chapter considers over-regulation and under-regulation both as potential threats to freedom. It conceives political knee-jerks that see-saw between over- and under-regulation as posing particularly strong threats of domination. Responsive regulation was developed as an integrated and balanced approach to these threats to freedom. Its balance is particularly richly improved by integration with restorative justice. Responsive regulation is often thought of narrowly as an approach to business regulation. This chapter explains what responsive regulation means through discussing the way it was developed in the regulation of a particular human service, aged care.

Types of Regulation

In the human services, as with all domains where regulation is important, we can think of three kinds of responsive regulation. One is state regulation of the providers of a human service. Regardless of whether a service provider is a private firm or a government agency, there are other parts of government that have responsibilities to regulate them to ensure that they do not pay bribes, that the food they provide is not contaminated, the care they provide is not abusive, for example. A second kind of regulation by the state is of individual citizens. A child protection agency regulates mothers and fathers to ensure they do not neglect or abuse their children. A third kind is regulation of the state and of business by citizens, by civil society organizations. This third kind of regulation has a particularly strong role in responsive regulatory theory as a check and balance on the other two kinds of regulation.

We will illustrate these three kinds of regulation in aged care regulation, which was the most important substantive field in the development of harnessing of restorative to responsive regulation. In the process, we seek to begin to set up the argument of our concluding chapter that the human services suffer from a want of attention to questions of regulatory theory.

When John and Valerie Braithwaite, with many collaborators, started their comparative research on nursing home regulation in the late 1980s, well over 40 per cent of nursing home residents in the

DOI: 10.4324/9780429398704-2

United States were being physically restrained. Most commonly, they were confined to a chair with a lap restraint for just part of the day. We observed more devastating examples of restraint, however, where individuals were tied for long periods at the lap, with their wrists also to the arms of a chair, their ankles to its legs. Sometimes there was a punitive aspect to this abuse of the freedom of the elderly. Usually there was some principled rationale, such as that the resident had been pulling down the curtains when their hands were free, or that they were at risk of a fall. Good nurses and care workers know, however, that there are almost always better ways of solving these underlying problems by talking them through with the resident and their relatives.

So there began an 'Untie the Elderly Campaign' led by the National Citizens' Coalition for Nursing Home Reform (Braithwaite, Makkai, & Braithwaite, 2007). The campaign pointed out that the incidence of physical restraint in US nursing homes was probably more than eight times that in the UK. Campaigning called for and achieved legislative and regulatory changes that caused US aged care to become at least as good as British aged care in this regard. The Untie the Elderly Campaign also made heroes of restraint-free American homes. It put their Directors of Nursing and Administrators on the platform during their campaign meetings on Capitol Hill to explain how they achieved zero restraint. AMP (Awareness, Motivation and a Pathway) were all needed to untie the elderly (Honig et al., 2015). These American restraint-free homes showed simple Pathways to freedom, because the campaign leaders knew that Awareness of better outcomes in Britain and regulatory pressure from civil society to Motivate change were not enough.

So this was an example of civil society organizations regulating state regulators to change the state regulatory system, and also of civil society directly regulating private, state and charitable providers of aged care. It was a brilliant campaign that sequenced many regulatory strategies. One was to popularize its research results on the most common reasons administrators gave for physical restraint. This was to fend off litigation from the families of residents over falls. The research found that there was hardly any successful litigation for falls occurring as a result of failing to restrain a resident, but a considerable amount of successful litigation as a result of deaths caused by excessive restraint, as when a resident slid down in their chair and strangled on their lap restraint (Evans & Strumpf, 1989; Special Committee on Aging, United States Senate, 1990: 22–56).

Changes to nursing home inspection protocols and priorities occurred at the end of the 1980s as a result of the legislative victory of the Untie the Elderly Campaign. For most aged care facilities it was enough for the inspectors to arrive after the law changed and point out something administrators and staff already knew as a result of the campaign: that the expectation now was that facilities document continuous reduction in the use restraints if they were to stay out of trouble with inspectors. Most private, charitable and state providers of aged care achieved continuous improvement quickly. They had been persuaded by the campaign that it would make life better for them, as by reducing litigation costs, as well as better for their residents. Braithwaite et al.'s (2007) research showed there were hold-outs and hard-liners of ingrained disciplinary traditions. Increasing numbers of civil penalty orders were imposed on them after they ignored warnings. When the civil penalties also failed to change them, many were suspended from receiving new admissions funded by Medicare or Medicaid until they reduced their levels of restraint. This was a more severe penalty that would put the firm at risk of bankruptcy if it continued for too long. For a tiny number of facilities it was necessary to threaten proceedings to remove their licence if they did not change. In this chapter we will describe this kind of sequencing and escalation of regulatory responses as responsive regulation. In a short space of years all aged care providers did change, though some more transformatively than others.

The history of the United States can be read as a story of struggle for freedom. The period 1987–1992 when the elderly were freed from their chains was one of the most important and decisive moments in that history. National shame about such a recent past of keeping our grandparents in chains saw the nation in denial about this as another example of a past of other oppressed minorities in chains. During those few years, the incidence of physical restraint in US nursing homes fell from well over 40 per cent of all residents to well under 4 per cent. It fell a lot further still in the next two decades (Braithwaite et al., 2007). Cynics who believe that business always games new regulatory laws predicted that nursing homes would substitute by putting more of their troublesome charges under chemical restraint. The cynics were proved wrong. Chemical restraint was also caught up in the regulatory reform and also dramatically reduced (Castle & Mor, 1998; HCFA, 1998: vol. 1, viii). Game playing with the regulatory reform was averted because aged care providers were genuinely persuaded that the reform was in so many ways a good one. They saw what was needed to build a more decent society for our grandparents, and they took day-to-day professional pride in achieving restraint reduction at least until a new found of gaming the law took hold in the next century.

So, we can see each of the three kinds of responsive regulation that we described at the beginning of this chapter. We see responsive regulation of private, public and charitable providers of human services by state regulators. We see regulation of the state (first regulation of the Congress by civil society, then of the regulators by the Congress and civil society in combination). The National Citizens Coalition for Nursing Home Reform was regulation of the regulators by civil society. We see also a transformation of the way individual citizens were regulated by providers. Instead of tying up that elderly woman who was pulling at the curtains, a discussion was triggered about why she was so bored, so angry. From the perspective of this book, among the wonderful things about the way this was done moves to more restorative processes in aged care. Residents and Relatives Councils were newly empowered in conversations in a circle that included many in wheelchairs and sometimes residents wheeled in on their beds. These empowering conversations were often about what can be done to reduce the boredom and anger and improve the quality of care of residents. Representatives of these councils were also empowered to sit in the large circle of managers, staff representatives and inspectors in exit conferences at the end of nursing home inspections to decide on changes needed. Finally, care planning meetings in this era in the United States ceased being meetings only of care professionals to discuss revisions to a resident's care plan. Relatives were required to receive an invitation in advance so they could support and speak up for their relative. The regulatory reforms also required the resident to receive an invitation to the meeting.

While these authors started thinking about restorative and responsive regulation in the way business regulation was conducted in exit conferences after coal mine safety inspections (Braithwaite, 1985), the most important domain of R&D turned out to be a human service, aged care, where responsive practices of regulating business, regulating the state and regulating individuals were all critical to understanding how a freer society was created through the interaction between the regulatory state and regulatory society.

The Challenge of Understanding Responsive Regulation

Responsive regulation is about being responsive to those we are regulating; being responsive to the environment; responsive to democratic impulses—seeking to respond to the needs articulated by the regulated, and then, perhaps most importantly of all, being responsive to the history of encounters between the regulator and the actor on the other side of the fence. Restorative justice and responsive regulation are both relational forms of justice (see Llewellyn, Chapter 9 this volume) that can reduce domination.

Restorative and responsive justice both aim to privilege dialogue over punishment and aim progressively to solve problems by bringing more parties into the circle when circles fail. Responsive regulation is distinguished by its dynamic strategy—by signalling that a regulator will escalate responses if required. Regulators signal that they will not go away until all stakeholders are safe from the kind of domination of concern in the regulatory encounter. It involves human services providers consulting with stakeholders not only about what services are most valuable and that should therefore be provided, but also about the dynamic sequencing of strategies. This strategy is normally the strategy of first resort; that is normally the strategy of last resort; and these are the strategies we consider in between the first and last resorts.

Nursing home regulation illustrates the dilemma well. We have long periods of quiet when we hear nothing in the media about what is happening in the nursing home industry. Then one will burn down, or there are incidents of sexual assault in a nursing home, or reports are made to the police about a particular nursing home chain where more than a dozen people have died from causes seemingly related to neglect. A cycle of political scandal unfolds. Media exposure of the horror triggers public outcry that, in turn, puts pressure on the industry and on the government that is supposed to be regulating the industry. In the aftermath of the scandal comes recognition that change is needed. Governments come under pressure to do something tougher. Usually, this means tougher enforcement, for example sending someone to prison, imposing fines, shutting down a nursing home, removing a provider's licence or taking someone up to the top floor of corporate headquarters and off-loading them on the media scrum waiting below to write a story on their fall from grace.

What is also expected is law reform. However, what we often find unfortunately is that the reform that occurs is ritualistic. That is to say, it provides rituals of comfort to the community (Power, 1997). The reform that takes place gives the appearance that something is being done, so that political leaders can stand up and say, "Well we have now implemented these new procedures and all our staff will be trained in these steps". But rarely will this process prevent a relapse. Sure enough, no relapse occurs again for a while, because there is a media attention cycle with scandal and reform. The media have a wave of interest in a particular topic, then lose it, because they want to entertain their readers with something scandalous in a new arena. The media rarely continue to focus on the same regulatory agency—unless it is hit by another scandal immediately after the first. Attention will not stay on the same responsible politicians forever. They will soon be chasing after another politician, and that gives the agency a period of quiescence outside the limelight.

Often what we find in the many different business regulatory regimes we have studied is that these rituals of comfort, established in that climate of fending off the scandal, acquire a terrible life of their own. Levels of enforcement that may have been appropriate in the immediate aftermath of the scandal persist in a time when the business culture has changed, when perhaps the scandal's lessons have been learned and people are actually behaving in a more socially responsible fashion. There has been no reflection on or re-evaluation of the regulatory demands as the regulated environment changes. Most importantly, there is no cool head scrutinizing the regulatory demands that worked well, brought no change or were counterproductive. Regulators and regulated actors alike become slaves to the regulatory demands put in place in the aftermath of the scandal.

Then what can sometimes happen is that an industry or professional association will orchestrate a campaign with politicians in economic portfolios attacking bureaucrats for foisting ridiculous levels of red tape upon them. Consequently, there will be a call for deregulation. Those rituals of comfort may then be abolished and replaced with self-regulatory frameworks. Unfortunately, the baby may be thrown out with the bath water. That is to say, no-one will have reflected on the positive elements of the rituals of comfort. And neither will they have reflected on how the rituals were becoming ritualistic; that is, why they were being followed for their own sake, as opposed to being used as tools to reflect, with discretion and wisdom, on what would be the most responsive way of dealing with a problem.

This cycle of high regulatory control by the state followed by self-regulation continues, regardless of the regulatory domain. What we find is a see-sawing between the highly punitive regulation of a problem, and trust in self-regulation and corporate social responsibility. Consequently, the regime designed to serve a particular public interest fails to evolve. There is no cumulative learning and continuous improvement in the design of the regime. Rather there is this cycle of moving back and forth between the ritualism of 'getting tough' at one extreme, and that of 'removing all red tape to make it easier for people to do their job' at the other. The capacity of the regulatory system to solve growing problems then fails to grow.

Transcending the See-saw: Thinking About Regulatory Pyramids

Responsive Regulation, by Ayres and Braithwaite (1992), helped to think of regulation very broadly as 'steering the flow of events' (Parker & Braithwaite, 2003), where the idea of responsive regulation is to be creative in the steering tools selected.

A key idea in all of this is a regulatory pyramid. Above is a very straightforward example of such a pyramid that might apply to the regulation of something like a nursing home (Figure 2.1). There is no such thing as a standard pyramid or a pyramid that is the right way of being responsive; the right

A responsive regulatory pyramid

FIGURE 2.1 The Regulatory Pyramid

thing is to be responsive in different ways depending on different situations. The idea of this particular example of a pyramid is to start at the bottom of the pyramid and regulate through persuasion in the first instance. This means we talk to people and say, "It's awful that people are lying every day in urine-soaked sheets. What can you come up with to change that?" Sometimes just asking such a question stimulates real change. That is a 'persuasion' example. What then if inspectors return to find there is still a problem with urine-soaked sheets? Perhaps the appropriate response then is to issue a warning letter—a formal shot across the bow.

Warning letters work variably; they have differential effectiveness in different areas. In Japan, for example, letters can be very effective, because Japanese businesses take seriously a letter from the State, whereas Australian businesses tend not to take them so seriously. In the tax arena, letters can be surprisingly effective. For example, when a tax agency has a large number of small and medium-sized businesses which have paid no tax for the past three years (and that is all the tax office knows about them), the agency can send a computer-generated, though cleverly crafted letter to these businesses, as the Australian taxation office has done, to the effect of "We have noticed that you have not paid any tax for three years". A considerable proportion of the businesses then pay tax in the next year. This is a cheap intervention that generates a large amount of revenue (Braithwaite, 2005).

If the warning letter fails, one of the standard regulatory responses is to impose civil penalties. This does not mean a criminal process but an 'on the spot' fine. In nursing home regulation, we have seen that it usually escalates to the more effective form of a ban on the admission of new residents, until such time as the facility complies. This can be a highly effective kind of civil penalty because it means that the business can return to normal with the admission of new residents as soon as the problem is resolved, and until then it can concentrate on improving quality of care for a smaller group of residents. The cost to the organization is significant while it is in force—the business loses money every day that they are unable to admit new residents to their facility. But as soon as the problem is fixed, that civil penalty will be removed. Should the short, sharp measure of civil penalties fail, the regulator might proceed to the next step on the pyramid, a more punitive approach such as laying criminal charges in the courts.

People find it strange sometimes that licence suspension and revocation would be at the peak of the pyramid above a criminal penalty. For human services providers, however, removing their licence to provide those services is really like capital punishment. Closing a business is corporate capital punishment. So is closing a government subunit that provides some human service. The worst outcome for owners, shareholders, workers and users of the service is to have the provider sink into bankruptcy because it is no longer an approved provider. People lose their livelihoods because there is little likelihood of the organization trading its way out of trouble if it no longer can provide services. The same is true of 'regulation inside government', when one part of the state regulates another (Hood et al., 1999). If a state anti-corruption commission or a government audit office closes another government operating unit in the human services and a new state provider is built from scratch, this can have more dramatic consequences for everyone involved than targeting a responsible individual to go to prison.

Redundancy as a Principle of Pyramid Design

One of the reasons for having layers in the enforcement pyramid is that most of the tools that we use to solve problems, whatever the problem, will not work most of the time. This is as true of relational approaches as of any other. Relational approaches to restorative and responsive regulation often fail. We may focus attention on controlling a particular problem, but its complexity will often mean that the intervention will not hit the mark—in some circumstances even being counterproductive. So what we do is to have some redundancy in our controls through using a mix of strategies (Gunningham, Grabosky, & Sinclair, 1998). The nature of the mix is important however. Obviously, we must prudently assure that strategies are not contradictory. One part of the strategy can be effective while it undermines some other aspect of the strategy. Equally importantly, we do not want strategies to be too similar. When we look at mixes of strategies empirically, we find that people are not very creative about developing layered strategies for risk prevention. That is to say, they think of many techniques, but most are too alike. This is illustrated by James Reason's (1990) "Swiss Cheese" model of risk prevention (Figure 2.2).

Reason's work focused on aircraft safety. How do we resolve a situation in which a pilot who has been drinking alcohol crashes the plane into the mountain? We have a co-pilot present, but the co-pilot may have been the pilot's drinking buddy. Or, how do we resolve a situation in which a pilot is disoriented by a white-out in a snow storm? If we rely on a co-pilot, both pilots are likely to be simultaneously affected by the optical illusion. This is the idea of the holes in Figure 2.2 being in alignment—we don't have sufficiently diverse strategies to act as checks and balances against one another. It would be better to have the plane flown by a pilot and a computer than to have it flown by two pilots or two computers. Be it a computer virus, be it drunkenness or white-out, we require different checks and balances to successfully manage risk. Covering the weaknesses of one strategy with the strengths of another is an underlying principle in designing regulatory pyramids. To have a pyramid that relies only on economic sanctions of different levels of intensity is to ignore the insights provided by Reason. If money is no object to the regulated actor posing a risk to the community, that regulated actor will continue to buy his or her way out of trouble with the regulator. The regulatory system needs to be designed in such a way that if strategy A fails to contain the risk, strategy B will still have a fair chance of being successful, because it seeks to contain risk in an entirely different way. Persuasion, education, social sanctions, psychological sanctions and economic sanctions provide a diverse array of strategies for consideration in designing pyramids. Later we will introduce the idea of praise and reward to further diversify the strategies available for more effectively addressing risk. In nursing home regulation,

FIGURE 2.2 Swiss Cheese Model of Risk Prevention

Source: James Reason (1990).

when Australian inspectors routinely offered praise when compliance was achieved, this was one of the strongest predictors of improved quality of care (Makkai & Braithwaite, 1993). The child development literature likewise shows the importance of building intrinsic motivation for ethical conduct by praise for being a good little boy or girl (Altschul, Lee, & Gershoff, 2016; Gunderson et al., 2018).

A Second Principle of Pyramid Design: Optimum Harm Minimization

Another general principle in the design of a pyramid is that there is a regulatory optimum to be sought which is unique to the particular time and context in which the problem is situated. For effective resolution, the same problem does not necessarily demand the same solution each time it occurs. Responsiveness to the problem means taking into account the context because it is always changing and histories differ. Consider the earlier example where scandal has embroiled a regulatory agency. Where the optimum lies following the huge public scandal that has the agency in a corner is far removed from where it lies during a period of regulatory quiescence. Tough measures sometimes must come into play after regulatory failures, soft measures when regulated actors are cooperatively engaged in compliance. And this is not only for political reasons. When controls are not successfully operating and the media exposes regulatory failure, there is a decline of confidence in the law and its enforcement because nothing is seen to be done. Honest regulated actors who are playing by the rules will begin to think, "Well I must be the only mug around here who is spending my budget to maintain compliance with these environmental rules", if it is environmental regulation of a government agency or a business. Consequently, their commitment to voluntary compliance will erode if, in the context of that public scandal, there is an absence of firm action against non-compliers. In more normal conditions, however, we may not need such a heavy-handed enforcement approach, in which case this balance will be different.

Most social problems are either under-regulated or over-regulated. Finding the mix of strategies that optimize harm minimization is no easy challenge. Figure 2.3 represents how Stephen Mugford (1991) developed the idea of harm minimization in relation to the regulation of harmful drugs, from legal ones like tobacco to illicit drugs like heroin.

Mugford pointed out that we can have over-regulation of illicit drugs, meaning that the industry goes underground. As a result, there are more impurities in drugs, and people die from this. Alternatively, we can have under-regulation, as has traditionally been the case with tobacco. For much of its history, tobacco could be readily purchased at relatively low prices by anyone, including adolescents, with

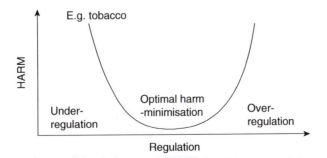

FIGURE 2.3 Regulation for Harm Minimization

alarming health consequences, including lung and throat cancer and cardio-vascular disease. Finally, we can have an optimum level of regulation, where we bring the issue into the open and arrive at an approach which avoids the excesses of harm from these various pathologies of under-regulation, whilst not accelerating harm by criminalization.

In the regulation of pharmaceuticals, most societies strike a more interesting kind of balance than they do with either tobacco or heroin. That is, there is a prescription regime that has built within it various checks and balances. To sell pharmaceuticals, like cigarettes, through the supermarket might be dangerous under-regulation. We see regulation escalating upwards to a degree with drugs that can be bought over the counter, but only from a pharmacist who provides warnings for use; and then escalating further when a doctor's prescription is required for their use. We can also see the problems that arise if access to therapeutic drugs goes too far. At this other end of the spectrum, we could suffer terrible therapeutic losses by criminalizing the use of many pharmaceuticals that we rely on to cure disease and restore health.

Optimum harm minimization can be challenging. Child protection is an excellent example. Public outrage over the death of a child from a family known to child protection authorities can lead to closer monitoring and assessing of families, perhaps even removing children and placing them in foster care more quickly than usual as a precautionary measure. Such a package of intervention strategies may not only amount to over-regulation, but also may perpetuate the same risk, increasing stress on families and carers, stress that jeopardizes the quality of care provided for children. If stress is a risk factor, adopting corrective measures that increase stress will allow the problem to mushroom rather than be contained. The prospect of over-regulation creates another set of problems. Instead of lifting standards of care across the community, over-regulation that continues beyond the crisis may result in resource-poor families keeping children out of school and away from health services for fear of harsh intervention from child protection authorities. Over-regulation may also reduce the number of foster carers who are willing to engage with the child protection system: They may be willing to care for children, but not willing to deal with a complex set of rules that the authorities impose upon them.

Principles of optimum harm minimization and risk prevention affect the suite of strategies that are assembled for a regulatory intervention. In thinking through the child protection situation, it becomes clear that good regulatory design depends on having a deep understanding of how children are cared for in families and how families manage their life situation. Such understanding becomes even more important when the strategies are arranged within a regulatory pyramid. The regulatory pyramid makes assumptions about how various strategies will be interpreted by regulated actors. Before a pyramid is implemented, regulators must be sure that the meaning they attach to the steps of the pyramid corresponds to the meaning attached by regulated actors. Each step up the regulatory pyramid is intended to be more intrusive by the regulator as we discussed earlier with the nursing home regulation example. Checks need to be made to ensure that those being regulated see the regulatory pyramid as incremental in the same way as the regulators do.

Assumptions About Regulated Actors and Strategies

To understand the different meanings attached to different steps in a regulatory pyramid, we need to return to our basic structure (see Figure 2.4) and think about it in a more abstract way. At the base, we try to solve the problem by capacity development. In so doing, we form a certain kind of assumption about the regulated actor. At the base of this particular pyramid we assume that the regulated actor is a learning and rational citizen. If mistakes are made, they might not be repeated.

The next level up the pyramid is restorative justice as a regulatory strategy, where we assume the regulatory actor is virtuous and will respond to the restorative justice dialogue.

Then, failing that, we escalate to a deterrence-based strategy that could be something like those fines that we have in the more detailed pyramid in Figure 2.1. At this level we assume that individuals are swayed by the costs of persisting with their behaviour. They will pause to re-think their situation because the costs are mounting and the regulator is not going away or moving on to someone else. With the increased pressure from the regulator, they come to the decision that they may be better off if they adapt and change their behaviour to meet the expectations of the regulator.

In summary, constructing a regulatory pyramid means assembling multiple strategies that are sorted and assessed with three principles in mind: (a) Is the strategy adding value by delivering a redundancy that can prevent risk? (b) Is the strategy optimal for harm minimization? and (c) Does the strategy speak to the self that we want to influence (that is, the learning self, the virtuous self, the rational self and the incompetent and irrational self)?

At this point, a further refinement needs to be reflected upon. At each of these levels of the pyramids in Figures 2.1 and 2.4 we can have multiple stages. Responsive regulation is nimble and flexible. At different stages up the regulatory pyramid, a particular strategy may be tried and re-tried, providing there is some rationale for thinking that because the context has changed, a new attempt might be productive. For nursing homes in Figure 2.1, for example, a restorative justice circle could be held between civil penalty and criminal penalty. The idea would be to talk through the problem, with a backdrop of deterrent measures. Let us assume that this strategy fails. The problem re-occurs, and another restorative justice circle is convened. It fails and we convene another one in a rather different way with different and more people in the circle and see if it succeeds. And maybe if they all fail, we can try different layers of deterrence. We could try withdrawing funding on new admissions to the facility until it is fixed. If that fails then we could escalate up to something tougher, like criminal penalties, and incapacitation, such as licence suspension or revocation. Or, if we switch our thinking to illicit drug control, we may

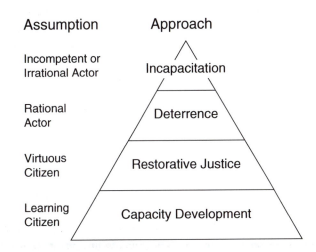

FIGURE 2.4   Regulatory Assumptions and Approaches

try restorative justice and court-imposed fines, but we may also come to the view that the drug dealer should be immediately put in prison, so that it is harder for them to endanger the community. Regulatory pyramids can never be used as templates. They need to be used responsively in relation to context, persons and threat to community, not only now but also into the future.

Possibly the most important idea, and the hardest for policy makers to get their heads around with regulatory pyramids, is that we have to think in a very particularistic way to construct them. This introduction to responsive regulation has provided an abstract way of talking about responsive regulation. We often miss the point that we design pyramids to achieve a practical task and to provide practical entries to different layers of the pyramid. To push our thinking a little more in this direction, the chapter moves on a little later to talk about the complementary idea of strengths-building pyramids.

Before doing that, however, consider an issue that causes consternation among some, and wild goose chases for others. The above discussion may leave the impression that responsive regulation is all about categorizing people. That is not as much the case as accepting that we are all very complex characters and have a range of selves we put forward when we are engaged with regulation. We all have some moments when we are capable of learning or thinking differently about a problem. We also have times when we just don't get it, when there are blocks to our accepting what is being asked of us. We all have moments when we are virtuous, and moments when we are not. We have some moments when we are rational actors and probably more when we are not. As regulators it is important to understand that regulators and regulated actors have one important thing in common. We share a very large number of moments when we do not act in a particularly competent or rational way. That is not to say we cannot or will not change if nudged in the right direction and given an opportunity (Thaler & Sunstein, 2008). Responsive regulation prefers to gently coax and caress change, but if necessary it pushes change coercively, after proffering opportunities to meet regulatory expectations. What this means is that all of us have multiple selves according to the particular context in which we are acting, and any of those selves can come to the fore depending on how we define the context we find ourselves in.

Understanding Multiple Selves

To understand responsive regulation is to understand that we have these multiple selves. Regulation can be designed to get us to put our best self forward in a situation. Imagine we are projecting the 'rational actor self' in a particular situation and ask, "What's in it for me?" What responsive regulation is trying to do is to move us down the pyramid to the virtuous self and the learning citizen role (see Figure 2.4) where the regulator's appeal is to ask us if we would not want to do that simply because it is the *right* thing to do and can we not be persuaded to want to do the right thing all the time? We have seen that this was very much how the "Untie the Elderly" Campaign succeeded. In other words, the regulator seeks to drive the nature of the self that is presenting in the regulatory situation further down the pyramid toward more virtuous selves, more learning selves.

The idea of the pyramid then, if we can go right back to Figure 2.1, is that we want most action to be down at the base of the pyramid. We start at the base and work up. Then if we get up to higher levels of the pyramid and things start to improve, we want to de-escalate. We move back down the pyramid. That there is the least space at the peak of the pyramid reflects the fact that it should be extremely rare that we resort to licence revocation. But the paradox of the pyramid is that if we lop the top off, we can only escalate up to something like civil penalties. The design of the pyramid is to keep driving us down to the base: The peak of the pyramid exists to both give the regulator the capability to escalate up the pyramid, and the regulated actor the incentive to keep things down at the base. If we lop the top off and have a pyramid that only goes halfway up to civil penalties for instance, the logic is reversed. The pressure will be to escalate from the warning letter to civil penalties. Why will the pressure be to escalate up to civil penalties? Precisely because the regulated actors know that is as far as things can go. They have greater incentive to be game-playing rational actors, because the worst thing that could happen to them is visible and they are prepared for managing their worst-case scenario. In areas like occupational health and safety regulation in the United States, we have seen a standard civil penalty regime operating. Regulated actors break the rules in relation to their workplace, get a slap on the wrist and a fine. Paying the fine just becomes a cost of them doing business. In such regulatory contexts voluntary compliance tends to fail; normative commitment to doing the right thing corrodes. Instead, the truncated nature of the regulatory options produces a calculative optimizing attitude to occupational health and safety obligations.

Supports and Sanctions: A Regulatory Pyramid and Strengths-based Pyramid

The idea of the regulatory pyramid is that non-compliance is posing some sort of risk and therefore requires some form of risk containment. The regulatory pyramid is about the idea of prompt responses before the problem escalates. Conversely, the emphasis in the strengths-based pyramid is more on opportunities assessment and opportunities enhancement. The strengths-based pyramid is about waiting to support strengths that bubble up from below. Adding strengths-based pyramids to regulatory pyramids seeks to emphasize that we are too often obsessed with risks and not enough with opportunities.

The strengths-based pyramid is about hope for seizing opportunities; regulatory enforcement pyramids are ultimately about fear of sanctions. Strengths-based pyramids are about establishing institutions focused on building community hope, empowering communities to solve their own problems. Good leaders of institutions like universities sit back, see where excellence is bubbling up from below within the institution and say, "That is terrific. Let's get behind it". This is a strategy that builds and regulates through a strengths-based approach, in contrast to top-down restructuring that might crush the innovation this is bubbling up (Gunningham & Sinclair, 2002).

We see then that regulatory pyramids of sanctions and strengths-based pyramids of supports do different things. A regulatory pyramid pushes standards above a floor. A strengths-based pyramid is about pulling standards up through a ceiling. If the purpose is to dramatically lift standards, regulators handicap their effectiveness by focusing only on the poor performers, that is, on minimal standards and on the enforcement pyramid. In addition they need a strengths-based pyramid to help them focus on excellence, recognizing the accomplishment of the high flyers and using them as a benchmark for pulling everyone's standards up. This can happen in cultures of industry compliance (Gunningham & Sinclair, 2002), but it can also happen among adolescent peer groups. The young person who finds a new way of being, that takes his or her life into a new trajectory, can help to raise up everyone in his or her peer group, just as firms that are leaders can raise the standards of everyone across their industry in work safety for instance. The key idea is that one going up through the ceiling can help pull others up through the floor. And that is part of the philosophy of a strengths-based approach.

So how can we use regulatory and strengths-based pyramids? They can, and most effectively are, used in combination. Regulators generally have the dual role of pushing standards above the floor and pulling standards up through ceilings. If we have a set of problems or a set of risks, one way we can set out to solve them is to focus and target the risk. Restorative justice helps with that because it puts the problem, rather than a stigmatized person, in the centre of the circle. In doing so, we consider ways of containing risk. One approach is to prevent people from engaging in a certain behaviour—the traditional regulatory pyramid approach. However, if we were to apply the strengths-based philosophy, we would focus on individual, family and collective strengths and try to expand out from their strengths until they absorb the weaknesses. Both can be effective ways of steering the flow of events. The argument is not that one should be used and the other not. The strengths-based critique is that too much public policy is about risk-management and not enough is about strength-building.

If there is an under-performing person within a human services organization that is letting the team down, creating disasters week in and week out, one way to solve that problem is by targeting the risk that person poses to the organization. We can re-train, discipline and regulate them in some way, so that the risk is no longer a problem. Another way to think about such problems, however, is to see how the strengths of other people might compensate for that person's weaknesses. A human resource manager using a strengths-based approach might say to an under-performer and the work team: "Wouldn't it be better for you to move into this area of responsibility, where you have real strengths, and where the person in the job at the moment is not as good at that as you are. You will absorb their weaknesses with your strengths, and this other person over here absorbs your area of responsibility, where they have strengths that are greater than your weaknesses". In this way, problems are dealt with by using the strengths of people who are already there, and growing those strengths through nurturing them, rather than trying to discipline the weak link. We do that in managing problems in organizations all the time, but we perhaps do not think about it in regulatory terms as a strategy of using strengths-based rather than risk-based intervention.

Below in Figure 2.5 is just one example of complementing a regulatory (or what we shall now call enforcement) pyramid with a strengths-based pyramid, which is from the nursing home regulatory research (Braithwaite et al., 2007).

The two pyramids in Figure 2.5 are also often called a pyramid of sanctions and a pyramid of supports. At the base of the two pyramids we have an education and persuasion approach. In the regulatory pyramid it is focused on the problem, informing the regulated actor about what they should do to avoid

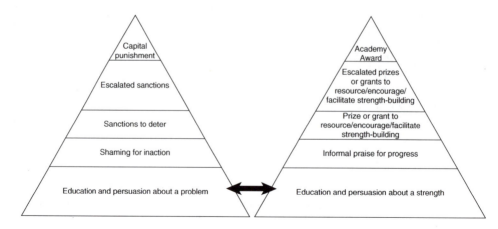

FIGURE 2.5 Enforcement Pyramid and Strengths-based Pyramid

risks, perhaps risk of injury in the workplace. In contrast, an education and persuasion approach on the strengths-based pyramid would focus on the opportunity regulated actors have to improve their well-being based on a strength that they have, perhaps a good way of lifting a patient. From this strength, other improvements will be sought and other strengths introduced to safeguard against risk. Let us consider the case of nursing home regulation in relation to these two types of pyramids. Inspectors may give informal praise when they inspect the nursing home, for example: "That is terrific what you have done there". We have seen that praise in our empirical research was found to be a powerful predictor of improved compliance of the nursing home, that is, improved quality of care two years on (Makkai & Braithwaite, 1993). Praise for improvement is a simple thing that inspectors do that does not increase the cost of regulation.

A strengths-based approach can also be used to target particular facilities that are known to have potential while also facing problems. By opening doors for them to learn more, regulated actors can see what the gold standard is, can be encouraged to reach that standard, and in the process, manage their risks. At the level of say an individual child or a family that has a child protection problem, the strengths-based philosophy would give rise to questions like, "What are the strengths of this individual child? What are the strengths of this family or the school that the child goes to?" And, "Which of all of those strengths, if we concentrated on just one, would be the most strategic in absorbing the risks that exist around the life of that child?" There might be another strength on our list of strengths, which is a really impressive strength, and from which we could grow many more strengths, but it might not be a very strategic one to target in terms of absorbing the particular risks that are putting that child at risk, or that family at risk.

It is the same when we award a prize. These are not prizes in the imperialist tradition of knighthoods in the British Empire for a life of serving the disciplinary objectives of the empire. Nor are they like rankist prizes[1] of academic imperialism for a life lived in a discipline that is superior to the lives of others in disciplining of young minds into the regulated paths of that discipline. We give out these prizes for specific continuous improvements in the quality of care given in nursing homes. The nursing home has done something really innovative that we want the whole industry to take notice of, because if they all take notice of it, it will help them all pull themselves up through ceilings and above the floors the standards set. With escalated prizes and academy awards, we can escalate up to these more exceptional rewards. Similarly, we can have an escalated set of regulatory sanctions. Indeed, the idea is that the pyramids are complementary. You would more than likely be doing both—ideally, you would start at the base of the strengths-based pyramid, and see how far it could take you. For regulators, it is much more satisfying to start by escalating up this strengths-based pyramid. An inspector goes into the nursing home, sees some things are improving and targets those things because that is an inspiring new development: and if they get this improved management system really working then they are going to solve a lot of the risks that might otherwise have led the inspector to escalate up with sanctions. So, the inspector concentrates on moving up the strengths-based pyramid, and encourages the regulated actor to have staff awards for some action that is critically important, or a scheme where residents are able to fill out a piece of paper to thank a staff member for something particularly kind. Inspectors need to encourage all of these sorts of positive things. And if they are producing greater improvements through the pyramid of supports and absorbing the risks that are causing most concern, then we have the desired outcome without damaging social relationships or imposing costs. If on the other hand, there still are major risks that are not being absorbed, then the inspector would move across to the enforcement pyramid, and would signal preparedness to escalate up this pyramid with these more costly regulatory interventions. So, inspectors can, and usually will be escalating up both regulatory pyramids simultaneously.

We have only started working with enforcement and strengths-based pyramids together. How that should be done is far from resolved. To privilege strengths-based pyramids is an empowering philosophy. It allows regulated actors to become the more dominant shapers of the pace. But many regulators have protective obligations under the law, and there is a threshold where a regulator just cannot sit on their hands and allow regulated actors to go at their own pace when some terrible risk is not being managed. Knowing when to move to enforcement from strengths-based pyramids is a hard question, relying very much on the knowledge and wisdom of experienced regulators who have a deep understanding of regulated actors and the contexts in which they work. What we do know, however, is that regulation currently errs on the side of enforcement because of the mistaken belief that this provides the best protection and too often in doing so relational and cultural safety is undermined.

Be Wary of the Nuclear Option

Thinking about strengths-based interventions in a regulatory area where, for example, children's lives are at risk may seem to some managers to be part of the problem. Child protection has been heavily dominated by social work philosophy and practice, and empowerment is one of the central tenets of social work. For those managers with doubts about the usefulness of strengths-based approaches in high-risk areas like child protection, consider a radically different kind of regulatory challenge that has been well researched—nuclear safety regulation. In this area the reaction of regulators has been that "there is no riskier activity than a nuclear power plant; we must have a tough regulatory strategy with formal guarantees of enforcement because we just cannot afford to have a nuclear melt-down".

After the investigation into the Three-Mile Island disaster in the United States, where America almost faced its first nuclear plant meltdown, regulators and the commission of enquiry (Kemeny, 1979) reached a surprising conclusion (Rees, 2009). They found that due to the emphasis on detailed regulatory control and tough oversight enforcement, checking against risks in a highly 'rulish' regulatory regime, people operating the nuclear power plant became rule-following automatons. They became ritualists—following rituals of comfort so that people out there might think they would be safe from a nuclear meltdown (Braithwaite, 2008: Chapter 6). When something went wrong, they frenetically searched for "Which rules haven't we followed", instead of thinking systemically about the safety management system. Indeed, they could not think in a problem-solving way because the enforcement system had prevented them from developing systemic wisdom.

The learnings from Three-Mile Island led to a radical shift in the enterprise of regulating for nuclear safety. The regulatory regime moved to one that was less prescriptive, less obsessed with enforcement and more self-regulatory and relational (or communitarian as Joseph Rees (2009) put it in his classic work). The emphasis was more on thinking and learning than it had been before. This was a more strengths-based, wisdom-building regulatory regime. The effect of that change has been impressive. Regulators have quite a good way of measuring nuclear safety risk which is to measure how many SCRAMS there are—automated shutdowns of a nuclear power plant as a result of systems passing safety thresholds. In the ten years after Three-Mile Island across the United States and then globally, the risk of SCRAMS reduced from 7 to 1 per facility per year, and the following decade up to 1990 it reduced from 1 to 0.1—another ten-fold reduction. The regulatory technology in relation to nuclear plants has improved through being more strengths-based rather than doing what seems to come naturally with a very extreme risk—that is to keep focused on those risks and to prescriptively regulate them under formal enforcement controls.

Conclusion

The process of building responsive regulatory pyramids takes place with a number of relationship-building principles that sit alongside a regulatory agency's formal mission. We can think of these as the key principles of restorative justice that include listening, empowering, healing, procedural justice and widening the circle when problems are not reaching resolution. The most difficult of problems require us to be thoughtful about our willingness to use a variety of both supports and sanctions. Responsiveness also requires us to be thoughtful about the dynamic sequencing of supports and sanctions. Most of all it requires communication of the message that we are willing to fail, learn and adapt fast because the world is a very complex place (Harford, 2011). Yet the regulator, and the community that supports it, will not go away until the problem is solved and the community is safe.

Responsive regulation as a model of how to escalate community concern has been applied in Australia and its region (the Pacific, South-East Asia, particularly New Zealand) and in parts of Europe such as the United Kingdom, Ireland and the Netherlands (Ivec & Braithwaite, 2015). However, there is no regulator we know in North America that could be described as a responsive regulator. While Valerie and John Braithwaite's work on responsive regulation has been much more cited by scholars than their work on restorative justice, the response of *practitioners* in North America has been quite the opposite. Thanks to the work of so many wonderful North American scholarly and practice champions restorative justice has had a wide, if not deep, impact on practice across North America and the world. In fact, it is very difficult, if not impossible, to visit any country in the world that does not have some kind of restorative justice program led by some inspiring restorative justice thinkers. In human services, restorative roots may be shallow in most countries, but at least they are taking root.

This is not true of responsive regulation, which has had little impact on the human services in any country, nor on scholarly writing in the human services field (though see Burford & Adams, 2004 and the associated special issue; Healy & Dugdale, 2011: Harris, 2011; Ivec, Braithwaite, & Harris, 2012; Dow & Braithwaite, 2013). Our hope is that this volume might change this and help stimulate new synergies in the relationship between restorative justice and responsive regulation in the human services. The final chapter of the book draws together the lessons of that politics of hope for a restorative and responsive regulation of human services that builds a freer society.

Note

1. Rankism means an elitist regulatory strategy of signalling that some people are better than others for no strong reason. Sexism and racism are just the two most common kinds of rankism. In many former colonies we see a continuation of colonial institutions in their academies in the tradition of the Royal Society that create an upper class of scholars and accomplish that by allowing existing members of the academic elite to "black-ball" the election of new fellows to the academy.

References

Altschul, I., Lee, S. J., & Gershoff, E. T. (2016). Hugs, not hits: Warmth and spanking as predictors of child social competence. *Journal of Marriage and Family*, 78(3), 695–714.

Ayres, I., & Braithwaite, J. (1992). *Responsive regulation: Transcending the deregulation debate*. New York: Oxford University Press.

Braithwaite, J. (1985). *To punish or persuade: Enforcement of coal mine safety*. Albany: SUNY Press.

Braithwaite, J. (2005). *Markets in vice, markets in virtue*. Sydney/New York: Federation Press/Oxford University Press.

Braithwaite, J. (2008). *Regulatory capitalism: How it works, ideas for making it work better.* Cheltenham, UK: Edward Elgar.

Braithwaite, J., Makkai, T., & Braithwaite, V. (2007). *Regulating aged care: Ritualism and the new pyramid.* Cheltenham, UK: Edward Elgar.

Burford, G., & Adams, P. (2004). Restorative justice, responsive regulation and social work. *Journal of Sociology and Social Welfare, 31*(1), 7–26.

Castle, N. G., & Mor, V. (1998). Physical restraints in nursing homes: A review of the literature since the Nursing Home Reform Act of 1987. *Medical Care Research and Review, 55*(2), 139–170.

Dow, K. L., & Braithwaite, V. (2013). *Review of higher education regulation report.* Canberra: Commonwealth of Australia.

Evans, L. K., & Strumpf, N. E. (1989). Tying down the elderly: A review of the literature on physical restraint. *Journal of the American Geriatrics Society, 37*(1), 65–74.

Gunderson, E. A., Sorhagen, N. S., Gripshover, S. J., Dweck, C. S., Goldin-Meadow, S., & Levine, S. C. (2018). Parent praise to toddlers predicts fourth grade academic achievement via children's incremental mindsets. *Developmental Psychology, 54*(3), 397–409.

Gunningham, N., Grabosky, P. N., & Sinclair, D. (1998). *Smart regulation—designing environmental policy.* Oxford: Oxford University Press.

Gunningham, N., & Sinclair, D. (2002). *Leaders and Laggards: Next generation environmental policy.* Sheffield, UK: Greenleaf Publishing.

Harford, T. (2011). *Adapt: Why success always starts with failure.* London, UK: Hachette Digital.

Harris, N. (2011). Does responsive regulation offer an alternative? Questioning the role of formalistic assessment in child protection investigations. *British Journal of Social Work, 41*(7), 1383–1403.

Health Care Financing Administration (HCFA). (1998). *Report to congress: Study of private accreditation (deeming) of nursing homes, regulatory incentives and non-regulatory initiatives, and effectiveness of the survey and certification system.* Baltimore, MD: Health Care Financing Administration.

Healy, J., & Dugdale, P. (2011). Patient safety first: Responsive regulation in health care. *Journal of Nursing Regulation, 2*(2), 60.

Honig, M., Petersen, S., Herbstein, T., Roux, S., Nel, D., & Shearing, C. (2015). A conceptual framework to enable the changes required for a one-planet future. *Environmental Values, 24*(5), 663–688.

Hood, C., James, O., Scott, C., Jones, G. W., & Travers, T. (1999). *Regulation inside government: Waste watchers, quality police, and sleaze-busters.* Oxford: Oxford University Press.

Ivec, M., & Braithwaite, V. (2015). *Applications of responsive regulatory theory in Australia and Overseas: Update (2015).* Retrieved from http:// http://regnet.anu.edu.au/sites/default/files/publications/attachments/2015-05/Occasional%2520Paper%252023_Ivec_Braithwaite_0.pdf.

Ivec, M., Braithwaite, V., & Harris, N. (2012). "Resetting the relationship" in Indigenous child protection: Public hope and private reality. *Law & Policy, 34*(1), 80–103.

Kemeny, J. G. (1979). *Report of the president's commission on the accident at Three Mile Island. The need for change: The Legacy of TMI.* Washington, DC: The President's Commission on the Accident at Three Mile Island.

Makkai, T., & Braithwaite, J. (1993). Praise, pride and corporate compliance. *International Journal of the Sociology of Law, 21,* 73–91.

Mugford, S. K. (1991). Drug legalization and the "Goldilocks" problem: Thinking about costs and control of drugs. In M. Krauss & E. Lazear (Eds.), *Searching for alternatives: Drug-control policies in the United States* (pp. 33–50). Stanford, CA: Hoover Institution Press.

Parker, C., & Braithwaite, J. (2003). Regulation. In P. Cane & M. Tushnet (Eds.), *The Oxford handbook of legal studies* (pp. 119–145). Oxford: Oxford University Press.

Power, M. (1997). *The audit society: Rituals of verification.* Oxford: Oxford University Press.

Reason, J. (1990). *Human error.* Cambridge: Cambridge University Press.

Rees, J.V. (2009). *Hostages of each other: The transformation of nuclear safety since Three Mile Island*. Chicago: University of Chicago Press.

Special Committee on Aging, United States Senate. (1990). *Untie the elderly: Quality care without restraints, 101st congress, December 4, 1989.* Washington, DC: US Government Printing Office.

Thaler, R. H., & Sunstein, C. R. (2008). *Nudge—Improving decisions about health, wealth and happiness*. New Haven, CT: Yale University Press.

3

FAMILIES AND SCHOOLS THAT ARE RESTORATIVE AND RESPONSIVE

Valerie Braithwaite

Introduction

This chapter seeks to normalise responsive regulation as a natural part of family life and identify restorative practice as an integral part of problem solving that makes responsive regulation work in family settings. Intuitive understanding of responsive regulation and restorative justice are more widespread in western culture than human service professionals recognise. For instance, the familiarity of these ideas in the child-rearing space has made it more natural to translate ideas of responsive regulation and restorative justice into the school setting to deal with bullying through whole-of-school approaches. Yet there are obstacles to expanding the reach of the approach, involving ideology, low trust in the community, state-led technocratic regulation and overly zealous political control.

Normalising Responsive Regulation and Restorative Practices

What responsive regulation does not mean is consistency in *the way we respond to* problem behaviour. Expressed baldly like this, responsive regulation sounds like bad parenting. Ideal child-rearing practices always place consistency at the top of the list. What consistency means in the parenting context, however, is that a parent is consistent in setting standards for a child, in particular, being consistent in pointing out to a child what is acceptable and unacceptable behaviour. In other words, shouting in a sibling's face is not acceptable at home, nor in the park with a stranger, nor at school with a teacher.

It does not follow that if one is consistent in calling out misbehaviour, consistency in what one does to manage the behaviour is best practice. As a child in the 1950s I remember the response of parents and authority to misbehaviour being very consistently punitive—a smack or the strap or the cane. What changed in parenting over the next half century was the practice of authoritarian parenting, that is, a parenting style that both consistently called misbehaviour to account *and* consistently responded in a punitive fashion. In the second half of the last century, a tome of research relegated authoritarian parenting to the scrap heap, at least in the eyes of western experts (Darling & Steinberg, 1993; Larzelere, Morris, & Harrist, 2012; Power, 2013; Rudy & Grusec, 2006; Steinberg & Silk, 2002). In its place

DOI: 10.4324/9780429398704-3

emerged a philosophy of good parenting best described as democratic parenting (also referred to as authoritative parenting by Baumrind, 1978). A less efficacious form of laissez faire parenting also made its presence known in these bodies of research, arguably more as a reaction against authoritarian parenting than a coherent philosophy of how to raise a child who could fit into society.

While laissez faire parenting was permissive on both calling out misbehaviour and correcting it, democratic parenting called out misbehaviour but then evoked a range of strategies for its correction, the central plank being dialogue with the child directed toward understanding the misbehaviour and its consequences. The child might be asked "Why did you do that?", "Did you see what effect it had?", "Have some time out while you cool down", "Straight home and bed for you", "No more watching cartoons on television, it is teaching you bad habits". The array of responses was endless because the assumption was that in order to change the behaviour, a parent needed to work with the child both to understand its causes, explain why the behaviour was undesirable and to rechannel behaviour down a more socially accepted path.

Repeated displays of a particular form of misbehaviour were also better managed through democratic parenting. Should unacceptable behaviour continue, a parent is held responsible first and foremost for its correction in western culture. Nagging or just repeatedly and consistently responding in the same way without changing the behaviour is not good enough. A parent with a democratic parenting style in such circumstances was likely to respond with a plan of action: "If you do this again, we need to consider other ways . . ."; "If you do this again, we will have to develop strategies together for you to practice at home . . ."; "If you do this again, we will go together and talk to your teacher . . ."; "If you do this again, I think it is reasonable to remove some of your privileges—do you agree that . . .". A democratic parenting style, in response to persistent misbehaviour, will escalate the intensity of the intervention to change the behaviour. In general, a parent will increase the dialogue, increase remedial action, involve others and increase the seriousness of consequences until the problem starts abating. All the while, the parent relates to the child with respect and affection. Democratic parenting requires warmth in the relationship to be effective; hostility is counterproductive (Power, 2013; Rudy & Grusec, 2006; Shin, 2009).

Democratic parenting of this kind is an example of responsive regulation: Consistently staying on message to correct misbehaviour, but being responsive by analysing the situation and selecting discerningly from an array of possible strategies to correct the behaviour. In the democratic parenting tradition this would extend to being willing to ask for help and build a community of support around the child and parent if need be to get things on track. There is consistency in disapproving of a behaviour but not disapproving of the child herself. There is critical self-reflection on the part of the parent, but not total self-condemnation for herself as a parent. Her worth is reflected in the efforts she invests to correct the child's misbehaviour.

A parent's response will differ with different children, in different contexts and with variation in seriousness of the harm of the misbehaviour. This is at the heart of responsive regulation. The crucial question is always to account for the response, to explain one's actions, not to do the same thing repeatedly regardless of context. If a child shouted at her mother and then crumpled into a ball of shame, no further disapproving action from a parent is required. The child disapproves of herself. Lesson learnt. If a child escalates in violent outbursts against her mother, in spite of efforts by a bevvy of family and professionals to remedy the situation, intervention may be necessary to separate mother and child for a while. Whichever the scenario, the priority is to prevent harmful behaviour. To do otherwise is to harm the child—she is likely to be tagged a behavioural problem, a bully. While stopping the harmful behaviour, social scaffolding for the child remains critical so that she can learn that certain behaviour is unacceptable and needs to be controlled. The child through being supported while held accountable for her actions learns to self-correct. In other words, the process allows the child to learn about being regulated by others and self, to trust and be trusted, to use one's social scaffolding to build one's character and understand social life.

Learning this process of self-regulation through social scaffolding from others is an essential part of learning to fit into society (Bandura, 1986, 1997). And it never stops. Learning to follow school rules and getting on with fellow students and teachers morphs into understanding employer expectations and working well alongside others, which morphs into being a good citizen in the community, in time being a good parent oneself, and lastly, if life is long, being a loved and cared-for person in a nursing home.

Does this process of self-regulation mean we become automatons of compliance? There is not much evidence of that in the world. The real question surrounds the conditions under which we break out from being automatons (Braithwaite, 2009). Do we do it in rage or on an impulse to release tension or get something we want? Do we break out because we didn't quite appreciate the significance of the rules and their meaning? Or do we think through our non-compliance, sometimes taking advantage of the system, sometimes rebelling because we object to how the system operates. Non-compliance can result from one or more of these conditions. Non-compliance can be a force for good, if the system is out of sync with people's needs. The hope of democratic parenting is not that non-compliance will not occur but rather that non-compliance can be discussed, is well reasoned, explicable and does not do harm to others; and when it occurs, people learn from their mistakes and self-correct.

Why What Is Good for Families Is Good for Schools and Society

It is through continuous socially informed learning with others that responsive regulation is useful not only for problem solving in families but also for protecting our democracy and human rights. Responsive regulation is sensitive to non-compliance that stems from rage or ignorance or defiance or political protest. Different responses are made depending on circumstance. Sometimes coordination is imposed or coerced through responsive regulation to safeguard stability and ensure smooth transitions to new laws or policies. But that is not done without deliberation, transparency and accountability. Sometimes as a result the rules are changed. Responsive regulation pushes us toward compliance, but not without providing opportunity for us to reflect on the system with which we are expected to comply. If rules are unfair or oppressive, or expect too much of a person, the process of responsive regulation allows for dialogue to explain behaviour and consider alternative, more acceptable pathways for the future.

Dialogue is necessary to familiarise an authority with context so that it is possible to be responsive. In order to understand context, authorities have to unshackle from official accoutrements and trappings and connect with the lives of people—listen, understand and work with them to find a better pathway forward. Restorative justice circles for resolution of conflict and restorative practices more generally are examples of mechanisms for building shared understandings of context and commitment to a pathway forward.

The purpose of this first section to the chapter is to reiterate a very simple point from some 30 years ago (J. Braithwaite, 1989). Every parent who has read a 'how to book' on raising a child knows about responsive regulation. They also know the basics of restorative justice—to acknowledge harm, understand consequences and find a way forward that repairs the harm and/or relationships. Responsive regulation and restorative justice are practiced within families routinely and mindlessly, in the family room or at the dining room table. It is therefore not surprising that these ways of thinking and engaging have been most readily translated into schools. Hopkins (2002) refers to restorative justice in the UK as "a natural development of where many schools are already or are moving towards" (p. 146). It is more surprising that restorative justice and responsive regulation have not reached further into practices of our human service institutions.

Formal Schooling—a Tough Gig

The value of formal education has been valorised to the point that adults often forget the challenge schooling poses for children. It is here that they face the extraordinarily difficult, and often-underestimated, task of learning to "fit in" with people who they don't know while also participating in a structured set of learning activities many of which they can't do the first time round. In the process of learning, children watch their peers closely, not only for guidance and assurance, but also inevitably as a point of comparison. Competition and cooperation define work and play. It is normal for children to become involved in games where one person wins and next time another person wins. Bullying younger kids, weaker kids, kids who look different, those who fit in less well, or learn more slowly, or too quickly becomes mixed up with the game where there is a tussle for being the best. As Dixon and Smith (2011) put it, bullying is part of a game of one-up/one-down. The problem lies when children become locked in a relationship with one consistently 'up' (that is, bullying) and the other consistently 'down' (being bullied).

Bullying is a relational problem of domination. As such it is different from the one-up/one-up game where children are pitting themselves against each other, competing on a task, and learning the art of being a winner sometimes, and a loser at other times. We need to learn to have a healthy appetite for one-up/one-up play and steer away from one-up/one-down play. This is one of the lessons we have to learn at school. It lends itself well to resolution through restorative justice and responsive regulation.

What We Know About Bullying

Bullying is not just a school problem. This is partly why its management within schools is difficult. Increasingly, bullying is recognised as a societal problem from the streets housing the homeless to the homes of Hollywood's rich and famous. Bullying is linked to sexual harassment and assault, domestic violence, workplace harassment, HR dismissal tactics, rage toward health providers (from ambulance to hospital), police culture, child protection practices, youth and refugee detention facilities, prisons, trolling and social media, and of course, our education systems from kindergartens to universities.

Bullying refers to one individual or group repeatedly seeking to dominate another person, physically or psychologically, in jest or in order to control another's behaviour. A well-accepted definition is: Bullying involves persistent, offensive, abusive or intimidating behaviour that makes the target feel threatened, humiliated, stressed or unsafe (Di Martino, Hoel, & Cooper, 2003). A substantial body of empirical research has shown the deleterious effects of bullying on people's health and well-being, ranging from loss of confidence, withdrawal from social life, low life satisfaction and unhappiness through depression, anxiety, mental and physical disorders, and, in some cases, suicide (Hymel & Swearer, 2015 for children; Balducci, Fraccaroli, & Schaufeli, 2011 for adults).

Public anti-bullying campaigns in recent years have reached their peak with media coverage of tragic outcomes such as bullying-induced suicide. At such times, public outcry converges on messages of law and order and punishment of offenders: The simple solution is perceived to be stopping bullies through enforcing anti-bullying laws (present across countries, for one US example see www.nytimes. com/2011/08/31/nyregion/bullying-law-puts-new-jersey-schools-on-spot.html). Somewhere missing from the public discourse are two important empirical findings which limit the likely success of simply enforcing anti-bullying laws, as important as they may be for setting acceptable standards of conduct.

First, bullying and victimisation for a significant proportion of children and adults go hand in hand. There are a minority of individuals who are persistent bullies. But those who are most socially and psychologically at risk are bully-victims. They flip between being the victim and the bully and back again, carrying the insecurities and social awkwardness of victims and the aggressiveness and impulsivity of bullies (Olweus, 1993).

Second, and this is often overlooked, most of us learn about the harm done by bullying through experience, through our own mistakes in competitive playfulness or social insensitivity. Soft bullying is part of everyday life and results in self-correction. Serious bullying is a pattern of hurtful behaviour that is not self-corrected when we see the pain we cause others. The factors that determine whether we learn or we don't learn are many and complex. Moreover, they interact. Family child rearing and family relationships matter, school culture, teaching and peer relations matter, personality matters and highly contextual issues like what is happening when bully and victim meet matters. And then there are sites of bullying beyond the school which adds to the complexity—walking to and from school, parks, public transport and on the internet. Against this body of research that has accumulated over some 40 years, legislation or anti-bullying organisational policy is an inadequate response. Learning not to bully involves more than learning a rule and fearing punishment for breaking the rule.

The Phenomenon of the Bully-Victim

A substantial literature documents the bully-victim as being most at risk psychologically and socially (Haynie et al., 2001; Kumpulainen & Räsänen, 2000; Veenstra et al., 2005). Both Helene Shin and Eliza Ahmed have made a significant contribution to understanding how children become bully-victims and why children caught in bullying incidents need understanding and responsiveness from authorities as early as possible; not neglect until an incident triggers school expulsion or police intervention.

Shin has been analysing biennial survey data on bullying conducted as part of Growing Up in Australia: the Longitudinal Study of Australian Children (LSAC). The survey, supported by the Australian government, set out to track growth and development of 10,000 children and families from all parts of Australia (www.growingupinaustralia.gov.au/). Shin has focused on one cohort of the study (Cohort K), around 4,000 children who were aged 12–13 years at Wave 5, 14–15 years at Wave 6 and 16–17 years at Wave 7. The Wave 7 survey was conducted in 2015–16.

The majority of children reported involvement in bullying in the past month as victim or offender or both in the 12–13 age group (60%). Middle school is the time when bullying is often reported to peak (see Olweus, 2013; Wang, Iannotti, & Luk, 2012). Around half (29%) reported being victims but not bullies, while a further 25% reported that they were both victims and bullies. This reflected a substantial proportion of at-risk children: The story became more dire when cyberbullying was taken into account.

In the LSAC analyses undertaken by Shin and her colleagues, cyberbullying, while far less common than traditional bullying in this age group, nevertheless was linked to traditional bullying and the children most likely to cross-over were bully-victims (Shin, Braithwaite, & Ahmed, 2016). In cyber space, they were most likely to be victims. The risks facing this most vulnerable group increased with time rather than decreased (Braithwaite & Shin, 2018). At follow-up, many children in the Wave 5 sample had transitioned out of being part of bullying encounters: At 16–17 years of age, only 1 in 3 reported involvement. But the trajectory of those who had not was toward being a victim or bully-victim. Children who found themselves in the bully-victim role, particularly on-line, reported lower school belonging, higher depression, self-harm and suicide ideation, and poorer overall health and parental relationships. Such children also spent more time on-line, presumably on social media.

Shin's work has been important in showing diverse needs within the group of children affected by bullying. They need a responsive regulatory approach that is sensitive to context and a complex range of issues that span school life, home life, use of the internet and peer interactions. And those in greatest need—bully-victims—need assistance in managing their relationships which appear to be causing distress both at home and at school. For this group, restorative practices hold particular appeal. But given the risk to bully-victims of being engulfed in continuing bouts of bullying with serious mental and physical health consequences, more options for intervention are likely needed.

Eliza Ahmed used the Life at School Survey (1969–1999), an earlier study of 32 schools in Canberra, Australia, to draw similar conclusions about the different needs of children caught up in bullying incidents (Ahmed & Braithwaite, 2004a, 2004b, 2005, 2006, 2012). Ahmed developed the schema for grouping children as bullies, victims, bully-victims and nonbully-nonvictims. While the bully-victim numbers were smaller in this sample, their risks were evident. Bully-victims tended to report more authoritarian parenting and family disharmony, not liking school, being in trouble at school and seeing little control of bullying at school. The bullying problem arose from many sources, both social and individual. Ahmed collected data from children aged 9–12 years in primary school, and then with Brenda Morrison followed up these children 3 years later when they were in secondary school.

Like Shin, Ahmed followed the trajectories of children who had been classified as bully only, victim only, bully-victim and nonbully-nonvictim. Those who were bullying when they were aged 9–12 years were likely to be still bullying when aged 12–15 years. There was a tendency for bully-victims, if they changed groups, to transition to the bullying-only group (Ahmed & Braithwaite, 2012). Since this time, most schools have introduced anti-bullying programs and bullying has become a point of concern for parents in selecting a school for their children. Children may be less locked into roles of bullying and victimisation today than was the case at the time of Ahmed's study. In this respect it is of note that Rigby and Smith (2011) report a drop in bullying from 1990 to 2009 which they consider in part due to a stronger focus on the better management of bullying.

While Ahmed's work was conducted before the explosion in school anti-bullying programs, the research design has some distinctive features that explain why anti-bullying laws and policy is not enough and why schools need to invest in the integration of social-emotional-relational interventions along with effective disciplinary control measures. Ahmed provides deeper insights into the emotional architecture that can hold children in the bullying space. This emotional architecture is sustained by factors associated both with how the school is run and how children engage with each other. Those wishing to find someone to blame for bullying will be disappointed: The answer is complex.

The Emotional Architecture That Sustains Bullying

Ahmed's data showed that students who believed there was tolerance of bullying at school (no action was taken to stop it) were more likely to have transitioned into bullying (as bullies or bully-victims)

3 years on. These findings support Ttofi and Farrington's (2011) meta-analysis which highlighted the effectiveness of anti-bullying programs that implemented social control measures in the school (school rules, supervision, teacher training) as opposed to programs that focused on improving the social skills of students. But Ahmed's data shows that it is also important for children to accept bullying as a socially undesirable practice that they want to avoid. In other words, preventing bullying also requires active and on-going efforts at self-regulation within schools.

The emotional architecture identified by Ahmed as critical to whether or not bullying becomes a problem at school is shame management. Shame describes the emotion that we feel when we have failed to live up to a shared social standard either in relation to a moral code or a performance standard. Sometimes we break codes without realising it is a shared standard of proper conduct. School is full of such learnings for young children. Learning not to bully is a specific case of our journey to civility.

Revised reintegrative shaming theory sets out conditions for learning what is appropriate behaviour and what is not, so that we can find our place in society and enjoy it as a source of support and productive activity. The key feedback loop on which we rely is shaming (sensing or imagining others' disapproval). Shaming works for us when we learn how to manage it well (Ahmed et al., 2001). J Braithwaite argued for shaming that was reintegrative (disapprove predatory actions, support the predatory person) not stigmatising (disapproving and socially rejecting the whole person). Both kinds of shaming can impact a person's ethical identity (goodness and capability of self) if the criticism comes from a respected source (Harris, 2011). But reintegrative shaming provides us with the social scaffolding to learn and recover. Stigmatising shaming grinds us into the dirt, breaking spirits and capacity to recover because of its holistic condemnation of us.

Just as shame can be delivered in different ways, shame is *received and interpreted* differently by different individuals. Adaptive shame management means that when we feel shame, we interpret it in these terms: If the criticism is true, we acknowledge the problem and seek to correct it or make amends. If the criticism is not true, we seek to clear our name. When shame is not managed in a socially adaptive way, others are blamed for the problem, responsibility is denied and anger is displaced onto others. Shame acknowledgement is most likely to occur when a person feels safe to openly face wrongdoing or failure, that is, under conditions of reintegrative shaming and supportive social bonds. Shame displacement is most likely when a person's ethical identity is threatened, when shaming is stigmatising and a person feels unsafe to share failings with others. Children involved in bullying as victims or bullies are the least likely to feel safe at school, and some will feel unsafe at home. Special efforts are required to create "safe space" for resolution and learning.

Ahmed and colleagues used shame acknowledgement and displacement to explain a pattern of bullying others at school in studies in both Australia and Bangladesh. Shame displacement and bullying tolerance accompanied transition into bullying. Shame acknowledgement and control of bullying marked desistence from bullying. Effects of shame management and social control were not uniform across groups of bullies, victims, bully-victims and nonbully-nonvictims. Interventions may need to be flexible and responsive to prior bullying experiences. One-shot anti-bullying programs with before-and-after measures of empathy and social responsibility will not suffice. Interventions involving supervision and sanctioning may create a safer school environment quickly, but developing shame management capacities will take time and be shaped by belonging and liking for school and family, and bullying experiences. Shin and Ahmed's work suggests that some children abandon hope for an existence beyond a bullying culture. Reigniting hope may require skill and imagination and patience. At the same time, harm to other children must be contained. Reigniting hope and controlling harm over extended periods of time requires a long-range plan of action that is inclusive and flexible to accommodate different circumstances. It can't be restricted to restorative justice interventions or to off-the-shelf anti-bullying programs.

The kind of approach being advocated here could benefit from responsive regulatory thinking: See the child, observe the family and school experiences of that child, note the consequences of the child's behaviour, listen to the child and together develop a plan of action with a range of interventions for learning the art of self-regulation, with help from appropriate social scaffolding at school and at home. If an intervention does not work, possible explanations are reviewed and something else is tried. What is tried with one child will be different from another. This is more likely to be the case if the problem is serious and persistent because the bullying troubles are likely to be underpinned by a complex set of factors. Responsiveness should follow a pattern which escalates intrusiveness or intervention, starting with conversation that allows a child to correct his or her own mistakes and ending with a child losing valued privileges in order to protect others from harm. Such privileges are restored as soon as harm is redressed or eliminated.

Soft Bullying—We Probably Have All Done It![1]

Most of us learn not to bully by accident. As children we try bullying as part of the game that Roz Dixon and Peter Smith (2011) call one-up/one-down. If we are smarter, stronger and faster we may well try our hand at dominating unfairly (beyond the rules of competitive play). But for most of us we very quickly realise that is not the right way to behave. We may experience retaliation, or a teacher, parent or friend may call us to account, or we may directly see that we have caused harm and lost a friend. In the normal course of events, we try to make up for it and we learn that bullying did not feel so good, it did not bring rewards, and we decide not to try it again. This is called soft bullying in that we do it naively or carelessly without thinking things through and are easily dissuaded from doing it again. In contrast, serious bullying is not a mistake. It is repeated, possibly even escalated in response to the hurt caused to another.

Ahmed's data from 1996 and 1999 illustrated this principle well. In 1996, children told us of their bullying efforts, mostly done in groups, not alone. When asked about their feelings of shame at the time, and whether they acknowledged shame or displaced shame, they did both. Children who bully have a taste of both acknowledgement and displacement. This is the important part of experiential learning—and a part that resonates with adult experience. Shame makes us all vacillate—did we do the wrong thing or was it someone else's fault? We "toggle" between feelings of acknowledgement and displacement as we sift through our recollections of the event and try to make sense of our experience. The important point here is that if children have the opportunity to experience both acknowledgement and displacement, then teachers and parents have a role to play in turning these experiences into positive learning experiences. Teachers and parents can capitalise on these experiences to encourage learning of positive shame management; and they can place checks on actions that may inadvertently open the door to negative shame management.

The central thesis therefore is that the majority of children learn from their experience of bullying another child. If they are open to school efforts to counter bullying, they will develop shame management skills that lessen their desire to bully others. They will learn to find safety and acknowledge shame (Ahmed & Braithwaite, 2012). Others, particularly those who cannot find safe space at school, are more likely to cling to shame displacement and continue bullying.

So after a school implements all the preventive measures that Ttofi and Farrington (2011) find effective, and after investing in developing interpersonal skills from showing respect for others, expressing needs, to peaceful conflict resolution and shame management, what happens when bullying continues?

Managing Institutional Resistance

There are likely to be both cultural and individual scenarios where bullying persists and proves difficult to contain. Highly competitive schools that honour power and domination and exercise social control through status hierarchies and the rule book historically have been incubators of bullying, harassment and sexual abuse. Government enquiries across the western world into child sexual abuse in the Catholic Church and other religious and charitable institutions provide evidence of the kind of educational culture that allows bullying (among other undesirable forms of domination) to take hold. In short, it is difficult to outlaw dominating through bullying with another form of domination emanating from authority.

Olweus's (1993) whole-school approach to countering bullying addresses specifically the problem of bullying school cultures and has had a profound impact in communities where the value-focus is on social harmony and cooperation for learning and development. With Olweus's whole-school intervention, adults are expected to assume the role of responsible and authoritative role models (Olweus & Limber, 2010). They show warmth and offer support to students. At the same time, they are strong in setting limits on unacceptable behaviour by using non-physical, non-hostile negative consequences in response to breaking rules. Importantly, the whole-school approach has the goal of eliminating domination from relations among students, teachers, parents and administrators. Morrison (2007) has extended the whole-school approach in a restorative and responsive regulatory direction, moving from preventive measures to resolution with those children affected, and then to broadening the circle to include others to resolve more persistent and serious problems (professionals, other school members, parents). Morrison argues for greater empowerment of children in creating safe space at school. The approach has received considerable support internationally (Schiff, 2018). Not all schools, however, have been won over to this pedagogical approach. Values loom large in how individuals and institutions deal with bullying (Braithwaite, 2000; Morrison, 2007). Wong et al. (2011) attribute the greater success of whole-school restorative justice interventions in Hong Kong to the schools being part of a broader Chinese culture where collective values are held in high regard.

Values refer to ideal goals in life and modes of conduct. They guide us when we need a moral compass to tell us what is best. These values are both social and personal in nature and cluster around two themes, both of which are important for our social adaptation (Braithwaite, 1985, 1997, 2009b). The first are harmony values relating to getting along with others, cooperation, being considerate and helpful to others, finding peaceful and respectful ways of resolving conflict, and having an interest in well-being and self-improvement. The second cluster of values relate to security, ensuring that in competition for scarce resources, self-interest is accommodated and there are rules to determine how the game is played. Security values tout a society that is strong, united, with a stable order, with pathways for competition for status and success. The former set of values tend to be more strongly endorsed than the latter, but both types of values are considered desirable. Different values guide our behaviour in different contexts as we assess how best to advance our social survival. Harmony values, for instance, have strength when trust and social coherence are strong in a community. When the world is seen as a more threatening and adversarial place, security values gain ascendancy—security values underpin actions that protect from those who would do us harm.

It follows that some educational settings are going to have a higher tolerance for a bullying culture than others depending on the degree to which security values are allowed to be prioritised over harmony values in the educational agenda. Moreover, a drift into a bullying culture will be more likely when institutional values confer legitimacy on forms of domination, even if bullying is not one of the approved forms.

Military academies, some elite private schools, schools run by some religious sects may fall into this category and need a set of interventions specifically tailored to the bullying problem at hand. The law and its enforcement through school inspectorates and accreditation boards may have a crucial role to play in ensuring a school allocates time and resources to address bullying effectively. This would be yet another example of responsive regulation at work. Voluntary cooperation cannot always be assumed. A school culture may not easily accommodate anti-bullying programs and resistance may be of an order where such programs sit on a book shelf without being meaningfully implemented. In such cases, there is little to be gained by an authority "nagging". Firmer action and intervention are needed which may involve legal coercion to address bullying. Possibly legal action is required against those who have allowed abuse to occur in the school. Responsive regulation favours voluntary, cooperative interventions, but makes coercive measures available, should harm persist.

Using Responsive Regulation with Difficult Behaviour

The above case involves respected institutions with considerable power resisting the introduction of anti-bullying policies and procedures. The individual scenario, in schools at least, is more often about socially marginalised children with behaviours that are difficult to manage. Many schools are challenged by children, who for want of a better term, have been seriously damaged or have entrenched behavioural problems and who are unresponsive to normal interventions. Invariably such children are subject to a barrage of interventions—disapproval, intense interrogation, separation from others, detention, counsellors, doctors and medication, suspensions—and then they are expelled. The battle with the child often extends to being a battle with the parent as well (Braithwaite et al., 2003). Parents can adopt "dismissive defiance" (Braithwaite, 2009a) toward authorities which means that they cut themselves off from relational resolution of the kind made possible by a restorative justice framework.

Some school authorities have opted for punitive measures to control difficult children. Schiff (2018) describes the tension in the US between schools favouring a restorative justice approach and schools that have chosen, or been forced into (under pressure from school boards and government) a zero-tolerance bullying policy backed up with suspension and expulsion. Schiff assembles evidence of the harmful effects of the more punitive approach. Punishment can appear arbitrary to students, consistently applying a rule rather than consistently calling out unacceptable behaviour. Families become estranged from school, students risk feeling less connected, they may fall behind in lessons and school achievement, become involved in risky, delinquent or illegal behaviour, and become involved in the justice system. In short zero-tolerance bullying policies provide children with a "school-to-prison" pipeline.

The US appears to be following a different path to other countries through becoming embroiled in a highly adversarial and polarised debate between advocates of policies supporting punishing and harmful social control measures and those favouring a dialogic approach to teach children to respect and support each other and resolve conflict peaceably (Morrison & Riestenberg, in press; Schiff,

2018). Zero-tolerance bullying policy with its heavy reliance on suspension and expulsion is akin to authoritarian parenting and appears to be equally ineffective. Children who have come from communities plagued by poverty, underemployment, violence, poor nutrition and family breakdown are re-traumatised by a punitive, uncaring school system. Needless to say, such children dislike school as much as the schools dislike them. Undoubtedly, US schools have become something of an outlier in the western world because of the high incidence of school shootings and the understandable fear that it generates. That said, US data is showing that restorative approaches are proving successful in reducing school suspensions (Gregory et al., 2018; also see Morrison & Riestenberg, in press; Schiff, 2018).

Much international research in the field of bullying is around the effectiveness of particular programs. There is a debate around using programs in their "pure form" or mixing components of programs, adapting them to context. Most schools appear to combine different components (Smith, 2016). Components include improving positive peer-to-peer relations and bystander intervention, teaching emotion regulation and conflict resolution, building social skills around empathy, respect and tolerance and developing teacher and parent skills for bullying prevention and resolution (Smith, 2016). Other components place a stronger emphasis on imposing control over bullying through better supervision, school rules and disciplinary sanctions, improving teacher-student relations and classroom management and introducing cooperative group work among students (Ttofi & Farrington, 2011). There has been a tendency to contrast social-emotional and relational interventions with the use of control and disciplinary measures, somewhat reminiscent of the US debate discussed above, but not as extreme: Smith (2016) suggests professional epistemological differences may underpin "either-or" thinking around these two forms of bullying prevention, sometimes referred to as anti-punitive and punitive measures. This chapter urges a combination of social-emotional and disciplinary interventions integrated around responsive regulation and the principles of respect and procedural justice. This makes room for sanctions that encourage children to take new non-bullying pathways and should be distinguished from the punishments described by Schiff (2018) that cut off opportunities for rehabilitation and destroy children's lives.

A responsive regulatory approach demands that productive options be made available for children who cannot fit into a mainstream school so that their education can continue in settings where they are safe and other students are safe. While such schools exist in most developed countries, access to them is rarely recognised as a necessary part of an anti-bullying social policy. More often, nothing is done for expelled children until a crime is committed (which almost inevitably occurs) and then problem children are locked up in youth detention centres away from society and away from any capacity to learn to find a productive niche in the world. Such institutions for young people are punishment by default. A responsive regulatory approach if adopted would map out a different trajectory. Punishment and incarceration would neither be accepted as the answer after school expulsion nor would it be allowed to become the default position. A responsive regulatory approach would not hesitate to place restrictions on a child's freedom if that child was likely to inflict harm on self or others. A child would be regulated, but that regulation would be designed to be non-stigmatising, educational, engaging and meaningful to the child. As David Best and Amy Musgrove (Chapter 12 this volume) would describe it, it would be regulation for recovery through creating an environment of safe normalcy for children needing to learn to find their place in social life. School-day treatment programs for delinquent and at-risk youth, following a restorative practice philosophy, have been successful in reducing reoffending (McCold, 2005).

The Flushing Action of Responsive Regulation

In the age of Trump we have heard much of draining swamps, but when problems persist within our institutions there is something to be said for flushing out the system. "Flush out" means to force out of hiding or make something more transparent and public. Bullying programs and policies are packaged and sold to meet legal or regulatory requirements. They may be implemented fully or partially, with self-evaluations and continuous improvement being practiced in some cases, but probably not in the majority of cases. Too often anti-bullying programs sit in the background, not connecting to core educational goals and their achievement (Nickerson & Rigby, 2017).

Review and adaptation to integrate a school's range of responses and to clarify the part that schools play in reducing bullying is a flushing exercise. Justifying and explaining an anti-bullying practice to others who may use other practices, some of which may be competing rather than complementary, means that different efforts to prevent bullying can be compared and contrasted, contested and streamlined to build into an integrative whole.

Within a responsive regulatory framework, options for dealing with bullying must be integrated. Responses are proportional, are differentiated in terms of severity and intrusiveness, and are geared toward reining in harmful behaviour, while furthering educational objectives. Students and parents are given a clear understanding of a school's approach and how the success of the approach should be judged.

Responsive regulation is often organised in terms of regulatory pyramids of sanctions and supports (see Chapter 2). First and foremost, educational materials about the cause and consequences of bullying are shared with everyone in the school. The first step of a pyramid is universal exposure to the standards of behaviour expected with explanations for why such standards are important. Step 1 ensures everyone associated with the school is on the same page in terms of what constitutes bullying, how it harms and how it should be dealt with as part of the core educational purpose of the school. Dialogue and consultation with teachers, parents and students might tweak or revise such an approach to build consensus around expectations and disciplinary consequences.

When specific instances of bullying occur, subsequent steps of management come into play as pyramids of sanctions and supports. On the supports pyramid, Step 2 might mean that students are praised for de-escalating a bullying incident or preventing an incident. A child who is known to bully others might be rewarded for walking away and not reacting to a bullying trigger. Appointing children to a position of honour as a school monitor or mediator might constitute Step 3, a further way of acknowledging positive contributions from students which creates a culture that prevents bullying. Continuing to show approval and support for pro-social activities by children gives rise to a supports pyramid as part of the school's anti-bullying regulatory approach. This activity is best institutionalised within a whole-school approach to bullying prevention: Everyone is working toward a positive and respectful school culture where domination of another in an arbitrary, non-accountable way is renounced.

On the sanctions pyramid, there can be many steps; and usually there are in schools, even if they are not formally recognised as such. Students might correct each other with a stop bullying message. Next a student might be called out for possible bullying by a supervising teacher or monitor. A little more intrusive might be an intervention where a teacher asks a child directly if they bullied another and why. More intrusive still might be an informal conversation of the teacher with all those involved in a bullying incident. Next might be a request to see the teacher after school or during the lunch break. Further bullying incidents might attract time out and detention. If the problem continues, parents might be involved, or other lead teachers, or the principal. If bullying is not curbed through these measures, restorative justice conferences might be organised in the school with an action plan to prevent recurrence. They might range from being small and informal with only a few participants to being full, formal conferences with a range of participants from inside and outside the school. Morrison (2007) presents a full description of how circles for managing bullying can be expanded within a school and how students are held account able and be required to make amends for the harm they have caused. The values of mutual respect and concern for the well-being of others are present at every step of the sanctions pyramid.

School suspension might become a tool of last resort, short of expulsion from school. Such a measure might be deemed necessary to minimise harm, not as a measure to punish a child. School suspensions and expulsions are least desirable and become flags that a school's anti-bullying practices are probably neither well integrated into educational purposes nor effectively preventing the development of a bullying school culture. In such circumstances, a school with suspensions and expulsions has been flushed out as needing to re-evaluate its efforts to prevent bullying within its educational core. US evidence shows reduced rates of suspension and expulsion when restorative justice programs are implemented, though it is of note that the racial disparity between black and white Americans remains problematic (Gregory et al., 2018; Schiff, 2018).

Community Support for Interventions

Having a suite of interventions and strategies to prevent bullying organised into hierarchies from the least intrusive (education and persuasion) to the most intrusive (expulsion) has community support. In a study of parents whose children took part in the Life at School Survey, parents were asked which of the following they thought was best for designing anti-bullying interventions:

(a) Discussions involving teachers, students and parents to sort out problems between children who bully and the children who are bullied
(b) Enforcing strict rules that forbid bullying and through disciplining guilty parties
(c) Discussions first and then through stricter enforcement of rules if the problem is not resolved

All measures received strong support from parents with the combination strategy receiving endorsement from 93% of parents (Braithwaite, 2000). This result was explained in terms of harmony and security values. Some parents favoured a more relational approach, others favoured rules and sanctions. They could agree, however, on a regulatory pyramid which gave relational strategies a chance, followed up by sanctions if the relational approach did not work. As for dissenters, they favoured a more permissive, non-interfering approach.

These findings regarding parents' wishes are consistent with the proposition at the beginning of this chapter: Parents naturally use the principles of responsive regulation and restorative justice. The findings are also worth noting for another reason. Job and Reinhart (2003) in a general population study of trust in major institutions found that trust rippled out from families. If families adopted child-rearing practices that fostered trust within them, that capacity to trust would spread out to other institutions as children matured. It would seem to be in the interests of our major institutions to emulate family practices. But they do not. Why do human service institutions that impinge on schools—institutions of justice, health, recreation and worship—-struggle to adopt a responsive regulatory and restorative justice approach?

Institutional Impediments

Problems of ideology that stem from values of harmony pitted against values of security may create tensions for governments formulating policy and regulatory philosophy. This means in effect that the political right will argue against regulation, espouse freedom and use law and punishment as a safety net to provide security. The political left will argue for protections and cooperation in safeguarding public interest, and will be reticent to use punishment, preferring a more democratic process for holding people accountable, providing reparation and resolving conflicts. Ideology may partly explain the polarisation that Schiff (2018) and Morrison and Riestenberg (in press) describe in US school policies. It cannot be the whole explanation, however. The majority of people are pure advocates for neither ideologies of left nor right. They prefer an institutional framework which gives both sides a chance to restore order (Braithwaite, 1997). That said, if a political system becomes hyper-adversarial, a regulatory philosophy that is an amalgam of left and right ideologies may be difficult to progress.

A further impediment to a responsive regulatory and restorative justice approach being pursued by governments is low trust. Low trust expressed by citizens toward their democratically elected governments is well documented globally, widely discussed and appears persistent, if not on a downward trust trajectory (OECD, 2013). Governments become sensitive to public exposure of any material that suggests that the "untrustworthiness" of government may be justified. So less widely acknowledged is that governments have low trust in citizens and want to exercise control over public discourse. Trust is relational and so lack of trust works both ways.

Governments have engaged in new forms of regulation which rely on big data, surveillance, risk management, documentation and compliance schedules to strengthen their capacity to control and know about issues of concern to them. Service outsourcing means that the provision of support from government to communities has become distant and impersonal. Examples of predatory capitalism garnering public funds for private profit have bred further distrust. Auditing technologies to check that providers are actually delivering contracted services interferes with capacity for responsiveness. Governments through their technocratic regulation come to understand little of context, and rely on crude metrics to impose solutions to problems that are intricate, complex and constantly changing their form. The metrics are combined with other forms of intelligence to assess the likelihood of non-compliance. Regulatory attention follows risk. Too often the priority is to ensure government pre-empts harm, imposes a solution and if not obeyed, punishes accordingly. As with authoritarian parenting, the regulatory philosophy is one of suspicion of citizens, particularly those who are thrown up by risk indicators, with a standard and consistent repertoire for punishments for wrongdoing.

The above description of how technocratic regulation has come to dominate governance practices worldwide provides insight into why and how government education departments and related agencies exert downward control on schools in ways that are the antithesis of what one might expect under a restorative justice approach. Suspension and expulsion for rule violation are decisions that can be imposed on schools by government, along with reporting and data collection requirements to hold schools and principals accountable through record surveillance. Disempowered principals and teachers can be forgiven for caving into such systems, even though their actions are detrimental to children and the teaching profession. Teachers lose their professionalism (they know children do not learn in a climate of low trust and fear), children lose motivated and inspired teachers and suspended and expelled children enter the pipeline to prison.

It is worth remembering that at the centre of these technocratic regulatory webs are highly adaptive and knowing human beings, adaptive in both pro-social and anti-social ways. If the regulatory controls put in place by government are seen to be non-beneficial or worse still, counterproductive, if they generate rather than deliver injustice, and if they elicit ridicule rather than a sense of moral obligation, cooperation from the community is unlikely to be genuine (Braithwaite, 2017). Responsive regulation and restorative justice require community input and cooperation. Also required is empowerment of the community to participate and initiate solutions. Working with government to develop a regulatory system that is more in touch with the real lives of citizens may be a step too far while government focuses on audit and control and citizens are sceptical about government intentions. In short, technocratic regulation can crush buy-in from citizens in local communities who of their own accord might well work collectively to resolve local problems.

Conclusion

The school environment is one where restorative and responsive regulatory ideas have been embraced as common sense, at least within the confines of the classroom. The school setting in effect extends best practice parenting, namely democratic or authoritative parenting as opposed to authoritarian parenting. Schools, like families, are sites of learning for cognitive development, social relationships and psychological well-being. A globalised, fast-changing world requires humans to excel at 'learning to learn'. At the heart of learning to learn is curiosity and awareness of new knowledge, rising to the challenge of mastering new knowledge, and trying and failing in the process until learning is consolidated. At school, as in the family, children need safety and supportive infrastructure for such learning to effectively take place.

School, however, is likely to be an intimidating and demanding setting for many children. Rules and schedules have to be learnt. New relationships have to be formed, not always with friendly people. The authority of a teacher is in itself a new experience for children when they first go to school. Students build a new identity in this strange, demanding environment, an identity which over the years will be constantly challenged by new people and new knowledge. In such an environment, bullying invariably will occur as an outlet for frustration, aggression, pent-up emotion or shame displacement.

Managing bullying is approached through both organisational and personal lenses. An organisational lens draws attention to the importance of leadership from the principal to control bullying, school rules and enforcement of rules, a skilled teaching workforce, quality teachers who are good at imparting new knowledge and maintaining classroom control, good supervision of children in and outside the classroom, and fostering cooperative and positive relationships among all members of the school community. A personal lens sets out explicitly to develop a child's social and psychological capacities. Programs are used to teach children to respect each other, to practice tolerance, control their anger, mediate in fights between other children and to better manage their negative emotions in the face of disappointment or provocation. Some encourage children to develop coping skills, to stand up for themselves or practice forgiveness. The approach empowers children to create safety in their school environment.

A merging of these two different kinds of lenses is commonly practiced in schools. When restorative justice and responsive regulation are practiced together, the organisational and personal lenses are fully integrated. Sometimes the integration is less perfect than desired. Sometimes, authoritarian regulatory practice is imposed from above, silencing school communities and rendering them powerless. When the integrity of a school's anti-bullying measures is disrupted, it is not uncommon for the source to be a knee-jerk reaction from government spurred by a media scandal and political imperatives for law and order.

But government does not bear all the blame. In part government interference occurs when there is failure in school communities across districts to work together and evaluate their anti-bullying measures and their effectiveness through a regulatory lens. Sometimes schools are quite happy to pass on children who they have failed to discipline to other schools or to authorities known for their more punitive approaches. Schools, like all institutions, engage in risk management—moving the problem along to someone else. Also of note is that schools, like many human service organisations, do not like to think of themselves as regulators.

Regulation simply means steering the flow of events—as kindly and transparently as possible. When do we do it? When harm is imminent. Regulation, when owned by people who care about the wellbeing of others, is no more than responsible care. In investigating the nature of emotional work, Lyndall Strazdins (2000) delineated three dimensions which are relevant to our family and work lives. Our emotional work encompasses companionship, also support. Both strengthen the feeling of connection we have with others. Emotional work also involves regulation—keeping people safe when their judgement lapses or when they are simply unaware of impending danger. Regulatory emotional work is not always comfortable, nor are we routinely thanked for it. It does, however, prevent harm when undertaken with care and respect.

Note

1. Olweus (1991) and Smith and Sharp (1994) define bullying as deliberate, repeated and harmful abuse of power where bullies' superior power may be physical or psychological (Egan & Todorov, 2009, p. 200). Technically soft bullying does not fit the definition of deliberately inflicting hurt on others. Soft bullying nevertheless gives rise to the feedback loop, "I hurt someone, I dominated them, I won't do that again".

References

Ahmed, E., & Braithwaite, V. (2004a). Bullying and victimization: Cause for concern for both families and schools. *Social Psychology of Education*, 7(1), 35–54.

Ahmed, E., & Braithwaite, V. (2004b). "What, me ashamed?" Shame management and school bullying. *Journal of Research in Crime and Delinquency, 41*(3), 269–294.

Ahmed, E., & Braithwaite, J. (2005). Forgiveness, shaming, shame and bullying. *Australian and New Zealand Journal of Criminology, 38*(3), 298–323.

Ahmed, E., & Braithwaite, V. (2006). Forgiveness, reconciliation, and shame: Three key variables in reducing school bullying. *Journal of Social Issues, 62*(2), 347–370.

Ahmed, E., & Braithwaite, V. (2012). Learning to manage shame in school bullying: Lessons for restorative justice interventions. *Critical Criminology, 20*, 79–97.

Ahmed, E., Braithwaite, J., Harris, N., & Braithwaite, V. (2001). *Shame management through reintegration*. Cambridge: Cambridge University Press.

Balducci, C., Fraccaroli, F., & Schaufeli, W. B. (2011). Workplace bullying and its relation with work characteristics, personality, and post-traumatic stress symptoms: An integrated model. *Anxiety, Stress & Coping: An International Journal, 24*(5), 499–513.

Bandura, A. (1986). *Social foundations of thought and action: A social cognitive theory*. Englewood Cliffs, NJ: Prentice-Hall.

Bandura, A. (1997). *Self-efficacy: The exercise of control*. New York: W.H. Freeman.

Baumrind, D. (1978). Parental disciplinary patterns and social competence in children. *Youth and Society, 9*, 239–276.

Braithwaite, J. (1989). *Crime, shame and reintegration*. Cambridge: Cambridge University Press.

Braithwaite, V. (1997). Harmony and security value orientations in political evaluation. *Personality and Social Psychology Bulletin, 23*, 401–414.

Braithwaite, V. (2000). Values and restorative justice in schools. In H. Strang & J. Braithwaite (Eds.), *Restorative justice: Philosophy to practice* (pp. 121–144). Aldershot, UK: Ashgate.

Braithwaite, V. (2009a). *Defiance in taxation and governance: Resisting and dismissing authority in a democracy.* Cheltenham, UK/Northampton, MA: Edward Elgar.

Braithwaite, V. (2009b). The value balance model and democratic governance. *Psychological Inquiry, 20*(2–3), 87–97.

Braithwaite, V. (2017). Closing the gap between regulation and the community. In P. Drahos (Ed.), *Regulatory theory: Foundations and applications* (pp. 25–41). Australian National University, Acton, ACT: ANU Press.

Braithwaite, V., Ahmed, E., Morrison, B., & Reinhart, M. (2003). Researching prospects for restorative justice practice in schools: The Life at School Survey 1996–1999. In L. Walgrove (Ed.), *Repositioning restorative justice: Restorative justice, criminal justice and social context* (pp. 165–185). Cullompton, UK: Willan Publishing.

Braithwaite, V. A., & Law, H. G. (1985). The structure of human values: Testing the adequacy of the Rokeach Value Survey. *Journal of Personality and Social Psychology, 49*, 250–263.

Braithwaite, V., & Shin, H. (2018) (in preparation)

Darling, N., & Steinberg, L. (1993). Parenting style as context: An integrative model. *Psychological Bulletin, 113*(3), 487–496.

Di Martino, V., Hoel, H., & Cooper, C. L. (2003). *Preventing violence and harassment in the workplace* (Report). Dublin: European Foundation for the Improvement of Living and Working Conditions.

Dixon, R., & Smith, P. K. (2011). *Rethinking school bullying: Towards an integrated model.* Cambridge: Cambridge University Press.

Egan, L. A., & Todorov, N. (2009). Forgiveness as a coping strategy to allow school students to deal with the effects of being bullied: Theoretical and empirical discussion. *Journal of Social and Clinical Psychology, 28*(2), 198–222.

Gregory, A., Huang, F. L., Anyon, Y., & Eldridge, G. (2018). An examination of restorative interventions and racial equity in out-of-school suspensions. *School Psychology Review, 47*(2), 167–182.

Harris, N. (2011). Shame, ethical identity and conformity: Lessons from research on the psychology of social influence. In S. Karstedt, I. Loader, & H. Strang (Eds.), *Emotions, crime and justice* (pp. 193–209). Oxford: Hart Publishing.

Haynie, D. L., Nansel, T., Eitel, P., Crump, A. D., Saylor, K., Yu, K., Simons-Morton, B. (2001). Bullies, victims and bully/victims: Distinct groups of at-risk youth. *Journal of Early Adolescence, 21*(1), 29–49.

Hopkins, B. (2002). Restorative justice in schools. *Support for Learning, 17*(3), 144–149.

Hymel, S., & Swearer, S. M. (2015). Four decades of research on school bullying: An introduction. *American Psychologist, 70*(4), 293–299.

Job, J., & Reinhart, M. (2003). Trusting the tax office: Does Putnam's thesis relate to tax? *Australian Journal of Social Issues, 38*(3), 299–322.

Kumpulainen, K., & Räsänen, E. (2000). Children involved in bullying at elementary school age: Their psychiatric symptoms and deviance in adolescence. An epidemiological sample. *Child Abuse & Neglect, 24*(12), 1567–1577.

Larzelere, R. E., Morris, A. S., & Harrist, A. W. (Eds.). (2012). *Authoritative parenting: Synthesizing nurturance and discipline for optimal child development.* Washington, DC: American Psychological Association.

McCold, P. (2005). *Follow-up research confirms positive effect of a restorative milieu on young offenders, eForum Archive, January 25.* Paper presented at the annual meeting of the American Society of Criminology, Nashville, Tennessee, November 16–19, 2004.

Morrison, B. (2007). *Restoring safe school communities: A whole school response to bullying.* Sydney: Federation Press.

Morrison, B., & Riestenberg, N. (in press). Reflections on twenty years of restorative justice in schools. In D. Osher (Ed.), *A collaborative handbook for education, mental health, child welfare, safety, and justice professionals, families, and communities.* CA: Praeger.

Nickerson, A., & Rigby, K. (2017). Prevention and Intervention for bullying in schools. In M. Thielking & M. Terjesen (Eds.), *Handbook of Australian school psychology: Bridging the gaps in international research, practice, and policy* (pp. 521–536). New York: Springer.

OECD. (2013). *Government at a glance 2013*. Paris: OECD Publishing.

Olweus, D. (1991). Bully/victim problems among schoolchildren: Basic facts and effects of a school based intervention program. In D. Pepler & K. Rubin (Eds.), *The development and treatment of childhood aggression* (pp. 411–48). Hillsdale, NJ: Erlbaum.

Olweus, D. (1993). *Bullying at school: What we know and what we can do*. Malden, MA: Blackwell.

Olweus, D. (2013). School bullying: Development and some important challenges. *Annual Review of Clinical Psychology, 9*, 751–780.

Olweus, D., & Limber, S. P. (2010). The Olweus bullying prevention program: Implementation and evaluation over two decades. In S. R. Jimerson, S. M. Swearer, & D. L. Espelage (Eds.), *The handbook of bullying in schools: An international perspective* (pp. 377–401). London, UK: Routledge.

Power, T. (2013). Parenting dimensions and styles: A brief history and recommendations for future research. *Childhood Obesity, 9*(Suppl 1), S-14–S-21.

Rigby, K., & Smith, P. K. (2011). Is school bullying really on the rise? *Social Psychology of Education, 14*(4), 441–455.

Rudy, D., & Grusec, J. E. (2006). Authoritarian parenting in individualist and collectivist groups: Associations with maternal emotion and cognition and children's self-esteem. *Journal of Family Psychology, 20*(1), 68–78.

Schiff, M. (2018). Can restorative justice disrupt the 'school-to-prison pipeline?'. *Contemporary Justice Review, 21*(2), 121–139.

Shin, H. H. (2009). *Talking to children clearly but respectfully: The effect of inductive reasoning and hostile parenting at age 4–5 on child's conduct problems at age 6–7 using LSAC Waves 1 and 2*. Paper presented at the 2nd LSAC Research Conference, December, 2009, Melbourne, AU.

Shin, H. H., Braithwaite, V., & Ahmed, E. (2016). Cyber-and face-to-face bullying: Who crosses over?. *Social Psychology of Education, 19*(3), 537–567.

Smith, P. K. (2016). School-based interventions to address bullying. *Eesti Haridusteaduste Ajakiri, 4*(2), 142–164.

Smith, P. K., & Sharp, S. (Eds.). (1994). *School bullying: Insights and perspectives*. London, UK: Routledge.

Steinberg, L., & Silk, J. S. (2002). Parenting adolescents. In M. H. Bornstein (Ed.), *Handbook of parenting: Vol. 1: Children and parenting* (2nd ed., pp. 103–133). Mahwah, NJ: Erlbaum.

Strazdins, L. (2000). Integrating emotions: Multiple role measurement of emotional work. *Australian Journal of Psychology, 52*, 41–50.

Ttofi, M. M., & Farrington, D. P. (2011). Effectiveness of school-based programs to reduce bullying: A systematic and meta-analytic review. *Journal of Experimental Criminology, 7*(1), 27–56.

Veenstra, R., Lindenberg, S., Oldehinkel, A. J., De Winter, A. F., Verhulst, F. C., & Ormel, J. (2005). Bullying and victimization in elementary schools: A comparison of bullies, victims, bully/victims, and uninvolved preadolescents. *Developmental Psychology, 41*(4), 672–682.

Wang, J., Iannotti, R. J., & Luk, J. W. (2012). Patterns of adolescent bullying behaviors: Physical, verbal, exclusion, rumor, and cyber. *Journal of School Psychology, 50*(4), 521–534.

Wong, D. S. W., Cheng, C. H. K., Ngan, R. M. H., & Ma, S. K. (2011). Program effectiveness of a restorative whole-school approach for tackling school bullying in Hong Kong. *International Journal of Offender Therapy and Comparative Criminology, 55*(6), 846–862.

4

BURNING CARS, BURNING HEARTS AND THE ESSENCE OF RESPONSIVENESS

Brenda Morrison and Tania Arvanitidis

Introduction

On June 15, 2011, in downtown Vancouver, British Columbia, a destructive riot broke out following Game 7 of the Stanley Cup finals. Precedent for the formal, prescriptive and punitive response by the police and courts was established by the 1992 case *R v Loewen*,[2] which determined general deterrence to be the principal sentencing purpose in riot cases, and retribution as necessary to meet this purpose. The previous year—2010—the inaugural Fasken Lecture was delivered in Vancouver: "The Essence of Responsive Regulation" (J. Braithwaite, 2011). Nine heuristics of the regulatory framework were discussed: attend to context; listen actively; engage resisters with fairness; praise committed innovation; achieve outcomes through support and innovation; signal a range of sanctions; engage wider networks; elicit active responsibility; evaluate and communicate lessons learnt. Through a formalized, rather than a responsive, regulatory response to the riots, Vancouver lost an opportunity for norm clarification, responsibility and education as a foundation for human capacity building and bridging at an individual, community, professional and institutional level.

Context: Riots and the Ritual of Formalized Criminal Justice

On June 15, 2011, British Columbia's National Hockey League Team, the Vancouver Canucks, played their seventh and final game of the Stanley Cup Finals against the Boston Bruins. The Canucks' loss against the Bruins was followed by one of the most destructive riots in the city's history. Not long after the riot, the Integrated Riot Investigation Team (IRIT), consisting of over 30 members of the Vancouver Police Department (VPD), Royal Canadian Mounted Police (RCMP), special prosecutors and municipal officers was set up to collect evidence and investigate suspected rioters. Several public statements made by team members promised hefty penalties and expressed a clear desire to see riot participants punished to the fullest extent of the law, as echoed by the Vancouver Police Chief Constable:

> Our diligence and thoroughness will ensure that we lay the highest number of charges and obtain the greatest number of convictions with the most severe penalties. We will not rest or bow to

DOI: 10.4324/9780429398704-4

pressure until all the evidence has been examined. We owe it to those who lost property and others who suffered losses to do this right. If you are in favour of speed, you are in favour of acquittals and lighter sentences.

(Vancouver Police Chief Jim Chu, 2011, August 17)

The IRIT delivered on its promise of formalized retributive accountability: between October 31, 2011, and July 24, 2014, 912 charges were laid against 300 alleged rioters (British Columbia Ministry of Justice, 2016), with the final riot participant being sentenced in February 2016 (Proctor, 2016). All riot suspects had one charge of participating in a riot (section 65) recommended against them, an indictable offense with a maximum penalty of two years' imprisonment. This decision has since been defended by the IRIT on the grounds that "this is the most serious charge we can lay and will ensure the most accountability from the courts" (Vancouver Police Department, 2011).

The retributive promise of accountability by the police and courts echoed calls from the greater Vancouver community to bring those responsible for the riot to justice. For example, a Metro Vancouver public opinion poll found that 95% of respondents agreed that *"the people who took part in riots should be prosecuted to the full extent of the law"* (Angus Reid Public Opinion, 2011). Yet not all who witnessed the riot demanded retribution in response, arguing that accountability would be more meaningful from offenders, victims and the community though restorative justice:

> I . . . cannot stand the thought of all those who rioted having no consequences, ineffective sentences, or filling up our prisons where they will learn more about crime and violence. I want offenders to directly face their victims and their community, understand the full extent of their actions, make amends, and learn some things of value [. . .]. Like it or not, they are a part of our community too.
>
> *(Zellerer, 2011)*

Restorative justice, as community accountability, was also echoed in the comprehensive independent riot review, *The Night the City Became a Stadium* as "a way for an offender to demonstrate remorse and a renewed commitment to the community" (Furlong & Keefe, 2011, p. 123).

Despite the commitment and efforts of Vancouver-based restorative justice agencies, restorative justice, a response offering direct accountability to the victims and community affected, was not considered a viable response in the aftermath of the riot. Instead, "the most severe penalties" were resourced in unprecedented measures, at a cost of nearly $5 million, surpassing the $3.78 million in damages (British Columbia Ministry of Justice and Attorney General, 2016). Sentencing included some form of custody for 94% of adults sentenced, despite the accompanying knowledge that 83% of these same adults carried no criminal record prior to their participation in the riot (British Columbia Ministry of Justice, 2016). Restorative justice was offered at $1,000.00 per case. In contrast, each case, on average, cost over $16,000.00.

The retributive response not only incurred high financial costs, the citizens of Vancouver also incurred the loss of deliberative opportunities to uphold justice through direct accountability, norm clarification and victim's right to participate and be heard (Christie, 1977). Riots are more than individual acts of harm; they are collective acts of harm that happen in our streets, in our neighborhoods and in our business centers. Riots are a collective act of street group violence that challenge us to broaden the lens of justice (Gavrielides, 2012). Given the community impact, the context of street group violence invites a holistic response that goes beyond a formalized regulatory response that creates a justice conveyor belt that is offender-centric, processing single riot cases, one after another. Applying the nine heuristics of responsive regulation to frame the use of restorative justice creates an opportunity to build institutional capacity to engage victims, offenders and community in a systemic process wherein the collective intent in achieving justice is to attend to context; listen actively; engage resisters with fairness; praise committed innovation; achieve outcomes through support and innovation; signal a range of sanctions; engage wider networks; elicit active responsibility; evaluate and communicate lessons learnt (J. Braithwaite, 2011).

Responsive Regulation and Restorative Justice

The nine heuristics work together to regulate civil society through dynamic responsive regulation rather than static formalized regulation. The cumulative creation of responsive regulatory theory has been a challenge to define, given its emergent and circular, rather than static and linear, nature. Yet, the essence of this dynamic regulatory framework is as broad as it is clear: learning and growth through norm clarification, responsibility and education as a foundation for human capacity building—at an individual, community, professional and institutional level (J. Braithwaite, 2002, 2011, 2016, 2017, 2018).

> Responsive regulation is about listening to the wisdom of practitioners in regulatory agencies, business and advocacy groups to discover deep structures of theoretical meaning in their struggles. . . . The idea of responsive regulation . . . is that wisdom grounded in practice leads theory; then that theory provides better lenses through which to see and transform practice. The gifts we scholars give, at their best, add a little yeast to that noble process.
>
> *(J. Braithwaite, 2018, pp. 69–118)*

This chapter aims to contextualize the potential of the nine heuristics of responsive regulation in the context of the 2011 Vancouver Stanley Cup Riot.

Context over Precedent: Active Engagement

Precedent is a normative legal instrument in formalized regulatory capacities, as demonstrated in the sentencing proceedings of the 2011 riot cases. The prosecution and conviction of as many riot participants as possible was defended by Crown Counsel on the grounds that such a response was "required in the public interest" and necessary to ensure consistency with precedent established in *R v Loewen* (1992). The appellant, George Loewen, was charged with two counts of mischief and one count of participating in a riot, following the 1991 Penticton, B.C., riot. In sentencing, the judge acknowledged that Loewen, under "normal" circumstance, would not receive a custody sentence, given he was 18 years old at the time of the offense, carried no criminal record, pled guilty early on in the trial, expressing remorse throughout his court hearings. Yet, Loewen was sentenced to 12 months in prison. Although his case was later appealed, and his sentence reduced to 6 months, in conjunction with one year of probation and 150 hours of community service work, the judge ruled that the imposition of a custody sentence remained appropriate in the circumstances—given Loewen's participation in a riot.

The precedent logic of the *Loewen* decision for the 2011 Vancouver rioters is that the sentencing principle of *general deterrence* and, to a lesser extent, the related sentencing principle of *denunciation*, must take precedence above all others when sentencing an individual charged with participation in a riot:

> This is not the time for unwarranted leniency nor by the same token for unwarranted severity. Care must be taken at the same time to preserve the message of general deterrence.
>
> *(at para 46)*

In the context of this sentencing aim, Loewen's custody sentence is not unusual, as it is typical practice within Canadian case law for the sentencing aims of general deterrence and denunciation to be fulfilled through the imposition of a custody sentence. What sets *Loewen* apart from similar cases as the leading precedent for sentencing riot participants is that the accused in this case was specifically acknowledged as a young, first-time offender during the sentencing process. In cases where these mitigating factors are present, it is the sentencing purpose of *rehabilitation* that must, ordinarily, be prioritized over *general deterrence* and/or *denunciation*, which then typically renders consideration of a custody sentence inappropriate. *Loewen* thus set the important and atypical precedent that, in the unique circumstance wherein an individual is charged for participating in a riot, the achievement of general deterrence must be considered the primary guiding principle during the sentencing process *even when* the presence of mitigating factors would ordinarily require a focus upon rehabilitation instead:

> Taking into account all of the foregoing circumstances I am of the view, that in this case the sentencing principle of not imposing a custodial sentence upon a first-time offender must yield to the imposition of a custodial sentence that will recognize the principle of general deterrence.
>
> *(at para 50)*

An exception to established case law of this magnitude can typically be justified only when the circumstances of the case are proven to be exceptional—that is, not "ordinary". *Loewen* was deemed exceptional, and the prioritization of deterrent over rehabilitative sentencing goals deemed necessary, due to the accused's crimes having taken place within the circumstances of a riot. *Loewen*, in other words, is crucial to establishing that the *context of a riot* is an *aggravating factor* that heightens the seriousness of a given crime:

> To take part in a riot is by mere presence to contribute to the excitement, fervour, intimidation and dangerousness of the unlawful assembly.
>
> *(at para 45)*

> A riot is, by its very nature, a serious threat to orderly society. If riots become prevalent, they will undermine many of the values of a free and democratic society.
>
> *(at para 47)*

Crimes committed in the context of a riot thus carry both a higher degree of *culpability*, and more severe *consequences*, than crimes committed in isolation for two primary reasons: The act encourages others to participate, and the act forms merely part of a larger, and more destructive, public disturbance.

The logic, thus, is that greater efforts on the part of justice officials are necessitated to deter people from participating in them.

Responsive Regulation: Beyond Regulatory Formalism

Responsive regulation moves beyond one-size-fits-all regulatory frameworks, offering a richer responsiveness to context, beyond aggravating factors. Given the serious and collective nature of riots, there is good reason to be responsive to the impact beyond a central focus on general deterrence. Responsive regulation recognizes that dangers exist in both maximalist and minimalist deterrent response to crime (J. Braithwaite, 2018), arguing that through community engagement offenders, together with victims and community, learn how minimally sufficient deterrence works.

> By relying on layered strategies, this approach takes deterrence theory onto the terrain of complexity theory. It integrates approaches based on social support and recovery capital, dynamic concentration of deterrence, restorative justice, shame and pride management, responsive regulation, responsivity, indirect reciprocity, and incapacitation. Deterrence fails when it rejects complexity in favor of simple theories such as rational choice.
>
> *(J. Braithwaite, 2018, p. 69)*

Responsive regulation asks what sanction—persuasion, deterrence, incapacitation—offers the most promise in delivering accountability, resolve, commitment, fairness, active responsibility, norm clarification and education? A regulatory pyramid of sanctions suggests to begin with the less interventionist remedies at the base of the pyramid, wherein persuasion and education offer opportunities for norm clarification that strengthens community to prevent further harm, in the context of active listening and responsibility. Specifically, to *think in context, and not impose preconceived theory* (Responsive Regulation Principle 1; RRP1).

Restorative justice is the foundation, or first stage, of a responsive regulatory pyramid, offering a community-based process to all affected parties—victims, offenders, community and professionals:

> Restorative justice is "a justice that puts its energy into the future, not into what is past. It focuses on what needs to be healed, what needs to be repaired, what needs to be learned in the wake of a crime. It looks at what needs to be strengthened if such things are not to happen again".
>
> *(Sharpe, 1998, p. 5)*

Sharpe (1998) offers five touchstones of restorative justice: invite full participation and consensus; heal what has been broken; seek full and direct accountability; reunite what has been divided; strengthen the community, to prevent further harms. Each of these elements are relevant to the experience of victims, offenders, community and professionals in the context of the riots; in other words, street group violence.

Beyond Precedent: Collective Commitment to Listen and Learn

Akin to restorative justice, a key principle of responsive regulation is *active listening, through structured dialogue that gives voice to stakeholders; settles agreed outcomes and how to monitor them; builds commitment by helping actors find their own motivation to improve; communicates firm resolve to stick with a problem until it is fixed* (RRP2). In the context of the 2011 Vancouver riot, not only did we fail to actively listen and learn from those most affected—victims, offenders, community and professionals—the courts regressed to precedence sentencing that precedes a number of significant reforms made to the Criminal Code in 1996, with the intention of reducing reliance upon custody in sentencing (Daubney & Parry, 1999; Roberts & von Hirsch, 1999). Included among these reforms are the addition to the *Code* of a statement codifying the many purposes and principles of sentencing (section 718), and of provisions that encourage the use of community sanctions in place of custody wherever offenders possess strong prospects for rehabilitation and are not deemed to be at risk to the public (section 717; section 742). Granting these sections greater significance is the principle of restraint now entrenched within section 718.2(e) of the *Code:* "All available sanctions other than imprisonment that are reasonable in the circumstances should be considered for all offenders" (Manson, Healy, & Trotter, 2008). Those who took part in the 2011 Vancouver riot appear, in other words, to have been sentenced with guidance both from a leading case which maintains that the serious context of a riot demands, under all circumstances, the incarceration of those responsible, and a *Criminal Code* that calls for the very opposite: restraint. Restraint offers the lead actors of our criminal justice system an opportunity to widen the lens of response and work from the base of the regulatory pyramid, as a first step.

Signal Denunciation with Restraint: Sanctions that Build Capacity

Subverting the *Code* during sentencing does not, of course, always lead to injustice. The parity principle—that offenders being sentenced for the same or similar offense must receive appropriately similar sentences—is entrenched in the *Code* alongside the *Purposes and Principles of Sentencing* (section 718), and an important part of the way in which Canada's criminal justice system practices fairness and consistency in sentencing. What matters less than the fact that sentencing judges *could* have exercised judicial discretion in favoring the supremacy of the *Code* over the precedent set by *Loewen,* then, is the larger question of why they *should* have: What, exactly, marks the 2011 Vancouver riot as so unique, so special, that it deserved a criminal justice response any different from those which followed the riots that came before? The 2011 riot is a unique event in Canada's history for quite a number of reasons. *Loewen* may, in isolation, closely resemble many of the individual riot cases that Vancouver Provincial Court saw sentenced after the 2011 riot, but this matters less than the fact that the 2011 riot itself occurred within a social and technological context vastly different from that which surrounded any other large-scale riot that had previously occurred in Canada—and this, as we argue, necessitates a legal response capable of adapting appropriately.

> History is a very important part of context. What is a sound regulatory policy in one period of a nation's history will be unsound during another. Responsive regulators must therefore "think in a stream of time" as the historians Richard Neustadt and Ernest May argue. They are detectives who ask a lot of journalists' questions—what, who, how, when, where, why—to get the time line of the story.
>
> (J. Braithwaite, 2011, p. 492)

Researchers in the social sciences have investigated for decades how and why human beings collectively organize and control their own behaviors in the presence of one another. The particular form of social disorder known as a "riot", however, continues to be perceived with considerable lack of understanding, witnessed in the manner by which research and media publications alike so often describe them as "senseless" or "pointless" (see Baron & Kerr, 2003; Forsyth, 2006; Schneider, 1992). Knowing that individuals who instigate riots within the context of sporting events have been identified within studies as more likely than other spectators to have a history of aggressive encounters, disorderly conduct and prior criminal convictions (Arms & Russell, 1997; Mustonen, Arms, & Russell, 1996; Roversi, 1991; Russell & Arms, 1998; Trivizas, 1980), it is to some extent understandable that justice officials in the wake of the 2011 Vancouver riot attributed the disturbance to "criminals", "anarchists" and "thugs" (Wintonyk, 2011) and, subsequently, assumed that the imposition of harsh penalties would be the only meaningful way to deter similarly violent others from participation in future disturbances.

The rioters who participated in the 2011 Vancouver riot do not, however, appear to fit the above profile of "veteran" rioters well-experienced in the practice of instigating crowd violence, and eager for the opportunity to do so again. Rather, their status as first-time offenders who, by many accounts, had only a short time before the riot been peacefully watching the hockey game, and seemed to act impulsively and with no prior deliberation, is far more consistent with one of the most frequently cited explanations offered by social psychologists for how otherwise law-abiding people so often become "caught up" in riots, mobs and other forms of street group violence: that such individuals act as a result of experiencing deindividuation, defined by Postmes and Spears (1998, p. 238) as "a psychological state of decreased self- evaluation and decreased evaluation apprehension causing antinormative and disinhibited behavior". The phenomenon of deindividuation is fairly well established, having been portrayed in social psychology texts as having recognizable and predictable effects on human behavior since the 1980s (see Baron & Kerr, 2003; Forsyth, 2006; Paulus, 1980; Shaw, 1981)—and although the varying theoretical models that have been put forward over the years to explain how and why deindividuation occurs have been both numerous and contradictory, an extensive meta-analysis conducted by Tom Postmes and Russell Spears (1998) concluded that *anonymity, group membership* and *reductions in self-awareness* are strongly correlated with conformity to situation-specific norms that emerge spontaneously within group settings—for example, the "norm" of taking part in a sports riot.

An interview by Gavrielides (2012, p. 38) with an individual charged for participation in the 2011 Vancouver riot lends credence to the suggestion made by deindividuation theories that participation in riots may be attributable, for many, to unseen group pressures and crowd influence. When asked what led him to join the crowd, the participant explained:

> I honestly do not know what happened to me. I can't really explain it. I rarely go downtown—I just went for the game and when I saw lots of people rioting . . . well, it looked exciting at the time. I joined and I remember it was as if I was watching myself do things I would never do.

Arvanitidis (2013) found similar themes in her examination of reasons for judgment given for the first 20 participants convicted for their involvement in the riot. In *Peepre*,[3] the accused was described to have "appeared mortified by his conduct on display in the video played for the Court" (2012, para. 24); in *Williams*,[4] the accused wrote in a letter of apology that he "does not understand how he went from being a normal guy who went to work every day to someone who did what he did that night" (2012, para. 26); in *Dorosh*,[5] the accused states that "he does not know why he committed this offense and feels like an 'idiot'" (2012, para. 22), many others acknowledged regret, shame and took full responsibility (Arvanitidis, 2013).

The contextual differences between the 1991 Penticton and 2011 Vancouver riots, together with the emerging empirical evidence on the social psychology of street group violence, was an opportunity to signal a responsive regulatory approach that both upheld the changes to the criminal code while harnessing the regulator capacity of a range of stakeholders, including downtown businesses and the local community affected. The local restorative justice network collaborated to design a process that *engaged those who resist with fairness, showing them respect by construing their resistance as an opportunity to learn how to improve regulatory design* (RRP3).

Procedural justice bridges restorative justice with criminal justice. Tyler (2006, p. 307) identified three approaches to dealing with rule braking: procedural justice, restorative justice and moral development.

> Each argues that the long-term goal when dealing with rule breaking is to motivate rule breakers to become more self-regulating in their future conduct. This goal is undermined by punishment-focused models of sanctioning. Sanction-based models, which dominate current thinking about managing criminals, have negative consequences for the individual wrongdoer and for society. It is argued that greater focus needs to be placed on psychological approaches whose goal is to connect with and activate internal values within wrongdoers with the goal of encouraging self-regulatory law-related behavior in the future.

More recently, Murphy's (2017, for overview) work on policing shows that when attention is given to procedural justice—the quality of treatment and decision making—people's willingness to cooperate with the police can improve as well as encourage them to voluntarily comply with the law.

> This is because procedural justice can promote identification with authorities and reduce negative emotion and resistance. It can also build public perceptions of the legitimacy of authorities, leaving people to feel more obligated to obey their instructions and laws.
>
> *(Murphy, 2017, p. 55)*

Police are important gatekeepers to the criminal justice system and the regulation of civil society.

Capacity Building through Innovation that Signals a Range of Sanctions

Stephen Reicher (2011), following the 2011 London, UK, riot, argues for the importance of locating empirically grounded explanations for why riots occur, and warns of the dangers of dismissing such attempts at understanding as "making excuses" for people who, some insist, deserve only to be punished. Following this astute observation, one cannot help but wonder the extent to which a fear of being perceived as "sympathetic" towards riot participants inclined the myriad recommendation reports that were published in the 2011 riot's aftermath to claim, with little supporting evidence, that they already understood why the riot occurred. Both the City of Vancouver (2011) and Vancouver Police Department (2011) attributed blame to the availability and regulation of alcohol consumption. The Furlong and Keefe report (2011) attributed the cause of the riot to: "People who either wanted to make trouble or thought it looked like fun" (p. 1). Curiously, none of these reports sought understanding from the very people who took part in the riot in the first place—and in the absence of their voices, these reports' claims are little more than baseless assumptions that lend legitimacy to long-standing punitive justice practices (Reicher, 2016). How can we be so sure that riot participants are "troublemakers" who respond only to the threat of harsh penalties without first hearing their side of the story? And wouldn't knowing their stories—understanding what it was that caused these otherwise law-abiding young people to turn on their own communities—strengthen our ability to respond to such events in the future?

In the context of responsive regulation active listening involves giving voice to all stakeholders (e.g., offenders, direct and indirect victims, community, business owners; police, first responders); settles agreed outcomes and how to monitor them; builds commitment by helping actors find their own motivation to improve; communicates firm resolve to stick with the problem until it is fixed (J. Braithwaite, 2011, p. 501). Through working together responsive regulation builds capacity: *praise of those who show commitment, through support of their innovation; nurturing motivation to continuously improve; helping leaders pull laggards up through new ceilings of excellence* (RRP4).

Karstedt's (2017) analysis of street group violence acknowledges the contagion effect, wherein behavior spreads to proximate areas if conductive conditions prevail, suggesting lever-pulling policing strategies based on four principles: selective focusing on known offenders; communication and dialogue of potential escalation of sanctions; future orientation of potential criminal behavior; and broad range and escalation of intervening actions in the case of non-compliance. Each principle is consistent with responsive regulation.

The Opportunity to Hear from Victims—A Regulatory Signal of Support

In addition to the damage done to businesses and personal property, the 2011 riot was enormously traumatic for many of those caught up in the chaos. Many police officers, bystanders and employees, whose businesses were targeted, reported having been directly assaulted by rioters, some while attempting to intervene and stop them (Howe, 2013). Countless more experienced deep psychological harm and trauma from being trapped in the vicinity of the riot, including several hundred theatergoers who found themselves unable to safely leave the Queen Elizabeth Theatre that was situated in the riot zone (Matas, 2011)—with among the most traumatized by the riot being those employees who found themselves trapped inside their place of work when their businesses were attacked, including about 27 employees forced to lock themselves in the basement of a London Drugs that suffered extensive looting and vandalism throughout the riot. It is not only through these obvious harms that victims of crime suffer, however; as has been well documented within the dual fields of restorative justice and victimology, crime victims are frequently denied a meaningful voice in state-based sentencing processes, leaving them feeling dehumanized, disempowered and unable to find closure (see Strang, 2003; Van Camp, 2014, 2017).

In this context, it is noteworthy that the sentencing approach taken in the 2011 Vancouver riots did not consider reparative goals a priority. Rather, judges were primarily concerned with satisfying, in accordance with *Loewen*, the overarching sentencing goals of general deterrence and denunciation (Arvanitidis, 2013). The criminal justice system is offender centric, not victim centric; at best, victims become witnesses to the crime they experienced. The crime is against the State. Restorative justice, within a responsive regulatory framework, offers an opportunity to give victims a voice.

Here, we find one of the first lost opportunities to deliver to victims the restoration so many of them may very well have desired: Many riot participants who were sentenced received not custody sentences to be served in a custodial institution but rather *Conditional Sentence Orders (CSO)*, a custody alternative that allows offenders to serve out a sentence of imprisonment in the community, with mandated conditions placed upon them. Because the conditions that sentences judges may attach to such orders include reparative gestures—up to and including participation in a restorative justice process—the creation of conditional sentence orders is widely seen as an effort on the part of Canada's justice system to include restorative justice principles within the court sentencing process. Failure of the court sentencing process to include conditions that would allow for riot participants to make meaningful reparations to both their victims and the greater community may be attributable, in large part, to the fact that these provisions remain relatively new and quite ambiguous in their application; nonetheless, it remains unfortunate that the opportunity that the riot provided to clarify these provisions was not seized.

Elicit Active Responsibility

Restorative justice practice has been heavily informed by literature on the perceived deficits of retributive state-based criminal justice systems (Gavrielides, 2007), and as such, the approach focuses primarily on personalizing the justice process in order to deliver healing to those harmed. Material forms of reparation resultant from restorative processes include monetary restitution, service to the victim, community service and apologies (see Strang, 2003; Van Camp, 2014, 2017), though typically of greater value to both victims and researchers are the emotional benefits that restorative justice can offer. Recent reviews have found that, across a variety of crimes and countries, many victims who choose to participate in restorative justice conferencing are satisfied with both the process and the outcomes reached, while additional studies have shown that victims who undergo restorative justice, when compared to those who undergo a court process alone, are less fearful of re-victimization, are more sympathetic and less angry toward their offender and are more likely to perceive the justice process as having been fair (Shapland, Robinson, & Sorsby, 2011; Sherman & Strang, 2007; Strang et al., 2013; Van Camp, 2014, 2017). By requiring offenders to repay their debts to their victims in tangible and meaningful ways, offenders, too, are held accountable for their actions—and additionally, are made to take "real accountability" through hearing about the consequences of their offending, thus enabling them to fully understand what they have done and why their actions were harmful (Shapland et al., 2011; Sherman & Strang, 2007; Strang et al., 2013; Van Camp, 2014, 2017).

Compared to those who go through a court process alone, offenders who participate in restorative processes have been found to be more likely to deliver repair or restitution to victims and feel remorse for what they have done (Shapland et al., 2011; Sherman & Strang, 2007; Strang et al., 2013). Further, meta-analyses (Sherman & Strang, 2007; Strang et al., 2013; Wong et al., 2016) have consistently found restorative justice to be more effective than state-based practices at lowering recidivism rates for participating offenders.

> Restorative justice conferencing now has the benefit of more numerous and more rigorous evaluations than perhaps any other criminal justice program. Some might say the world of RJ practice has been little influenced by this long program of research, bedevilled as it is by the cautiousness of policymakers around the Western world about applying it to those very cases for which research shows it to be most effective. Thus, RJ is still rarely used for serious and violent crime.
>
> (Strang, 2017, pp. 494–495)

Given the empirical support for community based restorative justice and the lack of empirical support for state-base punishment, there is good reason to believe that accountability and amends through restorative justice could elicit higher levels of responsibility post-riots. A central principle of responsive regulation is to *elicit active responsibility (responsibility for making outcomes better in the future), resorting to passive responsibility (holding actors responsible for past actions) when active responsibility fails* (RRP8).

Signaling a Range of Sanctions

One way in which restorative justice could have been offered to riot participants could have been pre-sentence or as a condition of sentencing. Put another way—one which, arguably, would have been much more meaningful in its impact—would have been in accordance with Braithwaite (2002)'s conceptualization of *responsive regulation*, which would see restorative justice offered as the first and primary justice response for riot participants, and sanctions that prioritize the sentencing goals of deterrence and incapacitation offered only when such face-to-face processes are proven inappropriate or ineffective; such a referral process is consistent with the *Code*, and legislated under section 717 (Daubney & Parry, 1999). As Braithwaite (2002) argues, offering restorative justice as the default response to crime would not only benefit individual victims and offenders, but potentially effect a grander change at the level of societal *perceptions* of justice. Specifically, responsive regulation would not only legitimize restorative justice processes in the eyes of the public, but also legitimize more punitive sanctions—as the latter would be resorted to only when more dialogic forms of justice have failed. If community-based restorative justice had been made available to riot participants who expressed remorse and a genuine desire to take responsibility, those riot cases unsuitable for a reconciliatory approach could then be processed much more speedily through state-base justice. This regulatory and collaborative process that involves the state and civil society *signals, but does not threaten, a range of sanctions to which you can escalate, including the signal that the ultimate sanctions are formidable and are used when necessary, though only as a last resort* (RRP6).

Engage Networks that Develop Capacities and Benefits

A further rationale for community-based restorative justice, over formalized state-based justice, is the potential it offers to reduce the fiscal cost of justice to taxpayers (see Lee et al., 2012; Matrix Evidence, 2009; Native Counselling Services of Alberta, 2001). On the face of it, the operating costs associated with restorative justice programming are typically much lower than those associated with the conventional criminal justice system (Shapland et al., 2011). In some jurisdictions this is, in part, because community-based volunteers and NGO staff often facilitate cases, resulting in less time, fiscal and resource commitment compared to court, in particular costs related to legal representation (Perry, 2002). Together, the result is a more efficient justice system.

The argument for alternatives to custody when processing such a significant number of cases efficiently finds even greater significance in the context of an overburdened court system. The 2011 Vancouver riot preceded the 2012 Review of the Provincial Justice System in British Columbia (British Columbia Ministry of Justice, 2012), which called attention to the fact that, despite a decrease in both provincial crime severity and crime rates, the number of cases being dealt with by the province's justice system had risen in recent years. The resulting slowing of the processing times for these cases has also led to increases in the time it takes to get to trial, the length of trials and in the number of cases being dismissed and/or stayed, all of which lead to increased processing costs as well (Tilley, 2012). The Review (2012) concluded that enhancing efficiency, reducing court costs and decreasing the volume of cases entering the justice system all must be considered primary goals for British Columbia's court system, including advocating for restorative justice. The IRIT's decision to sentence as many rioters in court as possible did not aid in achieving this goal; indeed, these same limited court resources were responsible for many charged for involvement in the riot having to wait up to 5 years for a sentence to be served. Conversely, had a community-based restorative justice process been implemented for appropriate cases, at the pre-sentencing stage, those cases before the courts could have been processed more efficiently and at far less cost.

The need to consider alternatives to custody in the aftermath of events like the 2011 Vancouver riot is heightened by the sheer volume of convictions that large-scale events like riots can bring into the criminal justice system within a relatively short period of time—in particular, through the use of such "crowdsourced policing" tactics as were employed in the aftermath of the 2011 riot. Included among the IRIT's evidence-gathering strategies was the establishment of a website that members of the public could then use to upload photographic and video evidence from the night of the riot directly to police (Furlong & Keefe, 2011)—a strategy that proved enormously successful, as evidenced by the fact that, by October 31, 2011, the team had already managed to process "over 30 terabytes of data" and "over 5,000 hours of video" (Vancouver Police Department, 2011). In this unexpected way, the 2011 Vancouver riot proved to be notably different from previous riots in Canada's history by the thousands of individuals present at the disturbance who had on their personal portable devices equipped with photo and video capabilities, which were made use of to obtain visual evidence of the rioters' behavior. The precedent set by *Loewen* did not account for this rapid and significant change in the ease with which incriminating photographic and video evidence from large-scale public disturbances could be obtained by members of the public and made available to police: indeed, *Loewen* makes far more sense when accompanied by the expectation that a city-wide riot will see a few dozen participants sentenced at most; less so when that number increases to a few hundred.

Finally, the reaffirmation, at a time of potential reforms, that individuals charged with participating in a riot must be sentenced in accordance with the aims of general deterrence and denunciation, and that the context of the riot necessitates a custody sentence even when mitigating factors are present, has set a precedent that limits the extent to which rehabilitative and restorative measures can be pursued if—or when—Canada experiences another riot of this size and scale again. This is a substantial consequence given the effort and expenditures now known to have gone into bringing participants in the 2011 riot to justice—indeed, one may argue it to be flat-out unsustainable when criminal justice resources are inherently limited. Are justice officials to continue to press charges and recommend hefty custody sentences for all identified participants in large-scale criminal events that follow the 2011 Vancouver riot, in accordance with a decades-old precedent from a technological era that saw the capacity for community vigilante justice far more underdeveloped than it is today?

Riots have direct impact, along with secondary and tertiary impact. The impact on a justice system already working at capacity was significant, and impacted other cases before the courts. The stain on the justice system—both financial and operational—could have been lessened through engaing wider networks of justice actors, particularly community-based partners, including restorative justice providers. A central principle of responsive regulation is harnessing *network pyramidal goverance by engaging wider networks of partners as you move up the pyramid (RRP7)*. Given this principle, community-based restorative justice providers could have been used at any stage of the justice response. For example, in the context of breach of sentencing conditions, community based restorative justice providers could work with courts, probation and police to harness active responsibility and direct accountability.

Signal Support and Education to Riot Participants

While the IRIT eagerly crowdsourced photo and video evidence from riot witnesses in the weeks that followed the riot (Schneider & Trottier, 2012, 2013), vigilante efforts with similar aims sprang up simultaneously on social media platforms. In the mere hours that followed the riot, public groups on the social media website Facebook with names such as "[the] Vancouver Riot Wall of Shame", "Vancouver Riot Pics: Post Your Photos" and "Report Canuck RIOT Morons" were created to enable those present at the riot to upload photographs, videos and any other evidence incriminating to alleged rioters (Robinson et al., 2011). Consistent with the IRIT's goals, the stated intent of these groups was to expose rioters in a public venue in order to coerce them to turn themselves in (and, later, to assist the IRIT in their investigative efforts). Yet almost immediately, those who joined the groups took to using them for a second purpose: to unreservedly insult, shame and even threaten those suspected of having participated in the riot (Beaumont, 2011; Dhillon, 2011). On some occasions, this "naming-and-shaming" escalated to the degree that highly personal information pertaining to alleged rioters—including phone numbers, home addresses and the names of family members—were published online, leading many of these individuals to fear for their personal safety (Mann, 2011; Ryan, 2012). Harris's (2017) analysis of "naming-and-shaming" suggest that while these strategies tend to focus on social impact—loss of face or humiliation—the role of shame is much more complex: "Shame is invoked when individuals question whether they have violated their values and, when experienced, represents a threat to the person's sense of who they are" (pp. 70–71).

Studies that have since examined the purpose that these acts of "naming-and-shaming" served for those who took part suggest a key function in helping participants rebuild and reaffirm a sense of shared community identity (see Lavoie et al., 2014; Schneider & Trottier, 2012, 2013)—and further, that this identity reaffirmation process altered not only how those who took part in it viewed themselves, but also those individuals who participated in the riot. Schneider and Trottier's (2012, 2013) qualitative examinations of user responses to the 2011 Vancouver riot on the social media website Facebook, for example, found that the riot was perceived as threatening to the identities of other social media users, and that users coped with this threat by collectively using social media to *redefine* and *reinforce* their current social identities in ways that highlighted their superiority relative to the "other" group—that is, the rioters (see also Branscombe et al., 1999; Branscombe & Wann, 1994; Ellemers, Spears, & Doosje, 2002; Ethier & Deaux, 1994). Focused on what was arguably the largest and most popular Facebook group for posting photos and video evidence incriminating to rioters following the riot—a group named "Vancouver Riot Pics: Post Your Photos"—they found that many of the examined posts saw users post to the group purely to reaffirm and validate the social identities of one another via labels such as "real Vancouverite", "Canucks fan", "real fan" or "true fan", and that these labels were used to portray the "in-group" ("real Vancouverites" or "real fans") in a favorable light, while derogating the "out-group" (participants in the riot). Arvanitidis (2015) found that language indicative of social identity threat had notable overlaps with language both indicative of feelings of *shame* and *embarrassment*, and language indicating *support for punishment*.

There is no disputing that those who took part in these public humiliation tactics are responsible for their own actions; yet there is an argument to be made that responsibility must also be shared by those with the powerful voices in the aftermath of the riot, who also were some of the earliest campaigners for the now-accepted narrative of a "world-class" city victimized by "criminals", "anarchists" and "thugs"—though not, interestingly, the thousands of hockey fans well known to have been present prior to the riot. News stories and editorials discussing the riot in the days that followed were heavy with emotional language indicative of shame, embarrassment and anger, though none top the *Vancouver Province*'s front-page headline of "Let's Make Them Pay" (Beasley-Murray, 2011)—an impassioned encouragement for online vigilantes to continue to post images and videos of alleged rioters, in shameless disregard for the criminal justice system's presumption of innocence. It comes as little surprise, then, that Schneider and Trottier (2012, 2013)'s research found many users who posted to the "Vancouver Riot Pics: Post Your Photos" Facebook group believed the group to have been surveilled by members of the IRIT, and that their actions provided direct assistance to the IRIT's investigative efforts.

Those with the most powerful voices in the aftermath of a community-wide criminal event have a social responsibility to consider how the imposition of unfounded labels like "hooligans" and "thugs", and the use of novel evidence-gathering tactics like "crowdsourced policing", legitimize those dangerously unregulated forms of self-surveillance and community vigilantism that were witnessed in the aftermath of the riot (see Kohm, 2008; Trottier, 2012). Perhaps more importantly, they must also recognize that, insomuch as the myth of "us. vs. them" provides a convenient way to legitimize the harsh punishment of those involved in the riot, it creates just as immense an obstacle to their eventual reintegration back into their communities. The hundreds of first-time offenders sentenced for their participation in the 2011 riot must now contend not only with the burden of a criminal record, but also the unshakeable stigma that comes from being labeled a much-reviled "rioter"—one that no amount of evidence to the contrary may ever be able to shake (Dripps, 2003). The regulatory capacity of those in power would be more productive to *signal the preference to achieve outcomes by support and education that builds capacity to self-regulate for the normative good* (RRP5). Rather than amplifying regulatory mechanisms that stigmatize and exclude, responsive regulation puts resources into a future that supports self-regulation through processes of support, education and reintegration that build human capacities.

Learn, Evaluate, Communicate

The foundations of responsive regulation, together with restorative justice, are learning and growth that fosters responsibility and human capacity building at the individual, community and professional level. Besides the significant fiscal and operational costs and burdens of the criminal justice response to the 2011 riots, there have been significant costs to human capacity building, particularly for those sentenced and victimized. We have yet to learn the true impact of the effect of the riot on individuals—victims and offenders—along with community. No report, to date, includes their voices (Reicher, 2016). This is a significant step to building understanding to prevent such harm from happening again.

The report on the 2011 riot prosecutions concludes with the assurance that "considerable resources" were spent to hold those who took part in the riot accountable, and with the hope that these prosecutions "will deter—even prevent—the reoccurrence of events like the 2011 riot" (British Columbia Ministry of Justice, 2016, p. 20). It's a normative ideal, but one that also sidesteps the rather awkward reality that the 2011 Vancouver riot was far from novel—evidenced not only in the riot that took place only 17 years earlier in 1994, but in the many football and hockey riots that preceded it as well. Indeed, what perhaps truly marks the 2011 riot as unique when compared to the disturbances that came before was the far more evident effort that followed, on behalf of both law enforcement officials and the community at large, to protect Vancouver's reputation as a "world-class city" by any means necessary. The street group violence eroded the pride Vancouverites held. Through swift punishment, and subsequent public humiliation of those deemed "unworthy" by both the criminal justice process and the public, the response alienated those deemed not fit to belong to the "real Vancouver". Perhaps the biggest failed lesson made in the city's response to the riot, then, was the greater failure to recognize a deeper value of a "world-class city" that nurtures belonging and inclusion for all citizens. Our response to street group violence offers those impacted an opportunity to collectively denounce the behavior and stand up for the values that make a city great. This includes those who make decisions that threaten social order or those who suffer the most harm—and to realize that "real" cities, including the "real" Vancouver, have riots—as they also have social tensions, social divisions and crime.

A Vancouver that truly wants to prove itself to be a "world-class city" and set an example for the rest of the world should perhaps consider doing so not by publicly shaming and excluding wrongdoers in a continuous effort to uphold a perfect public image, but through recognizing that "real" communities include even those who have done wrong—and that they are strengthened in their recognition that preserving the potential that lies within each and every member of their community is worth far more than the desire for retribution. To be a resilient city we must learn and grow together. Resilience comes from reflecting on and learning from our own actions and inactions. It comes from leaning into difficult conversations, wherein we *learn, evaluate how well and at what cost outcomes have been achieved and communicate lessons learnt* (RRP9). There is good evidence that the community does have a role to play in closing the gap between individuals and those who regulate them (V. Braithwaite, 2017).

At the level of the criminal justice system, this may very well require an embracing of a "tripartisan" approach to justice—one that recognizes justice to be more than simply an exercise in handing down punishment, to instead be an opportunity for norms-clarification that is accomplished only through the involvement of community and the reframing of justice as an exercise in democracy.

Notes

1. *R. v. Loewen,* [1992] B.C.J. No. 1454
2. *R. v. Loewen,* [1992] B.C.J. No. 1454
3. *R. v. Peepre,* 2012 BCPC 328 (CanLII)
4. *R. v. Williams,* 2012 BCPC 345 (CanLII)
5. *R. v. Dorosh,* 2012 BCPC 370 (CanLII)

References

Angus Reid Public Opinion. (2011). *British Columbians want Vancouver rioters and looters to face justice* [Data set]. Retrieved from http://angusreidglobal.com/wp-content/uploads/2011/06/2011.06.20_Riots_ BC.pdf.

Arms, R. L., & Russell, G. W. (1997). Impulsivity, fight history and camaraderie as predictors of a willingness to escalate a disturbance. *Current Psychology Research and Reviews, 15*(4), 279–285.

Arvanitidis, T. (2013). *From revenge to restoration: Evaluating general deterrence as a primary sentencing purpose for rioters in Vancouver, British Columbia* (Master's thesis). Retrieved from http://summit.sfu.ca.

Arvanitidis, T. (2015). *"It takes a community to keep these idiots in line": Examining biased and "othering" language on social media following the 2011 Vancouver Stanley Cup riot.* Manuscript submitted for publication.

Baron, R. S., & Kerr, N. L. (2003). *Group process, group decision, group action.* Philadelphia, PA: Open University Press.

Beasley-Murray, J. (2011, June 24). Please stop saying you're the 'real' Vancouver. *The Tyee.* Retrieved from https://thetyee.ca/Opinion/2011/06/24/RealVancouver/?PageSpeed= noscript.

Beaumont, P. (2011, June 30). *Vancouver rioters named and shamed in internet campaign.* Retrieved from www.theguardian.com/world/2011/jun/30/vancouver-rioters-internet-campaign.

Braithwaite, J. (1989). *Crime, shame, and reintegration.* Cambridge: Cambridge University Press.

Braithwaite, J. (2002). *Restorative justice and responsive regulation.* London, UK: Oxford University Press.

Braithwaite, J. (2011). The essence of responsive regulation. *UBC Law Review, 44*(3), 475–520.

Braithwaite, J. (2016). *Restorative justice and responsive regulation: The question of evidence* (Working Paper No. 51, Canberra, AU: School of Regulation and Global Governance (RegNet)). Retrieved from http://regnet.anu.edu.au/research/publications/paper-series.

Braithwaite, J. (2017). Types of responsiveness. In P. Drahos (Ed.), *Regulatory theory: Foundations and applications* (pp. 117–132). Canberra: ANU Press.

Braithwaite, J. (2018). Minimally sufficient deterrence. *Crime and Justice: A Review of Research, 47*(1), 69–118.

Braithwaite, V. (2017). Closing the gap between regulation and the community. In P. Drahos, (Ed.), *Regulatory theory: Foundations and applications* (pp. 25–42). Canberra: ANU Press.

Branscombe, N. R., Ellemers, N., Spears, R., & Doosje, B. (1999). The context and content of social identity threat. In N. Ellemers, R. Spears, & B. Doosje (Eds.), *Social identity: Context, commitment, content* (pp. 39–58). Malden, MA: Blackwell.

Branscombe, N. R., & Wann, D. L. (1994). Collective self—esteem consequences of out-group derogation when a valued social identity is on trial. *European Journal of Social Psychology, 24*(6), 641–657.

British Columbia Ministry of Justice. (2012). *Review of the provincial justice system in British Columbia.* Retrieved from www.ag.gov.bc.ca/public/JusticeSystemReview.pdf.

British Columbia Ministry of Justice and Attorney General. (2016). *B.C.'s prosecution service—Report on the 2011 Vancouver Stanley Cup riot prosecutions.* Victoria, BC: Ministry of Justice and Attorney General.

Christie, N. (1977). Conflict as property. *The British Journal of Criminology, 17*(1), 1–15.

City of Vancouver. (2011). *Internal review of the 2011 Stanley Cup riot.* Retrieved from https://council.vancouver.ca/20110906/documents/specAppendixA1.pdf.

Daubney, D., & Parry, G. (1999). An overview of bill C-41 (The Sentencing Reform Act). In J. V. Roberts & D. P. Cole (Eds.), *Making sense of sentencing* (pp. 31–47). Toronto: University of Toronto Press.

Dhillon, S. (2011). *When rioters trashed Vancouver, Twitter fanned the flames—and gathered the evidence.* Retrieved from www.theglobeandmail.com/news/british-columbia/when-rioters-trashed-vancouver-twitter-fanned-the-flames—and-gathered-the-evidence/article4182089/.

Dripps, D. A. (2003). Fundamental attribution error: Criminal justice and the social psychology of blame. *Vanderbilt Law Review, 56*(5), 1385–1438.

Ellemers, N., Spears, R., & Doosje, B. (2002). Self and social identity. *Annual Review of Psychology, 53*, 161–186.

Ethier, K. A., & Deaux, K. (1994). Negotiating social identity when contexts change: Maintaining identification and responding to threat. *Journal of Personality and Social Psychology, 67*(2), 243–251.

Forsyth, D. R. (2006). *Group dynamics* (3rd ed.). Pacific Grove, CA: Brooks/Cole.

Furlong, J., & Keefe, D. J. (2011). *The night the city became a stadium: Independent review of the 2011 Vancouver Stanley Cup playoffs riot.* Vancouver: Government of British Columbia.

Gavrielides, T. (2007). *Restorative justice theory and practice: Addressing the discrepancy.* Monsey, NY: Criminal Justice Press.

Gavrielides, T. (2012). *Waves of healing: Using restorative justice with street group violence.* London, UK: Independent Academic Research Studies.

Harris, N. (2017). Shame in regulatory settings. In P. Drahos (Ed.), *Regulatory theory: Foundations and applications* (pp. 59–72). Canberra: ANU Press.

Howe, G. (2013, March 12). *Another 33 people charged in Vancouver Stanley Cup riot.* Retrieved from www.ctvnews.ca/canada/another-33-people-charged-in-vancouver-stanley-cup-riot-1.1191989.

Karstedt, S. (2017). Scaling criminology: From street violence to atrocity crimes. In P. Drahos (Ed.), *Regulatory theory: Foundations and applications* (pp. 465–482). Canberra: ANU Press.

Kohm, S. A. (2008). Naming, shaming and criminal justice: Mass-mediated humiliation as entertainment and punishment. *Crime, Media, Culture: An International Journal, 5*(2), 188–205.

Lavoie, J. A. A., Eaton, J., Sanders, C. B., & Smith, M. (2014). 'The wall is the city': A narrative analysis of Vancouver's post-riot apology wall. In M. D. Johns, S. S. Chen, & L. A. Terlip (Eds.), *Studies in symbolic interaction* (Vol. 43, pp. 203–222). Bingley, UK: Emerald Group Publishing.

Lee, S., Aos, S., Drake, E., Pennucci, A., Miller, M., & Anderson, L. (2012). *Return on investment: Evidence-based options to improve statewide outcomes.* Olympia, WA: Washington State Institute for Public Policy.

Mann, B. (2011). *Social media "Vigilantes'" I.D. Vancouver rioters—and then some.* Retrieved from www.huffington post.ca/bill-mann/vancouver-riot-social-media_b_889017.html.

Manson, A., Healy, P., & Trotter, G. (2008). *Sentencing and penal policy in Canada: Cases, materials, and commentary.* Toronto: Emond Montgomery Publications.

Matas, R. (2011, June 15). *Bystanders share experiences of the riots after the Stanley Cup loss.* Retrieved from www.the globeandmail.com/news/british-columbia/bystanders-share-experiences-of-vancouver-riots-after-stanley-cup-loss/article583505/.

Matrix Evidence. (2009). *Economic analysis of interventions for young adult offenders.* Retrieved from www.bctrust.org.uk/wp-content/uploads/2011/01/Matrix_ Economic_analysis-T2A-2009.pdf.

Murphy, K. (2017). Procedural justice and its role in promoting voluntary compliance. In P. Drahos (Ed.), *Regulatory theory: Foundations and applications* (pp. 43–58). Canberra: ANU Press.

Mustonen, A., Arms, R. L., & Russell, G. W. (1996). Predictors of sports spectators' proclivity for riotous behaviour in Finland and Canada. *Personality and Individual Differences, 21*(4), 519–525.

Native Counselling Services of Alberta. (2001). *A cost-benefit analysis of hollow water's community holistic circle healing process.* Ottawa, ON: Public Safety Canada. Retrieved from www.publicsafety.gc.ca/res/cor/apc/_fl/apc-20-eng.pdf.

Paulus, P. B. (Ed.). (1980). *Psychology of group influence.* Hillsdale, NJ: Erlbaum.

Perry, J. (2002). Introduction: Challenging the assumptions. In J. Perry (Ed.), *Repairing communities through restorative justice* (pp. 1–18). Alexandria, VI: Magnet Print Brokers.

Postmes, T., & Spears, R. (1998). Deindividuation and antinormative behavior: A meta- analysis. *Psychological Bulletin, 123*(3), 238–259.

Proctor, J. (2016, February 19). 2016 Stanley Cup rioters sentenced for assault of good Samaritans. *CBC News.* Retrieved from www.cbc.ca/news/canada/british-columbia/stanley-cup-rioters-sentenced-assault-good-samaritans-1.3456478.

Reicher, S. D. (2011). Reading the riot actors. *New Scientist, 211*(2830), 30–31.

Reicher, S. D. (2016, October 28). *The power of a riot: Justice, identity and belonging.* Retrieved from www.sfu.ca/publicsquare/upcoming-events/city-conversations/2016/Oct-28-2016.html.

Roberts, J.V., & Von Hirsch, A. (1999). Legislating the purpose and principles of sentencing. In J.V. Roberts & D. P. Cole (Eds.), *Making sense of sentencing* (pp. 31–47). Toronto: University of Toronto Press.

Robinson, M., Kane, L., Duggan, E., & Law, S. (2011, June 17). Vancouverites fight back against rioters through social media. *Vancouver Sun.* Retrieved from www. vancouversun.com/news/ Vancouverites+fight+back+again st+rioters+through+social +media/4958109/story.html.

Roversi, A. (1991). Football violence in Italy. *International Review for the Sociology of Sport, 26*(4), 311–331.

Russell, G.W., & Arms, R. L. (1998). Toward a social-psychological profile of would-be rioters. *Aggressive Behaviour, 24*(3), 219–226.

Ryan, D. (2012). *Rioting teen Nathan Kotylak and family face backlash, forced to leave home.* Retrieved from www.vancouversun.com/technology/Rioting+teen+Nathan+Kotylak +family+face+backlash+forced+leave+h ome/4972283/story.html.

Schneider, C., & Trottier, D. (2012). The 2011 Vancouver riot and Facebook. *BC Studies, 175*(Autumn 2012), 59–72.

Schneider, C., & Trottier, D. (2013). Social Media and the 2011 Vancouver Riot. *Studies in Symbolic Interaction, 40*, 335–362.

Schneider, H. J. (1992). Criminology of riots. *International Journal of Offender Therapy and Comparative Criminology, 36*(3), 173–186.

Shapland, J., Robinson, G., & Sorsby, A. (2011). *Restorative justice in practice: Evaluating what works for victims and offenders.* New York: Routledge.

Sharpe, S. (1998). *Restorative justice: A vision for healing and change.* Edmonton, AB: Victim Offender Mediation Society.

Shaw, M. E. (1981). *Group dynamics: The psychology of small group behaviour* (3rd ed.). New York: McGraw-Hill.

Sherman, L., & Strang, H. (2007). *Restorative justice: The evidence.* London, UK: The Smith Institute.

Strang, H. (2003). *Repair or revenge: Victims and restorative justice.* Oxford: Oxford University Press.

Strang, H. (2017). Experiments in restorative justice. In P. Drahos (Ed.), *Regulatory theory: Foundations and applications* (pp. 483–498). Canberra: ANU Press.

Strang, H., Sherman, L., Mayo-Wilson, E., Woods, D., & Ariel, B. (2013). *Restorative Justice Conferencing (RJC) using face-to-face meetings of offenders and victims: Effects on offender recidivism and victim satisfaction. A systematic review.* Oslo: Campbell Systematic Reviews. Retrieved from campbellcollaboration.org/lib/project/63/.

Tilley, K. (2012). *The causes of B.C.'s criminal justice system crisis.* Retrieved from http://bccla.org/wpcontent/uploads/2012/05/20120401-Justice-Denied-report1.pdf.

Trivizas, E. (1980). Offences and offenders in football crowd disorders. *British Journal of Criminology, 20*(3), 276–288.

Trottier, D. (2012). *Social media as surveillance: Rethinking visibility in a converging world.* Burlington, VT: Ashgate.

Tyler, T. (2006). Restorative justice and procedural justice: Dealing with rule breaking. *Journal of Social Issues, 62*(2), 307–326.

Van Camp, T. (2014). *Victims of violence and restorative practices: Finding a voice.* New York: Routledge.

Van Camp, T. (2017). Understanding victim participation in restorative practices: Looking for justice for oneself as well as for others. *European Journal of Criminology, 14*(6), 679–696.

Vancouver Police Chief Jim Chu's Statement on Pace of Riot Investigation. (2011, August 17). *Georgia straight.* Retrieved from www.straight.com/news/vancouver- police-chief-jim-chus-statement-pace-riot-investigation.

Vancouver Police Department. (2011). *Vancouver police department 2011 Stanley Cup riot review.* Retrieved from http://vancouver.ca/files/cov/2011-stanley-cup- riot-VPD.pdf.

Wintonyk, D. (2011, June 16). *'Criminals, anarchists, thugs' behind post-cup riot.* Retrieved from https://bc.ctvnews.ca/criminals-anarchists-thugs-behind-post-cup-riot-1.658053.

Wong, J., Bouchard, J., Gravel, J., Bouchard, M., & Morselli, C. (2016). Can at-risk youth be diverted from crime? A meta-analysis of restorative diversion programs. *Criminal Justice and Behavior, 43*(10), 1310–1329.

Zellerer, E. (2011, June 24). *Restorative justice would help Vancouver heal after riot.* Retrieved from www.straight.com/news/evelyn-zellerer-restorative-justice-would-help-vancouver-heal-after-riot.

5

FAMILINESS AND RESPONSIVENESS OF HUMAN SERVICES

The Approach of Relational Sociology

Elisabetta Carrà

Introduction

Within the framework of relational sociology, a body of studies and research has shown that as regard to both social policies and human services, the most promising models were family-focused. Familiness has become a distinctive feature of the relational approach to the study of welfare systems and human services. After an examination of literature on family-based approaches and welfare regime models—with particular attention paid to processes that trend towards what is called *defamilization*—the relational sociological approach is presented as a theoretical framework for evidence-based family-centered practices. An exploratory model for analyzing familiness of services and practices is described. In conclusion, an example of a responsive regulatory pyramid is provided that maps possible pathways towards familiness and suggests ways to regulate ever-present risks of an escalation of defamilization.

Familiness and Responsiveness of Human Services: The Approach of Relational Sociology

In recent years, studies in the relational sociology framework (Donati, 2014a; Donati & Archer, 2015; Donati, 2015)[1] have increasingly revealed strengths of family-focused policies (Carrà, 2016b; Donati, 2012c) or family associations (Carrà, 2017; Donati & Prandini, 2007). Good practices in services to the family (Carrà, 2014a), *familiness*[2], has become, little by little, a distinctive relational genre in the study of welfare systems and human services: *Familiness* is a quality that is shown empirically to add value (Carrà, 2012b; Carrà & Bramanti, 2017; Donati, 2012a).

Interest in the concept of *familiness* has advanced in parallel with increasing reassessment of the influential classification of welfare regimes developed by Esping-Andersen (Esping-Andersen, 1990): this is based on a negative ideological vision of the family, leading to the classification of Mediterranean welfare systems as "familistic" and to advocate their defamilization (Donati & Prandini, 2007), through

DOI: 10.4324/9780429398704-5

provisions and practices which make wellbeing independent from family and intergenerational relationships (Lohmann & Zagel, 2016; McLaughlin & Glendinning, 1994).

Within the relational approach, *familiness* can be seen as a logical conclusion of the debate on the personalization of welfare provision (Barnes & Prior, 2009; Duffy, 2011; Prandini & Orlandini, 2015; Sabel et al., 2010).

Personalization, an innovative model to design human services, has started to spread in European welfare regimes since the early 2000s (Needham & Glasby, 2014): referring to 'person' rather than an individual highlights that the human being is a subject embedded *within* a network of relations, beginning with the *family*, which firstly mediates between its members' wellbeing. It entails, on one hand, the need to tailor a service on users' personal features and, on the other hand, the propensity to address their needs, by enabling relational processes, based on co-design and co-production (Andersen, 2007). To personalize welfare systems public authorities, third-sector organizations and social professionals should "reset" their identities, their functions and roles, in order to enable their users to take every opportunity that social innovation provides: so-called flourishing, Aristotelian happiness (*eudaimonia*), the ultimate good for the human being, conceived as the full realization of all her capabilities (Stiglitz, Sen, & Fitoussi, 2009).

The drive to personalization originates from the post-modern process of "individualization" (Beck, 1992; Beck & Beck-Gernsheim, 2002). Within the area of human services it has caused an unstoppable momentum to provide even more specific, fragmented and standardized services: this is leading to an endless decomposition of individuals' needs, whilst the person's unity and capabilities are liquefied (Bauman, 2001). Prandini and Orlandini (2015)—referring to literature on co-production of goods and services (Bovaird & Loeffler, 2012; Needham, 2008; Verschuere, Brandsen, & Pestoff, 2012)—argue, on the contrary, that personalization actually requires a more participative way of providing welfare services, based on the engagement of subjects with their own networks of relationships.

Hence, the family network must be primarily involved, since family is the first provider of strongly personalized care: in this respect, *familiness* ought to be considered the highest level of personalization (Carrà, 2003, 2013). Nevertheless, within the relational approach, awareness is growing that *familiness* is an ambiguous concept as well as ideologically contested (the above-mentioned defamilization trend). It appeared necessary to conduct a deep analysis of literature on family-centered practices, in order to find sound arguments for this model.

From another perspective, studies on responsive regulation (Braithwaite, 2011; Drahos, 2017) present strong similarities with narratives of personalization and co-production. Personalization and co-production undoubtedly resemble some of the nine principles of responsive regulation (Braithwaite, 2011): the second ("actively listen", "give voice to stakeholders", "settle agreed outcomes and how to monitor them", "build commitment"); the seventh ("engage wider [and wider] networks of partners"); the eighth ("elicit active responsibility"); and the ninth ("learn [by doing]").

Starting from these premises, the structure of this chapter shall be as follows: (1) after an examination of the family-based and evidence-based literature; (2) the defamilization model will be discussed and a theory of family social capital as a fundamental resource for society will be argued; (3) then, the relational sociological approach will be presented as a theoretical framework for evidence-based family-centered practices; (4) finally, an exploratory model for analyzing *familiness* of services and practices will be illustrated. Concluding (5), a proposal of a responsive regulation pyramid for *familiness* will be provided, in order to draw up the road map towards *familiness* and the ever-present risk of an escalation of defamilization.

Whole-Family Approaches and the Family Impact Lens: Evidence-Based Supports to *Familiness*

Within the relational sociology framework, the case for promoting *familiness* of policies and programs is supported through top-down arguments, looking at family relationships as an essential factor of society that must be acknowledged, promoted and enhanced. Considerable research shows bottom-up that *whole-family approaches* tend to be more effective than individual-based strategies (Morris et al., 2008), especially when *family impact* is adopted as a lens for policies and practices (Bogenschneider et al., 2012a, 2012b; Epley, Summers, & Turnbull, 2010).

Whole-Family Approaches

In the late 1990s a substantial body of research and literature outlined the value and effect of involving children's networks in child welfare services (Morris & Burford, 2007). In this perspective, the UK Children Act 1989 (Department of Health, 1998) stated that children are best supported within their networks. Similar conclusions were reached in the US, where several studies found that having social supports is associated with positive outcomes in prevention and intervention in health, education, justice and child welfare (Biegel, 1984; Burford & Hudson, 2000; Collins & Pancoast, 1976; Kemp, Whittaker, & Tracy, 1997; Werger, 1994; Whittaker & Garbarino, 1983). Primarily narrowed to childcare (Broad, 2001; Bullock, Gooch, & Little, 1998; Thoburn, Lewis, & Shemmings, 1995), whole-family practices have gradually included families who, in a broad sense, were experiencing multiple challenges. In 2008, the UK Cabinet Office published *Think Family: A Literature Review of Whole Family Approaches* (Morris et al., 2008) and this encouraged policies and practices based on a more holistic and contextualized understanding of people's lives and more joined-up approaches to delivering services (Tew et al., 2015).

Morris and Burford (2007) reported that whole-family approaches suffered a slowdown, due to the difficulties in agreeing on which dimensions were most important.

In 1996, after analyzing a wide literature, 10 recurring standards of *family centeredness* were identified by Allen and Petr.[3] Based on such indicators, a broad and widely shared definition was provided: "Family-centered service delivery, across disciplines and settings, views the family as the unit of attention. This model organizes assistance in a collaborative fashion and in accordance with each individual family's wishes, strengths, and needs" (Allen & Petr, 1996, p. 64). More than 10 years later, a new review reduced standards from 10 to 5,[4] noting that "inclusion of family choice and a strengths-based perspective in definitions of family centeredness has increased whereas family as the unit of attention has declined" (Epley et al., 2010). The latest research has outlined the relevance and the discriminatory role of social capital (Malin, Tunmore, & Wilcock, 2014), understood as an asset or a hindrance to take into account in designing an intervention. In this direction, other researchers (Epley et al., 2010) point out that evaluation systems of interventions addressed to families with children generally assess only child outcomes and not family outcomes as well.

In Italy, the National Observatory of the Family had been supporting for some years research on good practices, based on the involvement of the family network (Carrà, 2008a, 2014b; Carrà & Pavesi, 2015; Donati, 2012a): however, they have remained localized experiences without undergoing an evaluation research process, despite the Italian government in 2012 passing a National Plan for the Family, providing expressly family-based services and regular assessment of the results.

From Individual Impact to Family Impact

As stated above, the latest trends in family-centered conceptualizations call for not only child outcomes to be assessed, but also family outcomes. Along these lines, a model has developed in the US since 1988[5] by the Family Impact Institute which seems to meet this requirement through strong arguments based on extensive empirical research and field trials, showing the close interconnection between personal and family wellbeing and the necessity to implement policies explicitly addressed to the family.

The Family Impact Institute over the years has provided many tools to guide the design and assessment of legislation and programs, to get a positive impact on family relationships (Bogenschneider et al., 2012b). The family impact lens consists in five evidence-based principles (family responsibility, family stability, family relationships, family diversity, family engagement), each linked to a set of checklists to be used for designing and analyzing policies and practices.

Ultimately, the most eye-opening findings imply standards for family-centered practices (Allen & Petr, 1996; Epley et al., 2010) and family impact principles (Bogenschneider et al., 2012a, 2012b). The latter do not merely foreshadow standards for family-based practices, but go beyond, by empirically supporting the need that family must be the cornerstone of policies and programs, in strong harmony with the relational perspective.

It should be into account that all these approaches are informed by family systems theory (Bowen, 1974; Brofenbrenner, 1979; Minuchin, 1974): it holds that individuals can best be understood within the context of the immediate systems with which they interact, and it therefore considers multiple and inter-related influences on individual and family outcomes (Ooms, 1984). According to relational sociology, this vision appears still inadequate to provide well-founded reasons to support theoretically the effectiveness of whole-family practices and their positive impact on family relationships.

Defamilization, Welfare Regimes and Family Social Capital

Before entering into the relational approach, specific attention must be paid to the defamilization model, insofar as it could undermine family-centered approaches.

Defamilization is a goal of those welfare regimes which strive to make individuals independent from family and intergenerational relationships (McLaughlin & Glendinning, 1994); (Lohmann & Zagel, 2016). As shown by Donati and Prandini (2007), it is based on a vision of the family, the so-called amoral familism (Banfield, 1958), looking at family social capital as a hindrance rather that a facilitator of societal wellbeing.

The most widespread classification of welfare regimes distinguishes between *liberal* welfare typified by Anglo-Saxon countries, *socialist* welfare typical of the Scandinavian countries, *conservative or corporate* welfare typical of the countries of central Europe and the so-called familistic welfare in the Mediterranean countries (Esping-Andersen, 1990). This classification is often read to imply a negative ideological vision of the family and adopts an individualistic philosophy that leads to considering the Scandinavian model [but this is conceived as a socialist model that therefore does not fit with individualism] as preferable and foreshadows the defamilization of Mediterranean regimes (Esping-Andersen, 1999, 2009). Goods and care services provided by families should be replaced by public facilities, in order to increase a wider and more significant participation of married women in the labor market. The countries following this path would be those reaching higher levels of decommodification, solidarity among citizens, equality and individualization. This model is known as the Scandinavian paradox of statist individualism (Berggren & Trägårdh, 2011; Daun, 2010; Trägårdh, 2014) or solidaristic individualism (Movitz & Sandberg, 2013): according to this perspective, a strong state and a strong individual are not mutually exclusive, since state interference can strengthen personal autonomy. The concept is mainly used with reference to the Swedish welfare state, one of the most advanced in the world, in which socialism does not mean collectivism, as welfare policies and family law are aimed at making individuals autonomous from family (women from men, children from parents, elderly from young people), church and private charities.

In the social democratic Scandinavian culture, we can find underlying credit for the thesis of amoral familism (Banfield, 1958), which—beyond the intentions of Banfield—tended to discredit the family role in creating public good, by pitting family norms against community norms. The family seems to play a merely secondary role in research and literature on social capital: most authors tend to share the (sometimes implicit) idea that the degree of cooperation, trust and solidarity developed in the family's inner dynamics is inversely correlated with the family building social capital for the public sphere. As Coleman (1988, 2000) stated, family capital has an important function in building the new generation's human capital; however, he pointed out that strong families are becoming ever more residual in Western countries and their crucial role of social capital generation has to be replaced by some substitute formal organization. While Putnam (1994, p. 73) asserted that family is "the most fundamental form of social capital" (p. 73), he did not detail how the family supports social capital. His approach (1994) is based on civic involvement, cooperating horizontal connections, generalized trust and associative life. Family is instead associated with "familism" in Putnam's approach, which in turn is associated with lack of generalized trust and lack of cooperating horizontal networks. Familism is a "private" case in its "expressive" nature on this view of social capital, and should not influence the system's "instrumental" orientation (Cartocci, 2002).

On the contrary other studies and research (Edwards, Franklin, & Holland, 2003; Franklin, 2004; Mutti, 2003; Sciolla, 2003; Stone & Hughes, 2000, 2002) have explored the connections between social capital in the family and civic and social commitment. Empirical evidence shows that the family's social capital—defined as the reciprocal orientations of the family's members which are able to generate trust and therefore cooperative actions (Donati, 2013)—is intimately connected to the emergence of pro-social attitudes in individuals, particularly in terms of social trust and participation in civil associations (Donati, 2003; Prandini, 2003, 2005). Thus relational sociology considers family bonds as a sort of 'paradigm' of social capital, as the original place of trust and cooperation among members (Donati & Prandini, 2007; Donati, 2014b). In this perspective, defamilization cannot be the aim of a new welfare model (Donati, 2012b): family relations and their wellbeing are the cornerstone of policies, programs and practices (Bogenschneider et al., 2012b; Bogenschneider & Corbett, 2011). This can be argued based on the idea of relational wellbeing and relational reflexivity, illustrated in the following pages.

A Theoretical Framework for Evidence-Based Family-Centered Practices: Relational Sociology

Within contemporary sociological debates, Archer's morphogenetic theory (2003) and Donati's (2010) relational approach provide the theoretical framework and the conceptual categories to support the idea that individuals' wellbeing is closely interwoven with their family relationships' wellbeing and it cannot be pursued unless a family lens has been adopted and the whole family is engaged in the process of producing wellbeing (Carrà, 2012a, 2013).

Referring to Archer's and Donati's theoretical approaches, individual welfare aspirations can more easily be pursued when the subjects establish trust-based cooperative networks to include as many people as possible as facilitators of reciprocal life projects (Carrà, 2008b). The argument moves from the consideration that any individual's welfare project is an action tending to social *change*, by turning uneasiness into comfort, or preventing future uneasiness.[6]

Archer (1995, 2003) sees morphogenesis as the result of a corporate agency of social subjects, that is, a joint action with other people, initiated by individual agents to change the structural and cultural conditions considered inadequate with respect to personal interests. Within socio-cultural interaction, groups and individuals mobilize resources and form alliances in their pursuit of material goals and reflexively constituted ideals: the possibility to start a social change (morphogenesis) depends on each person's will to initiate a joint project (a corporate action) together with others with a similar interest in making their way of living (*modus vivendi*) sustainable.

According to Donati, Archer makes a fundamental contribution to the understanding and management of the relationship between *care giver* and *care taker* (Donati, 2006): practitioners and users, through their reflexivity, can mobilize the resources present in society in order to fulfil their own plans; thanks to her competence, a practitioner can base her own project on more effective strategies than the users can. However, a change process (morphogenesis) could only take place if the operator's and user's projects meet within a corporate form of agency.

In the light of Donati's relational perspective, human beings are essentially *in relationship*; thus, the sustainability of a subject's projects is closely linked to the choices made by other subjects: an inextricable web of resources and projects makes people interdependent; individuals can be potential facilitators to each other, as long as they keep a cooperative, rather than competitive, attitude. Reticularity can be a trap of mutually hindering projects, or a support if the nodes become opportunities for corporate agency.

To transform the network into a resource, cooperative skills must be promoted, showing that the possibility to fulfil personal aspirations increases if each person acts cooperatively within their primary networks and life communities. In this perspective, social interventions must feature a sort of *dialogical, relational reflexivity*, as suggested by Donati (Donati, 2010). It can emerge from a fabric of relationships characterized by trust, cooperation and reciprocity, that is, by the presence of social capital (Carrà, 2008a, 2017; Donati, 2014b). In other words, a *modus vivendi* can be sustainable only if people offer and receive support reciprocally in order to pursue this sustainability.

As regards the practitioner-user relationship, the final product of a shared project will belong to *neither of them* but to their relationship, and will be a form of wellbeing coinciding with neither's expectations but transcending both. Donati calls it "relational good" (Donati, 2012, 2016, 2017), a concept reminiscent of that of "social justice as a virtue" (Novak & Adams, 2015), required by responsive regulatory practices in both practitioners and family members (see Adams, Chapter 6 this volume). Moreover, relational reflexivity involves *all* subjects within the operator's and recipient's relationship network (other professionals and services, the beneficiary's family and members of her network): where relationships work towards a common good, each node in the network receives positive feedback. Hence, interventions aimed at producing/recovering wellbeing operate through relationship networks, needing a cooperative orientation towards reciprocity (Folgheraiter, 2003, 2007).

The Importance of Family Relationships

Among social networks, in the relational perspective, the family is a crucial one, the *matrix* of all social bonds: it is the place where subjective and inter-subjective rights are mediated; where an individual first experiences the need to be supported and give support; where cooperation is needed to achieve super-individual goals; where one learns that cooperation to produce a common good generates wellbeing for oneself too (Bosoni & Mazzucchelli, 2016; Rossi & Carrà, 2016). Such ideas go beyond family system theory (Bowen, 1974; Brofenbrenner, 1979; Minuchin, 1974) that highlights the interconnectedness among social systems, but sees family only as an intermediate concentric circle between individual and society.

The family is a *sui generis* relationship—as Donati (2012c) suggests—because in it an inter-gender, inter-generational mediation takes place, as well as one between the individual and society. Furthermore, the family represents a sort of island within post-modern society: it is, in fact, a sphere of relationships oriented towards the totality of the human person (Donati, 1995). Today's complex, fragmented, individualized society tends to lose sight of the person (Luhmann, 1988) while focusing, instead, on social roles: a firm's employee, a service user, a doctor's patient, a schoolchild's parent. Within the family alone all these different roles are reassembled as belonging to one subject, such as a working father, who needs to contact public services to obtain assistance, is affected by a certain pathology and must therefore see a medical doctor, and has a child who goes to school; within a family there will be an overall wellbeing situation if all members, by reassessing their own expectations according to others', can help build a balanced solution that is sustainable in its entirety, rather than individually. The family experiences this composition as either sustainable or non-sustainable. Thus, family represents primary social capital: social interventions should aim to strengthen it *in se* (Donati & Prandini, 2007), and not consider it instrumentally, as a means (Malin et al., 2014).

The solutions to the serious problems affecting today's families will not come mainly from professional services or even public programs: instead, each family in the community and each subject within it should take personal action and feel responsible for providing her own specific, irreplaceable contribution. This perspective has strong similarities with the model of Recovery capital (Cano et al., 2017) where the heart of a strengths-based care system derive from personal, family and community social capital (see Best and Musgrove, Chapter 12 this volume).

An Explorative Model for Analyzing *Familiness*

According to the evidence-based literature, reinterpreted in the light of the relational approach, a model—currently still in the developmental phase—is being used to outline *familiness* of human services and practices.

Relational sociology utilizes a classic conceptual framework, the AGIL scheme drawn up by Parsons in 1937, and interprets it as a "conceptual compass" which allows the sociologist to orient himself or herself in the context of a potentially open-ended reflection (multidimensional and contingent) on society and social phenomena. AGIL analyzes a relationship in order to understand whether, how and to what extent they are present, how they relate to each other, how they influence each other and finally which configuration the observed relationship actually has. AGIL identifies the relational conditions in which a social phenomenon emerges: in this case, the *familiness* of an intervention or a human service. According to Donati (2010), every phenomenon or sociological concept always is a combination of structural (*religo*) and cultural dimensions.[7] Thus, AGIL is constituted by the two axes East-West and North-South of the compass: on the two poles (A-I) of *religo*, there are structural/functional resources on A and internal regulation on I; on the two poles of *refero* (L-G), there are on L culture, meanings, symbols, values that steer the relationship and the goals of the relationships on G.

It is time to apply AGIL to *familiness*, that is, to identify which are its resources, its rules of functioning, its culture and its goals. In order to accomplish this task, it is necessary to take into account: standards of family centeredness (Allen & Petr, 1996; Epley et al., 2010; Malın et al., 2014; Morris et al., 2008; Morris, 2012); family impact principles (Bogenschneider et al., 2012a); dimensions of family social capital (Carrà, 2017; Donati, 2014b); some key concepts of personalization such as flourishing and capabilities (Stiglitz et al., 2009), co-design and co-production (Bovaird & Loeffler, 2012; Needham & Glasby, 2014; Needham, 2008; Prandini & Orlandini, 2015; Verschuere et al., 2012); principles of responsive regulation (Braithwaite, 2011); and the concept of relational reflexivity (Donati, 2014a).

All of these elements can be consolidated in the following requirements of *familiness*:

- to include social networks and primarily family relationships;
- to give voice to stakeholders;
- to rely upon a dialogical relational reflexivity;
- to empower and enhance users' capabilities;
- to impact on the whole family;
- to expand family social capital.

Four questions can enable reorganization of this multidimensionality through the AGIL compass with respect to:

1. Structural dimensions (*religo*):

    - A: who designs, realizes and assesses the intervention? Individuals alone, people in relationships, families, networks of families?
    - I: how are they engaged in the intervention? Do stakeholders have a voice or are they banished to a passive role? Is a dialogical reflexivity played by professionals and users?

2. With respect to the cultural dimensions (*refero*):

    - L: which is the approach to the problem? Are users' capabilities considered a good to enhance?
    - G: what is the purpose? Individual wellbeing or relational wellbeing? Is family social capital eroded or expanded? Is there a positive impact on family relationships?

Considering A, there could be interventions whereby the designer is a single professional, or a team of professionals, or a professional and a user together, or a professional/a team with a user/many users in relationships (e.g., a family/many families, families without professionals, etc.).

Considering I, stakeholders in the strict sense (troubled people human services support) could be held in a passive position and the decision-making process could be steered only by professionals' reflexivity; alternatively, stakeholders could have a full say and a dialogical reflexivity could be carried out by a "corporate agency" of users and professionals.

Considering L, the interventions could aim to support and empower users' capabilities or could be totally substitutive and disable users and their networks of relationships. Interventions could be responsive to users' needs/expectations or they could be carried out in a standardized and impersonal way. This is the risk of human services templates.

Considering G, professionals could be concerned only about the impact of the intervention on the individual: this would have the unintentional effect to erode family social capital; conversely, they could adopt a whole-family perspective and—according to the five principles of the family impact lens—they could strive for enhancing family responsibility, supporting family relationships, fostering family stability, stimulating family engagement and harnessing in an engaged way the specificity of each family.

Based on the AGIL scheme, a map of *familiness* has been drawn up as a tool to analyze a practice or a service: this tool is both quantitative and qualitative since methods to collect information about each of the four dimensions have been qualitative so far; however, in order to provide a visual representation of *familiness*, the researcher is required to translate the descriptive evaluation in a score within a scale from 0 to 2, graded at intervals of .25. The four scores provide a radar graph. This visualization allows outlines of the different shapes of *familiness* or non-*familiness*. An example is provided by Figure 5.1, relating to an education *family group conference*. Radar graphs provide a visual representation of the analysis synthetized in Table 5.1.

This constitutes the first step of a research project aimed at testing the model of *familiness*, applying it to *family group conference* (FGC). The research is part of a randomized controlled trial (RCT), conducted in Italy between 2013 and 2015, in order to evaluate the effectiveness of the FGC in easing discomfort of students in grades 6 and 7 (Argentin, Barbetta, & Maci, 2015). FGCs, firstly applied in youth justice and child welfare, offer a democratic and inclusive process for family decision-making, engaging all significant others and not just immediate family (Burford & Hudson, 2000; Burford, 2011, 2013). The FGC has now been put into use in the decision-making relating to the care of vulnerable adults and supporting the recovery of people with mental distress (Broadhurst et al., 2010; de Jong & Schout, 2011; Morris & Connolly, 2012). The Italian trial follows previous implementations

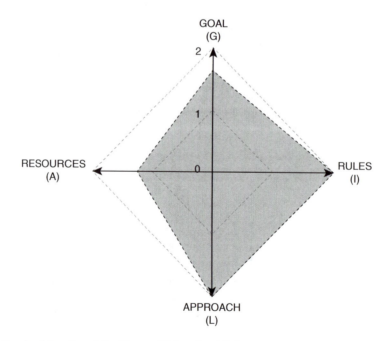

FIGURE 5.1 Graph of the alleged familiness of Education FGCs

TABLE 5.1 Alleged familiness of Education FGC

Dimensions	Scores	Explanation
RESOURCES (A)	1.25	FGC should involve family and all significant others: parents, child, teachers, facilitator, advocate
		It does not involve other families and does not foster families networking
GOAL (G)	1.625	Average between *Family Impact* score and *Social Capital* score
Family Impact	2	Average between the *five Family impact principles* scores
1. Family responsibility	2	FGC should avoid substitution of family in its education task
2. Family relationships	2	FGC should include whole-family relationships
3. Family stability	2	FGC should foster family stability, that could be weakened by child discomfort at school
4. Family diversity	2	FGC should implement personalized project for each family
5. Family engagement	2	FGC should stimulate family participation in school
Social Capital	*1.25*	Average between *Trust, Mutuality, Cooperation* scores
• Trust	1.25	FGC should reinforce trusting relations between child, parents and teachers with a limited impact on secondary (associative) and generalized social capital
• Mutuality	1.25	FGC should be based on a more equal relationship between all the participants with a limited impact on secondary (associative) and generalized social capital
• Cooperation	1.25	FGC should promote a greater school-family cooperation with a limited impact on secondary (associative) and generalized social capital
RULES (I)	2	FGC should give voice to all stakeholders and promote a relational reflexivity at three levels: child-teachers, family-teachers, child-family
APPROACH (L)	2	FGC should extend the family power to design autonomously an educational project

in education, where the FGC appeared as an effective way of working with attendance and behavior problems in schools (Argentin et al., 2015; Hayden, 2009; Holton & Marsh, 2007).

The new project should check the *Family Impact* of education FGCs and their ability to restore social capital, strengthen social ties and stimulate trusting and mutually supportive relations (De Jong et al., 2015). Qualitative interviews and focus groups will be conducted with the purpose of confirming or not the alleged *familiness* of Education FGCs and to identify more analytical indicators for each measured dimension in order to rest the scoring process for the quantitative dimensions of the research on a less subjective bases.

Conclusion: Moving Towards a Responsive Regulatory Pyramid for *Familiness*?

The idea of designing a responsive regulatory pyramid of *familiness* immediately turned out promising, firstly for its plasticity—it is "a cumulative creation" in Braithwaite's words (2011). Secondly it provides a model where opposites may have room and apparently irreconcilable elements may be composed within a single framework. This may be the case for defamilization and *familiness*. Figure 5.2 mirrors the proposals as developed by others (Dukes, Braithwaite, & Moloney, 2014; Healy, 2011).

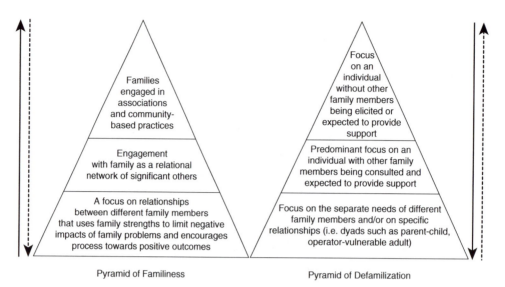

FIGURE 5.2   The responsive regulatory pyramids of familiness and defamilization

Thus, in the perspective of responsive regulation, social practices should always strive for a high level of *familiness*, resorting to a low level of *familiness* (defamilization) only when there are no other possibilities.

The path towards *familiness* goes down the pyramid on the right and moves up the left one, in order to personalize services and stimulate an increasingly larger involvement of primary and secondary social networks (Bogenschneider et al., 2012b; Carrà, 2017; Morris et al., 2008; Morris & Connolly, 2012; Tew et al., 2015).

When welfare regimes aim at defamilization, they gradually move from the acknowledgment of the importance of family and social networks to a narrow view focused on single family members, towards full individualization (Bambra, 2007; Chau, Foster, & Yu, 2017; Esping-Andersen, 1990; Lohmann & Zagel, 2016; McLaughlin & Glendinning, 1994).

Although whole-family approaches have reached their peak in the first decade of the 2000s (Morris et al., 2008), subsequent studies on their implementation outlined an explicit and implicit increasing individualization of policy and service responses in relation to families (Morris, 2012). Widening the idea of 'family' beyond a narrow focus on parents (usually mothers) and parenting, or singular operator and vulnerable adults (Tew et al., 2015) seems even more difficult. Defamilization-oriented approaches combined with economic downturn has caused more individually focused services to attract ongoing core funding, whereas innovative projects engaging with whole families receive only time-limited funding.

Referring to the Italian context, cuts to mainstream services, caused by austerity, had greatly stimulated the spread of family associations, that is, families coming together to share their problems and together find solutions to their needs (Carrà, 2017). This has led to a proliferation of family-focused practices, carried out by self-organized families. Some enlightened local authorities seized this as an opportunity to re-conceive ways of delivering services and passed laws promoting family associations.

This could be an innovative road map to foster a bottom-up propagation of *familiness* in a world even more individualized. In this perspective, it might be a positive and significant signal to the attention for family associations recently paid by Chilean academia (Carrà, 2016a), looking at this phenomenon as a new means to support the so-called reconstruction of we-ness (*reconstrucción del nosotros*) (Yévenes, 2016) within a highly fragmented and individualized society.

Notes

1. In contemporary sociology, the conviction seems to be emerging that if we are to understand ongoing socio-cultural processes, a privileged place needs to be given to the subject of social relations (see www.relational studies.net). In the last three decades a series of scholars have developed a "relational" sociological theory in a more or less systematic manner: the first version was formulated by Pierpaolo Donati (Donati, 1983), and subsequently other quite different versions appeared (Archer, 2012; Bajoit, 1992; Crossley, 2011; Emirbayer, 1997; Laflamme, 1995; White, 1992). This work refers to the founder's version, Donati's relational sociology.

2. It is difficult to properly translate in English '*familiare*'. This could be literally translated *familial*, but it does not resonate as a noun (*the familial*). Thus, searching in literature, *familiness* has been chosen, a concept introduced in economics by Habbershon and Williams (1999): it refers to the unique set of resources of a family business which arise from the interactions between the family system as a whole, individual family members and the business itself. Numerous scholars have further developed the idea of *familiness*, seeing it as a specific construct in the field of family business research, and one which may constitute a key part of an explanatory theory of family business. In this sense, it can provide an appropriate framework to identify the sources of advantage for family businesses and for the analysis of the relationship between benefits and performance of family businesses (Habbershon, Williams, & MacMillan, 2003). Pearson, Carr, and Shaw (2008) note that *familiness* can be a source of competitive advantage and generate wealth and value for the company, and propose a theory which elaborates on *familiness* from the perspective of social capital theory.

3. See Allen and Petr (1996, pp. 63–64):
   regarding the family as the unit of attention or concern; involving parents or forming a collaboration/partnership between parents and professionals; addressing needs of the consumer; providing specific types of services; relying upon family choice or decision making; emphasizing the strengths or capabilities of families; maintaining children in their own homes; attending to the uniqueness or culture of families; empowering families; following principles of normalization.

4. They are family as the unit of attention, family choice, family strengths, the family–professional relationship and individualized family services.

5. The Family Impact Seminar was launched by private funding in 1976 (Ooms, 1984).

6. Archer's *Morphogenesis* offers a key interpretation of social change, with particular effectiveness in explaining the relationship between structure and agency without falling into classical reductionisms of holism or individualism. *Holism* (change depends on a mechanistic determinism whereby man is denied the possibility to interfere with its laws) and *individualism* (the minor or major changes which, in time, modify society are originated by the subject) are usually attributed to Èmile Durkheim and Max Weber.

7. Donati refers to *religo* and *refero* respectively in the Durkheim and Weber traditions.

References

Allen, R. I., & Petr, G. C. (1996). Toward developing standards and measurements for family-centered practice in family support programs. In G. Singer & L. Powers (Eds.), *Redefining family support: Innovations in public-private partnerships* (pp. 57–84). Baltimore, MD: Paul H. Brookes.

Andersen, N. Å. (2007). Creating the client who can create himself and his own fate—the tragedy of the citizens' contract. *Qualitative Sociology Review, 3*(2), 5–29.

Archer, M. (1995). *Realist social theory: The morphogenetic approach.* Cambridge: Cambridge University Press.

Archer, M. S. (2003). *Structure, agency and the internal conversation.* Cambridge: Cambridge University Press. doi: 10.1017/CBO9781139087315.

Archer, M. S. (2012). *The reflexive imperative in late modernity.* Cambridge: Cambridge University Press. doi: 10.1017/CBO9781139108058.

Argentin, G., Barbetta, G., & Maci, F. (2015). Cercare soluzioni altrove. Una sperimentazione sull'uso delle *Family group conferences* come strumento di prevenzione del disagio scolastico. In A. Bassi & G. Moro (Eds.), *Politiche sociali innovative e diritti di cittadinanza* (pp. 185–203). Milano: FrancoAngeli.

Bajoit, G. (1992). *Pour une sociologie relationnelle*. Paris: Presses Univ. de France.

Bambra, C. (2007). Defamilisation and welfare state regimes: A cluster analysis. *International Journal of Social Welfare, 16*(4), 326–338. doi: 10.1111/j.1468-2397.2007.00486.x.

Banfield, E. C. (1958). *The moral basis of a backward society*. Glencoe, IL: Free Press.

Barnes, M., & Prior, D. (Eds.). (2009). *Subversive citizens. Power, agency and resistance in public services*. Bristol: Policy Press.

Bauman, Z. (2001). *Liquid modernity*. Cambridge: Polity Press.

Beck, U. (1992). *Risk society*. London, UK: Sage Publications.

Beck, U., & Beck-Gernsheim, E. (2002). *Individualization. Institutionalized individualism and its social and political consequences*. London, UK: Sage Publications.

Berggren, H., & Trägårdh, L. (2011). Social trust and radical individualism: The paradox at the heart of nordic capitalism. In Global Utmaning (Ed.), *The nordic way* (pp. 11–26). Stockholm: Global Utmaning.

Biegel, D. E. (1984). Help seeking and receiving in urban ethnic neighborhoods. *Prevention in Human Services, 3*(2–3), 119–143. doi: 10.1300/J293v03n02-07.

Bogenschneider, K., & Corbett, T. J. (2011). *Evidence-based policymaking: Insights from policy-minded researchers and research-minded policymakers*. London, UK: Routledge.

Bogenschneider, K., Little, O., Ooms, T., Benning, S., & Cadigan, K. (2012a). *The family impact handbook*. Madison, WI: The Family Impact Institute.

Bogenschneider, K., Little, O., Ooms, T., Benning, S., & Cadigan, K. (2012b). *The family impact rationale*. Madison, WI: The Family Impact Institute.

Bosoni, M. L., & Mazzucchelli, S. (2016). Is the family really an outdated institution in Italy as well as in Europe? Findings from the European Values Study. *Socialinė Teorija, Empirija, Politika Ir Praktika, 13*, 24–40. doi: 10.15388/STEPP.2016.13.10040.

Bovaird, T., & Loeffler, E. (2012). From engagement to co-production: The contribution of users and communities to outcomes and public value. *Voluntas: International Journal of Voluntary and Nonprofit Organizations, 23*(4), 1119–1138.

Bowen, M. (1974). Alcoholism as viewed through family systems theory and family psychotherapy. *Annals of the New York Academy of Sciences, 233*(1), 115–122. doi: 10.1111/j.1749-6632.1974.tb40288.x.

Braithwaite, J. (2011). The essence of responsive regulation. *UBC Law Review, 44*(3), 475–520.

Broad, B. (Ed.). (2001). *Kinship care: The placement choice for children and young people*. Lyme Regis: Russel House.

Broadhurst, K., Wastell, D., White, S., Hall, C., Peckover, S., Thompson, K., . . . Davey, D. (2010). Performing 'initial assessment': Identifying the latent conditions for error at the front-door of local authority children's services. *The British Journal of Social Work, 40*(2), 352–370. doi: 10.1093/bjsw/bcn162.

Brofenbrenner, U. (1979). *The ecology of human development: Experiments by nature and design*. Cambridge: Harvard University Press.

Bullock, R., Gooch, D., & Little, M. (1998). *Children going home: The re-unification of families*. Aldershot, UK: Ashgate.

Burford, G. (2011). Il lavoro con le famiglie nella tutela minorile. In P. Donati, F. Folgheraiter, & M. L. Raineri (Eds.), *La tutela dei minori. Nuovi scenari relazionali* (pp. 102–110). Trento: Erickson.

Burford, G. (2013). *Family group conferences* in youth justice and child welfare in Vermont. In *Restorative justice today: Practical applications* (p. 81). Los Angeles, CA: Sage Publications. doi: 10.4135/9781452244228.n10.

Burford, G., & Hudson, J. (2000). *Family group conferencing: New directions in community-centered child and family practice*. New York: Aldine de Gruyter.

Cano, I., Best, D., Edwards, M., & Lehman, J. (2017). Recovery capital pathways: Modelling the components of recovery wellbeing. *Drug & Alcohol Dependence, 181*, 11–19. 10.1016/j.drugalcdep.2017.09.002. Retrieved from www.drugandalcoholdependence.com/article/S0376-8716(17)30483-0/fulltext.

Carrà, E. (2003). *Dentro le politiche familiari. Storia di una ricerca relazionale sulla l.r. 23 della Regione Lombardia "Politiche regionali per la famiglia"*. Milano: LED.

Carrà, E. (2008a). *Buone pratiche e capitale sociale. servizi alla persona pubblici e di privato sociale a confronto*. Milano: LED.

Carrà, E. (2008b). *Un'osservazione che progetta. strumenti per l'analisi e la progettazione relazionale di interventi nel sociale*. Milano: LED.

Carrà, E. (2012a). Famiglie fragili. In P. Donati (Ed.), *La famiglia in Italia. Sfide sociali e innovazioni nei servizi. Nuove best practices nei servizi alle famiglie* (Vol. II, pp. 207–222). Roma: Carocci.

Carrà, E. (2012b). *Residential care: An effective response to out-of-home children and young people?* doi: 10.1111/cfs.12020.

Carrà, E. (2013). Putting family first: A sociological analysis of Doherty's citizen professionalism and participatory approaches. *Italian Journal of Sociology of Education, 5*(3), 127–146. doi: 10.14658/pupj-ijse-2013-3-8.

Carrà, E. (Ed.). (2014a). *Families, care and work-life balance services. Case studies of best practices*. Milano: Vita & Pensiero.

Carrà, E. (2014b). Good practices for frail families care and intervention: A case study on an innovative foster care service. In E. Carrà (Ed.), *Families, care and work-life balance services. Case studies of best practices. Quaderno del Centro Famiglia, N. 28* (pp. 99–118). Milano: Vita & Pensiero.

Carrà, E. (Ed.). (2016a). *La identidad relacional del asociacionismo familiar: una teorización a partir de la experiencia italiana*. Santiago: Universidad Finis Terrae.

Carrà, E. (2016b). Politica familiare. In P. Terenzi, L. Boccacin, & P. Prandini (Eds.), *Lessico della sociologia relazionale* (pp. 181–185). Bologna: Carocci.

Carrà, E. (2017). Family associations as social capital for families and society. *Socialinė Teorija, Empirija, Politika Ir Praktika, 14*, 20–35. doi: 10.15388/STEPP.2017.14.10413.

Carrà, E., & Bramanti, D. (2017). Verso la misura della qualità familiare degli interventi: Un percorso entro la sociologia relazionale. *Sociologia e politiche sociali*, (1), 61–82. doi: 10.3280/SP2017-001004.

Carrà, E., & Pavesi, N. (2015). *Come promuovere interventi con e per le famiglie: L'esperienza del Friuli Venezia Giulia*. Milano. In A. Bassi & G. Moro (Eds.), *Politiche sociali innovative e diritti di cittadinanza* (pp. 223–237). Milano: FrancoAngeli.

Cartocci, R. (2002). *Diventare grandi in tempi di cinismo: Identità nazionale, memoria collettiva e fiducia nelle istituzioni tra i giovani italiani*. Bologna: Il mulino.

Chau, R. C. M., Foster, L., & Yu, S. W. K. (2017). The effects of defamilization and familization measures on the accumulation of retirement income for women in the UK. *Journal of Women & Aging, 29*(6), 551–561. doi: 10.1080/08952841.2016.1256737.

Coleman, J. S. (1988). Social capital in the creation of human capital. *American Journal of Sociology, 94*, S120.

Coleman, J. S. (2000). *Foundations of social theory*. Cambridge: Cambridge University Press.

Collins, A. H., & Pancoast, D. L. (1976). *Natural helping networks: A strategy for prevention*. Washington, DC: National Association of Social Workers.

Crossley, N. (2011). *Towards relational sociology*. London, UK: Routledge.

Daun, Å. (2010). Individualism and collectivity among swedes. *Ethnos, 56*(3–4), 165–172. 10.1080/00141844.1991.9981433. https://doi.org/10.1080/00141844.1991.9981433.

de Jong, G., & Schout, G. (2011). Family group conferences in public mental health care: An exploration of opportunities. *International Journal of Mental Health Nursing, 20*(1), 63–74. doi: 10.1111/j.1447-0349.2010.00701.x.

De Jong, G., Schout, G., Pennell, J., & Abma, T. (2015). Family group conferencing in public mental health and social capital theory. *Journal of Social Work, 15*(3), 277–296. doi: 10.1177/1468017314547675.

Department of Health. (1998). *Patterns and outcomes in child placement*. London, UK: HMSO.

Donati, P. (1983). *Introduzione alla sociologia relazionale*. Milano: FrancoAngeli.

Donati, P. (1995). Famiglia. In E. Scabini & P. Donati (Eds.), *Nuovo lessico familiare* (pp. 15–29). Milano: Vita & Pensiero.

Donati, P. (2003). La famiglia come capitale sociale primario. In P. Donati (Ed.), *Famiglia e capitale sociale nella società italiana. Ottavo rapporto Cisf sulla famiglia in Italia* (pp. 31–101). Cinisello Balsamo (MI): Edizioni San Paolo.

Donati, P. (2006). Introduzione all'edizione italiana. In M. S. Marcher (Ed.), *La conversazione interiore. come nasce l'agire sociale* (pp. 9–42). Trento: Erickson.

Donati, P. (2010). *Relational sociology: A new paradigm for the social sciences*. London, UK/New York: Routledge.

Donati, P. (2012). Beyond the market/state binary code: The common good as a relational good. In M. Schlag & J. A. Mercado (Eds.), *Free markets and the culture of common good* (pp. 61–81). New York: Springer.

Donati, P. (Ed.). (2012a). *La famiglia in Italia. Sfide sociali e innovazioni nei servizi. Nuove best practices nei servizi alle famiglie* (Vol. II). Milano: FrancoAngeli.

Donati, P. (2012b). *Family policy. A relational approach*. Milano: FrancoAngeli.

Donati, P. (2012c). Le politiche sociali di fronte alla modernizzazione riflessiva: Tra morfogenesi sistemica e morfogenesi sociale. In I. Colozzi (Ed.), *Dal nuovo al vecchio welfare. percorsi di una morfogenesi* (pp. 17–35). Milano: FrancoAngeli.

Donati, P. (2013). The added value of social relations. *Italian Journal of Sociology of Education, 5*(1), 19–35. doi: 10.14658/pupj-ijse-2013-1-2.

Donati, P. (2014a). Morphogenic society and the structure of social relations. In M. S. Archer (Ed.), *Late modernity—trajectories towards morphogenic society* (pp. 143–172). Heidelberg/New York/Dordrecht/London, UK: Springer.

Donati, P. (2014b). Social capital and associative democracy: A relational perspective. *Journal for the Theory of Social Behaviour, 44*(1), 24–45. doi: 10.1111/jtsb.12026.

Donati, P. (2015). Manifesto for a critical realist relational sociology. *International Review of Sociology, 25*(1), 86–109. doi: 10.1080/03906701.2014.997967.

Donati, P. (2016). The family as a source of relational goods (and evils) for itself and for the community. *Italian Journal of Sociology of Education, 8*(3), 149–168.

Donati, P. (2017). The good life as a sharing of relational goods. *Relational Social Work, 1*(2), 5–25. Retrieved from http://rsw.erickson.international.

Donati, P., & Archer, M. S. (2015). *Relational subject*. Cambridge: Cambridge University Press.

Donati, P., & Prandini, R. (2007). The family in the light of a new relational theory of primary, secondary and generalized social capital. *International Review of Sociology, 17*(2), 209–223. doi: 10.1080/03906700701356812.

Drahos, P. (Ed.). (2017). *Regulatory theory*. Canberra: ANU Press. doi: 10.22459/RT.02.2017.

Duffy, S. (2011). Personalisation in social care—what does it really mean? *Social Care Neurodisability, 2*(4), 186–194. doi: 10.1108/20420911111188434.

Dukes, G., Braithwaite, J., & Moloney, J. P. (2014). *Pharmaceuticals, corporate crime and public health*. Cheltenham, UK: Edward Elgar. doi: 10.4337/9781783471102.

Edwards, R., Franklin, J., & Holland, J. (2003). *Families and social capital: Exploring the issues*. London, UK: London South Bank University.

Emirbayer, M. (1997). Manifesto for a relational sociology. *The American Journal of Sociology, 103*(2), 281–317.

Epley, P., Summers, J. A., & Turnbull, A. (2010). Characteristics and trends in family-centered conceptualizations. *Journal of Family Social Work, 13*(3), 269–285. doi: 10.1080/10522150903514017.

Esping-Andersen, G. (1990). *The three worlds of welfare capitalism*. Cambridge: Polity Press.

Esping-Andersen, G. (1999). *Social foundations of postindustrial economies*. Oxford: Oxford University Press.

Esping-Andersen, G. (2009). *The incomplete revolution: Adapting to women's new roles*. Malden, MA: Polity Press.

Folgheraiter, F. (2003). *Relational social work. Toward networking and societal practices*. London, UK: Jessica Kingsley Publishers.

Folgheraiter, F. (2007). Relational social work: Principles and practices. *Social Policy and Society, 6*(2), 265–274. doi: 10.1017/S1474746406003526.

Franklin, J. (Ed.). (2004). *Politics, trust and networks: Social capital in critical perspective*. London, UK: London South Bank University.

Habbershon, T. G., & Williams, M. L. (1999). A resource-based framework for assessing the strategic advantages of family firms. *Family Business Review, 12*(1), 1–25. doi: 10.1111/j.1741-6248.1999.00001.x.

Habbershon, T. G., Williams, M., & MacMillan, I. C. (2003). A unified systems perspective of family firm performance. *Journal of Business Venturing, 18*(4), 451–465. doi: 10.1016/S0883-9026(03)00053-3.

Hayden, C. (2009). Family group conferences—Are they an effective and viable way of working with attendance and behaviour problems in schools? *British Educational Research Journal, 35*(2), 205–220.

Healy, J. (2011). *Improving health care safety and quality. Reluctant regulators*. Farnham, UK: Ashgate. doi: 10.4324/9781315588049.

Holton, L., & Marsh, P. (2007). Education family group conference. In C. Ashley & P. Nixon (Eds.), *Family group conferences—where next? Policies and practices for the future* (pp. 131–156). London, UK: Family Right Group.

Kemp, S. P., Whittaker, J. K., & Tracy, E. M. (1997). *Person-environment practice: The social ecology of interpersonal helping*. Hawthorne, NY: Aldine De Gruyter.

Laflamme, S. (1995). *Communication et émotion. Essai de microsociologie relationnelle*. Paris: Harmattan.

Lohmann, H., & Zagel, H. (2016). Family policy in comparative perspective: The concepts and measurement of familization and defamilization. *Journal of European Social Policy, 26*(1), 48–65. doi: 10.1177/0958928715621712.

Luhmann, N. (1988). Sozialsystem familie. *System Familie, 1*(1), 75–91.

Malin, N., Tunmore, J., & Wilcock, A. (2014). How far does a whole family approach make a difference. *Social Work & Social Sciences Review, 17*(2), 57–62.

McLaughlin, E., & Glendinning, C. (1994). Paying for care in Europe: Is there a feminist approach? In L. Hantrais & S. Mangen (Eds.), *Family policy and the welfare of women, cross-national research papers* (pp. 52–69). Leicestershire: European Research Centre, Loughborough University of Technology.

Minuchin, S. (1974). *Families and family therapy*. Cambridge: Harvard University Press.

Morris, K. (2012). Thinking family? The complexities for family engagement in care and protection. *The British Journal of Social Work, 42*(5), 906–920. doi: 10.1093/bjsw/bcr116.

Morris, K., & Burford, G. (2007). Working with children's existing networks—building better opportunities? *Social Policy and Society, 6*(2), 209–217. doi: 10.1017/S1474746406003472.

Morris, K., & Connolly, M. (2012). Family decision making in child welfare: Challenges in developing a knowledge base for practice. *Child Abuse Review, 21*(1), 41–52. doi: 10.1002/car.1143.

Morris, K., Hughes, N., Clarke, H., Tew, J., Mason, P., Galvani, S., . . . Burford, G. (2008). *Think family: A literature review of whole family approaches*. London, UK: Cabinet Office Social Exclusion Task Force.

Movitz, F., & Sandberg, Å. (2013). Contested models: Productive welfare and solidaristic individualism. In Å. Sandberg (Ed.), *Nordic ligths. Work, management and welfare in scandinavia* (pp. 31–90). Stockholm: SNS Förlag.

Mutti, A. (2003). La teoria della fiducia nelle ricerche sul capitale sociale. *Rassegna Italiana Di Sociologia,* (4/2003), 515–536. doi: 10.1423/11195.

Needham, C. (2008). Realising the potential of co-production: Negotiating improvements in public services. *Social Policy and Society, 7*(2), 221–231. doi: 10.1017/S1474746407004174.

Needham, C., & Glasby, J. (Eds.). (2014). *Debates in personalisation*. Bristol: Policy Press.

Novak, M., & Adams, P. (2015). *Social justice isn't what you think it is*. New York: Encounter Books.

Ooms, T. (1984). The necessity of a family perspective. *Journal of Family Issue, 5*(2), 160–181.

Parsons, T. (1937). *The structure of social action*. New York: MacGraw Hill.

Pearson, A. W., Carr, J. C., & Shaw, J. C. (2008). Toward a theory of *familiness*: A social capital perspective. *Entrepreneurship Theory and Practice, 32*(6), 949–969. doi: 10.1111/j.1540-6520.2008.00265.x.

Prandini, R. (2003). Capitale sociale familiare e socialità: Un'indagine sulla popolazione italiana. In P. Donati (Ed.), *Famiglia e capitale sociale nella società italiana. Ottavo rapporto Cisf* (pp. 102–155). Cinisello Balsamo (MI): Edizioni San Paolo.

Prandini, R. (2005). Capitale sociale, differenziazione sociale e il nuovo patto sociale negli Stati Uniti d'America: Come contestualizzare le più recenti ricerche di Robert D. Putnam. *Non Profit, 1*, 151–178.

Prandini, R., & Orlandini, M. (2015). Personalizzazione vs individualizzazione dei servizi di welfare: Fasi, attori e governance di una semantica emergente. *Studi Di Sociologia, 53*(4), 353–373.

Putnam, R. D. (1994). *Making democracy work: Civic traditions in modern Italy*. Princeton, NJ: Princeton University Press.

Rossi, G., & Carrà, E. (2016). The relational approach and the family. *Socialinė Teorija, Empirija, Politika Ir Praktika, 13*(13), 7. doi: 10.15388/STEPP.2016.13.10040.

Sabel, C., Saxenian, A., Miettinen, R., Kristensen, P. H., & Hautamäki, J. (2010). *Individualized service provision in the new welfare state: Lessons from special education in Finland*. Helsinki. Sitra.

Sciolla, L. (2003). Quale capitale sociale? Partecipazione associativa, fiducia e spirito civico. *Rassegna Italiana Di Sociologia, 2*, 257–290. doi: 10.1423/9465.

Stiglitz, J. E., Sen, A., & Fitoussi, J. (2009). *Report by the commission on the measurement of economic performance and social progress*. Retrieved from www.stiglitz-sen-fitoussi.fr/en/index.htm.

Stone, W., & Hughes, J. (2000). What role for social capital in family policy and how does it measure up? *Family Matters, 56*, 20–27.

Stone, W., & Hughes, J. (2002). *Social capital: Empirical meaning and measurement validity.* (Research Paper No. 27). Melbourne: Australian Institute of Family Studies.

Tew, J., Morris, K., White, S., Featherstone, B., & Fenton, S. (2015). What has happened to 'Think family'— challenges and achievements in implementing family inclusive practice. In *Parental mental health and child welfare work* (pp. 59–64). Hove, UK: Pavilion Publishing and Media.

Thoburn, J., Lewis, A., & Shemmings, D. (1995). *Paternalism or partnership? Family involvement in the child protection process.* London, UK: HMSO.

Trägårdh, L. (2014). Statist individualism. The Swedish theory of love and its Lutheran imprint. In J. Halldorf & F. Wenell (Eds.), *Between the state and the eucharist: Free church theology in conversation with William T. Cavanaugh* (pp. 13–38). Eugene, OR: Pickwick Publications.

Verschuere, B., Brandsen, T., & Pestoff, V. (2012). Co-production: The state of the art in research and the future agenda. *VOLUNTAS: International Journal of Voluntary and Nonprofit Organizations, 23*(4), 1083–1101. doi: 10.1007/s11266-012-9307-8.

Werger, G. C. (1994). *Understanding support networks and community care: Network assessment for elderly people.* Aldershot, UK: Avebury.

White, H. C. (1992). *Identity and control: A structural theory of social action.* Princeton, NJ: Princeton University Press.

Whittaker, J. K., & Garbarino, J. (1983). *Social support networks: Informal helping in the human services.* Hawthorne, NY: Aldine De Gruyter.

Yévenes, A. M. (2016). Prólogo. In E. Carrà (Ed.), *La identidad relacional del asociacionismo familiar: Una teorización a partir de la experiencia italiana* (pp. 9–10). Providencia (CL): Ediciones Universidad Finis Terrae.

6

FAMILIES AND FARMWORKERS

Social Justice in Responsive and Restorative Practices

Paul Adams

Introduction

This chapter develops two themes that are implicit in restorative and responsive approaches to human services. One is that of empowerment, especially in highly disempowering contexts that involve the coercive power of the state, the power, for instance, to remove children permanently from their parents and terminate parental rights. The other is the dependence of restorative and responsive practice, not only on processes and values that support it, but also on the habits and dispositions, the qualities of character—in short, the virtues—required for and developed by such practice.

Empowerment and the virtues, in turn, depend on cultural, social, and legal elements that either enable those involved, lay and professional, to act virtuously to meet their moral obligations or make it harder for them to do so (Feser, 2005). They raise, too, the central question for social work and human services of the proper relation of formal to informal care and control. What is the proper role of the authorities in working with the already present helping systems and networks within families and communities to strengthen their capacity to keep their members safe and when is it necessary to substitute formal mechanisms of care and control that can take over from problematic or failed informal systems?

The regulatory pyramid (see Chapter 2) in its various forms developed by Braithwaite and colleagues in the field of regulatory theory and responsive regulation shows that the relation between empowerment and coercion, and hence between formal and informal care and control, is a dynamic one. Whether the regulatory intervention is aimed at ensuring the safety of children or of a power station, it may move up or down the regulatory pyramid.

Most care and control in families and communities is informal, occurring outside the direct involvement of state or professional policing. Where official regulation becomes necessary, it starts where possible, in the responsive approach, at the base of the regulatory pyramid. Regulation there involves more informal and empowering interventions that rely on the good will and capacity of the "virtuous actor," a lightly supervised form of family self-regulation. It taps into and supports the informal mechanisms of care and control already present in families and communities rather than substituting for them.

DOI: 10.4324/9780429398704-6

At the same time, all concerned understand that escalation to a higher level of coercion is inexorable if the problem is not fixed. Where intervention fails to elicit a level of family self-regulation adequate to protect the children concern for whose safety gave rise to professional and state involvement, regulation shifts from the restorative, empowering approach at the base of the pyramid to more coercive measures at the apex, where only the most recalcitrant cases end up. There the actor, whether parent or management of a nursing home or power station, proves incompetent or irrational. A high level of coercion (to the point of termination of parental rights or revocation of an operating license) may then be necessary.

No less important, the regulatory pyramid contains, in its responsiveness to the behavior of the regulated, the possibility of moving back down the pyramid. As the regulated actor, responding to and working in partnership with the regulator, increasingly demonstrates the will and competence to come into and remain in compliance with the required standards, the regulatory relation shifts from coercion to empowerment.

Empowerment

In a much-quoted passage in their book on *Family Group Conferencing* (FGC), Burford and Hudson (2000) endorse the view common to proponents of FGC and to community-minded social workers that "lasting solutions to problems are ones that grow out of, or can fit with, the knowledge, experiences, and desires of the people most affected" (p. xxiii). Implicit in this formulation is an understanding that there exist, even in distressed families and communities, patterns, and networks of care and control, ranging from informal helping networks (that might include neighborhood women—"aunties"—who keep an eye out for untoward behavior, to structured meetings of or between family groups) that enable people to resolve challenges without state or professional involvement. There is a wealth of wisdom, knowledge, and resources, creative patterns of problem-solving, that themselves are expressions of ways cultures have found, over generations and millennia, to address problematic situations, address injustices, and make things right.

Such patterns and practices precede state and professional interventions, both in time—they developed prior to modern bureaucratic-professional states—and in the sense that they are responses of first resort. In most cases, bad behavior of children, youth, and adults is addressed informally, within family and civil society, without intervention of the state or professionals.

In Hawai'i, with its traditional indigenous practice of *ho'oponopono*, and New Zealand, with its Maori practice of *whānau hui*, we have examples of restorative justice practices both preceding modern states and operating outside their purview. They take the form of structured family group meetings aimed at making things right. Many or most cultures evolved such restorative justice mechanisms and some persist in and alongside the bureaucratic-professional state. Modern family group conferences that are part of the state's statutory responsibility for child protection offer a more formal practice, a form of state-supervised family self-regulation. Unlike traditional processes used by indigenous people within their own communities, the legally established practices of family group conferencing or, in Hawai'i, 'Ohana Conferencing,' are ways in which the child protection system works with all ethnic groups. They tap into a family's own knowledge, wisdom, resources, creativity, initiative, and desires for their own children and families, but without abdicating the state's legal responsibility for child protection. For this reason, the plans for keeping the children safe that emerge from these processes tend to cover a much wider range of options than the few standard plans, like anger management or drug or alcohol treatment, that social workers on their own come up with (Adams & Chandler, 2004; for other applications of restorative justice in Hawai'i, see Walker, 2013, 2017).

Virtues

Restorative and responsive human services are commonly discussed in terms of processes or values. The process of conferencing in FGC and similar family group meetings brings together those involved in the situation (an offense or harm) coming together to restore victims, offenders, communities. Among the values of such processes are healing, moral learning, community participation and caring, and respectful dialogue (Braithwaite, 2002).

Restorative and responsive practices are virtue-driven, in MacIntyre's (1990) term. They involve certain virtues that are required for and developed by those practices. Values may refer to principles or standards, or strongly held beliefs, but virtues are those habits of the heart and mind (Tocqueville, 2000), stable and firm dispositions to do the good, that form our character. A virtuous physician, for instance, is one who applies the required knowledge and skills with such virtues as prudence or practical judgment, compassion and caring, intellectual honesty, humility, and trustworthiness. Pellegrino and Thomasma (1993) have proposed just such a list for the medical profession. A similar list could be compiled for social workers or other human service professionals.

Certain virtues seem particularly important for restorative and responsive practices. Such family- and community-centered practices as FGC de-emphasize and decenter the professional-client relationship from the heart of a network of relationships with which the family is involved and of which it is only one, temporary, element. The professional aim is not to place a pre-determined solution in the lap of the family, much less to give them an ultimatum—"Do this if you want to get your children back!"—but to enable the family to tap into their own wisdom, knowledge, and resources (including those of creativity and initiative). Among the virtues necessary for such practices is that of equanimity, the virtue, in this context, of accepting that one is not and should not be in control of a family. The virtuous professional, without abdicating responsibility for keeping the children safe, holds back from imposing his or her own preferred solution.

Attention to the virtues required for and developed by responsive and restorative practices shifts the focus from beliefs and processes to the habitual behavior and character of practitioners. It recalls the social work emphasis, until recently, on the "professional use of self" as a key element of the professional-client relationship and so of good practice.

Social justice

In social work, social justice usually refers to a state of affairs—an ideal but non-existent one by comparison with which existing states are measured and found wanting. It serves as a kind of regulative ideal. Many proponents of expanded government spending or new social programs support their positions by appealing to "social justice." The implication is that opponents of the program or spending plans in question are ipso facto proponents of social injustice. Used that way, social justice is essentially a rhetorical device to which there is no answer. Either one must accept the proposed plan or policy on pain of being condemned out of one's own mouth as socially unjust, or one must reject the concept entirely, as Hayek (1976) and many libertarian and conservative writers have done. No-one, in their own view, supports social injustice.

Understanding social justice as a virtue, however, is more helpful as well as true to the term's origins and development within Catholic social teaching. Taking this approach, Novak and Adams (2015) say this of the virtue of social justice:

> Social justice names a new virtue in the panoply of historical virtues, a set of new habits and abilities that need to be learned, perfected, and passed on to new generations—new virtues with very powerful social consequences.
>
> *(pp. 22–23)*

It is not that the virtue is completely new. As a sub-virtue of the cardinal virtue of justice, it can be understood as oriented to general justice, to the good of the community rather than to what is due to individuals (commutative justice). Those Greek soldiers who in 480 B.C. held the pass at Thermopylae to the last man against a vast Persian army were practicing social justice in this sense, doing their duty to the common good of the polis. Rather, it is new in the sense that democracy, as observed by Tocqueville (2000), offered unique opportunities and required new initiatives for citizens far from the centers of political power to join together in order to achieve a common good—a good they could not have achieved as individuals nor relied on others (the state, social superiors) to deliver to them. Democracy, in his view, rested on this art of association.

As a virtue, social justice is social in two senses. Its aim is social, to improve the common good of society as a whole, whether on a small scale (building a new well or school or church) or large (building a union and uniting with other unions, or a national or international voluntary organization). These and other activities are social—the social activities of a free and responsible people.

Secondly, this virtue is social in its constitutive practices. As Novak and Adams (2015) put it, "The practice of the virtue of social justice consists in learning new skills, both of leadership and of cooperation and association with others, to accomplish ends that no one individual can achieve on his own. At one pole this new virtue is a social protection against atomic individualism, while at the other pole it protects considerable civic space from the direct custodianship of the state" (p. 23).

Responsive and regulatory practices require and build the virtue of social justice in both practitioners (professionals) and citizens (family members). Most clearly in FGC and related forms of family group decision-making, they require that professionals exercise their leadership skills to bring the appropriate people together, even those who may not have spoken to each other for years, but who might now be prepared to set other issues aside and give priority to the needs of the children. They must know when to remind others of that purpose, when to provide information that can inform the family's development of a plan to keep the children safe, and when to hold back (and remind other professionals to do the same) so the family can develop its own leadership and take responsibility for its own solutions.

If we understand the process of FGC as one of supervised family self-regulation, we can see the conference as building and modeling the skills of social justice, of leadership and cooperation with others in and beyond the family. It is, as Braithwaite (2004) has argued, a democracy-building, community-enhancing practice. "Restorative and responsive justice can be a strategy of social work practice that builds democracy bottom-up by seeing families as building blocks of democracy and fonts of democratic sentiment" (p. 199). It fosters the art of association, which lies at the heart of democracy (Tocqueville, 2000).

Responsive and Restorative Practices—Without the State?

Regulation, self-regulation, making things right are central to human life and flourishing at all levels from the body's physical systems to systems of societal governance. In the human services, regulatory and restorative practices typically assume the involvement of professionals who are paid or licensed by the state and directly or indirectly have immense power over the family. The emphasis then should be on helping those professionals who are used to wielding such power to hold back (but not disengage), keeping the coercive element of the job in the background until more restorative and responsive methods have proven futile.

We can see the power of a responsive, social justice-driven approach to regulation if we examine a situation where the regulation has entirely bubbled up from below with no direct role of the state. Necessarily, then, we find such a situation where human services are not involved although there is great human need and serious injustices and infringement of human rights are common. Human services are involved in alleviating some of the results of the poverty wages, unsafe and inhumane working conditions and housing, forced labor, sexual abuse, and violence, but are powerless to pull people together to address the underlying conditions that give rise to such problems. Bringing people together to create systemic change in all these areas was the challenge confronting the Coalition of Immokalee Workers (CIW).

In 1960, Edward R. Murrow's television documentary, *Harvest of Shame*, exposed the appalling conditions of agricultural migrant labor in the United States, specifically in Immokalee, Florida, the hub from which tomato pickers began and worked long hours for poverty wages in southwest Florida and then followed the crops and the seasons north to New Jersey. It showed the persistence of what to most Americans were unimaginable conditions of neglect and human rights abuses. One grower is quoted as saying, "We used to own slaves, now we just rent them." Tellingly, Murrow (1960) ends on a note that portrays the workers as powerless to help themselves, to come together to improve their situation through their own labor organizing or lobbying, as workers had done in other industries. Their only hope lay in the efforts of others. "The migrants have no lobby. Only an enlightened, aroused and perhaps angered public opinion can do anything about the migrants. The people you have seen have the strength to harvest your fruit and vegetables. They do not have the strength to influence legislation. Maybe we do. Good night, and good luck."

At the end of the 20th century, conditions of poverty wages, wage theft, slavery and debt peonage, sexual abuse, violence, and intimidation persisted. (For an important discussion of these conditions, their historic roots in Florida agriculture, their persistence, and the innovative and transformative approach developed by the Coalition of Immokalee Workers, see Asbed & Hitov, 2017. Asbed is a cofounder of the CIW and the Fair Food Program (FFP), and is also a principal architect of the Worker-driven Social Responsibility model. Hitov is a cofounder of the FFP and is principally responsible for drafting the binding Fair Food Agreements discussed below. He is the CIW's General Counsel.)

Traditional labor organizing of migratory and transient farmworkers was even more difficult considering the undocumented status of many and their language and ethnic divisions. Confronting the employers, themselves squeezed by the consolidation in the food industry and the purchasing power of corporate buyers to force down prices and hence wages and working conditions, remained difficult. Case-by-case "impact litigation" and government regulation, audited by a tiny Department of Labor staff assigned to cover a vast area, were powerless to change the systemic abuses in the fields (Marquis, 2017).

Beginning in 1993, a small group of workers, many with experience as activists in the dangerous and violent environment of Haiti during the demise of the Duvalier dictatorship and its aftermath, began meeting weekly in a room borrowed from a local church. Over several years, as the CIW grew and brought in more workers, it developed a new approach. Through a range of actions and activities that included strikes, marches, cooperation with law enforcement to end several notorious cases of enslavement of farmworkers, as well as recruitment and education of the farmworkers based in Immokalee, the CIW developed an analysis of the wider situation of the agricultural economy and came up with a new strategy. They practiced the virtue of social justice at a high level and developed it in those they recruited.

The CIW's weekly discussions, leadership development workshops, and strategy retreats led to a new analysis and line of attack. The participating workers realized that change would not come through confronting the growers, who had no room to maneuver due to the downward pressure on prices (and so, wages and the work environment) the corporate buyers exerted on them. It would not come from government either, but a new starting point was needed. They came to the realization that if the enormous fast-food chain Taco Bell could use its purchasing power to force down prices, the process could be reversed to force up prices and improve wages and working conditions. The key vulnerability was the brands on which the large buyers, especially the fast-food giants who dominated the market, spent many millions of dollars to develop and protect. The growers were not vulnerable on this score—how many consumers had even heard of them or knew which ones sold to which big corporations? Instead, through demonstrations, marches, boycotts, and other actions, the CIW pressured Taco Bell—and after them McDonalds, Subway, Trader Joe's, and many other corporate buyers—to sit down with the farmworkers to take responsibility for ending the abuses to which farmworkers were subject.

The new strategy produced change on a scale hitherto unseen in Florida agricultural labor. The CIW launched the Campaign for Fair Food which led to the Fair Food Program (FFP), a unique farmworker- and consumer-driven initiative and, from 2011, the Fair Food Standards Council (FFSC), which carries out the monitoring and enforcement of the FFP. The program brings the corporations, growers, and farmworkers together to the table. They agreed on a price premium of a penny per pound that goes directly from the corporate buyer to its suppliers, and on a human-rights-based Code of Conduct. Participating growers in turn agree, as a condition of being able to sell to the participating corporate buyers, to pass the price premium on to their workers as a Fair Food bonus; comply with the Code of Conduct that includes zero tolerance for forced labor, child labor and sexual assault; and cooperate with a worker-triggered complaint resolution mechanism that includes investigation, corrective action plans, and, at the regulatory apex, suspension of a farm's participating grower status and so its ability to sell to participating buyers. The sanction then, comes, not from the state, but the market.

The CIW is responsible for compliance with the program. It explored the possibilities of engaging an existing non-profit organization to monitor and audit participating growers in order to ensure compliance with the Code and investigate complaints. In particular, they tested the possibility of working with Verité, a global non-profit that has partnered with hundreds of multinational brands in more than 70 countries with the aim of ensuring that working conditions are safe, fair, and legal. Finding, however, that their own situation in the tomato fields of Florida required more specific knowledge of the industry and much more thorough and patient processes, the CIW set up its own independent monitoring organization, the Fair Foods Standards Council. The FFSC ensures compliance with each element of the program. It is responsible for implementing, monitoring, and enforcing the Fair Food Program. Its monitoring and auditing are unprecedentedly thorough.

Marquis (2017) of the RAND Corporation has described the strategy, organizing principles, approach, and methods of the FFSC in her detailed account, *I Am Not a Tractor: How Florida Farmworkers Took on the Fast Food Giants and Won.* Here I want to highlight two aspects of this regulatory environment.

First, the movement to regulate bubbled up from below, led by the farmworkers themselves, those whose predecessors Murrow had found to be so beaten down as to be incapable of acting on their own behalf. Other approaches, such as "impact litigation" of specific cases of abuse, efforts to organize along traditional union lines that identified the worker-employer relationship as the central locus of action, and engagement of the churches in providing material help and publicity, had been tried over many years. The CIW did not reject them and built allies among the churches and student activists. But they stepped back to analyze more carefully why such measures, even where necessary, were insufficient and had dangers of their own. Through their own direct experience of the work, the growers, and each other, the CIW came to see the need for a new strategy and developed a plan of action to implement it.

The movement from below that built the CIW and, in turn, the Campaign for Fair Food, the Fair Food Program, and the Fair Food Standards Council, required in its participants, and developed from the start, the virtue of social justice. Its leaders saw the need to bring together people who had been seen by others, and experienced themselves, as isolated and hopeless in their subjection and poverty, to realize a common good that none could have achieved on his or her own. Coming in many cases from Haiti, Guatemala, and Mexico, they needed to deploy and develop the "art of association" in the new and difficult context of the Florida tomato fields, where they worked long hours for poverty wages in dangerous conditions. They learned the skills of leadership needed in this setting, of drawing in new members through the means available to them, such as the space offered for weekly meetings, film screenings, skits, and discussions in the local Catholic Church. They learned and prioritized leadership development with the widest participation in determining the group's activities and tactics—their slogan is "*Todos somos lideres*"—We are all leaders. They developed leadership from within their own ranks, building alliances with supporters in the churches, among students, lawyers, and philanthropists, but always insisting that leadership of their collective efforts must derive from, in the Burford and Hudson phrase, the "knowledge, experiences, and desires of the people most affected." They stressed education of the workers of different backgrounds and languages as they came to Immokalee to work in the fields, education not only in terms of human rights and remedies (limited as these were at the start) but also in the larger picture of the food industry and their place in it. They understood the need for ongoing discussions of their situation and the possibilities for action. They held strategic leadership retreats to analyze the situation in depth—their own position and the nature of the industry in which they worked—and to develop a perspective and plan of action. It was out of such meetings and processes that the decisive shift in strategy emerged, from traditional labor dispute and impact litigation methods to the worker-led, industry-wide focus on the corporate buyers who dominated the market and had the power to force wages and working conditions up as well as down and the incentive to do so to protect their brands.

The monitoring body, the FFSC, required and developed virtues required for and developed by its specific practices. As with CIW leaders, the capacity to think systemically and analytically was essential. FFSC investigators spend long hours and days in the heat of the fields, listening patiently to workers, gaining trust, and asking key questions as they go about their work of detailed, objective fact-finding. In addition to the interpersonal skills and integrity needed for this work, they also need to think analytically and systemically to identify patterns and to go beyond the anecdotal (Espinoza, 2017). In addition, investigators need both the courage and strength of youth and the cardinal virtue of practical judgment (*phronesis*, the virtue acquired only with maturity, as Aristotle says). In the words of FFSC director Judge Laura Espinoza, they "need stamina and wisdom, stamina and professionalism . . . the maturity and sophistication to develop a rapport with [farm] management and workers" (Marquis, 2017, p. 119). They need "Analytical skills, writing skills, quantitative skills" (p. 121) and in addition the virtues, especially courage and prudence or practical judgment, required in the farm fields, where they do much of their work. As Judge Espinoza explained to Marquis (2017), the audit teams "are dealing with grizzled and often crude farm managers and crew leaders who will roll over you if given the opportunity. You need to be able to stand your ground but in a manner that is constructive" (p. 121).

It is easy to think, in the context of child protection and family group conferencing, of the encounter between, on one hand, the modern state—with its bureaucratic norms and legal rights and processes (and its professional social work "family regulators")—and, on the other, families with rich traditional or indigenous cultures with well-established methods of restoring justice and regulating their own members to keep children safe or address other harms. The question then is, how does each learn from the other, allowing the strengths of each to constrain the excesses of the other? In the case of the Florida farmworkers, their families, and communities, the actors are different, as are the regulatory dynamics and processes.

The knowledge, experience, and desires of the CIW were not static or time-honored values of a traditional culture. The founders and leaders of CIW were formed in struggles in other countries (Haiti was particularly important in this regard). They drew on the experience and ideologies of other struggles in the Caribbean and South America, on the concepts of Brazilian educator and philosopher Paulo Freire (1970) and the critical pedagogy movement. They had themselves to learn, analyze, and adapt their thinking and methods of organizing to the new and different circumstances of Immokalee.

Second, the kind of regulation of the industry that the processes of struggle and negotiation among workers, growers, and buyers produced did not emerge, in the manner of many demands for "social justice," out of claims or demands on the state. State legislation and its enforcement through government regulation had very little to do with the systemic changes in the industry. These came, rather, from the practice of the virtue of social justice by those who joined together in the CIW and the worker-led initiatives it spawned, coming together to analyze and understand their own situation in its wider context and bring the voice of the farmworkers to the table with the growers and corporations. The CIW had to carve out a new approach to an apparently intractable problem of farm labor relations and develop a new way to regulate the industry that went far beyond both the purview of the US Department of Labor and the existing methods of social responsibility auditing (Marquis, 2017).

CIW counsel, Steven Hitov, asked whether he hoped that the standards, monitoring, and enforcement methods of the Fair Food Program, perhaps the best workplace monitoring program in the United States, would be picked up by the federal government, said this. "So, when people ask me, where do you see this going? Do you expect it to become law? I hope not! I've worked on the Hill. It would be watered down and compromised . . . diluted to pass. Even if the idea is good to start, what will come out will be the minimum of what they [the corporations and the growers] have to do" (Marquis, 2017, p. 65).

Human services agencies and farmworkers confront many of the same problems—of poverty, violence, sexual abuse, lack of decent and affordable housing, and so on. But they come at them from quite different directions and from different positions. In their different ways, though, both are involved in regulatory processes and aim to set things rights or restore justice. The role of the state and legal norms and processes are also different. And those who come to the table in one case, like FGC in child welfare—family members and professionals who have concerns and information to share, along, in some cases, with statutory responsibility for child safety—are very different from those who come together to join in the regulatory task involving farmworkers, growers, and corporate buyers. The buyers, themselves subject to other kinds of regulation, become in this context regulators—via codes of conduct, if they are vigorously enforced by third parties (but not the state)—of the growers (Drahos & Krygier, 2017).

In short, the dichotomies in which we tend to think in human services and child welfare, even when the aim is to promote responsive and restorative services, dichotomies of family and state, professionals and citizens or service users, of regulator and regulated, even of formal and informal services (which has long seemed to this author to be the central question of social work) may be too limiting. The virtue of social justice, however, of bringing people together to serve the common good, and the skills and habits it entails, remains central to the virtue-driven restorative and regulatory processes discussed here. They depend on and build the virtues, and, in particular, social justice as the distinctive virtue of democracy.

References

Adams, P., & Chandler, S. M. (2004). Responsive regulation in child welfare: Systemic challenges to mainstreaming the Family Group Conference. *Journal of Sociology & Social Welfare, 31*(1), 93–116.

Asbed, G., & Hitov, S. (2017). Preventing forced labor in corporate supply chains: The fair food program and worker-driven social responsibility. *Wake Forest Law Review, 52*, 497–531.

Braithwaite, J. (2002). *Restorative justice and responsive regulation.* New York: Oxford University Press.

Braithwaite, J. (2004). Families and the republic. *Journal of Sociology & Social Welfare, 31*(1), 199–215.

Burford, G., & Hudson, J. (Eds.). (2000). *Family Group Conferencing: New directions in community-centered child and family practice.* Hawthorne, NY: Aldine de Gruyter.

Drahos, P., & Krygier, M. (2017). Regulation, institutions, and networks. In P. Drahos (Ed.), *Regulatory theory: Foundations and applications* (pp. 1–22). Canberra: Australian National University Press. Retrieved November 15, 2017, from http://press-files.anu.edu.au/downloads/press/n2304/pdf/ch01.pdf.

Espinoza, L. S. (2017). Personal interview, Ave Maria, FL, December 20.

Feser, E. (2005). *Social justice reconsidered: Austrian economics and Catholic social teaching.* Hayek Memorial Lecture delivered at the 2005 Austrian Scholars Conference, Auburn, AL. Retrieved December 15, 2017, from www.edwardfeser.com/unpublished/papers/socialjustice.html.

Freire, P. (1970). *Pedagogy of the oppressed.* New York: Herder & Herder, 1970.

Hayek, F. (1976). *The mirage of social justice, Vol. 2 of Law, legislation and liberty.* Chicago: University of Chicago Press.

MacIntyre, A. (1990). *Three rival versions of moral enquiry: Encyclopaedia, genealogy, and tradition.* Notre Dame, IN: University of Notre Dame Press.

Marquis, S. L. (2017). *I am not a tractor: How Florida farmworkers took on the fast food giants and won.* Ithaca, NY: ILR Press.

Murrow, E. R. (1960). *Harvest of shame.* CBS television documentary. Retrieved November 15, 2017, from www.youtube.com/watch?v=yJTVF_dya7E.

Novak, M., & Adams, P. (2015). *Social justice isn't what you think it is.* New York: Encounter Books.

Pellegrino, E. D., & Thomasma, D. C. (1993). *The virtues in medical practice.* New York: Oxford University Press.

Tocqueville, A. (2000). *Democracy in America* (H. C. Mansfield & D. Winthrop, Ed. & Trans.). Chicago: University of Chicago Press.

Walker, L. (2017). Restorative practices for juveniles in Hawai'i, United States. In K. Jaishankar (Ed.), *Interpersonal criminology: Revisiting interpersonal crimes and victimization* (pp. 87–96). Boca Raton, FL: CRC Press.

Walker, L., & Greening, R. (2013). Huikahi restorative circles: A public health approach for reentry planning. In K. S. van Wormer & L. Walker (Eds.), *Restorative justice today: Practical approaches* (pp. 173–183). Thousand Oaks, CA: Sage.

7

CHILDREN'S HOPES AND CONVERGING FAMILY AND STATE NETWORKS OF REGULATION

Joan Pennell, Kara Allen-Eckard, Marianne Latz, and Cameron Tomlinson

Introduction

Children involved with human services are within converging networks of regulation—family and state institutions. Families may experience the state intervention as an unjust intrusion into their lives. To shield children from the resulting friction, families and agencies often make decisions with little input from their young charges. Conversely, the friction may spark dialogue in which children express their hopes, and together families and agencies generate plans guided by collective hope. A potential mechanism for including children in collaborative planning are family meetings. This chapter considers the extent of child inclusion in family meetings within a US state, based on two surveys: the first with interdisciplinary advisory bodies responsible for recommending systemic change in public child welfare and the second with professionals from different agencies working with individual children and families. The conclusions emphasize that participatory practice models require reinforcement from intersecting family and state networks of support and accountability.

Children's Hopes within Converging Family and State Networks of Regulation

Children involved with human services are bound within converging networks of regulation—family and state institutions. Parents and other caregivers welcome much-needed agency supports that they have requested in order to care for their young charges. Conversely, if families have little choice over state provisions, they may experience services as an unjust intrusion into their personal lives. Families are likely then to react through resistance, disengagement, or game playing to undermine agency rules (Braithwaite, 2017). In turn, agencies experience the families as non-compliant with state standards and react by ordering services and issuing sanctions. The friction is not limited to family–state relationships. The involved agencies may dispute among themselves who is responsible for service delivery, service costs, and legal liability. These system-level clashes further exacerbate tensions with families, who may well have conflicting agency expectations imposed on them.

DOI: 10.4324/9780429398704-7

During the friction, children are often sidelined, unable to express their hopes for the future. As a result, young people lose the opportunity to exercise a meaningful say in their affairs in conjunction with their families and involved services. Such exclusion contravenes the rights of children to have input into administrative rulings affecting their well-being and their connection to family and culture (United Nations, 1989, 2008). In response, child-and-family-serving systems around the globe have sought to put into effect restorative approaches in which the family group—that is, the children, their families, relatives, and other close supports—take part (van Wormer & Walker, 2013; Zinsstag & Vanfraechem, 2012).

Implementation studies of restorative programs indicate that involving young people in deliberations increases their sense of being treated fairly, nurtures their capacity to participate, and builds their sense of self-efficacy (Gal, 2015). These same studies, however, repeatedly report difficulties in institutionalizing child-inclusive forums in which family groups and agencies reach decisions together. Theory and research on responsive regulation identify strategies for overcoming these difficulties.

From a regulatory perspective, institutionalizing child inclusion requires not only offering restorative approaches but offering the meetings within supportive networks of human services. Generating these supportive networks depends on a tripartite system of governance that de-centers state authority, encourages civic participation, and sustains a sense of hope as a community (Drahos & Krygier, 2017). These tripartite systems are required both within the family group forums and across the systems hosting the forums. In a multilevel, polycentric network of governance, state authorities are positioned to strengthen family systems and only as needed, to intervene to protect children's human rights (Braithwaite, 2004). In child protection services, the often-referenced pyramid of responsive regulation can be depicted with educational programming at its broad base and resting on top are restorative approaches, next deterrents such as supervised visits, and at the apex incapacitation including removal of children from their homes or termination of parental rights. Giving preference to supports over coercion in child protection means climbing up the regulatory pyramid to more controlling mechanism only as needed and then climbing quickly down as soon as possible.

In the southeastern USA, North Carolina offers a site in which to test the utility of regulatory theory in explicating the possibility of child inclusion in family group forums. In North Carolina, these forums are referred to as *child and family team meetings* (CFTs). The name in itself highlights child inclusion within a family-state collaboration or "team." To encourage cross-system collaboration, this same term for the meetings is used by child welfare, mental health, juvenile justice, public health, and schools.

Interdisciplinarity is further promoted through statewide and county collaboratives. One of these collaboratives is an interdisciplinary advisory body called a *Community Child Protection Team* (CCPT) responsible for reviewing the performance of public child welfare and recommending systemic changes. Thus, CCPTs are a potential mechanism for effecting a tripartite system of governance at the system level and for assessing the delivery of CFTs at the practice level.

Accordingly, this chapter considers the extent of child inclusion in CFT meetings within North Carolina from two perspectives: (a) interdisciplinary Community Child Protection Teams at the system level and (b) professionals from different agencies working with individual children and families at the practice level. Two surveys examined their respective views. The first survey accessed 71% of the state's 100 counties. The second surveyed service providers from different child-and-family-serving agencies, with a sample of 507 participants. The researchers analyzed the data from these two vantage points to address the following three questions: How often do children participate in their CFT meetings? What are the barriers to their inclusion? What are the strategies for overcoming these barriers? The term *children* is used in this chapter to refer to zero up to 18 years of age.

The chapter begins by reviewing factors affecting children's inclusion in family meetings. Next attention turns to the North Carolina context and the policies and collaborations that support child participation in CFT meetings. Then, the research methods for surveying community teams and professionals are described, and their results are summarized. Based on these findings, the authors reflect on how professional practices affect child inclusion and identify systemic strategies for fostering tripartite systems of regulation and nurturing a culture of hope and participation.

Children's Inclusion in Family Meetings

Most jurisdictions that encourage children's participation in family meetings uphold their inclusion as a best practice or an agency policy. A notable exception is *Aotearoa* New Zealand where children's participation was established from the outset as a human right. New Zealand legislation passed in 1989 mandated family group conferences (FGC) as a means of involving the children, young persons, and their families in child welfare and youth justice decision-making. This act reflected protests by Maori (Indigenous peoples) against Eurocentric approaches that they had experienced as eroding their families and tribes and leading to removal of their young relatives (Rangihau, 1986). The underlying philosophy was that children belong with their families and that government must respect cultural traditions and partner with communities (Hassall, 1996). Although emphasizing children's rights to take part, the legislation empowered FGC coordinators to restrict participation depending on factors such as the child's level of maturity or best interests.

In the early days of implementation in *Aotearoa* New Zealand, FGCs in child welfare had children in attendance 79% of the time (Paterson & Harvey, 1991). This rate likely reflected both the legislative mandate and initial enthusiasm for the model. The New Zealand rate is higher than the attendance at child welfare conferences found by an international study conducted in 2003–2004 (Nixon, Burford, & Quinn, 2005). The researchers distributed the survey to human service programs of which they were aware. The 225 respondents came largely from the United States, United Kingdom, and Canada. The survey cannot be considered representative of practice at the time but does offer insights about the inclusion of children.

The survey asked respondents to indicate the frequency of child attendance, and 191 (85%) provided estimates (Nixon et al., 2005). For meetings focused on child welfare, 60% of respondents reported that children were present half the time or more. The level of child attendance in child welfare was lower than that reported for all other focal areas: domestic violence at 69%, youth and adult justice/corrections at 74%, child mental health at 79%, and schools at 83%. A follow-up question asked respondents to describe "any restrictions on children's attendance" (Nixon et al., 2005, p. 35). Their responses assist in understanding the lower rate for child welfare. Two-thirds of those responding to this question reported they limited children's attendance on the basis of age and the nature of the subject under discussion. Child welfare conferences are more likely to pertain to younger children and to the maltreatment of these children or sensitive family issues such as substance use.

The same restrictions as well as additional ones on children's participation in different countries are evident in more recent reports regarding meetings in child welfare, family court, schools, and youth justice. Gal (2015) observes that some of the concerns are about the children and some about the professionals themselves. The service providers fear that children will lack the capacity to make decisions or will be hurt by taking part. Professionals, particularly in court settings, acknowledge worries that they will not be able to talk with children or they may be emotionally overwhelmed by hearing what the children suffer in their lives. In addition to worries about secondary trauma, the workers may see involving the children as requiring too much time, effort, and resources.

Examining effective strategies for overcoming professional reluctance, Gal (2015) advises, "Initial education followed by hand-on experience may enhance professionals' willingness to engage in participatory practices; broader exposure to such pioneering practices may extend child participation beyond local initiatives to create a culture of child participation" (p. 454). In other words, what professionals learn and do at work is important but so is the broader context in which they are operating. Such is evident in the development of child and family teams in the United States and specifically in North Carolina.

Child and Family Teams in North Carolina

Unlike FGCs in New Zealand, child and family teams (CFTs) emerged in the United States from child mental health as a part of a larger reform effort to wrap a system of care around children with serious behavioral health issues. This unified approach is intended to be child-centered, family-focused, community-based, multisystem, culturally competent, and in least restrictive/intrusive settings (Stroul & Friedman, 1986, pp. 16–24). Thus as the case with FGCs, CFTs are conceived as both supporting individual children and their families and mobilizing system-wide change. CFTs, however, diverge from FGCs in regards to who develops the plans and how often the group meets.

FGC plans are made by the family group with the involved authorities responsible for approving the action steps and authorizing necessary resources, and the family group may meet once or on a limited basis. Contrasting FGCs with CFTs, Burchard and Burchard (2000) point out that CFT plans are co-constructed by the team and the professionals who serve as partners rather than experts and that the team often meets on a weekly basis in order to provide ongoing support to family members, especially mothers. Burchard and Burchard further observe that family participants at CFT meetings are likely to be fewer in number than at FGCs. CFT principles encourage the participation of children but unlike in New Zealand's FGC, children are not entitled members. Nevertheless, in North Carolina, cross-system collaborations and agency policies support their inclusion. The collaborations have representation from many of the same agencies and family advocacy groups, making for cross-fertilization of ideas on CFTs.

A long-serving, interdisciplinary advisory group occurring across North Carolina is the Community Child Protection Team (CCPT). The local teams are charged with reviewing cases of child maltreatment and making recommendations on improving public child welfare. State legislation (North Carolina General Statute §§ 7–1406–1413) became effective in 1993 and mandated each of the 100 counties to establish its own CCPT. The statute specifies the required agency members while leaving room for additional appointees, including family partners who have received services and can offer family perspectives. Subsequently, CCPTs also became the means by which North Carolina was permitted to meet the expectations of federal legislation, the Child Abuse Prevention and Treatment Act (CAPTA) as amended in 1996 (Public Law 104–235). CAPTA requires that each state create citizen review panels, usually three per state. Thus, North Carolina's requirement of one CCPT for each of its 100 counties far exceeds the federal mandate and emphasizes local participation.

Federal statute and the congressional record accord an "expansive mandate" to citizen review panels: evaluate the policies, procedures, and practices of child protection services; reach out for public comment on child protection's performance; make recommendations for system reform and dissemi-nate these to the state and public; and advocate for system reform and increased supports and resources for child protection workers (Vadapalli, 2017, p. 541). This broad mandate distinguishes citizen review panels from other external review processes such as guardian-ad-litem and judicial review that focus on individual cases. Federal statute encourages diverse membership, including former victims of child maltreatment. In addition, federal program instruction does not prohibit the participation of child pro-tection services. The participation of child protection supports a much-needed exchange of informa-tion between the agency and community participants about a complex, constantly evolving, and often controversial system (Collins-Camargo, Buckwalter, & Jones, 2016). The underlying assumption of the federally mandated citizen review panels and the North Carolina CCPTs is that state-community part-nership improves child protection services.

In keeping with the state and federal statutory requirements, the North Carolina CCPT Advisory Board (2017) conducts annual surveys of local CCPTs. The surveys serve as a basis for making policy recommendations to the North Carolina Division of Social Services. The authors of this chapter are at a university center that manages and analyzes the surveys on behalf of the board. Among other matters, the advisory board decided in its 2014 survey to examine the role of child and family teams (CFTs) in wrapping services around children and their families. This focus reflects that as reported in the subse-quent 2015 survey completed by 87 CCPTs, agencies involved directly in CFT meetings also tend to be present *very frequently* at their county CCPT meetings: social services (90%), mental health (61%), health care (61%), public health (58%), and guardian ad litem (54%).

The other mandated members—law enforcement, community action agency, school superinten-dent, county board of social services, and district attorney—more often attend the CCPT meetings on an intermittent basis. A minority of CCPTs has family partners as team members, and usually these partners attend *occasionally*. The composition of the North Carolina CCPT Advisory Board is intended to mirror the local CCPT membership and includes representation from many of the same agencies as identified in state statute and has family and youth partner members.

The CCPT membership overlaps extensively with that of the North Carolina Collaborative for Children, Youth and Families founded in 2000 to provide a forum in which different groups involved in child-and-family services exchange ideas and promote a system-of-care approach. To reinforce family voice, the NC Collaborative is co-chaired by a family partner and an agency or university partner. The North Carolina Collaborative (2007) endorsed a definition of CFTs that highlights family and child inclusion in decision-making: "family members and their community support that come together to **create, implement and update** a plan **with** the children, youth/student and family" [emphasis in original].

Within the state, efforts to include families and children in decision-making through CFTs have been spearheaded by system-of-care initiatives in multiple agencies: child mental health, child welfare, courts, juvenile justice, public health, and schools (Gifford et al., 2010). Agency policies do not require but do encourage the attendance of children and youth. For instance, child mental health policy states: "In partnership with the beneficiary, the beneficiary's family, and the legally responsible person, as appropriate, the Licensed or QP [Qualified Professional] is responsible for convening the Child and Family Team" (North Carolina Division of Medical Assistance, 2013, p. 34).

The state child welfare manual reads: "Involving children/youth in the CFT meeting is a critical and complicated issue. However, it is not a question about whether the children/youth should be involved in the process, but rather how they should be involved in the process" (North Carolina Division of Social Services, 2009, p. 13). This statement is reinforced by the federal Preventing Sex Trafficking and Strengthening Families Act of 2014 (Public Law 113–183) clause that "if a child has attained 14 years of age, the permanency plan developed for the child, and any revision or addition to the plan, shall be developed in consultation with the child."

Supporting the adoption of CFTs in multiple systems, the university center in which the authors are based carries out training, technical assistance, and evaluation across the state. In 2015, the North Carolina Division of Social Services asked the center to revise and adapt its training addressing strategies for including children and youth in CFTs to a more accessible online format. This delivery format presented the center with an opportunity to expand its participants to a larger cross-system audience, encompassing public agency, community, and family partners. With this in mind, curriculum developers felt that it was necessary to have a current understanding of attitudes and practices related to including children and youth in the various CFT processes across the state.

Informal feedback from practitioners in statewide child welfare training events indicated that most were aware of the policy directives regarding the desire to include children and youth in the CFT process. When the trainers solicited specific examples of child or youth inclusion in meetings, however, most did not include the physical presence of young persons at the meetings. Participants more often shared examples of how adult team members represented young people as well as acknowledging their own concerns about including children and youth in person.

The center developed a survey to gain a clearer sense of how these hesitations of professionals from different systems were affecting their inclusion of children in CFT meetings. The survey also intended to get a picture of how workers were engaging children in CFT meetings and of what resources might be necessary to increase child participation. The items on the service provider and CCPT surveys differed and were not directly comparable with each other. Nevertheless, the surveys provided insights about child participation in CFTs from two different perspectives—individual service providers and interagency teams.

Method

The university center conducted two surveys: (a) Community Child Protection Teams (CCPTs) survey and (b) service provider survey. Both surveys used the software tool Qualtrics to administer the survey, ATLAS.ti to code qualitative data according to themes related to child participation, and SPSS to conduct descriptive data analyses. The surveys did not collect personal information on respondents, and both were determined to be exempt by the host university's research ethics board.

CCPT Survey

The CCPT survey was designed to cover the local teams' activities and experiences in their county for the calendar year 2014. No county had more than one CCPT; thus, the potential pool of respondents was the same as the number of counties. The survey instrument encouraged CCPT chairs to schedule an "opportunity for input and review" by the local team. The extent to which CCPT chairs conferred with their teams is unknown, but anecdotal information indicates that many checked with their teams before responding. From the 100 counties, 71 CCPTs completed the survey. These teams represented well all state regions and counties with small to medium to large populations.

The North Carolina CCPT Advisory Board chose to focus the survey on barriers to children and families served by public child welfare having access to mental health, substance use, and developmental disabilities services. The board further wanted to explore how CFTs and community collaborations improved access to these needed services. This study uses the survey items on the frequency of CFT attendance by different family members and organizations, system-level and family-level strategies used to improve CFT meetings, main challenges to holding CFT meetings, and recommended strategies for overcoming these challenges.

Service Provider Survey

Approximately half a year after the CCPT survey, the university center administered the service provider survey in August 2015. The service provider survey was designed to identify practices across the state for including children in CFTs and to use these findings to support curricular development. The center distributed the survey by email using a snowball sampling method. After filtering out respondents who were neither 18 years of age nor working with North Carolina children and removing incomplete surveys, the sample was reduced from 570 to 507. Four groups made up 85% of the 507 survey participants: guardians ad litem (GALs, 231, 46%), child welfare (115, 23%), behavioral health (42, 8%), and juvenile justice (41, 8%). The remaining 77 (15%) consisted of workers from other systems with only small percentages of family advocates, foster parents, and others completing the survey.

The survey asked the respondents to check the considerations that they took into account when deciding whether to include children in CFTs. Then they were asked to rate the frequency with which children were physically at the meetings, represented by a support person, or represented by some other means. The survey closed with one qualitative question about gaps in resources or information that would help the respondents include young people in CFTs.

Results

This section presents the results from the two surveys for each of the three research questions on child participation. A reminder, the service provider survey asked generally about CFT participation while the CCPT survey questions were focused on access for families served by public child welfare to mental health (MH), substance abuse (SA), and developmental disabilities (DD) services. Quotations are amended for readability.

How Often Do Children Participate in Their CFT Meetings?

CCPT Survey

The survey asked CCPTs to indicate the frequency of CFT attendance by family members and organizations in their counties. Table 7.1 shows that for families involved with child protection and requiring MH/SA/DD services, 57% of the CCPTs reported that children were *often* present while 34% indicated *sometimes* and 9% responded *never* or *rarely*. In contrast, 94% of the CCPTs rated mothers as *often* in attendance. The percentages of CCPT agreement on fathers and other family attending *often* were somewhat higher than for their children or young relatives, respectively 64% and 65%.

Among the organizations, social services was the most frequently present with nearly all (97%) CCPTs indicating *often*. Coming in second were guardians ad litem, *often* in attendance for 65% of the CCPTs. The higher attendance by social services and GALs is in line with their responsibilities for children served by public child welfare. The rate for mental or behavioral health is lower with their professionals *often* present according to 53% of the CCPTs. The CCPTs typically viewed the other

TABLE 7.1 CCPT Survey

In 2014, how often in your county did the following groups attend CFT meetings for children, youth, and/or their parents/caregivers who were served by public child welfare and who required access to services for mental health, substance abuse, or developmental disabilities? (n = 71)

Participants	n	Percentages				
		Never	Rarely	Sometimes	Often	Median[a]
Children/youth	68	1.5%	7.4%	33.8%	57.4%	4.00
Mothers	70	1.4%	0%	4.3%	94.3%	4.00
Fathers	69	1.4%	4.3%	30.4%	63.8%	4.00
Other family	69	1.4%	1.4%	31.9%	65.2%	4.00
Friends	69	2.9%	8.7%	55.1%	33.3%	3.00
Family/youth partners	60	13.3%	11.7%	38.3%	36.7%	3.00
Social Services	70	1.4%	0%	1.4%	97.1%	4.00
Guardian ad Litem	71	1.4%	4.2%	29.6%	64.8%	4.00
Mental or Behavioral Health	70	2.9%	5.7%	38.6%	52.9%	4.00
Schools	68	1.5%	20.6%	52.9%	25.0%	3.00
Juvenile Justice	67	9.0%	20.9%	46.3%	23.9%	3.00
Public Health	65	26.2%	26.2%	6.2%	6.2%	2.00
Domestic Violence	66	18.2%	36.4%	37.9%	7.6%	2.00
Child advocacy organization	54	25.9%	33.3%	33.3%	7.4%	2.00
Family advocacy organization	51	29.4%	39.2%	21.6%	9.8%	2.00
Faith organization	57	17.5%	47.4%	31.6%	3.5%	2.00
Cultural organization	49	40.8%	51.0%	8.2%	0%	2.00

a Medians are calculated with *never* 1, *rarely* 2, *sometimes* 3, and *often* 4.

categories of participants, including friends and family/youth partners, as present *sometimes* or *rarely*, or they did not venture an estimate.

Service Provider Survey

Based on their experience, respondents were asked to rate how frequently children were physically at the meetings. As seen in Table 7.2, respondents reported that children were *often* physically present at the meeting 33% of the time. Children and youth were *rarely or never* at the meetings a combined 30% of the time. Further analysis found differences in response by the respondents' role. Juvenile justice indicated that children were *often* present at the highest rate (85%), followed by behavioral health (61%). The percentage of *often* responses was lower for child welfare (33%) and far lower for GAL (17%).

What Are the Barriers to Their Inclusion?

CCPT Survey

The CCPT survey asked the open-ended question, "What are the main challenges in your county to holding CFT meetings?" This question was not specific to child inclusion but the identified

TABLE 7.2 Service Provider Survey

In your experience, how often are children/youth . . .? (n = 507)

	n	Never	Rarely	Sometimes	Often
Physically at the meeting	486	46 (9%)	99 (20%)	182 (37%)	159 (33%)
Represented at the meeting by a support person	473	21 (4%)	62 (13%)	120 (25%)	270 (57%)
Represented at the meeting by other means[a]	393	44 (11%)	73 (19%)	134 (34%)	142 (36%)

a The survey stated, "Representation may include a photo, a letter, or some other reminder of the child/youth."

challenges affected their participating in meetings. Many CCPTs responded at length to this question, and only six (8%) out of 71 did not specify any challenges. Their responses were coded into categories of challenges.

The two most commonly identified types of challenges pertained to logistics: (a) scheduling, availability, or meeting time issues for families and professionals (cited 31 times) and (b) transportation or meeting location issues for families (cited 23 times). For instance, a CCPT noted that children were prevented from attending when the meetings were held during school hours. Another CCPT observed, "Many of our children are placed outside of the county. Therefore, anyone willing to be involved in a CFT must often travel away from our home county."

A different set of challenges related to engaging groups of participants: families (15 times), mental health professionals (seven times), other professional or community partners (eight times), and children (two times). The absence of professionals such as from child mental health, schools, and juvenile justice was viewed as a major obstacle to developing productive plans for the children. Other barriers concerned attitudes on child participation. One CCPT wrote, "There is room for improvement on involving the children and youth in CFTs. There is often reluctance to involve them because of the difficult issues being discussed, possibility for hostility, and wanted to protect the child/youth from the heaviness of the meeting." Similar issues on child inclusion were identified in the service provider survey.

Service Provider Survey

The survey asked, "When thinking about including children/youth in a CFT, I consider the following," and then listed possible considerations that could affect their assessment on including children. Table 7.3 shows that most respondents agreed that these considerations were relevant to their evaluative process. Breaking out the responses by role found that over 75% of respondents from child welfare, behavioral health, and juvenile justice considered all these considerations. In contrast, GALs less commonly checked that they considered the amount of responsibility (61%), specific details (70%), exposure (73%), and availability of support (68%). Behavioral health and child welfare had unanimity or near unanimity on considering children's emotional well-being (respectively 100% and 96%) and developmental capacity (respectively 98% and 97%), and almost all behavioral health respondents took into account specific details (98%). The top consideration for juvenile justice was purpose (95%), and the top considerations for GALs were emotional well-being (91%) and developmental capacity (90%).

TABLE 7.3 Service Provider Survey

When thinking about including children/youth in a CFT, I consider the following. . . (n = 507)

Inclusion Considerations	Number	Percentage
Child/youth emotional well-being	464	92%
Child/youth developmental capacity to participate	460	91%
Purpose of the CFT meeting	434	86%
Potential exposure to inappropriate information or behavior at the CFT	401	79%
Specific details of the case[a]	388	77%
Availability of support for the child/youth in the meeting	385	76%
Amount of responsibility participation places on the child	344	68%

Note: Respondents asked to check all items that apply.

a The survey stated, "Case considerations may include things such as legal status of the parents, mental or physical health of the caregivers, or other family situations such as domestic violence."

What Are the Strategies for Overcoming These Barriers?

CCPT Survey

After asking CCPTs to identify barriers to holding CFTs, the survey posed its final question, "What does your CCPT recommend as strategies for overcoming these challenges?" The majority (80%) described strategies, with the responses between two and 183 words in length. They provided strategies for increasing the participation of families and professionals through outreach and training (26 times), better collaboration and communication among partners (13 times), arranging alternatives to in-person participation (nine times), providing transportation for families (seven times), and prioritizing family needs in terms of scheduling and venues (five times). A number of CCPTs referred to the role of family partners in supporting family participation and explaining to families the benefits of CFTs.

In regards to specifically involving children, a few CCPTs volunteered strategies. For children placed outside the county, a CPPT observed, "DSS often transports or arranges for transportation for families to participate in the location of the child." Another CCPT noted, "Youth Participation—We are now offering 2:30 and 5:30 time slots for CFTs. We can encourage teams to have the meetings at the school." Yet another CCPT explained the benefits of having the youngest children present, "Often encourage family to bring babies/toddlers to meeting to give sense of how they are responded to in the setting and humanizes the meeting."

Service Provider Survey

The survey asked respondents to score based on their experience the extent to which strategies are used for representing children through support persons or other means such as a photo or letter. As seen in Table 7.2, 57% responded that a support person *often* represented the children, and 36% agreed that other means were *often* used. Both these percentages are higher than the 33% for children *often* being physically at the meeting. A breakdown by role found marked differences in the frequency with which support persons *often* represented children: 71% GAL, 56% juvenile justice, 47% child welfare, and 34%

behavioral health. Differences were also found for how *often* other means are used to represent children: 41% child welfare, 40% GAL, 31% juvenile justice, and 20% behavioral health.

The service provider survey inquired about "what information or resources would help to include children/youth in more CFT meetings." Over one-third of the original respondents (190) offered input to this open-ended question. The most frequent responses (27) identified the need for resources to support children's participation by educating them about CFTs or obtaining their input either through a representative or by supporting their participation at the meeting. Specifically, one respondent requested, "A small packet that uses drawings . . . and words to describe the CFT and why we want to hear from the child, in language that is affirming and to help minimize any fears." Other resources requested included additional training (24) and resources specifically to educate parents (17) and professionals (eight) about how to support safe child participation in CFTs. Additional responses reflected systemic resource needs including more time to ensure that children were properly prepared for taking part in CFTs (11), transportation options for the families and their children (nine), and neutral facilitators to support the CFT process (three).

Discussion

Strengths and Limitations of the Research Method

Both surveys yielded information pertinent to the three research questions. Their findings, though, cannot be directly compared because the survey instruments did not ask the same questions. The generalizability of the study findings is limited by the snowball sampling used for the service provider survey, the lack of information about who within each local team completed the CCPT survey, and the restriction of data collection to one US state. Future research is needed that has clear sampling frames, collects more information about survey respondents, and compares data from different states and countries.

Nevertheless, the limitations of each survey is offset, in part, by the strengths of the other survey. The CCPT survey accessed the perspectives of interdisciplinary teams in 71% of the state's 100 counties. This survey also made it possible to better judge the representativeness of the viewpoints expressed in the service provider survey. Unlike the CCPT survey, the service provider survey made it possible to drill down to the views of individual professionals from different child- and family-serving organizations. The sample size of over 500 respondents made it possible to detect patterns in their answers. The two surveys were administered closely in time, with the CCPT survey preceding the service provider survey by half a year. Another strength of the study is that the North Carolina context assists with studying patterns of child inclusion. Discussion across North Carolina human services systems is enhanced by their having an agreed-upon term for the meetings—"child and family teams"—and a consensual agreement on the definition of CFTs. At the heart of this definition is the inclusion of children and their families in decision-making.

Patterns of Child Inclusion

The responses to the two surveys indicate, for the most part, awareness of issues pertaining to child inclusion: the CCPT survey had little missing data on children's attendance and the service provider survey yielded a rapid response from professionals based in different organizations. As the case with a multicountry survey (Nixon et al., 2005), the responses to both North Carolina surveys also point to inconsistent inclusion of children at the meetings.

The CCPT survey used the term "attend" with 57% of the teams checking *often* on children's attendance. The service provider survey used the more precise language of "physically at the meeting" with only 33% of respondents saying that children were *often* present. When asked about representation by a support person, 58% of the service providers checked *often*, a comparable percentage to 57% from the CCPT survey on children attending CFT meetings. It is likely that some CCPTs considered representation of children as a form of attendance, especially since agency policies in the state encouraged but did not require that children be present.

Breaking down the results of service provider survey by agency affiliation revealed some disciplinary differences in perspectives on children's inclusion. Four groups made up 85% of the 507 service provider respondents: GAL (46%), child welfare (23%), behavioral health (8%), and juvenile justice (8%). The higher participation rates of GALs and child welfare tilted overall findings toward their experiences. Notably, GALs and child welfare, who would have been working with the same child population, were the least likely of these four groups to respond that children were *often* physically at the meetings. These findings are in line with those reported by Nixon et al. (2005) that conferences focused on child welfare matters had the least children in attendance. The service provider survey found that juvenile justice had the highest rate at 85%, probably reflecting the older ages of their charges and the focus of their meetings on the youth's behaviors. One juvenile justice court counselor simply stated, "I think the child/youth should always be present at the meetings."

GALs responded at the highest rate that children and youth were *often* represented at CFT meetings by a support person. This may reflect systemic expectations for advocacy on behalf of children in juvenile court. As one GAL stated on the survey, "I don't think that the children should be in meetings. That is why I am there. To advocate for the child (be their voice)." As found by the CCPT survey, GALs are not present at all child protection meetings and, thus, are not available always to offer such representation. Moreover, representation does not have to be an alternative to children's attending.

Practice guidance on family meeting recommends that children be accompanied by a support person of their selection to stay by them and speak for them if needed (American Humane Association and the FGDM Guidelines Committee, 2010). Children are able to select support persons whom they trust to look out for them, but as the case with other participants, support persons need preparation for the conference (Pennell & Anderson, 2005; Pennell & Burford, 1995). A somewhat different approach is to have the children accompanied by an advocate, internal or external to their family group. A British study found that the majority of children opted for an advocate independent of the family group, and the children reported that an advocate (with adequate preparation) enhanced their sense of empowerment within the family group and the professional decision-making (Dalrymple, 2002). Upholding children as participants in their own right reconfigures the convergence of family and state networks of regulation.

A Culture of Child Inclusion

Child support persons or advocates alter normative and power structures within the meetings. Having a child advocate runs counter to norms that children belong under the authority of their parents, and having a child support person challenges the role of parents, especially mothers, as necessarily providing such caring. The presence of a child advocate or support person begins to shift the power alignment so that children are more likely to express their hopes and have their hopes acknowledged. In the midst of displays of high emotions at conferences, the children's physical presence reminds the adults that the purpose of the meeting is to safeguard the children and their families (Holland & Rivett, 2008). This reminder can ease not only clashes within the family group but also among the service providers in attendance and between the family and agency systems. As a result, children gain hope by seeing important adults in their lives making responsible decisions together.

In line with international findings (Gal, 2015), both North Carolina surveys identified concerns that including children could harm them or was logistically not feasible. A point of departure from the international reports is that none of the North Carolina respondents expressed personal fears about the emotional toll that engaging the children would have on them or about their capacity to reach out to the children. It is possible that the North Carolinians felt prepared for working with the children or that they refrained from giving what might appear as a socially undesirable survey response. Hesitation about how to involve children was possibly heightened by trauma-informed training recently introduced into the state for mental health professionals, child welfare workers, and foster parents.

A trauma-informed awareness was evident in the advice of one service provider respondent from mental health: "I think it would be important for children to have someone to help process before and after the meeting. . . . in order to make sure they have not been traumatized by the meeting." The trauma-informed trainings quite rightly increased sensitivity to the emotional safety of children who have experienced adverse life events and highlighted the need to consider the unique circumstances of children's situation when involving them in CFT meetings. At the same time, trauma-informed language could be used to excuse the omission of children from forums that might have enhanced their sense of self-worth and family and community connections.

The recommendations of survey respondents point to the need for more training and resources to support the inclusion of children at the meetings. Curricular development and delivery by training teams that include youth and family partners with direct experience as service recipients can orient the workshop participants to the impact of not being included in major life decisions. This partnership training model is precisely the approach adopted by the university center to translate findings from the service provider survey into an online curriculum capable of reaching a broad audience. The transfer of learning to the workplace requires support from other systemic strategies as well.

Both the CCPT and service provider surveys raised awareness about the state's commitment to child inclusion. This commitment is endorsed by the North Carolina Collaborative for Children, Youth, and Families (2007) in its definition of CFTs that emphasizes creating plans "**with** children/youth and their families." This definition reflects the active participation of family partners in its construction and their advocacy of system-of-care approaches. Within North Carolina and more largely the United States, children's participation is upheld as a best practice rather than a right as stated in the United Nations' (1989) *Convention on the Rights of the Child*.

Legislation as in *Aotearoa* New Zealand specifies children's participation as a human right and appears to increase their attendance but is not sufficient on its own. A New Zealand review of FGCs in 2012 reaffirms the original guiding FGC principles but urges adoption of a series of recommendations to improve delivery (Nixon, 2012). The recommendations include holding more conferences to meet demand, enhancing cultural outreach particularly to Maori communities, inviting children more often to the conferences, preparing children to participate, convening conferences at child-friendly times and venues, presenting information in simpler terms to participants, and involving more comprehensively service providers required to meet the increasingly complex situations of children and their families.

These recommendations demonstrate similarities between the New Zealand and North Carolina experiences. To be effective, endorsements by respected institutions, whether local or international, need reinforcement through monitoring. Otherwise, children's participation is likely to remain inconsistent (Crampton & Pennell, 2009).

One vehicle for monitoring is the Child and Family Services Reviews conducted by the US Children's Bureau of states' child welfare systems. Among the performance measures is an item on the inclusion of parents and children in case planning. States that do not meet expectations are subject to financial penalties. Another avenue is having a case-tracking system in place for monitoring children's participation in family meetings; this would reinforce the importance of children's input and would be a way to document that the local agency is meeting federal and state expectations. Workers and their agencies, however, are likely to react to the surveillance if they are not engaged in determining corrective measures with state authorities. A third means is citizen review of child maltreatment cases to examine the extent to which children and their families are included in planning. CCPTs are the mechanism for citizen review of child welfare in North Carolina, and the annual CCPT surveys ascertain trends in what factors set children at risk and what steps can counter these risks. The expansive role of citizen review panels supports CCPTs in acting on their findings, but a common characterization of the panels as a "watchdog" can spark conflict between panels and child welfare agencies and undermine the panel's role as an asset for child welfare (Vadapalli, 2017, p. 540).

All these approaches to monitoring can be and are experienced as punitive by states and their workers and can provoke resistance, disengagement, and game playing. This does not have to be the end-result according to regulatory theorists and researchers. Engaging agencies and workers in examining the data and working out solutions together can only serve children and their families well. This is the approach of the NC CCPT Advisory Board at which community and state participants sit at the same table to exchange ideas and figure out action steps together. Moreover, this inclusive approach parallels what is desired within the family meetings.

Advancing children's inclusion, whether as a human right, a statutory requirement, an agency policy, or a best practice, necessitates continual bolstering. To sustain human services responsive to the views of children requires intersecting, system-level strategies—interagency collaborations, partnership training, process and outcome evaluation, citizen review, and performance monitoring. All of these strategies, if handled in a collaborative manner, infuse external perspectives into the child welfare system and move the system toward a multiparty system of regulation that strengthens community-state partnership.

The broad base of this system of responsive regulation is the family meeting that teaches children and adults about participatory decision-making and generates a sense of engagement, fair play, and mutual trust. Supporting children as decision-making participants in their own right redefines the convergence of family and state networks of regulation around rather than over youngsters. This redefinition has the potential to renew children's hopes and restore child-adult relationships to the ideal of Tali Gal's (2015) "culture of child participation."

References

American Humane Association and the FGDM Guidelines Committee. (2010). *Guidelines for family group decision making in child welfare.* Englewood, CO: Author. Retrieved from www.ucdenver.edu/academics/colleges/medical school/departments/pediatrics/subs/can/FGDM/FGDM_Resources/Documents/FGDM%20Guidelines.pdf.

Braithwaite, J. (2004). Families and the republic. In P. Adams (Ed.), Restorative justice, responsive regulation, and social welfare. *Journal of Sociology and Social Welfare* [Special issue], *31*(1), 199–215.

Braithwaite, V. (2017). Closing the gap between regulation and the community. In P. Drahos (Ed.), *Regulatory theory: Foundations and applications* (pp. 25–41). Canberra: ANU Press, Australian National University. Retrieved from https://press.anu.edu.au/publications/regulatory-theory/download.

Burchard, J. D., & Burchard, S. N. (2000). The wraparound process with children and families. In G. Burford & J. Hudson (Eds.), *Family group conferencing: New directions in community-centered child and family practice* (pp. 140–152). Hawthorne, NY: Aldine de Gruyter.

Collins-Camargo, C., Buckwalter, N., & Jones, B. (2016). Perceptions of state child welfare administrators regarding federally-mandated citizen review panels. *Children and Youth Services Review, 62*, 83–89. doi: 10.1016/j.childyouth.2016.01.022.

Crampton, D. S., & Pennell, J. (2009). Family-involvement meetings with older children in foster care: Intuitive appeal, promising practices and the challenge of child welfare reform. In B. Kerman, M. Freundlich, & A. N. Maluccio (Eds.), *Achieving permanence for older children and youth in foster care* (pp. 266–290). New York: Columbia University Press.

Dalrymple, J. (2002). Family group conferences and youth advocacy: The participation of children and young people in family decision making. *European Journal of Social Work, 5*(3), 287–299. doi: 10.1080/714053160.

Drahos, P., & Krygier, M. (2017). Regulation, institutions and networks. In P. Drahos (Ed.), *Regulatory theory: Foundations and applications* (pp. 1–22). Canberra: ANU Press, Australian National University. Retrieved from https://press.anu.edu.au/publications/regulatory-theory/download

Gal, T. (2015). Conclusion—From social exclusion to child-inclusive policies: Toward an ecological model of child participation. In T. Gal & B. Faedi Duramy (Eds.), *International perspectives and empirical findings on child participation: From social exclusion to child-inclusive policies* (pp. 451–463). Oxford: Oxford University Press.

Gifford, E. J., Wells, R., Bai, Y., Troop, T. O., Miller, S., & Babinski, L. (2010). Pairing nurses and social workers in schools: North Carolina's school-based child and family support teams. *Journal of School Health, 80*(2), 104–107.

Hassall, I. (1996). Origin and development of family group conferences. In J. Hudson, A. Morris, G. Maxwell, & B. Galaway (Eds.), *Family group conferences: Perspectives on policy and practice* (pp. 17–36). Monsey, NY: Willow Tree Press.

Holland, S., & Rivett, M. (2008). 'Everyone started shouting': Making connections between the process of family group conferences and family therapy practice. *British Journal of Social Work, 38*(1), 21–38.

Nixon, P. (2012). *Final recommendations on improving family group conferences to achieve better outcomes for New Zealand's most vulnerable children.* Wellington, NZ: Child, Youth and Family, Ministry of Social Development.

Nixon, P., Burford, G., & Quinn, A (with Edelbaum, J.). (2005, May). *A survey of international practices, policy & research on family group conferencing and related practices.* Retrieved June 11, 2017, from www.und.edu/dept/aquinn/fgdcreports.pdf.

North Carolina Collaborative for Children, Youth and Families [NC Collaborative]. (2007). *Child and family teams.* Retrieved July 17, 2016, from www.nccollaborative.org/wp-content/uploads/2015/05/27508.pdf.

North Carolina Community Child Protection Team Advisory Board. (2017, May). *2016 end of year report* [to North Carolina Division of Social Services]. Raleigh, NC: Author. [Prepared by J. Pennell, J. Coupet, M. Thompson, H. Benton, J. Chilton, & J. McKelvy.] Retrieved from https://drive.google.com/drive/folders/0B0QNfwmT2VNrVGtuNS1WenNURzQ.

North Carolina Division of Medical Assistance. (2013). *Enhanced mental health and substance abuse services.* Retrieved July 17, 2016, from http://trilliumhealthresources.org/pagefiles/1264/enhancedmhsu8a.pdf.

North Carolina Division of Social Services. (2009). *Family Services manual, Vol. 1. Chapter VII—Child and family team meetings.* Raleigh, NC: Author. Retrieved July 17, 2016, from https://www2.ncdhhs.gov/info/olm/manuals/dss/csm-55/man/CSVII.pdf.

Paterson, K., & Harvey, M. (1991). *An evaluation of the organization and operation of care and protection family group conferences.* Wellington, NZ: Department of Social Welfare.

Pennell, J., & Anderson, G. (Eds.). (2005). *Widening the circle: The practice and evaluation of family group conferencing with children, youths, and their families.* Washington, DC: NASW Press.

Pennell, J., & Burford, G. (1995). *Family group decision making: New roles for 'old' partners in resolving family violence: Implementation Report* (Vol. I). St. John's, NF: Memorial University of Newfoundland, School of Social Work. Retrieved from https://faculty.chass.ncsu.edu/pennell/fgdm/ImpReport/index.htm.

Rangihau, J. (1986). *Pau-te-Ata-tu (Daybreak): Report of the Ministerial Advisory Committee on a Maori perspective for the Department of Social Welfare.* Wellington, NZ: Department of Social Welfare, Government Printing Office.

Stroul, B. A., & Friedman, R. M. (1986). *A system of care for severely emotionally disturbed children and youth.* Washington, DC: Georgetown University Child Development Center, CASSP Technical Assistance Center.

United Nations, General Assembly. (2008). *Declaration on the rights of indigenous peoples.* Geneva, Switzerland: 107th Plenary Meeting. Retrieved July 10, 2016, from www.un.org/esa/socdev/unpfii/documents/DRIPS_en.pdf.

United Nations, Office of the High Commissioner for Human Rights. (1989). *Convention on the rights of the child.* Retrieved July 10, 2016, from www.unhchr.ch/html/menu3/b/k2crc.htm.

Vadapalli, D. K. (2017). Citizen review panels in child protection: Misunderstood, neglected, and underutilized. *Children and Youth Services Review, 79,* 539–546. doi: 10.1016/j.childyouth.2017.07.008.

van Wormer, K. S., & Walker, L. (Eds.). (2013). *Restorative justice today: Practical applications.* Los Angeles, CA: Sage Publications.

Zinsstag, E., & Vanfraechem, I. (Eds.). (2012). *Conferencing and restorative justice: International practices and perspectives.* Oxford: Oxford University Press.

8

BLACK MOTHERS, PRISON, AND FOSTER CARE

Rethinking Restorative Justice

Dorothy E. Roberts

Introduction

This chapter has three overarching aims. First, I examine the case of black mothers involved in the prison and foster care systems as possible subjects of a restorative justice framework. Second, by examining the case of black mothers, I want to think more broadly and critically about the meaning of restorative justice. Who are the victims and who needs to make amends? Who needs to be reconciled and who should be held accountable? To whom should justice be restored? Finally, I call on scholars and advocates to imagine a restorative justice approach that goes beyond reforming the carceral state to fundamentally transforming the meaning of justice for black mothers and then, perhaps, the meaning of restorative justice itself.

The U.S. prison and foster care systems are marked by glaring race, gender, and class disparities: the populations in both systems are disproportionately poor and black and poor black mothers are overinvolved in both systems (Richie, 2002; Roberts, 2002). In 2010, about one-third of children in foster care were black and most had been removed from black mothers who were their primary caretakers (US Department of Health and Human Services, 2011). About one-third of women in prison were black and most were the primary caretakers of their children (Glaze & Maruschak, 2010).

This statistical similarity is striking, but its significance is not self-evident. Some see the disproportionate number of black mothers involved in prison and foster care as the unfortunate result of their disadvantaged living conditions. Others argue that the statistical disparities in both systems reflect the appropriate response to black mothers' antisocial conduct that puts their children and the larger society at risk of harm. Some do not perceive a relationship between the two systems because prisons inflict punishment whereas child welfare agencies provide services. However, both prisons and foster care have been sites for restorative justice (Harris, Braithwaite, & Ivec, 2009; Morrison, 2002; Toews & Harris, 2010). A restorative justice approach has been applied to reconcile incarcerated people, as well as parents accused of child maltreatment, with the victims of their wrongdoing and with their communities.

In my view, the prison and foster care systems work together to monitor, regulate, and punish black mothers in ways that help to extend an unjust carceral state: they help to preserve social inequality in

DOI: 10.4324/9780429398704-8

a neoliberal age of shrinking social programs and increasing government surveillance (Crenshaw, 2012; Roberts, 2012). This particular systemic intersection penalizes the most marginalized women in our society while blaming them for their own disadvantaged position. Given the role prison and foster care play in black mothers' lives, what role can restorative justice play? Can restorative justice address these women's needs and redress the suffering they have experienced resulting from their involvement in these systems? Can restorative justice provide a way not to reconcile these women within these systems but to liberate them from these systems?

Black Mothers in the Prison and Foster Care Systems

Over the last several decades, the United States, as well as other nations, has embarked on a pervasive form of governance known as neoliberalism that transfers services from the welfare state to the private realm of family and market while promoting the free market conditions conducive to capital accumulation (Harvey, 2007). Neoliberalism, however, does not entail solely a unidimensional "combination of market competition, privatized institutions, and decentred, *at-a-distance* forms of state regulation" (Braithwaite, 2000, emphasis added). At the same time that governments are dismantling the social safety net, they have intensified their coercive interventions in poor communities, especially communities of color. The welfare, prison, foster care, and deportation systems have all become extremely punitive mechanisms for regulating residents of the very neighborhoods most devastated by the evisceration of public resources (Di Leonardo, 2008; Giroux, 2004; Wacquant, 2009). These neoliberal forces of privatization and punishment operate within and in support of a racist and sexist political order that makes black mothers especially vulnerable to carceral regulation. Thus, the prison, welfare, and child welfare systems became more punitive since the 1970s as black mothers made up increasing shares of their populations (Mink, 2002; Roberts, 2002). Moreover, calls to expand these systems' punitive functions were based on myths about black mothers' reckless sexuality and childbearing (Collins, 2000; Haley, 2016; Harris-Perry, 2011; Roberts, 1997). In short, prison and foster care became intertwined aspects of an expanding carceral state that relies on the devaluation of black mothers.

Black Mothers Involved in Prison

Since the 1970s, law enforcement policies in the United States have caused an astronomical rise in the rate of incarceration that surpasses that of any other democracy in history and any other nation in the world today (Hartney, 2006; O'connor, 2014; Wagner & Rabuy, 2017). With more than 2 million people locked up in state and federal prisons and jails and 3.7 million people on probation, the United States leads the world in carceral control of citizens (Wagner & Rabuy, 2017). The incarceration rate of black men is especially staggering: 6 percent of black men ages 30–39 were imprisoned in 2014—six times the rate of white men (Carson, 2015). Numerous scholars have demonstrated that mass incarceration serves as a "new Jim Crow" that institutionalizes black political subordination (Alexander, 2012; A. Y. Davis, 2011; Gilmore, 2007; Hinton, 2016). Locking up enormous numbers of black people interferes with their democratic participation by robbing them of voting power, material resources, social networks, and legitimacy required for full political citizenship and for organizing local institutions to contest repressive policies (Roberts, 2004).

Women are the fastest-growing segment of the prison population in the United States and black female incarceration rates are the highest among women (Geer, 2000). There was an 828 percent increase in the number of black women behind bars for drug offenses between 1986 and 1991 (Geer, 2000). For most of incarcerated women, prison constitutes a culminating victimization that results from multiple forms of vulnerability and violation, including domestic violence, sexual abuse, drug addiction and other health problems, and homelessness (Richie, 1996, 2012). U.S. law enforcement treats the health problem of drug addiction as a criminal offense and black women are the most vulnerable to this inhumane approach (Zerai & Banks, 2002). Mothers who depend on public assistance to care for their children are increasingly treated as criminals—welfare fraud, for example, is now a felony offense instead of an administrative violation (Gustafson, 2012). Thousands of black women in prison today—mostly for nonviolent offenses—need treatment for substance abuse, support for their children, or safety from an abusive relationship, not criminal punishment.

Most incarcerated women are mothers who were the primacy caretakers of their children (Glaze & Maruschak, 2010). While judges used to show mothers leniency, they are now more often compelled by mandatory sentencing laws to give mothers prison terms. As a result, the number of children with a mother in prison nearly doubled between 1991 and 2007 (Glaze & Maruschak, 2010). Owing to racial disparities in the U.S. incarceration rate, 7 percent of black children had a parent in prison in 1999, making them nearly nine times more likely to have an incarcerated parent than white children (Glaze & Maruschak, 2010). By age 14, one in four black children, born in 1990, had a parent imprisoned, compared with one in 25 white children (Wildeman, 2009).

Black Mothers Involved in Foster Care

The prison system's regulation of black mothers is intensified by these very same women's disproportionate involvement in the foster care system. Before the civil rights movement, black children were disproportionately excluded from openly segregated child welfare services that catered mainly to white families (Billingsley & Giovannoni, 1972). Yet by 2000, black children made up the largest group of children in foster care (Roberts, 2002). A black child was four times as likely as a white child to be in the foster care system. Black children are still grossly overrepresented: even though they represent only 15 percent of the nation's children, they make up 30 percent of the nation's foster care population (United States Department of Health and Human Services, 2011). In some cities and states, the disparity is much greater. Child protection in many large cities functions mainly to monitor, regulate, and disrupt minority families.

Most children in foster care were forcibly removed from their mothers by state agents. These mothers are then intensely supervised by child welfare authorities as they comply with agency requirements in order to be reunified with their children (Lee, 2016; Roberts, 2002). Failing to meet these requirements is grounds to terminate their parental rights. This state intrusion is typically viewed as necessary to protect maltreated children from parental harm. But placement of children in foster care is usually linked to poverty, racial injustice, and inadequate state supports for struggling families (Briggs, 2012; Lee, 2016; Roberts, 2002).

Policies and programs that focus on rehabilitating mothers pay little attention to the political function of massive state removal of black children from their families. The racial disparity in the child welfare system reflects a political choice to address the startling rates of child poverty by investigating mothers instead of tackling poverty's societal roots (Roberts, 2002). It is no accident that child welfare philosophy became increasingly punitive as black children made up a greater and greater share of the caseloads. Since the 1970s, the number of children receiving child welfare services in their homes has declined dramatically, while the foster care population has skyrocketed (Roberts, 2002). As the child welfare system began to serve fewer white children and more black children, state and federal governments spent more money on out-of-home care and less on in-home services.

Congress's restructuring of welfare in 1996, ending the entitlement to public aid, coincided with the passage of the Adoption and Safe Families Act in 1997, which emphasized adoption as the solution to the rising foster care population (Roberts, 2002). Both were neoliberal measures that shifted government support for families toward reliance on low-wage work, marriage, and adoptive parents to meet the needs of children living in poverty (Mink, 2002; Smith, 2007). This coincidence marked the first time the federal government mandated that states protect children from abuse and neglect without a corresponding mandate to provide basic economic support to poor families (Courtney, 1998). Both systems, then, responded to a growing black female clientele by reducing services to families while intensifying their punitive functions. The main mission of child welfare departments became protecting children not from social disadvantage but from maltreatment inflicted by their mothers. Moreover, as neoliberal policies deprived poor black neighborhoods of needed services, residents increasingly were forced to rely on child welfare agencies' provision of family support that hinges on charges of child maltreatment and relinquishment of child custody to the state (Roberts, 2008).

This punitive foster care approach, like that of prisons, is legitimized by stereotypes of black maternal unfitness. In a qualitative study of Michigan's child welfare system, the Center for the Study of Social Policy Racial Equity Review discovered that many social workers negatively characterized or labeled African American families, mothers, and youth in particular and failed to fairly assess or appreciate their unique strengths and weaknesses (Center for the Study of Social Policy, 2009). For example, social workers often assumed that black parents had substance abuse problems without making similar assumptions about white parents. The report concluded, "The belief that African American children are better off away from their families and communities was seen in explicit statements by key policy makers and service providers. It was also reflected in choices made by [the Department of Human Services]" (Center for the Study of Social Policy, 2009, p. ii).

One of these discriminatory choices is for caseworkers to be more aggressive in their decision to remove black children from their homes rather than provide services to their families. A study of the intersection of race, poverty, and risk in removal decisions concluded that the racial disparity occurred because it takes more risk of maltreatment for a white child to be placed in foster care compared to the risk for a black child (Detlaff et al., 2011; Rivaux et al., 2008). This devaluation of the bonds between black children and their mothers discounts the harm inflicted on both parties when the children are removed from their homes.

The child welfare system's punishment of black mothers helps to perpetuate a neoliberal response to caregiving that relies on individual parents' private resources instead of public support for families. By attributing poor black families' hardships to maternal deficits, the child welfare system hides their systemic causes, devalues black children's bonds with their families, and prescribes foster care and adoption in place of social change and services. Casting black children's need for services as the fault of abusive mothers avoids confronting racism in the child welfare system and in the broader society—while discounting the harms inflicted on children by unnecessarily separating them from their families.

System Intersection

Prisons and foster care function together to discipline and control poor and low-income black women by keeping them under intense state supervision and blaming them for the hardships their families face as a result of societal inequities. Stereotypes of black maternal irresponsibility that fueled more punitive forms of public aid to families converge with stereotypes of black female criminality that support mass incarceration. As Angela Davis observes, the prison-industrial complex "relies on racialized assumptions of criminality—such as *images of black welfare mothers reproducing criminal children*—and on racist practices in arrest, conviction, and sentencing patterns" (A. Davis, 1998, p. 12). Together, these disparaging myths about black mothers form an ideological scaffold for an expanding carceral state.

These punitive systems intersect in the lives of black mothers when prison and foster care policies make it extremely difficult for incarcerated women to retain legal custody of their children. When their children are placed in out-of-home care, incarcerated mothers face obstacles to maintaining contact with them and to meeting other requirements imposed by child protective services. As Ronnie Halperin and Jennifer L. Harris note, "To avoid having their parental rights terminated, incarcerated women, like their counterparts in the community, must participate in case planning, remain involved in their children's lives, and demonstrate their commitment and ability to reform, typically by enrolling in corrective programs as set forth in the case plan" (Halperin & Harris, 2004, p. 340). But the conditions of incarceration coupled with prison and child welfare policies make it 'virtually impossible' to meet these requirements from behind bars (Halperin & Harris, 2004; Hager & Flagg, 2018).

A chief threat to reunification is the difficulty of visiting with children while in prison. Jails and prisons have "elaborate and time-consuming" visitation procedures, including requirements for prior notification, and caseworkers must arrange transportation and supervision of children in care during visits (Ross, Khashu, & Wamsley, 2004). As a result of all these obstacles to visitation with their children, more than half of all mothers in prison receive no visits at all from their children (Halperin & Harris, 2004). Incarcerated mothers then risk permanently losing custody of their children because it is considered in a child's best interests not to wait for his or her mother's release to have a stable family life. Judges often construe a mother's failure to visit with her child as abandonment and grounds for terminating parental rights.

Even when incarcerated mothers are able to keep legal custody of their children, the collateral penalties inflicted on them pose affirmative barriers to maintaining a relationship with their children once they are released from prison. A host of state and federal laws impose draconian obstacles to a mother's successful reentry in her community by denying drug offenders public benefits, housing, education, and job opportunities and barring formerly incarcerated women from many occupations held predominantly by women, such as childcare workers, certified nurse's aides, and beauticians (Brown, 2010). For many incarcerated mothers, the convergence of prison and foster care, without guaranteed public aid, means losing custody of their children permanently.

Appling Restorative Justice to Black Mothers

The experiences of black mothers involved in the prison and foster care systems force us to critically examine restorative justice analysis. Restorative justice breaks away from the retributive paradigm that punishes past wrongdoing to focus instead on "making the future safer" by reconciling offending and victimized individuals to each other and/or to their communities (Braithwaite, 2000, p. 230; Strang, 2002; Zehr, 2005). The dominant conception of restorative justice is a form of mediation that resolves individual conflicts between offenders, victims, and other community members (Braithwaite, 2000; Zehr, 2005) or shaming that reintegrates offenders into the community and encourages future compliance with the law (Braithwaite, 1989; Tyler et al., 2007). As Ivec, Braithwaite, and Harris have noted, "the central idea of restorative justice is to talk through the harm and use the strengths of individuals in the group, including the perpetrator(s) of the harm, to make amends" (2012, p. 98).

The restorative justice paradigm is better suited than the retributive paradigm for addressing black mothers' involvement in the prison and foster care systems because it focuses on needs rather than punishment and extends beyond individuals to include the community. However, the dominant conception of restorative justice falls short of the paradigm's radical potential. Applied to the criminal justice and child welfare systems, the central idea of restorative justice, as currently conceived, reconciles people who have committed crimes and parents who have maltreated their children with the victims of their wrongdoing. Under this framework, restorative justice might entail developing programs within these systems to help black mothers to be better mothers. The goal is to reform these systems so they can better facilitate repairing relationships between individual offending mothers and those they have harmed (Armour & Sliva, 2018).

Recognizing the role institutionalized discrimination and violence play in the prison and foster care systems changes the identities of perpetrator and victim. What does restorative justice mean for black mothers when they themselves have been victimized by these systems? What does it mean to "restore" these mothers when the systems that are supposed to administer justice actually promote societal structures and ideologies that oppress them? Dominant conceptions of restorative justice fail to address these questions and therefore do not differ radically enough from the retributive approach (Riley, 2017). If restorative justice seeks to restore justice to victims of violence, then the state should make amends to black mothers as much as help black mothers make amends for any harm they committed. Surely, what black mothers and their families have suffered at the hands of the state far outweighs any damage most of these mothers have caused. Ironically, a study of gender-specific factors in restorative justice in England and Wales noted that, because women are more likely than men to commit nonviolent "victimless" crimes, such as shoplifting, there may be fewer opportunities for them to participate in restorative conferencing (Masson & Österman, 2017).

The carceral systems of prison and foster care and their histories of racist state violence are not simply the background context in which restorative justice operates or the mechanisms that provide resources to the parties involved in the reconciliation process. Rather, these systems are themselves sources of injustice that a restorative justice paradigm should contest and ultimately help to dismantle.

Transforming Restorative Justice

Restorative justice for black mothers involved in the prison and foster care systems requires that we hold the institutions themselves accountable for their role in systematic harm to the individuals involved. Carceral systems cannot be viewed as the backdrop or facilitators; dismantling them must be at the very center of efforts to achieve justice for the most marginalized groups, including black mothers. Instead of asking the state to help black mothers to be better mothers, restorative justice should demand that the state end its systematic violence against them. Restorative justice does not require reforming carceral institutions but abolishing them (A. Y. Davis, 2011; Riley, 2017; Roberts, 2017). Family group decision making and feminist anti-carceral approaches to domestic violence provide helpful insights into how restorative justice might focus on dismantling unjust carceral systems.

Family Group Decision Making

To a large extent, contemporary U.S. social policy has written off the most disadvantaged families and the communities they belong to and subjected them to carceral remedies. Family group decision making (FGDM) can be part of the resistance to these policies of shrinking supports and intensified punishment. FGDM gives voice to those families and communities: it respects what they have to say rather than imposing authoritarian requirements on them; it capitalizes on their strengths rather than scrutinizing their deficits; it aims to support them rather than tear them apart (American Humane, 2013; Crampton, 2007; Merkel-Holguin, n.d.). Countering the way coercive state supervision of black mothers contradicts a democratic relationship between communities and government, the practice of FGDM promotes the democratic ideals of voice, freedom, equality, and respect. Moreover, research has shown that FGDM can reduce the disruptive impact child welfare systems have on families by decreasing the placement of children in foster care, increasing the numbers placed with relatives, and increasing exits of children from out-of-home care to reunification (Lambert, Johnson, & Wang, 2017; Merkel-Holguin, Nixon, & Burford, 2003; Pennell, Edwards, & Burford, 2010).

FGDM, however, is typically a supplement rather than an alternative to the investigative, regulatory, and punitive dimensions of the child welfare system (Feldman, 2017). In resolving the individual conflicts that led to the family's involvement with state child protection authorities, FGDM may not attend to the institutionalized forces that made the family vulnerable to investigation in the first place. Indeed, state authorities may see taking systemic injustice into account as interfering with the reconciliation process because it relieves parents from taking sufficient responsibility for their own behavior. Moreover, FGDM may give families a limited voice in crafting remedies for their needs without any authority or resources to implement their views. In order for FGDM to reach its potential, we must develop ways of engaging in this practice both inside and outside the confines of prison and foster care to contest these systems themselves and envision more equitable and humane institutions to meet families' needs. By facilitating nonpunitive dialogue, a restorative justice model could potentially enable black mothers currently identified as offenders and those identified as the victims and communities they have harmed to see their common oppression by carceral systems and to work together to dismantle them.

A Feminist Anti-Carceral Approach to Domestic Violence

Black and other women of color feminists have developed a sophisticated analysis of state protection and state punishment that moves beyond victimization to resistance (Roberts, 2014). Their radical approach to domestic abuse starts from the premise that policies to protect black women must address intimate and institutional violence simultaneously and therefore cannot rely on state systems, such as police, prisons, and foster care, which themselves unjustly target black communities for violence (INCITE!, 2016). Kristine Riley has similarly criticized the current entanglement of restorative justice and the criminal justice system in interventions into the sex trade, proposing an "intersectional feminist praxis" that "operates independently of the justice systems" (Riley, 2017, p. 1168). The anti-carceral approach situates family violence within a broader context of state violence against black people, as well as inequitable social structures, including male domination but also barriers created by poverty, racism, and government policies that trap many women in violent homes (Smith et al., 2006). Anti-carceral feminists have tied domestic violence to a continuum of social and state violence that, to quote Angela Davis again, "extends from the sweatshops through the prisons, to shelters, and into bedrooms at home" (A. Davis, 2000, p. 2).

These scholars and activists have cautioned against participating in a criminal justice regime that incarcerates astronomical numbers of black men, women, and children, causing devastating consequences to their families and communities. Moreover, black women are at heightened risk of being victimized by police brutality, including when they seek protection against violence in their homes

(Ritchie, 2017). At the same time, state and federal governments have refused to allocate similar resources to programs and services that would make women less vulnerable to violence. As noted above, "tough on crime" post-conviction penalties, such as federal lifetime bans on receiving welfare benefits, post-secondary financial aid, and public housing, intensify the vulnerability of formerly incarcerated women.

This anti-carceral analysis points to developing restorative justice strategies that can contest multiple, intersecting forms of systemic injustice and can develop collective efforts within communities to address private violence—efforts that rely on the strengths and accountability of community members rather than on punitive state intervention. This approach also insists on the accountability of the state for perpetrating institutionalized violence on marginalized communities.

Conclusion

By replacing the retributive paradigm with concern for people's needs, communities, and desire for reconciliation, restorative justice holds potential for contesting the expanding carceral state that strips the most marginalized communities of needed resources while subjecting them to increasingly punitive forms of control. Dominant conceptions of restorative justice, however, fail to meet this potential because they do not account for institutionalized discrimination, surveillance, and violence perpetrated by the very state systems relied on for restorative processes. I have argued that centering the experiences of black mothers in the prison and foster care systems can help us rethink the restorative justice approach. Rather than treat these women as offenders who need to make amends to their families and communities, restorative justice should hold the state accountable for harming all of them. Family group decision making and feminist anti-carceral approaches to domestic violence provide helpful insights into how we might develop a restorative justice framework that contributes to dismantling unjust carceral systems and creating an equitable and humane society.

References

Alexander, M. (2012). *The new Jim Crow: Mass incarceration in the age of colorblindness*. New York: The New Press.

American Humane. (2013). Promising results, potential new directions: International FGDM research and evaluation in child welfare. *Protecting Children, 18*(1–2).

Armour, M., & Sliva, S. (2018). How does it work? Mechanisms of action in an in-prison restorative justice program. *International Journal of Offender Therapy and Comparative Criminology, 62*(3), 759–784. https://doi.org/10.1177/0306624X16669143.

Billingsley, A., & Giovannoni, J. M. (1972). *Children of the storm: Black children and American child welfare*. New York: Harcourt, Brace, Jovanovich.

Braithwaite, J. (1989). *Crime, shame and reintegration*. Cambridge: Cambridge University Press.

Braithwaite, J. (2000). The new regulatory state and the transformation of criminology. *The British Journal of Criminology, 40*(2), 222–238. https://doi.org/10.1093/bjc/40.2.222.

Briggs, L. (2012). *Somebody's children: The politics of transnational and transracial adoption*. Durham, NC: Duke University Press.

Brown, G. (2010). The intersectionality of race, gender, and reentry: Challenges for African-American women. *American Constitution Society for Law and Policy*, 1–18.

Carson, E. A. (2015). *Bureau of Justice Statistics (BJS)—Prisoners in 2014* (Prisoners). Washington, DC: U.S Dept. of Justice, Bureau of Justice Statistics. Retrieved from www.bjs.gov/index.cfm?ty=pbdetail&iid=5387.

Center for the Study of Social Policy. (2009). *Race equity review. Findings from a qualitative analysis of racial disproportionality & disparity for African American children & families in Michigan's child welfare system*. Michigan Race Equity

Review. Retrieved from https://ncwwi.org/index.php/resource-library-search/resource-topics/cultural-responsiveness-disproportionality/item/885-race-equity-review-findings-from-a-qualitative-analysis-of-racial-disproportionality-disparity-for-african-american-children-families-in-michigan-s-child-welfare-system.

Collins, P. H. (2000). *Black feminist thought: Knowledge, consciousness, and the politics of empowerment.* New York: Routledge.

Courtney, M. E. (1998). The costs of child protection in the context of welfare reform. *The Future of Children, 8*(1), 88–103.

Crampton, D. (2007). Research review: Family group decision-making: A promising practice in need of more programme theory and research. *Child & Family Social Work, 12*(2), 202–209. https://doi.org/10.1111/j.1365-2206.2006.00442.x.

Crenshaw, K. W. (2012). From private violence to mass incarceration: Thinking intersectionally about women, race, and social control. *UCLA Law Review, 59,* 1418–1472.

Davis, A. (1998). Masked racism: Reflections on the prison industrial complex. *Colorlines.* Retrieved from www.colorlines.com/articles/masked-racism-reflections-prison-industrial-complex.

Davis, A. (2000). The color of violence against women. *Colorlines, 3*(3). Retrieved from www.colorlines.com/articles/color-violence-against-women.

Davis, A. Y. (2011). *Are prisons obsolete?* New York: Seven Stories Press.

Detlaff, A. J., Rivaux, S. L., Baumann, D. J., Fluke, J. D., Rycraft, J. R., & James, J. (2011). Disentangling substantiation: The influence of race, income, and risk on the substantiation decision in child welfare. *Children and Youth Services Review, 33*(9), 1630–1637. https://doi.org/10.1016/j.childyouth.2011.04.005.

Di Leonardo, M. (2008). Introduction: New global and American landscapes of inequality. In J. L. Collins, M. Di Leonardo, & B. Williams (Eds.), *New landscapes of inequality: Neoliberalism and the erosion of democracy in America* (pp. 3–20). Santa Fe, NM: School for Advanced Research Press.

Feldman, L. H. (2017). Using family group decision making to assist informal kinship families. *Child Welfare, 95*(4), 41–67.

Geer, M. (2000). Human rights and wrongs in our own backyard: Incorporating international human rights protections under domestic civil rights law—A case study of women in the United States prisons. *Scholarly Works, 388.* Retrieved from http://scholars.law.unlv.edu/facpub/388.

Gilmore, R. W. (2007). *Golden gulag: Prisons, surplus, crisis, and opposition in globalizing California.* Berkeley, CA/Los Angeles, CA: University of California Press.

Giroux, H. A. (2004). Public pedagogy and politic of neo-liberalism: Making the political more pedagogical. *Policy Futures in Education, 2*(3–4), 494–503.

Glaze, L. E., & Maruschak, L. M. (2010). *Parents in prison and their minor children* (Bureau of Justice Statistics Special Report No. NCJ 222984) (p. 21). Washington, DC: U.S. Department of Justice. Retrieved from www.bjs.gov/index.cfm?ty=pbdetail&iid=823.

Gustafson, K. S. (2012). *Cheating welfare: Public assistance and the criminalization of poverty.* New York: New York University Press.

Hager, E., & Flagg, A. (2018). *How incarcerated parents are losing their children forever.* New York: The Marshall Project. Retrieved from https://www.themarshallproject.org/2018/12/03/how-incarcerated-parents-are-losing-their-children-forever.

Haley, S. (2016). *No Mercy here: Gender, punishment, and the making of Jim Crow modernity.* Chapel Hill, NC: UNC Press Books.

Halperin, R., & Harris, J. L. (2004). Parental rights of incarcerated mothers with children in foster care: A policy vacuum. *Feminist Studies, 30*(2), 339–352. https://doi.org/10.2307/20458967.

Harris, N., Braithwaite, V., & Ivec, M. (2009). Rejoinder: A responsive approach to child protection. *Children and Families Australia, 4*(1), 69–75.

Harris-Perry, M. (2011). *Sister citizen: Shame, stereotypes, and black women in America.* New Haven, CT: Yale University Press.

Hartney, C. (2006). *US rates of incarceration: A global perspective* (p. 8). Madison, WI: National Council on Crime and Delinquency. Retrieved from www.nccdglobal.org/publications/us-rates-of-incarceration-a-global-perspective focus.

Harvey, D. (2007). *A brief history of neoliberalism*. Oxford: Oxford University Press.

Hinton, E. (2016). *From the war on poverty to the war on crime*. Cambridge: Harvard University Press.

Ivec, M., Braithwaite, V., & Harris, N. (2012). 'Resetting the relationship' in Indigenous child protection: Public hope and private reality. *Law and Policy, 34*(1), 80–103.

INCITE!. (Ed.). (2016). *Color of violence: The INCITE! anthology*. Durham, NC: Duke University Press. Retrieved from www.incite-national.org/page/color-violence-incite-anthology.

Lambert, M. C., Johnson, L. E., & Wang, E. W. (2017). The impact of family group decision-making on preventing removals. *Children and Youth Services Review, 78*(C), 89–92.

Lee, T. (2016). *Catching a case: Inequality and fear in New York City's child welfare system*. New Brunswick, NJ: Rutgers University Press.

Masson, I., & Österman, L. (2017). Working with female offenders in restorative justice frameworks: Effective and ethical practice. *Probation Journal, 64*(4), 354–371. https://doi.org/10.1177/0264550517728784.

Merkel-Holguin, L. (n.d.). *What is FGDM?* (Putting Families Back into the Child Protection Partnership: Family Group Decision Making). Washington, DC: American Humane Association, National Center on Family Group Decision Making.

Merkel-Holguin, L., Nixon, P., & Burford, G. (2003). Learning with families: A synopsis of FGDM research and evaluation in child welfare. *Protecting Children, 18*(1–2), 2–11.

Mink, G. (2002). *Welfare's end*. Ithaca, NY: Cornell University Press.

Morrison, B. (2002). Bullying and victimisation in schools: A restorative justice approach. *Australian Institute of Criminology,* (219), 1–6.

O'Connor, R. (2014, May 1). *The United States prison system: A comparative analysis*. Thesis, Tampa, FL: University of South Florida. Retrieved from http://scholarcommons.usf.edu/etd/5086.

Pennell, J., Edwards, M., & Burford, G. (2010). Expedited family group engagement and child permanency. *Children and Youth Services Review, 32*(7), 1012–1019.

Richie, B. E. (1996). *Compelled to crime: The gender entrapment of battered black women*. New York: Routledge.

Richie, B. E. (2002). The social impact of mass incarceration on women. In M. Chesney-Lind & M. Mauer (Eds.), *Invisible punishment: The collateral consequences of mass imprisonment* (pp. 136–149). New York: The New Press.

Richie, B. E. (2012). *Arrested justice: Black women, violence, and America's prison nation*. New York: New York University Press.

Riley, K. (2017). Empowering justice: An intersectional feminist perspective on restorative justice in the sex trade. *American Journal of Economics and Sociology, 76*(5), 1157–1190. https://doi.org/10.1111/ajes.12204.

Ritchie, A. J. (2017). *Invisible no more: Police violence against black women and women of color*. Boston, MA: Beacon Press.

Rivaux, S. L., James, J., Wittenstrom, K., Baumann, D., Sheets, J., Henry, J., & Jeffries, V. (2008). The intersection of race, poverty and risk: Understanding the decision to provide services to clients and to remove children. *Child Welfare, 87*(2), 151–168.

Roberts, D. E. (1997). *Killing the black body: Race, reproduction, and the meaning of liberty*. New York: Pantheon Books.

Roberts, D. E. (2002). *Shattered bonds: The color of child welfare*. New York: Basic Books.

Roberts, D. E. (2004). The social and moral cost of mass incarceration in African American communities. *Stanford Law Review, 56*(5), 1271–1305.

Roberts, D. E. (2008). The racial geography of child welfare: Toward a new research paradigm. *Child Welfare, 87*(2), 125–150.

Roberts, D. E. (2012). Prison, foster care, and the systemic punishment of black mothers. *UCLA Law Review, 59*, 1474.

Roberts, D. E. (2014). Complicating the triangle of race, class and state: The insights of black feminists. *Ethnic and Racial Studies, 37*(10), 1776–1782.

Roberts, D. E. (2017). Democratizing criminal law as an abolitionist project. *Northwestern University Law Review*, *111*(6), 1597–1608.

Ross, T., Khashu, A., & Wamsley, M. (2004). *Hard data on hard times: An empirical analysis of maternal incarceration, foster care, and visitation* (pp. 1–19). New York: Vera Institute of Justice. Retrieved from www.vera.org/publications/hard-data-on-hard-times-an-empirical-analysis-of-maternal-incarceration-foster-care-and-visitation.

Smith, A. M. (2007). *Welfare reform and sexual regulation*. Cambridge: Cambridge University Press.

Smith, A., Richie, B. E., Sudbury, J., & White, J. (2006). *The color of violence: INCITE! Anthology*. Cambridge, MA: South End Press.

Strang, H. (2002). *Repair or revenge: Victims and restorative justice*. Oxford: Clarendon Press.

Toews, B., & Harris, M. K. (2010). Restorative justice in prisons. In E. Beck, N. P. Kropf, & P. B. Leonard (Eds.), *Social work and restorative justice: Skills for dialogue, peacemaking, and reconciliation* (pp. 118–148). New York: Oxford University Press.

Tyler, T. R., Sherman, L., Strang, H., Barnes, G. C., & Woods, D. (2007). Reintegrative shaming, procedural justice, and recidivism: The engagement of offenders' psychological mechanisms in the Canberra RISE drinking-and-driving experiment. *Law & Society Review*, *41*(3), 553–585.

US Department of Health and Human Services. (2011). *The AFCARS report preliminary FY 2010 estimates as of June 2011* (The AFCARS Report). U.S. Department of Health and Human Services, Administration for Children and Families, Administration on Children, Youth and Families, Children's Bureau. Retrieved from www.acf.hhs.gov/sites/default/files/cb/afcarsreport18.pdf.

Wacquant, L. (2009). *Punishing the poor: The neoliberal government of social insecurity*. Durham, NC: Duke University Press.

Wagner, P., & Rabuy, B. (2017). *Mass incarceration: The whole pie 2017*. Northampton, MA: Prison Policy Initiative. Retrieved from www.prisonpolicy.org/reports/pie2018.html.

Wildeman, C. (2009). Parental imprisonment, the prison boom, and the concentration of childhood disadvantage. *Demography*, *46*(2), 265–280.

Zehr, H. (2005). *Changing lenses: A new focus for crime and justice* (3rd ed.). Scottdale, PA: Herald Press.

Zerai, A., & Banks, R. (2002). *Dehumanizing discourse, anti-drug law, and policy in America: A "crack mother's" nightmare*. London, UK: Ashgate.

9

RESPONDING RESTORATIVELY TO STUDENT MISCONDUCT AND PROFESSIONAL REGULATION

The Case of Dalhousie Dentistry

Jennifer J. Llewellyn

Introduction

I write this chapter on the relationship between restorative justice and responsive regulation on the third anniversary of a case that embodies their relationship in all its complexity and promise.

On December 16, 2014, four female fourth-year students in the Faculty of Dentistry at Dalhousie University in Halifax, Nova Scotia, Canada, brought forward complaints under the University's Sexual Harassment Policy about offensive materials posted on a private Facebook group site (called the "Gentleman's Club" Facebook group) by 13 male members of their class. The women's complaints were not limited to the posted materials but concerned the climate and culture at the Faculty reflected in, and perpetuated by, the posts. The women chose to proceed with their complaints through a restorative justice process available as an informal resolution option under Dalhousie University's Sexual Harassment Policy. All 13 men initially agreed voluntarily to participate in the restorative justice process selected by the complainants to investigate and try to resolve the matter. Ultimately, 12 of the 13 identified Facebook members followed through on their agreement and participated in restorative justice. The Faculty of Dentistry and the University also agreed to participate fully in the restorative justice process related to the climate and culture aspects of the complaints.

The restorative process ran intensively for almost five months, concluding successfully on May 6, 2015. It was an integrative response to the many aspects of the Facebook situation: professional regulation, educational discipline, and institutional and professional climate and culture. As the familiar metaphoric representation of restorative justice indicates, this process required as restorative justice pioneer Howard Zehr (2005) so profoundly sets out, a changing of the lenses commonly employed to address such issues to allow the light and depth required for relational seeing and knowing. Through such a lens we can see restorative justice and responsive regulation woven together in the response at Dalhousie.

Restorative Justice and Responsive Regulation: Responding to Relational Complexity

Before looking at the Dalhousie example further, it is important to consider the nature of the relationship between restorative justice and responsive regulation it illustrates. The relationship is a reciprocal

DOI: 10.4324/9780429398704-9

one whereby each requires the other to be fully realized. John Braithwaite's (2002) ground-breaking work identified restorative justice practices as promising and essential elements in responsive regulation. This is true but restorative justice offers more to responsive regulation than effective practice foundational to the responsive regulation pyramid (Braithwaite, 2002, pp. 30–34). The modern development of restorative justice began as practical reforms to justice processes aimed at greater participation and empowerment of affected parties, including victims, offenders, their support communities, and the wider connected communities. These practical reforms took hold in response to the perceived failures of criminal justice often absent or ahead of research and theory. The evolution of restorative justice, oriented in response to the urgent needs of individuals, groups, and communities failed by the traditional justice system, has had a lasting impact on the understanding of restorative justice. Most accounts of restorative justice now ground it as a way of seeing crime and criminal harms—as an idea or an approach. The implications of this conceptual underpinning have, however, been limited, for the most part, to explaining or advocating for the use of its practices. This leaves untapped the potential of restorative justice as a theory of justice to affect our understanding of justice itself and the structures, systems, and institutions through which it is pursued. It is this broader notion of restorative justice that is key to fully appreciate the relationship with responsive regulation. From this starting point, restorative justice is not merely strategic practice for compliance within a responsive framework. It is essential for responsive regulation because it reveals relational complexity in ways that are required for responsivity.

The view of restorative justice that drives this chapter, as it did the approach at Dalhousie, starts from the understanding of restorative justice as a relational theory of justice (Llewellyn & Howse, 1998; Llewellyn, 2011). Justice on this account is fundamentally concerned with just relations. It seeks relations marked by respect, care/concern, and dignity. This approach to justice is rooted in a broader relational theory of the world. This theory applies to human beings and by extension the meaning of human justice as relevant to this chapter, but, it is not anthropocentric. Rooted in the relational and interconnected nature of the world, the approach is similarly relevant for questions of environmental justice and in relational to non-human animals (Deckha, 2011).

A relational theory of human beings is more than a factual description of the ways in which we live. It claims not only do we in *fact* live in relation (and relationship) with one another, we could not be otherwise (Llewellyn, 2011). This is true in its most basic biological and evolutionary sense but also in terms of how human beings come to know, to understand, and to define themselves (Meyers, 1997; Koggel, 1998; Mackenzie & Stoljar, 2000; Nedelsky, 2011; Downie & Llewellyn, 2011). A relational approach does not see relationship as a good, to be secured or promoted, but, rather, as a reality that must be taken into account. Relationality must be core to our understanding of justice and injustice and how we respond. Interactions and arrangements at interpersonal, institutional, or systemic levels will be judged as just depending on the extent to which they reflect or structure relations. Injustice is similarly defined relationally for restorative justice rather than defined by the breach of rules or necessarily tied to an offence or specific harm. Approached in this way, it is clear how restorative justice is relevant both in reaction to particular incidents of harm and responsive to existing/underlying unjust relations as in institutional, systemic, or social injustices (Harbin & Llewellyn, 2015).

Grounding restorative justice as a relational theory of justice defines and guides its application. It requires processes that take account of context, causes, and circumstances of incidents and issues to ensure comprehensive and integrated responses. This cannot be achieved through a fixed set of processes or practice elements. A principle-based approach to doing and assessing the work of justice is necessary. The answer, then, to whether a particular practice is restorative cannot be found simply by some measure of its practice elements (as in McCold & Wachtel's (2002) restorative typology) but in the extent to which it reflects core relational principles in its process and substance (Llewellyn et al., 2013). At a principled level restorative processes are:

- Relationally focused: resist isolated view of individuals or issues;
- Comprehensive/holistic: take account of contexts, causes, and circumstances and are oriented to understanding what happened in terms of what matters for parties;
- Inclusive/participatory: relational view of parties with a stake in outcome of the situation—those affected, responsible, and who can affect outcome, communicative, dialogical processes that support agency and empowerment;
- Responsive: contextual, flexible practice attentive to needs of parties;
- Focused on taking of responsibility (individual and collective) not on blame;
- Collaborative/non-adversarial;
- Forward-focused: educative, problem solving/preventative and proactive (Llewellyn et al., 2013; Llewellyn & Llewellyn, 2015).

The robust relational conception of restorative justice affirms and explains why inclusive, participatory, and dialogical processes should serve as a starting point for regulation. Insofar as restorative justice processes and practices give central attention to relationship they are better able to marshall the knowledge, authority, and relational capacity needed to ensure successful justice responses. In this way, restorative justice serves as a backdrop for the regulatory pyramid and can inform interventions at the base and all the way up. It also helps discern when and why less interventionist approaches might fail according to where existing relationships are unable to support healthy and just regulation.

This account of the relationship between restorative justice and responsive regulation posits restorative justice as more than strategy or operationalizing a theory of compliance. It is more than just *foundational* to responsive regulation by virtue of its place at the base of the regulatory pyramid. It is *fundamental* to the very idea of responsive regulation. It is possible to read Braithwaite (2002) as suggesting a more limited view, as he explains the "most distinctive part of responsive regulation is the regulatory pyramid. It is an attempt to solve the puzzle of when to punish and when to persuade" (p. 30). The pyramid helps answer: "what do we do when [restorative justice] fails, as it often will? What is our theory of when not to use restorative justice?" (p. 27). It does so, he claims, by responding

> to the fact that restorative justice, deterrence, and incapacitation are all limited and flawed theories of compliance. What the pyramid does is cover the weaknesses of one theory with the strengths of another. The ordering of strategies in the pyramid is not just about putting the less costly, less coercive, more respectful options lower down in order to save money and preserve freedom as non-domination. It is also that by resorting to more dominating less respectful forms of social control only when more dialogic forms have been tried first, coercive control comes to be seen as more legitimate.
>
> *(p. 32)*

This takes restorative justice, though, as a set of practices not a theory. As a relational theory of justice it offers more than collaborative and dialogical processes. It can identify the relational conditions and circumstances that require more structured interventionist responses and then inform processes and practices to secure those conditions until such time as capacity or commitment exists to relate in just ways reflective of respect, care/concern, and dignity. But, for this to be so, all levels of the regulatory pyramid must be reflective and anchored by these commitments. None can forgo the values they seek to secure and produce. As the pyramid suggests "law enforcers should be responsive to how effectively citizens or corporations are regulating themselves before deciding whether to escalate intervention" (Braithwaite, 2002, p. 29). This capacity must then be nurtured by the ways in which law enforcers intervene. This makes the case for a restorative approach to responsive regulation to ensure that at all levels of the pyramid interventions are guided by restorative principles so as to build the capacity among citizens and corporations to govern themselves in future such that de-escalation in the pyramid is possible.

At times responsive regulation will entail a departure from robustly collaborative and inclusive processes that are the hallmark of restorative justice. This departure does not, however, necessitate a retreat from the relational principles that mark a restorative approach to justice. These principles need to shape the decision to employ non-restorative practices in view of the overall relational goals of just responsive regulation. Greater intervention should then be considered *within* a relational approach as it may be required to establish conditions for dialogue, participation, and collaboration of parties. Escalation up the pyramid, then, with the increased use of authority and intervention entailed does not necessitate an abandonment of a relational approach. The increased exercise of authority and potential for domination characteristic of the peak of the pyramid is no less relational in nature than the less dominating, freer processes at the bottom of the pyramid. Recall, relationship here is not describing a good or positive interaction but focused on the fact of relationship. Domination is not less relational by nature than its more positive relational dynamics at play lower on the pyramid. Indeed, it is precisely because of this relational nature and implications of these responses at the top of the pyramid that we should be concerned to ensure that they are used in a way that does not replicate, reinforce, or become sources of injustice. If the focus of justice is achievement of the conditions of just relationship—of mutual respect, care/concern, and dignity—then mechanisms of justice must take care to model such relations to the extent possible and the overall system of responsive regulation aim to establish the conditions for such relations in future. This is particularly important because responsive regulation is a dynamic model (Braithwaite, 2002). Escalation will only be effective in supporting responsive regulation if it is approached in such a way that it does not undermine de-escalation to more informal and robust relational networks. For responsive regulation to be successful there must be a feedback loop whereby relational skills and capacity needed for de-escalation are modelled and developed through interventions higher up on the pyramid. Decisions about moving up and down the pyramid should be considered within a relational frame and not beyond it.

This commitment to ensure a restorative approach informs the entire pyramid does not mean that only relational mechanisms or responses can be employed within the pyramid. While there will certainly be a preference for such mechanisms it is possible to accommodate the use of other responses that are not themselves restorative in nature. A relational approach requires their use be considered and justified through a relational analysis. For example, at the top of the pyramid, as Braithwaite has contemplated, non-restorative responses might be required including, for example, in the criminal context, imprisonment; in child protection, removing children from parents who do not want to give them up; in the corporate sphere, removing licences from businesses; or in the educational context, suspension or even expulsion. Taking a relational approach to regulation would certainly prefer restorative interventions where possible (as reflected by the commitment to such processes as the base of the pyramid with escalation only as necessary). A restorative framing should and does make a difference in terms of the strategies or practices included within the regulatory pyramid. This is consistent with Braithwaite's (2002) own rejection of retribution and punishment within the values of restorative justice.

The most fraught issue in the values debate is whether values such as retribution, just deserts, fair punishment should be accommodated in a restorative justice framework. Many of the most distinguished restorative justice thinkers think they should. My own inclination is to think they should not. [. . .] I argue that in the conditions of late modernity our retributive values are more a hindrance to our survival and flourishing than a help. Hence restorative justice should be explicitly about a values shift from the retributive/punitive to the restorative. Retributive emotions are natural, things we all experience and things that are easy to understand from a biological point of view. But, on this view, retribution is in the same category as greed or gluttony; biologically they once helped us to flourish, but today they are corrosive of human health and relationships.

(p. 16)

A relational approach does not, though, insist on restorative processes. It does insist that responses, even if not restorative in their modality, are relationally considered in terms of their impact. A relational approach would require, for example, consideration of why an isolating mechanism might be used with respect to wider relational purposes. In this way it is possible a relational analysis could support the use of such mechanisms in certain circumstances.

In all circumstances, though, compliance with regulations and the mechanisms employed must be in service of justice—of promoting and protecting just relations. Whether within the criminal justice system or in the context of some other regulatory system justice must overlay responsive regulation. Braithwaite (2002) makes this assumption clear in his caveat that responsive regulation is concerned with compliance with *just* law, otherwise the dialogue would rightly be about the justness of the law and not regulating to secure compliance (p. 30). This commitment to justice cannot simply be the starting point for compliance but must invade all aspects of the enterprise of regulation. Absent this core commitment, responsive regulation can become manipulation in service of any end.

As much as restorative justice is essential to ensure just and effective responsive regulation, responsive regulation has a similar crucial role in restorative justice. Thinking about restorative justice through the lens of responsive regulation focuses attention on the dynamic nature of the work to regulate relationships key for justice. As described above, justice, understood relationally, is fundamentally about just relations—requiring relations marked by mutual respect, care/concern, and dignity. It is not, as some restorative justice practices might suggest, narrowly focused on reconciled interpersonal relations of the 'hug and make up' variety (Llewellyn, 2011). While this may sometimes be the result of restorative justice, it is not necessarily so. Just relations often entail the end of existing relational arrangements. The broader sense in which restorative justice conceives of, and approaches, its work towards just relations comes clear through the lens of responsive regulation. Relationships are not static or fixed and the work to secure just relations requires constant care and attention—it is regulatory work. To be effective, such regulation is best done by those closely involved with the relations at stake (whether at interpersonal, institutional, systemic, or societal levels). There will, though, be circumstances in which such 'self' regulation is not possible and intervention to assist and insist on compliance with just relational norms is required. In such cases, restorative justice insists the interventions must still focus on the relational nature of their aim and take an appropriate approach while always attending to the principle of inviting the person(s) to step up and use their own 'agency' to self-regulate.

Understanding the regulatory nature of the work of justice in this way requires restorative justice advocates to resist their own versions of regulatory formalism. It requires consideration of how and when to escalate to more formal interventions when self-regulation or dialogue-based processes between and among parties are not possible (yet, or at all) or sufficient to respond to the situation and establish conditions for just relations. If restorative justice is about more than simply achieving a settlement or agreement between the direct parties on a particular issue, it requires understanding what happened in light of context, causes, and circumstances to establish a plan for what needs to be done to make the future better. This work demands flexibility in terms of the process and a vision of restorative justice as more than a one-off intervention (no matter how restorative). It also makes clear that within a restorative process one might need to move up and down the pyramid. Restorative justice cannot then be identified with a certain set of practices or limited to what happens within them. It must be designed to adapt and adjust depending on the needs and responses of the parties during the process. An approach to restorative justice as purely an alternative justice practice or aligned with particular tools is not up to this task. Responsive regulation reinforces the necessity for a principle-based approach to restorative justice if it is to be capable of the responsivity required to secure just relations.

The relationship between restorative justice and responsive regulation does not thus flow in one direction or the other. One is not a servant of the other. It is a relationship of mutuality—of interdependence—born of their shared relational DNA. They are, on this account, travelling companions on the relational path toward justice. Responsive regulation without restorative justice would lack an important moral compass and risk getting lost to the tyranny or illegitimacy of manipulation for compliance through the strategic use/misuse of relationships. Likewise, restorative justice requires responsive regulation to navigate when and how to move up and down the regulatory pyramid without abandoning the relational insights that ground and stabilize the pyramid.

Dalhousie's Facebook Incident: A Case Study of Restorative Justice and Responsive Regulation

The response to the Facebook incident at Dalhousie University is a rich and layered case study of the interplay of restorative justice and responsive regulation in the face of relational complexity. Fully explored, it offers many insights and raises many questions and issues for consideration (Report From the Restorative Justice Process at the Dalhousie University Faculty of Dentistry, 2015). Below I take up three key points relevant to this relationship: 1) the restorative process revealed the relational complexity of the issues and the parties involved; 2) responsivity was essential to the success of the process; and 3) the regulatory environment was a significant challenge for the success of the process.

1) Restorative Justice: Revealing and Responding to Relational Complexity

Dalhousie Dentistry is a case study in the importance of a restorative approach to reveal relational complexity of the issues, the parties, and their roles.

a. Relational Understanding of the Issues

Perhaps the most fundamental difference the restorative justice approach made in the Dalhousie case was to the understanding of the issues involved. Traditional approaches to such matters, whether through the criminal justice system or university complaint and discipline processes, focus on regulating behaviour. This influence was evident in the initial reactions to the incident on- and off-campus. The Facebook site became the subject of significant public attention shortly after it came to light through the release of select screen shots of the most egregious content. The public reaction, led by some prominent academic leaders on campus, was swift. The site and the men involved were cast as concrete manifestation of the widespread problems of campus rape culture and misogyny. A public campaign was quickly organized demanding a response under the rallying cry 'expel misogyny.' The situation garnered an exceptional amount of public attention in mainstream and social media, including approximately 3,500 local and national news stories, a public petition demanding expulsion with over 50,000 signatures, and a trending hashtag on Twitter. The reaction linked the case to broader social problems and the culture and climate they create for women on campuses. However, the solution demanded centred primarily on the individual male students. The loudest calls focused on the individual actions of the men involved and sought criminal charges, and/or university and professional discipline. Wider questions about the climate and culture at the Dental School or the University were generally raised in terms of institutional culpability for the men's actions and to compel a strong institutional response to the men. The demands for accountability for the men and the institution were shaped by the same individualized conception of culpability required for punitive responses (Harbin & Llewellyn, 2015; Heiner & Tyson, 2017).

It is likely that this individualized focus and approach would have prevailed but for the fact that staff within student and security services on campus had some prior experience with restorative processes on campus. This was significant not merely because of the process alternatives available but for the capacity to think about situations through a relational lens. As a result, when several of the women impacted by the Facebook site came forward to make a complaint under the University's sexual harassment policy the staff were not hampered by a narrow individual focus of traditional processes but could see the issues, as the women described them, in all their relational depth and complexity.

The women clearly identified the conduct of the individual men in their class as unacceptable, harmful, and extremely hurtful. Their dentistry class was small, they knew each other well and were under no illusions about one another. They had more complex knowledge of the men involved and of the context for their behaviours. From the outside it might have been possible to portray this as an issue of 13 bad apples (even if remarkable that there could be so many rotten apples without a sick tree). From up close, though, the complexity was obvious. The women's story about the Facebook site could not be fully captured as a matter of personal harassment. They had a different—broader—account about what happened and what mattered most about what happened to them. They located the harms they experienced and the issues at stake in their personal interactions as nested within sets of wider relationships—with their peer group, at the Faculty, within the profession, and in society (on nested relationships see: Nedelsky, 2011). The men's comments and the existence of the Facebook site itself reflected attitudes, assumptions, and patterns within the culture of the institution in which they learned, the profession they sought to join, and the society in which they lived. The women did not excuse the men's behaviour with this more complex account but sought to more fully understand its significance and impacts.

A relational approach clearly revealed the intersecting issues and relationships at stake in this case including:

- The climate and culture within the Faculty of Dentistry that shaped relationships between and among students and Faculty, across different programs within the Faculty including dentistry and dental hygiene and across the decades (Report From the Restorative Justice Process at the Dalhousie University Faculty of Dentistry, 2015).
- The relationships between the Faculty and the profession—they were interdependent with the Faculty relying on the profession for instructional and financial support and the profession on the Faculty for professional preparation and development.

- Gender relationships within the profession.
- The relationship between the profession and the public—public trust was declining for dentistry specifically and generally with respect to self-regulated professions (Croutze, 2010; Smith, 2011).
- Relationship of Faculty and University administration with respect to University governance (MacKinnon, 2018).
- Societal issues related to gender violence and misogyny (including rape culture on university campuses) as reflected recently in the #metoo and #timesup movements.

What at first blush may have looked like an issue of personal harassment (even if one of many similar stories) was quickly recognized as a situation of significant relational complexity with a set of interconnected issues that could not be understood or addressed adequately in isolation.

b. Relational Understanding of the Parties and Their Roles

This more complex relational view of the issues involved changed and expanded the parties involved. One of the most significant misconceptions of the restorative process at Dalhousie in the public discourse was that it was a process in which "the two sides come together and discuss what an appropriate punishment should be" (CBC News, 2014). In contrast to this perception, from the outset the restorative process involved a much wider circle of participants than the male and female students directly involved. It included students from other years and programs within the Faculty of Dentistry, Faculty, staff, and administrators from Dentistry, members of the profession including provincial professional associations and regulators, University administrators, on-campus advocacy groups related to the issues of safety and inclusion, representatives from women's organizations and men's violence prevention organizations in the province, patients of the Faculty's clinic, and representatives of the wider community. Dealing with the relational complexity of the issues required what Mimi Kim refers to as "multidimensional holism," that is, "the consideration of multiple perspectives, including those of survivors, community allies, and those doing harm, in the process" (2012, p. 19). Engagement of those connected to the issues in appropriate and meaningful ways within the process required more than the recognition that these wider groups had an interest and should be consulted on the nature of the process or its outcomes. It had to take account of the different and more nuanced roles and responsibilities of these parties in relation to the issues at stake.

This challenged the prescribed and fixed roles familiar from the standard individual punitive and adversarial responses to such incidents. The temptation to sort parties on one side or the other as offender or victim with the related assumptions about blameworthiness or innocence and responsibilities versus entitlements was significant. Responding to the relational complexity of the situation meant appreciating that parties might have experienced harm and at the same time held some responsibilities related to what happened and/or what needed to happen next. This was true, for example, for the Faculty and University administrators who experienced damage to the institution's relationships and reputation from the men's conduct but also bore responsibilities for the climate and culture within the institution that enabled or tolerated such views and behaviour and for failures to respond to earlier complaints.

Similarly, the relational approach disrupted assumptions about the roles of the women and the men involved from the dentistry class. For example, the women who sought the restorative process were clear that their classmates needed to be held to account for their actions but argued that real accountability required the men be part of the solution and carry their responsibility to bring about change along with leaders from the Faculty, the University, and the profession. In their words,

> We were clear from the beginning, to the people who most needed to hear it, that we were not looking to have our classmates expelled as 13 angry men who understood no more than they did the day the posts were uncovered. Nor did we want simply to forgive and forget. Rather, we were look-ing for a resolution that would allow us to graduate alongside men who understood the harms they caused, owned these harms, and would carry with them a responsibility and obligation to do better.
>
> *(Report From the Restorative Justice Process at*
> *the Dalhousie University Faculty of Dentistry, 2015, p. 9)*

This would require the men involved to step into the process prepared to accept their responsibility for the harms caused by their actions and to be able to stand along side the women impacted to hold other parties to account for their contributions to the climate and culture that facilitated and perpetuated harmful patterns of interaction and behaviour. The women involved in the restorative process also came to recognize the complexity in their own roles:

> As we moved through the restorative process, eventually we also had to unpack the assumptions we as women brought with us. We are a part of a generation in which inappropriate sexualization is more common and widespread than ever before and we have become used to this. Because such attitudes are everywhere, we rarely take time to question them. For example, we had always known about the men's Facebook group but had always assumed that, as a rule, there were no posts about women in our class. We assumed though, and did not address the fact, that the mate-rial on the site was likely by times sexist, unprofessional, and inappropriate. It was only when we knew it was about us that we took real offense. This made us realize that we, as women, also contribute to the culture and climate that allows Facebook groups like the one at issue to per-sist and flourish. We had to ask ourselves: why we are only up in arms when it is about us, but unconcerned with the objectification of other women? Why was this tolerable? We needed this restorative process because we had work to do ourselves.
>
> *(Report From the Restorative Justice Process at*
> *the Dalhousie University Faculty of Dentistry, 2015, pp. 9–10)*

This honesty about the complexity of their roles resulted in significant criticism from those committed to a more formalistic approach. An external task force appointed by the University to quell public criti-cism chose to ignore the experience of the women who participated in the restorative justice process (most women from the class) in favour of the view of one female student who opted out. The women's response was also deemed "unnecessarily self-critical" and evidence of an undue burden placed on them (*Globe & Mail*, 2015). Two of the women involved in the restorative process later reflected:

> By acknowledging our understanding of the role we played in the culture at the school, we did not excuse the wrongs that were done by the men in the group, nor did we place the blame on ourselves as some have suggested. The men still had to be accountable for their actions, but we took the opportunity the restorative justice process provided to develop a deeper understanding of the issues that shaped climate and culture and to empower ourselves to affect the changes we

wanted to see because we felt this was also our right and responsibility. Restorative justice processes are about learning and are future focused, and we would not have been fully participating
in the process if, by the end, we were preceding exactly as we had before the process began.

[...]

Perhaps our decision to participate in the RJ process was too complicated a story, or we did
not seem like good enough victims to earn a place in the narrative the Task Force crafted of what
happened. Regardless of whether we warranted a place in the Task Force's story, restorative justice
was a path that we chose for ourselves, and the gains we made individually and as a collective of
young professionals will carry on.

(Llewellyn, Demsey, & Smith, 2015, pp. 48–49)

Recognition of the relational complexity of the issues at stake necessarily also affected the scope and
nature of the parties' involvement. Viewed as a matter of interpersonal harm within the institution,
the standard response would have focused on individual culpability despite the collective participation in the Facebook site. The institution would have stepped in and taken up its role to hold the men
accountable by prosecuting the case before the Dalhousie Senate Discipline Committee. The women's
participation would be limited after they filed the complaint. They would be the subjects of, but not
agents within, the process, something the women in the restorative process were clear they did not want.
"As the subjects of some of the offensive Facebook material, we wanted to be active participants in
responding to it. It became clear to us that only through the restorative justice approach could we play
the active roles we wanted" (Report From the Restorative Justice Process at the Dalhousie University
Faculty of Dentistry, 2015).

The centrality of the women impacted was a significant difference, but not the only one, a restorative approach made in terms of widening the circle of participants. Despite some common tag lines of
restorative justice as "victim-centred," such a singular focus would fail for many of the same reasons a
narrow offender-centred process does. Instead, restorative justice widens and re-centres processes relationally for more inclusive and dynamic involvement of all parties. This was significant for the women
harmed in this case not only in terms of their own roles but also their engagement with other parties
needed for a meaningful outcome.

The relational complexity visible through a restorative lens together with the widening of the parties
involved and the nuanced and multifaceted nature of their roles possible within a restorative process was
essential to responsive regulation. It allowed the involvement of a wider set of parties to provide insight,
influence, and contribute to the conditions required for future compliance. Braithwaite's well-known
example of nursing home regulation revealed the importance of moving away from a prescriptive and
punitive regulatory system to a restorative one involving the broad range of actors and stakeholders in
the industry (Braithwaite, Makkai, & Braithwaite, 2007). The wider engagement brought compliance
and produced better-quality outcomes and greater trust there, as it did at Dalhousie.

2) Responding to Relational Complexity—Responsive Regulation for Restorative Justice

Standard complaint processes are not designed to deal with relational complexity. They reflect a prescriptive and formal approach to regulating behaviour enforcing rules crafted to proscribe individual behaviour and to ensure accountability for transgressions. The women understood that under the

formal complaint process available to them what would be central about their story was the actions of the individual men and the solution available dictated by the code of conduct. Broader issues of climate and culture and other systemic matters would not be considered relevant within this process. These issues would be left for some other process to deal with, likely divorced from their harms. The women who undertook the restorative process did not want their experience to be reduced to mirco-relational issues between the men and women in the fourth-year dentistry class. They could not be separated from the macro relational issues that shaped and marked the culture and climate at the dental school, on the campus, in the profession, and beyond. Any response to the Facebook site needed to appreciate this relational interactivity whereby the interpersonal was influenced and reflective of a sexist and misogynist culture that at the same time contributed, reinforced, and perpetuated that culture. Being responsive required a process capable of revealing and attending to these connections to disrupt this cycle and bring real and lasting change.

It is a common misconception that restorative justice consists of a single circle or conference. The role of responsive regulation in achieving restorative outcomes makes clear the importance of designing processes that are dynamic, layered, and tailored to the needs of the parties and to allow for evolution in their understanding of the issues. Processes must be multi-leveled to account for different and intersecting relationships. In the Dalhousie case the restorative process worked with similarly situated individuals and groups (intra-party sessions), it brought certain parties together on issues of shared importance (inter-party sessions), and gathered many or all the parties connected to the situation together when appropriate (multi-party sessions). A flexible approach to the restorative justice process was required so that decisions about who needed to be involved, when, and in what ways could be made throughout the process in response to ongoing feedback from the parties. For example, the Dalhousie process began with significant work separately with the women impacted by the posts and the men involved in the Facebook group to deepen their understandings of the situation. As part of the work to support learning for the men they met together with other groups impacted by or connected with the issues involved. The women also met together with others who could offer support and help them contextualize their experience (e.g. women from organizations concerned with gender violence and those within the dental profession). Contrary to assumptions about restorative process, it was only after significant work by the men and support processes for the women that the two groups came together within the process to address the impact of the men's actions. Through this process the men and women also identified common concerns related to the climate and culture at the Faculty and within the profession. They committed to working collectively through the process to address these concerns. The process was not, however, a linear one moving from the interpersonal to the institutional and the professional level. It was attentive to the relationships and issues as they were evolving during the process. For example, late in the process, after the members of the class had been collaborating for some time, it became clear that time and new insights surfaced issues for the women regarding the impacts of the men's actions that required further attention. This necessitated a return to an inter-party dialogue. In this way, the wisdom of responsive regulation was operative. The process was not fixed or rigid but sufficiently flexible to ensure time to test learnings, understandings, and commitments to change—to allow for failures and retries (Braithwaite, 2002, 2016).

This was also true in terms of the regulatory responses to the Facebook group members. The Faculty referred members of the Facebook group to the Academic Standards Class Committee (ASCC) (responsible for professional standards for graduation) as a matter of unprofessional conduct. The ASCC agreed to defer its final determination in the matter for the 12 men participating in restorative justice to allow them to remediate their behaviour in line with required standards for professionalism through the restorative process. Before the restorative process was even underway, the University decided, in response to public reaction and concern, that the men should be suspended from clinic duties pending investigation. This decision was, in part, reflective of the expectations of formal regulatory responses that shaped debate about the case on- and off-campus. Nevertheless, with the restorative justice process came opportunity for responsive regulation in ways particularly important to the development of professional responsibility. As the men worked to understand the context and impact of their actions they were given the opportunity to return to the dental clinic and test their commitments to changed behaviour. The process was designed with a recognition that change is not linear and resistance and failure are part of the process (Kim, 2012; Heiner & Tyson, 2017). The process was designed, however, not simply to wait for failure in order to intervene with a different regulatory response. The men continued to meet within the restorative process during their return to clinic to reflect on how their changed perspectives affected their experience and work in the clinic. Working together within the restorative process they committed to supporting each other, learning with one another, and holding each other to account for compliance with new norms and behaviours as they returned to the wider educational and clinical environment. The restorative process provided a safe environment in which to test, fail fast, and adapt. Over the course of the process the male and female members of the class worked together to develop capacities and processes to support such regulation in the future. The importance of this for their future professional obligations was not lost on them.

> Dentistry is a self-governing profession, a fact we didn't think about in detail five months ago. Having been through the restorative justice process, we have seen first-hand the immense responsibility that comes with being accountable for ourselves and ensuring accountability for how our colleagues act. In the restorative process we became comfortable questioning the status quo and demanding of ourselves that we come to the table with honesty and integrity. We have come to circle with members of our class, but also with our faculty and every level of leadership at Dalhousie, each time posing the same underlying question—how can we be better?
> (*Report From the Restorative Justice Process at the Dalhousie University Faculty of Dentistry, 2015, p. 10*)

Key to the success of this restorative process at Dalhousie was the balance it enabled between healing and regulating through the marriage of responsive regulation and restorative justice. The focus was not simply on repair or healing the relationships harmed but to envisioning and establishing the conditions for the regulation of just relations in the future. The successful outcome was owed, in part, to the common commitment of healers and regulators, facilitated through the restorative process, to see beyond the horizon of conflict resolution and discipline for the Facebook site, to the culture and systemic work still ahead.

In this way, responsive regulation makes sense of the future-focused orientation of restorative justice. The process is aimed at establishing a plan amongst the parties to regulate future just relations. This was the outcome of the restorative justice process at Dalhousie. Contrary to traditional processes that result in judgements, orders, or lists of recommendations, the restorative justice process generated commitments to address what community accountability scholars call the "unfinished" (Heiner & Tyson, 2017). It was clear that the work undertaken within the process could not stop at its conclusion. The plan in the Dalhousie case contemplated the ongoing nature of the process of climate and culture change at the Faculty, the University, and in the profession. The parties within the process committed to be part of that continuing work and established a responsive approach to ensuring mutual compliance by intentionally involving those who would be key to ensuring change. For example, it engaged students across the other years of the program so that they could be part of carrying the work forward. The processes involved Faculty, staff, members of the profession, and the community. The process ended with a day of learning explicitly focused on considering a plan to ensure meaningful and lasting change on the issues at stake. The success of the process in this respect must be measured in the years to come in terms of the breadth, depth, and sustainability of the resulting changes in climate and culture on campus and beyond. In terms of the changes on campus, other students at the Faculty of Dentistry have continued to work through a restorative process to assess issues of climate and culture and to make changes to the ways in which they govern and relate to one another. These efforts were recently considered along with other impacts of a restorative approach on campus through an external review process that found significant positive impacts and outcomes and recommended expanded use of the approach (Case, 2017).

3) Concluding Reflections on the Dalhousie Dentistry Case and the Importance of the Regulatory Environment

The Dalhousie case is a rich example of the potential, if not necessity, of integrating restorative justice and responsive regulation. It also reveals, though, in powerful ways how important the regulatory environment is to the success of such an endeavour. Regulatory formalism as the systemic or ideological backdrop makes working responsively and restoratively difficult if not, sometimes, impossible. A regulatory backdrop that is inconsistent with the relational orientation of restorative justice and responsive regulation will be destabilizing, challenging, and likely to cause significant misunderstanding and conflict. This was the case at Dalhousie.

The restorative and responsive approach at Dalhousie was undertaken within an existing regulatory eco-system that was very formalistic. It is never smooth sailing the first time something is tried and certainly the restorative response at Dalhousie was a first in response to this sort of situation. Yet the ferocity of the response cannot simply be explained by novelty and lack of understanding. There were clear and persistent misconceptions of the restorative process maintained and fostered throughout despite clear contrary evidence. It became obvious that some of this misunderstanding was not the result of a lack of information or knowledge. It was the product of an inability and/or unwillingness to understand because it would disrupt the power of those with regulatory authority or who took comfort in established and formal systems. The restorative approach threatened or sacrificed their authority and certainty. The existing systems were not designed to respond to relational complexity but to provide certainty through prescriptive precise regulations and responses. The restorative justice process at Dalhousie proceeded in the face of a number of these formal regulatory processes including the University Senate discipline process, the criminal justice system, the Faculty Academic Class Standards Committee, provincial professional regulatory bodies, and an external task force appointed by the University. While each posed slightly different challenges for the restorative justice process, the source of the threat they posed was similarly rooted in regulatory formalism. Each process valued and required certainty of response over evidence of effectiveness. Further, each was designed to respond to a specific or narrow issue in isolation from, and to the exclusion of, other connected issues. The siloed nature of these processes prevented the integrated and comprehensive response required in the midst of complexity. In order for the restorative justice process with its responsive approach to regulation to proceed these processes had to stand down or collaborate. Much could be learned by exploring the interaction of each of these regulatory systems with the restorative process at Dalhousie. For the purposes of this chapter, though, it is sufficient and significant to note that these formal regulatory processes generated considerable expectations for some individuals and groups about what should have happened at Dalhousie. Indeed, the certainty offered by these systems resulted in considerable disappointment, occasionally rising to the level of outrage, that restorative justice had denied what was deserved or owed according to the existing formal processes.

While each process posed its own practical set of challenges for restorative justice in this case, it was the ideological commitments underpinning these systems that posed, perhaps, the greatest issue and continues to feed misrepresentations of the process. At its core the considerable controversy over the Dalhousie restorative justice process turned on a debate about the nature of the problem and related convictions about the solution. The concerns raised at the time that genuinely reflected misunderstandings of the process or worries for the safety and wellbeing of those impacted have receded. Indeed, in many cases such views have been transformed by the evidence of the success and lasting impacts of the process for the parties involved. For example, after the process concluded the media coverage shifted significantly (*Chronicle Herald*, 2015; *New York Times* Editorial Board, 2015; Johnson, 2016), viewing the process as a promising example. This view is shared by several universities and experts around the world now exploring a similar approach to address culture and climate on campuses and in professions that tolerate or perpetuate sexism, misogyny, homophobia, and other harmful forms of discrimination (Schulich School of Law, 2016; Campus Prism, 2017).

What has endured is a particular strain of discontent rooted in the certainty of regulatory formalism and a punitive logic so ingrained it has "effected an *epistemic occupation* such that many of us encounter profound difficulty imagining and conceptualizing the redress and prevention of violence (including state violence) without recourse to the heteropatriarchal violence of the state" (Heiner & Tyson, 2017). As a result, Heiner and Tyson argue,

> it can even seem wrong to consider noncarceral responses to violence, because dominant neo-liberal logic delineates only one intelligible schema of accountability for violence—that of an individual (non-state) agent—and only one general form of legitimate response: state-centric punishment (whether confinement, execution, or other form of social death). Alternative forms of community accountability and redress that break from state-centric carceral systems appear baffling, irresponsible, even monstrous. The choice seems to be confined to either ensnaring an individual with the punitive arms of the state or fomenting complete, unaccountable disorder.
>
> *(Heiner & Tyson, 2017, p. 2)*

Critics of the restorative response to the Facebook incident argue that relational complexity could not justify a departure from dealing with the men individually through the standard punitive discipline systems (CBC News, 2015). Surprisingly, perhaps, was that much of this resistance came from within the academic feminist community. The development of relational theory has been led by feminist scholars (Downie & Llewellyn, 2011; Koggel, 1998; Campbell, Meynell, & Sherwin, 2009; Nedelsky, 2011), but the critics saw the Dalhousie case differently. In their view, the place and time to take account of relational complexity was not here and not now—not when regulatory formalism would provide the certainty they felt was so needed. Though they certainly recognized the institutional, systemic, and societal problem of sexism and misogyny at stake in this case, it did not drive a more nuanced, relational, or complex appreciation of the behaviours and their causes, context, circumstances, or impacts. On the contrary, it heightened the expectation for justice as available through existing individually focused, punitive, and adversarial processes. When the women asked for a restorative approach that might forgo this response it was perceived as a failure of justice. For these opponents, if the men were not expelled or punished the injustice would not be vindicated and the wider prospects for change lost. The radical insistence of the women who chose restorative justice that what was needed was education to equip and prepare these men to be part of the solution did not fit such a formalistic vision of justice.

The orientation and expectation of regulatory certainty seemed to impact how such critics could see the situation. Through the lens of individual, singular focused systems and the expectations and entitlements, the relational and complex nature of the facts was clouded or distorted. For such critics the flexibility and dynamic nature of restorative justice and responsive regulation and the irreducible relational complexity they reveal destabilized claims for certain and fixed responses in ways that seemed unconscionable and untenable compromises of their principles. The Dalhousie process was grounded in relational principles that insisted that facts matter. The commitment to contextuality makes it a fundamental principle of a restorative approach to take careful account of the relational context on the ground. This makes being right and doing right by those involved messy and uncertain work, but, by the marriage of restorative justice and responsive regulation, not remotely unprincipled. By contrast, the principles and convictions underlying existing regulatory systems ignore the complex realities in the case in service of the certainty of rigid rules and fixed processes. One can appreciate that such certainty offers immediate comfort in an uncertain world. But it will be cold comfort when it ultimately fails to respond to the relational complexity of the world and those wrapped up in it. The Dalhousie process is an example of responsivity to relational complexity through restorative justice. It is a model of responsive justice for a complex world.

References

Braithwaite, J. (2002). *Restorative justice and responsive regulation*. New York: Oxford University Press.

Braithwaite, J. (2016). *Restorative justice and responsive regulation: The question of evidence* (Working Paper No. 51). Canberra: School of Regulation and Global Governance (RegNet).

Braithwaite, J., Makkai, T., & Braithwaite, V. (2007). *Regulating aged care: Ritualism and the new pyramid*. Cheltenham, UK: Edward Elgar.

Campbell, S., Meynell, L., & Sherwin, S. (2009). *Embodiment and agency*. Philadelphia, PA: Pennsylvania State University Press.

Campus Prism. (2017). *A report on promoting restorative initiatives for sexual misconduct on college campuses*. Saratoga Springs: Skidmore College Project on Restorative Justice.

Case, T. (2017). *Restorative justice learning debrief*. Halifax: Dalhousie University.

CBC News. (2014, December 17). *Dalhousie dentistry students to decide together justice for Facebook posts*. Retrieved from cbc.ca: www.cbc.ca/news/canada/nova-scotia/dalhousie-dentistry-students-to-decide-together-justice-for-facebook-posts-1.2876875.

CBC News. (2015, January 11). *Dalhousie professors' Facebook scandal complaint tossed*. Retrieved from CBC News: www.cbc.ca/news/canada/nova-scotia/dalhousie-professors-facebook-scandal-complaint-tossed-1.2896942.

Croutze, R. (2010). Preparing today for dentistry tomorrow. *Journal of the Canadian Dental Association, 96*.

Deckha, M. (2011). Non-human animals and human health: A relational approach to the use of animals in medical research. In J. Downie & J. J. Llewellyn (Eds.), *Being relational: Reflections on relational theory and health law and policy* (pp. 287–314). Vancouver: UBC Press.

Downie, J., & Llewellyn, J. J. (2011). *Being relational: Reflections on relational theory & health law*. Vancouver: UBC Press.

Harbin, A., & Llewellyn, J. J. (2015). Restorative justice in transitions: The problem of 'the community' and collective responsibility. In K. Clamp (Ed.), *Restorative justice in transitional settings* (pp. 133–151). Oxford: Routledge.

Heiner, B., & Tyson, S. (2017). Feminism and the carceral state: Gender-responsive justice, community accountability, and the epistemology of antiviolence. *Feminist Philosophy Quarterly, 3*(1), 1–36. doi:10.5206/fpq/2016.3.3.

Johnson, J. (2016, August 17). The Ghomeshi effect: Finally we're talking about sexual assault. When does the pain stop? *The Walrus Magazine.*

Kim, M. (2012). Moving beyond critique: Creative interventions and reconstructions of community accountability. *A Journal of Crime, Conflict & World Order, 37*(4), 14–35.

Koggel, C. M. (1998). *Perspective on equality: Constructing a relational theory.* New York: Rowan.

Llewellyn, J. J. (2011). Restorative justice: Thinking relationally about justice. In J. Downie & J. J. Llewellyn (Eds.), *Being relational: Reflections on relational theory & health law* (pp. 89–108). Vancouver: UBC Press.

Llewellyn, J. J., Archibald, B., Crocker, D., & Clairmont, D. (2013). Imagining Success for a Restorative Approach to Justice. *Dalhousie Law Journal, 36*(2), 281–316.

Llewellyn, J., Demsey, A., & Smith, J. (2015). An unfamiliar justice story: Restorative justice and education reflections on Dalhousie's Facebook incident 2015. *Our Schools, Our Selves, 43*–56.

Llewellyn, J. J., & Howse, R. (1998). *Restorative justice—a conceptual framework.* Ottawa: Law Commission of Canada.

Llewellyn, J. J., & Llewellyn, K. R. (2015). A restorative approach to learning: Relational theory as feminist pedagogy in universities. In T. P. Light, J. Nicholas, & R. Bondy (Eds.), *Feminist pedagogy in higher education: Critical theory and practice* (pp. 11–31). Waterloo, ON: Wilfrid Laurier University Press.

Llewellyn, J., MacIsaac, J., & MacKay, M. (2015). *Report from the restorative justice process at the Dalhousie university faculty of dentistry.* Halifax: Dalhousie University. Retrieved from https://cdn.dal.ca/content/dam/dalhousie/pdf/cultureofrespect/RJ2015-Report.pdf

Mackenzie, C., & Stoljar, N. (2000). Introduction: Autonomy revisited. In C. Mackenzie & N. Stoljar (Eds.), *Relational autonomy: Feminist perspectives on autonomy, agency and the social self* (pp. 3–31). Oxford: Oxford University Press.

MacKinnon, P. (2018). *University commons divided: Exploring debate and dissent on campus.* Toronto: University of Toronto Press.

McCold, P., & Wachtel, T. (2002). Restorative justice theory validation. In E. G. Weitekamp & K. Hans-Jurgen (Eds.), *Restorative justice: Theoretical foundations* (pp. 110–142). Portland: Willan Publishing.

Meyers, D. (1997). *Feminists rethink the self.* Boulder, CO: Westview.

Nedelsky, J. (2011). *Law's relations: A relational theory of self, autonomy, and law.* New York: Oxford University Press.

Schulich School of Law. (2016, June 27–28). *Proceedings of the International Restorative Conference.* Retrieved from YouTube: https://youtu.be/xGrA8UEou-M.

Smith, R. G. (2011). Putting professionalism on the agenda. *Journal of the Cananadian Dental Association, 48.*

The Chronicle Herald. (2015, May 22). Editorial: Dal report a frank look at misogyny. *The Chronicle Herald.*

The Globe and Mail. (2015, May 24). Editorial: At Dalhousie the women rescue the men from themselves. *The Globe and Mail.*

The New York Times Editorial Board. (2015, September 9). An alternative approach to campus justice. *The New York Times,* September 9 2015.

Zehr, H. (2005). *Changing lenses: A new focus for crime and justice.* Scottdale, PA: Herald Press.

10

RESTORATIVE JUSTICE AND RESPONSIVE REGULATION IN HIGHER EDUCATION

The Complex Web of Campus Sexual Assault Policy in the United States and a Restorative Alternative

David R. Karp

Introduction

Sexual assault policy on college campuses in the United States is a complex system guided by federal policy, state policy, and local mandates. When students violate sexual misconduct policies, campuses primarily rely on suspensions and expulsions, paralleling the criminal justice system's reliance on incarceration as a solution based on stigmatization and separation. Since the 1990s, restorative justice has made inroads as an alternative response to student misconduct, but application to sexual misconduct is rare. The Campus PRISM Project (Promoting Restorative Initiatives on Sexual Misconduct) is a network of academics and practitioners exploring a restorative approach within a responsive regulatory framework (Karp et al., 2016). This chapter describes the current web of policy as an example of regulatory formalism, which follows from the federal Title IX legislation on sexual harassment. Then it explains the restorative approach promoted by the Campus PRISM Project. This approach embraces a "whole campus" response including restorative circles for sexual assault prevention efforts, restorative conferencing in response to misconduct, and reentry circles for students returning from suspension.

Sexual assault on college campuses is a regulatory nightmare. Sexual assault is pervasive and traumatic and intractably linked to a wider culture of hook-ups, binge drinking, and hegemonic masculinity (Mitchell & Wooten, 2016). Many assaults happen behind closed doors between individuals who are drunk and whose sexual encounter often begins with some level of mutual consent. Conduct hearing boards often have little evidence to review besides the impaired memories of parties involved. As a result, finding a student in violation of a campus sexual assault policy is a substantial challenge for conduct administrators. Under such conditions of uncertainty, mistakenly exonerating a student can further traumatize a victim and keep a campus at risk. Mistakenly finding a student in violation can deeply stigmatize them with lasting social, educational, and professional consequences. No other conduct adjudication outcome is as consequential for the students involved, but built on such a shaky platform of evidence. Implementing policies and procedures in response to allegations of sexual assault that leads to positive outcomes is a daunting administrative task.

DOI: 10.4324/9780429398704-10

This chapter examines the contemporary approach to campus sexual assault policy and an alternative restorative justice response. The analysis follows from Braithwaite's (2002) theory of responsive regulation. In this model, the contemporary approach in the United States is consistent with "regulatory formalism" (p. 29), while the restorative justice approach is an example of responsive regulation. According to Burford and Adams (2004, p. 15), "regulatory formalism is reactive, and directed at extracting compliance divorced from the influence of the persons harmed. The outcomes of adversarial interventions are typically seen as heavy-handed, uninformed and unfair and thereby promote reactivity even from people whose interests may be harmed by their own refusal to comply." While not writing about campus sexual assault, this is a strong and apt critique of the current formalist approach. The chapter describes how campus sexual assault policy is an example of regulatory formalism and delineates the counterproductive and unanticipated consequences of this model. It then defines a restorative approach that, in many cases, might lead to better outcomes.

Sexual and Gender-Based Misconduct on the American Campus: Defining the Problem

Campus sexual assault has received significant social attention through campus activism in higher education, in the media, and by the Obama and Trump Administrations. Organizations such as "Know Your IX," popular books, such as *Missoula* (Krakauer, 2015), magazines, such as *Rolling Stone* (Ederly, 2014) and *Time* (Gray, 2014), and documentaries, such as *The Hunting Ground* (Dick, 2015), have highlighted the social problem, and more recently, books such as *Unwanted Advances: Sexual Paranoia Comes to Campus* (Kipnis, 2017) argue that the recent response to the issue has created even more problems. While a broader movement to address violence against women has existed for decades (Brownmiller, 2000), this new wave has focused its attention on campus policies and procedures through online activism, lawsuits, federal complaints, and increased pressure on the federal government to mandate and enforce new rules for reporting, victim services, and conduct procedures.

Although popular accounting focuses on rape, regulatory responses to campus sexual and gender-based misconduct include a wide range of offending behaviors such as sexual harassment, stalking, sexual touching, and intimate partner violence. Table 10.1 summarizes findings from a recent survey of 26,417 students at eight institutions in the University of Texas system during the 2015–16 academic year (Busch-Armendariz et al., 2017). Victimization is lower among heterosexual male students and higher for LGBTQ students.

TABLE 10.1 Rates of Campus Sexual and Gender-Based Victimization (University of Texas)

Sexual harassment (unwelcome advances, gestures, exposure, sexting/photos/videos)	25%
Stalking (persistent threatening/harassing tactics)	13%
Intimate partner cyber abuse	12%
Intimate partner violence	10%
Sexual touching (unwanted, forced kissing, touching, groping)	12%
Rape (sexual penetration through force, threat of force or incapacitation)	6%

Higher Education Sexual Assault Adjudication: Title IX Guidance and Regulatory Formalism

Regulatory formalism is epitomized by legislative mandates. A complex web of policies now exists at the federal, state, and campus levels dictating how campuses should respond to sexual assault (see Figure 10.1). It has become so difficult to understand and keep up with various guidance documents, court cases, and public pressures that cottage industries have developed to help campuses navigate the legal landscape. For example, the student affairs professional association ACPA recently launched "Compliance U," "the world's first comprehensive 24/7/365 professional and career development digital training platform for law, policy, governance, jurisprudence and compliance in higher education" (ACPA, 2017). The major strands of the regulatory web are as follows:

- VAWA (Violence Against Women Act of 1994) is a federal law that provides funding toward the investigation and prosecution of violent crimes against women and established the Office of Violence Against Women (OVW) in the Department of Justice. OVW provides funding as part of its "Campus Grant Program" to higher education institutions to improve victim services and reduce campus sexual assault, domestic violence, dating violence, and stalking.
- Title IX (Title IX of the Education Amendments of 1972) is a federal civil rights law passed as part of a federal amendment to the Higher Education Act of 1965. Under this law, sexual harassment on college campuses, including sexual violence, should be understood as a form of gender discrimination that creates a hostile climate and an obstacle to educational opportunity. "No person in the United States shall, on the basis of sex, be excluded from participation in, be denied the benefits of, or be subjected to discrimination under any education program or activity receiving Federal financial assistance." Colleges are required to respond immediately and appropriately to allegations of sexual harassment. Students who believe that their educational rights have been violated because the college did not respond properly can file a complaint with Department of Education Office of Civil Rights (OCR). At the time of this writing, from April 2011–September 2018, OCR has opened 502 campus investigations, and resolved 192 of them (Chronicle of Higher Education, 2018).
- The Clery Act (Jeanne Clery Disclosure of Campus Security Policy and Campus Crime Statistics Act of 1990) is a federal consumer protection law passed in 1990. The Clery Act was named after Jeanne Clery, a student who was raped and murdered in her residence hall at Lehigh University in 1986. The law requires colleges to track and publish crime statistics so that prospective students can be informed about the risks of attending a college. More recent amendments also require timely notifications to campus communities about incidents.
- The Campus SaVE Act (Campus Sexual Violence Elimination Act of 2013) was passed as an amendment to the Clery Act. Campus SaVE mandates educational programming for students, faculty, and staff on campuses to prevent campus sexual assault, domestic violence, dating violence, and stalking.
- State Laws. Several states have passed legislation to address campus sexual assault (Morse, Sponsler, & Fulton, 2015). Democratic states have supported campus efforts to promote affirmative consent, transcript notations, victim autonomy, and collaboration with law enforcement. In 2014, California passed a law that colleges must adopt "affirmative consent" policies requiring individuals to obtain "affirmative, conscious, and voluntary agreement to engage in sexual activity" (SB-967,

2014). Similar laws have been passed in Illinois, New York, and Connecticut (Affirmative Consent Laws, 2017). Republican states have sought to curtail what they believe to be federal overreach in campus guidance. Their primary concern has been to ensure due process for accused students by supporting their right to legal representation in conduct hearings. North Dakota, Arkansas, and North Carolina have passed legislation to guarantee this right.

- Campus Policies. Every higher education institution is responsible for developing its own student code of conduct and sexual and gender-based misconduct policy. Public universities may develop one policy across many campuses, such as the policy for the 64 State University of New York campuses (SUNY, 2017). Despite the general autonomy of campuses to develop individualized policies, they often rely on model policies developed by organizations such as ATIXA (Association of Title IX Administrators).

The result of national attention on campus sexual assault has been a complex regulatory system that operates at different levels of jurisdiction and now broadly includes a wide range of sexual behavior under its regulatory umbrella. Gersen and Suk (2016) describe this regulatory web as a new "sex bureaucracy," which has had a net-widening effect, incorporating more varied sexual experiences under the sexual assault umbrella. They worry that "the bureaucratic tendency to merge sexual violence and sexual harassment with ordinary sex" trivializes sexual assault and is "counterproductive to the goal of actually addressing the harms of rape, sexual assault, and sexual harassment" (p. 882). This bureaucracy has so broadened the scope of sexual assault that

> there is a significant disconnect between the current discussions in our country about the epidemic of campus rape, and the fact patterns involved in the allegations now routinely investigated as sexual misconduct. . . [Many] appear to be situations in which he and she (or he and he, or she and she) say much the same thing about the facts of the incident, but give different meanings to the experience. The different meanings need not be radically dissimilar to result in different determinations about sexual misconduct.
>
> *(p. 942)*

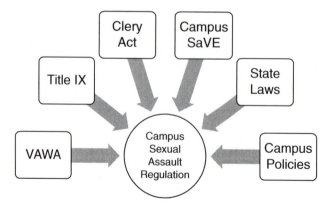

FIGURE 10.1 The Regulatory System for Campus Sexual Assault

These "different meanings" suggest that traditional definitions of sexual assault, rooted in a predatory conceptualization of offending, may no longer apply to many of the behaviors that are reported on college campuses.

Kevin and Amy: Unanticipated Consequences of Regulatory Formalism

The Association of Title IX Administrators (ATIXA) is an influential organization for interpreting the sex bureaucracy for campuses. The *ATIXA Gender-Based and Sexual Misconduct Model Policy* (Sokolow et al., 2015, pp. 13–14) provides the following case study as an educational tool to help sexual misconduct hearing board members make proper determinations in their cases.

> Kevin and Amy are at a party. Kevin is not sure how much Amy has been drinking, but he is pretty sure it's a lot. After the party, he walks Amy to her room, and Amy comes on to Kevin, initiating sexual activity. Kevin asks her if she is really up to this, and Amy says yes. Clothes go flying, and they end up in Amy's bed. Suddenly, Amy runs for the bathroom. When she returns, her face is pale, and Kevin thinks she may have thrown up. Amy gets back into bed, and they begin to have sexual intercourse. Kevin is having a good time, though he can't help but notice that Amy seems pretty groggy and passive, and he thinks Amy may have even passed out briefly during the sex, but he does not let that stop him. When Kevin runs into Amy the next day, he thanks her for the wild night. Amy remembers nothing, and decides to make a report to the Dean. This is a violation of the Non-Consensual Sexual Intercourse Policy. Kevin should have known that Amy was incapable of making a rational, reasonable decision about sex. Even if Amy seemed to consent, Kevin was well aware that Amy had consumed a large amount of alcohol, and Kevin thought Amy was physically ill, and that she passed out during sex.

New Policies Do Not Increase Reporting by Survivors

It is highly unusual for a student like Amy to file a complaint against a student like Kevin. Since OCR issued guidance in 2011, campuses have vastly expanded their formal support systems (Brown, 2017). However, this has not necessarily led to an increase in reporting. Prior research indicates that students rarely report sexual victimization: less than 20% seek assistance from sexual assault or women's centers; less than 11% report to the police; and less than 6% file a formal complaint through the campus conduct process (Holland & Cortina, 2017; see also Sabina & Ho, 2014; Khan et al., 2018). No recent studies indicate that reporting rates have increased despite the greater dedication of campus resources and development of formal adjudication systems. This may be especially true for students of color (Murphy, 2015). Holland and Cortina (2017) surveyed 840 undergraduate females in 2015 at a Midwestern university, with 284 (34%) reporting at least one sexual assault as a student. Only 16 (5.6%) disclosed their victimization to any of the three campus support offices—Residential Life, Sexual Assault Center, or Title IX Office. Only five students (1.7%) filed a formal complaint. The researchers examined reasons for nonreporting and many of them point to the need for an alternative approach. They believed the assault was insufficiently severe to warrant the formalist response, they did not think their case would be treated confidentially, they thought a formal hearing process would be too disruptive to them and their offenders. "In our study, reasons that survivors did not use the Title IX Office's formal grievance procedures mirrored top reasons that survivors do not report to the police . . . Thus, it may be beneficial to examine if there are effective alternatives to a quasi-criminal justice model. For instance, restorative justice" (p. 62). If survivors find the complaint process to be too intrusive, disruptive, and prolonged, they are not likely to make use of it as a resource.

Campus Communities Become Polarized and a Climate of Anxiety Grows

Adversarial processes heighten divisiveness on campus. For example, when Amy files a complaint against Kevin, one of the most common interventions by a university will be to invoke a "no contact order," warning each student to avoid one another and stop any communication between them (ATIXA, 2017). This order is likely to remain in place until the students graduate (or Kevin is expelled). The goal is to protect Amy from further harm, particularly through retaliation by Kevin. Although no contact orders are often helpful, one of their unintended consequences is ongoing anxiety about maintaining them. Students continually look over their shoulders, worrying about seeing the other on campus. Friendship groups become divided. Conflicts arise between supporters of Kevin and supporters of Amy. Campaigns begin on social media that call Amy a liar or Kevin a rapist. Amy's victim advocate is torn between encouraging Amy to pursue an increasingly stressful, quasi-public, adversarial process and a more private, inwardly focused healing process. Kevin begins to suffer from the public shaming common to sex offenders (Tewksbury, 2012). The adversarial response heightens anxiety, distrust, and campus polarization.

Adversarial Adjudication Exaggerates Biased Decision-Making

In this hypothetical case, so little information is provided that it is easy to embellish the story with a biased interpretation, one that is either favorable to a claim that Amy was assaulted or a claim that Kevin had legitimate consent. For many years, conduct administrators have been influenced by a study that suggests Kevin is likely to be a serial rapist. This study of college males was conducted in the 1990s by Lisak and Miller (2002). According to Coker's (2016, p. 171) review of the impact of this research on campus sexual assault policy, the dominant narrative is "(1) that *most* undetected rapists are predators; (2) that repeat assaulters (predators) account for most rapes; and (3) that the only appropriate response to predators is to remove them." If Lisak's study is an informal guide for policy and procedure, then hearing boards are likely to be biased against Kevin, assuming his motivation was to take sexual advantage of Amy through incapacitation. ATIXA's model policy encourages this conclusion.

Recent research complicates the dominant narrative by finding the serial predator model to be inadequate. A study by Swartout et al. (2015) does not dispute the severity of the campus sexual assault problem, but suggests that there is much more heterogeneity among those who commit sexual assault (or are accused of doing so), including those who, under the influence of alcohol, misperceive their partner's sexual intentions and decision-making capacity. Further evidence that college males often misperceive female sexual desire and consent was found by Lofgreen et al. (2017). Hearing board members that reject the predator model may be more likely to rule in Kevin's favor. Kevin, they might believe, may have had consent from Amy and not interpreted her behaviors as indications of incapacitation. Distinguishing "drunk sex" from incapacitation is complicated (McCreary, 2015). What is troublesome about Kevin is that he failed to observe or ignored warning signs of incapacitation. But what is troublesome about finding him in violation is Amy's sexual advances and explicit expression of consent. Forced to choose, with limited evidence at hand, it is likely that conduct administrators will be influenced by their beliefs about whether students are likely to be sexual predators. Presented with the same fact pattern, outcomes by hearing boards may be deeply influenced by adjudicator bias.

Accused Students Express Greater Denials of Responsibility

Regulatory formalism encourages rigid adherence to explicit policy. ATIXA seeks to provide clarity by stating unequivocally that Kevin is in violation. Kevin is likely to disagree. From his perspective, Amy initiated sexual activity and Kevin has verbally double-checked her consent. The line between drunk and incapacitated is not clear. He was not certain that she threw up or that she passed out. There are no other witnesses to attest to her incapacitation. Amy, herself, doesn't remember, which may indicate that she was incapacitated, but not a criterion that Kevin could have used to assess her ability to consent since she could lucidly verbally consent to sex in a "blackout" state, but not remember it.

Based on the scenario provided, we do not know if Kevin meant to cause harm or believed his behavior to be nonconsensual. We do know that Amy's harm was traumatic enough to persevere through the obstacles of reporting and file a complaint. In this case, the policy violation would typically lead to suspension or expulsion. In a zero-sum, high-stakes grievance process, Kevin is not likely to interpret this outcome as fair. Sherman (1993) argues that such a situation is more likely to lead to defiance than acceptance of responsibility. Rather than experiencing shame for causing harm, even if inadvertent, Kevin is likely to believe he is being unfairly labeled and stigmatized. This may increase gender hostility in accused students and lead to future transgressions. If Kevin is separated from the university, it is not clear that he will have learned anything except the system is unfair and that Amy is to blame for getting him in trouble. He will take these beliefs with him wherever he goes, perhaps to a place with little awareness about Kevin's behavior and fewer resources to support his growth, change, and development.

Accused Students Believe the Process Is Illegitimate and File More Lawsuits

If Kevin denies responsibility and believes he was treated unfairly, he may reject the legitimacy of the process (Tyler, 2006). Under the Obama administration, guidance by OCR was designed to clarify and make consistent the adjudication process, which might make it easier to find accused students in violation (Bartholet et al., 2017; Villasenor, 2016). For example, OCR has advocated for use of the preponderance of the evidence standard (the lowest standard of proof) and trauma-informed training of hearing board members (so they can see complainants as credible even when their actions may seem contradictory or unreliable due to memory impairment, changing statements over time, or behavioral reactions such as passivity during the incident). The backlash against these efforts has come in the form of lawsuits charging universities with failing to provide sufficient due process. Reviewing litigation of Title IX cases from 2014 to the first part of 2017, Pavela (2017) reports that accused students have prevailed in a majority of cases, either in preliminary or final rulings. Campuses are seeing more litigation as many students question the fairness of the hearing process. In 2018, the Trump administration has proposed changes that prioritize due process, which may shift the perception that the process is illegitimate from accused students to complainants (Carleton, 2018).

Disparities Grow between Rich and Poor, White and Black

If Kevin was poor or black, the likelihood that he would be found in violation may be increased (Halley, 2015; Rice Lave, 2016; Yoffe, 2017). Consider, for example, the Title IX case load at Colgate University during the three academic years of 2012–13 to 2014–15 (Yoffe, 2017). Although only 4 percent of Colgate's students are black, they accounted for 25 percent of sexual misconduct complaints and 15 percent of the students found responsible. Yoffe (p. 3) argues, "as the definition of sexual assault used by colleges has become wider and blurrier, it certainly seems possible that unconscious biases might tip some women toward viewing a regretted encounter with a man of a different race as an assault. And as the standards for proving assault have been lowered, it seems likely that those same biases, coupled with the lack of resources held by many minority students on campus, might systematically disadvantage men of color in adjudication, whether or not the encounter was interracial."

The stigma of being found in violation of sexual assault, the likelihood of suspension or expulsion, transcript notation, and the accompanying possibility of criminal prosecution all encourage accused students to hire lawyers to assist in their defense. No research demonstrates the effectiveness of lawyering up, but it probably reduces the chances of a student being found in violation, just as litigation has been effective in overturning such findings. Hiring a lawyer can cost a student tens of thousands of dollars (Kipnis, 2017), a fee that is inaccessible to most. Chances are less that students of color come from wealthy families and longstanding prejudice makes accusations against them more likely. It would not be surprising if poor students and students of color are more likely to be both accused of sexual assault and be found in violation of it.

Regulatory Formalism Undermines Female Agency

Did Kevin and Amy have non-policy-violation sex, as complicated, dissatisfying, and unpleasant as that might be, or is this an instance of sexual assault? The challenge is that it is so hard to know. ATIXA's solution is to tip in favor of the complainant. But in a recent case, charges were dropped against a University of Southern California student when a judge stated the complainant's sexual overtures indicated consent despite her intoxication (Alani, 2017). Kipnis (2017) argues that assuming college women cannot make their own sexual choices while drinking undermines female agency and perpetuates a presumption of female helplessness. "In a sexual culture that emphasizes female violation, endangerment, and perpetual vulnerability ('rape culture'), men's power is taken as a given instead of interrogated: men need to be policed, women need to be protected. If rape is the norm, then male sexuality is by definition predatory; women are, by definition, prey. Regulators thus rush in like rescuing heroes, doing what it takes to fend off the villains" (p. 14). Similarly, Iverson (2016, p. 24) argues that current campus policies create a "discourse of dependency [that] situates victims as reliant on others, namely university personnel, to mediate their experience, support them, and keep them safe." Not only does this discourse recapitulate a patriarchal framing of sexual assault as solely a victimization of women, it also marginalizes the sexual assault experiences of men and members of the LGBTQ community since they do not fit the prevailing heteronormative gender narrative (Wooten, 2016). While often referring to the goal of survivor empowerment, formalist policies may have the opposite effect of perpetuating gender stereotypes and discounting female agency.

The formalist approach was implemented to hold institutions accountable and strengthen campus responses to sexual assault. It has helped raise awareness and dedicate new campus resources to the problem. But it has also had troubling unintended consequences. It has not solved the problem of low reporting and may reify a concept of female helplessness. It helps perpetuate a serial predator model of male students, while failing to acknowledge the complexity of sexual encounters like Kevin and Amy's.

It discourages accused students from acknowledging harm, heightening adversarial, inequitable, and stigmatizing responses. Instead, what is needed is more authentic exploration by students, an exploration less focused on determining if a policy was violated than helping students like Kevin understand and take responsibility for Amy's experience of physical and emotional violation. Unlike the regulatory formalism of the "sex bureaucracy," in many cases a restorative approach may better respond to the problem of campus sexual assault.

Restorative Justice as Responsive Regulation

Several recent critiques of the current regulations have called for a restorative justice alternative (AAUP, 2016; ABA, 2017; Coker, 2016; Harper et al., 2017; Kaplan, 2017; Kirven, 2014; Koss & Lopez, 2014; Koss et al., 2014; Rice Lave, 2016). The Campus PRISM Project (Promoting Restorative Initiatives for Sexual Misconduct) comprises an international team of researchers and practitioners committed to reducing sexual and gender-based violence by exploring how a restorative approach may provide more healing and better accountability. It has a goal to "create space for scholars and practitioners to explore the use of RJ for campus sexual and gender-based misconduct (which includes sexual harassment, sexual assault, and other forms of gender-based misconduct) as an alternative or complement to current practices" (Karp et al., 2016, p. 2). The project's approach aligns with Braithwaite's (2002) regulatory pyramid (see Figure 10.2) by integrating RJ into the current regulatory scheme and offering preventive and first-alternative responses before turning to more adversarial interventions. Ultimately, the Project gives primacy to addressing harm and to creating the conditions in which it is safe enough for a student like Kevin to acknowledge causing harm and be actively accountable for it rather than perpetuate the conditions that provoke denials and minimization of responsibility.

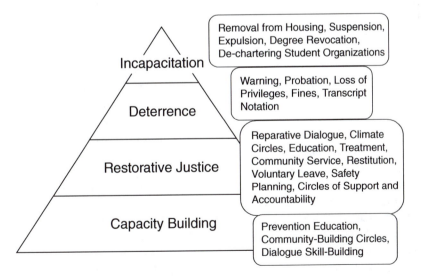

FIGURE 10.2   Braithwaite's Sanctioning Pyramid Adapted for Campus Sexual Assault Regulation

Sexual misconduct policies currently begin with the goal of offender incapacitation at the top of the pyramid. Most institutions recommend or mandate suspension or expulsion in a case like Kevin and Amy's. For a lesser violation, a student may be banned from campus housing. For a recent graduate, the degree may be revoked. If there was collusion by a student organization, such as a fraternity that conspires to incapacitate potential victims, the organization may be de-chartered and disbanded. These sanctions are designed to be retributive by providing a clear message of disapproval through the strongest punishments available to campuses. They also serve the purpose of incapacitation as measures intended to reduce the opportunity for reoffending.

The student may also be subject to deterrent sanctions, which are designed to impose a punitive cost. With these, the primary goal is an appeal to the rational decision-maker. By knowing the cost of misconduct, the student will choose to avoid it. This is lower on the pyramid because it still gives the student agency. Rather than banishment, the student is trusted enough to remain a member of the community, but expected to choose compliance. These sanctions include warnings, which are usually a letter maintained in a disciplinary file; probation, which may run for the duration of the student's attendance at the school and include a stipulation for more serious sanctions should the student reoffend; fines; and transcript notation, which becomes a permanent mark in the student record and disclosed to other educational institutions or employers upon request.

None of the above sanctions are designed to educate students, explore and address the harm caused by the incident, or treat students as moral beings capable of learning, growth, and development. It is possible, however, to begin with a restorative approach before resorting to deterrence or incapacitation. Most often, RJ is associated with face-to-face dialogue between victims and offenders. This is possible in sexual assault cases, but so are indirect forms of communication such as exchanges of writing or video recordings. Climate circles can be used to address broader community harms. Interventions focused on rebuilding trust and repairing harm include participation in educational workshops, counseling or treatment, restitution, and community service. Students may voluntarily take a leave of absence as a gesture of good faith. Overall safety planning may include the development of support and monitoring systems such as Circles of Support and Accountability (McMahon, Karp, & Mulhern, 2018).

One variation of Braithwaite's sanctioning pyramid includes a lower tier to highlight the importance of prevention efforts through capacity building (Braithwaite, 2017). Capacity building for the prevention of campus sexual assault would include prevention education, community-building circles, and skill-building education for campus community members to develop interpersonal communication competence. Community-building circles may enhance current prevention education efforts that primarily rely upon brochures, webpages, online workshops, and large auditorium presentations about campus sexual misconduct policy (Silbaugh, 2015). Circle practices offer members of the campus community a way to surface and explore issues related to sexual norms and behavior. They can be used for community building, personal and group reflection, facilitated discussions about sexual harm, rewriting cultural narratives about rape and hegemonic masculinity, and developing commitment to pro-social behavior along the stages-of-change continuum. RJ circles can be implemented as one-time events or a sustained series of dialogues.

In addition to Braithwaite's sanctioning pyramid, restorative justice practitioners, particularly in K–12 schools, often refer to a pyramid that illustrates a "whole school" approach that includes prevention, response, and reintegration. This pyramid does not order the priority of interventions, but instead illustrates a holistic implementation of restorative practices within a school community. Its original rendition drew upon a public health model (Morrison, 2007). Figure 10.3 adapts the K–12 RJ pyramid for "whole campus" application to campus sexual assault.

The whole campus approach includes three tiers of intervention. The first is designed for prevention education and intended for all members of the campus community—students, faculty, and staff. The goal is to build and strengthen relationships, foster trust, and develop interpersonal communication and conflict resolution skills. Circle practice offers an innovation through its emphasis on the intersection of information sharing, education, reflection, and community building. A circle-based approach incorporates the sharing of important technical and legal information that is universal to prevention education, but does so in a meaningful and intimate learning space. Circles provide a context that allows students to collectively analyze their personal views and experiences, at the same time making the learning process individually relevant. In circles, participants develop shared norms and community-based action plans, which can promote individual and group accountability as well as inclusive, restorative responses to harm.

Tier I prevention circles can take up a variety of topics for dialogue (Pointer, 2018). They may be used to articulate and set sexual standards for members of the campus community. Although codes of conduct are prescribed, the purpose of these circles is for participants to explore their own sexual values collectively. They may discuss the communication strategies of affirmative consent, the relationship between sex and drinking, and pressures students may feel to participate in a "hook-up culture" (Bogle, 2008; Wade, 2017). Students might examine their own experiences within a larger campus climate that may be supportive to them or may promote a more insidious "rape culture" (Burnett et al., 2009). Circles may be organized to explore trauma and strategies of resilience. Or they may simply offer safe spaces for students to share concerns or personal experiences. The following case study provides an example of a Tier I prevention circle facilitated at the University of California at Santa Cruz (Assegued, 2017).

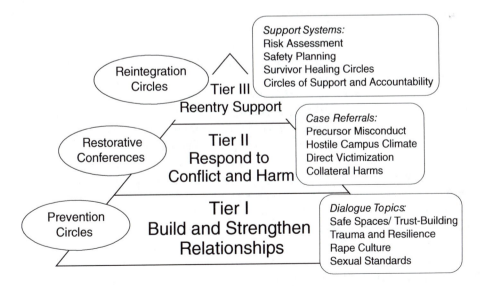

FIGURE 10.3 Whole Campus Restorative Justice Approach to Campus Sexual Assault

RESTORATIVE JUSTICE CIRCLE ADDRESSING SEXUAL VIOLENCE ON CAMPUS

In an effort to have an open dialogue and foster healing surrounding incidents of sexual violence and sexual harassment, Vicki Assegued, Restorative Justice Program Developer, Trainer and Facilitator at the University of California, Santa Cruz, organized a restorative community-building circle in 2017. Previously, Assegued had facilitated a restorative circle with students, faculty, and staff in an academic department that was reeling after a faculty member had been accused of sexually assaulting a graduate student. This healing circle provided so much social support, ideas for healing, and hope for the participants that Assegued was then asked to plan a circle to address sexual violence on campus, in general, and extend an open invitation to all members of the campus community.

Assegued collaborated with faculty from a working group, called Beyond Compliance, which seeks to reduce sexual violence and improve the campus sexual climate. Knowing the importance of the issue, but seeing that opportunities to openly discuss it were rare, the group wanted to invite the community to actively engage in a conversation within a structured, safe, and supportive format. They wanted to offer the chance for participants to express themselves openly and safely, to hear, acknowledge, and validate each other, to work collaboratively on solutions and to build a stronger sense of belonging to their wider community.

The circle agenda incorporated common elements of a restorative community-building process: creating a sense of connection, allowing people to discuss the harm associated with the topic, and brainstorming ways to address the harm and strengthen the community. Their circle began with a welcome to the 25 students, staff, and faculty in the circle, thanking them for coming, sharing the reasons for gathering, describing restorative justice and its benefits, and outlining how they would apply the principles together. They acknowledged the sensitive nature of the topic, introduced the support people who were there in case someone wanted to step out and talk one-on-one, and explained the use of the talking piece.

The three co-facilitators (Assegued and two faculty members she had trained) passed the talking piece around the circle for the first time, inviting participants to introduce themselves and express their hopes for addressing sexual violence on campus. Then, they divided into groups of four, being mindful to include mixes of students, staff, and faculty. The members of each small group discussed what inspired them to attend this gathering and what was most important for them to address about the topic of sexual violence on campus. After reassembling into the larger circle, a spokesperson from each group summarized their priorities.

Following this summary, the facilitators led an open, whole group discussion to brainstorm ideas about how to manifest their shared goals. They focused particularly on the importance of maintaining a strong community with transparency, trust, and openness for addressing issues of sexual violence. Ideas were captured on a large white pad for ongoing discussion and planning. Participants also shared upcoming events addressing sexual violence, giving everyone the opportunity to get more involved in the community.

In the closing round, they passed the talking piece again, with each person sharing how they felt about this restorative justice process and what it meant for them. Participants expressed their sincere appreciation for the opportunity. The facilitators closed the circle by summarizing and acknowledging what had taken place and thanking everyone for engaging in the process.

When an incident of harm occurs, Tier II restorative conferences can address the harm as an alternative or supplement to formal/adversarial hearings. Circle processes in response to harms can also be implemented. As of this writing, the Department of Education's Office for Civil Rights (OCR) has not provided guidance about the use of RJ for sexual and gender-based misconduct. In 2011, OCR briefly discusses informal resolution options and identifies mediation as permissible "for resolving some types of sexual harassment complaints," but inappropriate for sexual assault cases (U.S. Department of Education Office for Civil Rights, 2011). Because mediation and RJ are often confused, this stipulation has had a chilling effect on the application of RJ for sexual and gender-based misconduct. In 2017, OCR reversed the 2011 guidance and in a recently published document stated, "if a school determines that the particular Title IX complaint is appropriate for such a process, the school may facilitate an informal resolution, including mediation, to assist the parties in reaching a voluntary resolution" (U.S. Department of Education Office for Civil Rights, 2017, p. 4). This reversal will likely lead to increased use of restorative conferencing.

More commonly today, campuses are using conferencing for related harms. Collateral harms are those associated with an instance of direct victimization, but not the most immediate harms to the victim. For example, students may publicly criticize a harmed party in defense of the accused student or, alternatively, attack the accused student or that student's larger friend group. These ripple effects often play out over social media. Conferencing can also be used for harms to the campus climate, such as when a student group leads a "rape chant" (Foderaro, 2011) or a fraternity hangs a sexist banner during first-year orientation (Samuels, 2015). Campuses can readily use conferencing for precursor misconduct, such as binge drinking, hazing, or other behaviors that create the conditions in which sexual assault is most likely to occur. The following case study is a rare example of a restorative conference in response to an individual incident of sexual misconduct (Cirioni, 2016; Karp & Schachter, 2018; Lepp, 2018; Smith, 2017).

RESTORATIVE JUSTICE CONFERENCE IN RESPONSE TO A CAMPUS SEXUAL ASSAULT

Anwen and Sameer (pseudonyms) met in their first semester at a small, liberal arts college. They went on a date or two and then decided to remain friends. Fast forward to their second semester and they ran into each other at a party. Anwen noticed that Sameer was very intoxicated, but danced with him anyway. He became more sexually aggressive, isolating her in a private room. She tried to leave, but all of her friends had already gone, and she didn't have her dorm key or phone with her. Rather than assist her to get back to her room, Sameer persuaded her to go to his room instead. Once there, Anwen felt trapped and pressured into sexual activity she did not consent to and did not want. Afterwards, she said she walked "around for several days feeling disgust with myself, feeling a ghost hurt between my legs where he rubbed me, feeling dirty, blocking the thoughts."

Anwen stayed silent about her harm for the next three years. Throughout that time, she came into contact with Sameer on numerous occasions, especially through their roles as student orientation leaders. This incident and their following interactions affected her both socially and academically. In the spring of her senior year, Anwen reported the incident to the campus conduct administrator. She specifically requested that it be handled through an informal resolution process that would let her meet with Sameer so she could share how much she had been hurt by him. Otherwise, she did not want him to be suspended or expelled, nor did she want to involve the local police. Afterwards, Anwen explained, "What's important to me about the restorative justice process is that both people are given a space where they are empowered to make things better. I didn't want to take away his agency because that would just be reversing the roles." Sameer said, "Every time that I've wanted to punish myself beyond all belief she always said no, I want you to do better. Don't just take the easy route and lock yourself up or get yourself kicked off campus because that's not going to help anybody. She never wanted to punish me. She wanted me to learn. She wanted me to grow. She wanted me to prevent this from ever happening to others."

The conduct administrator met with Sameer, told him of Anwen's complaint, and Sameer immediately admitted to a sexual misconduct violation and expressed his deep remorse. He agreed that he did want to do whatever he could to meet Anwen's request and make up for what he had done. The administrator met individually with Anwen 12 times and Sameer seven times before bringing the two together. His conversations with Anwen were focused on regaining the power that she felt she had lost. The conversations with Sameer explored how he could take ownership and responsibility for his actions; what he could do to repair the harm he caused.

The facilitated RJ dialogue lasted for two hours. It allowed Anwen to share the pain she felt. Initially, she had felt isolated and intimidated. Later, she started to blame herself for not calling security. She felt guilty thinking that she led him on. These feelings of self-blame were triggered each time she saw him. Her role as an orientation leader was compromised due to his presence. Anwen's relationship with her new partner never felt whole because she prevented herself from feeling vulnerable with him. As a creative writing major, much of her work had been about the violation. She wanted Sameer to read her papers and write a response.

Sameer committed to fully hear about the harm he caused and to take responsibility. "For my end, this was just a fun hook up, but then from her end, this guy is pushing himself on me. It didn't sound like me; it sounded like a monster. That was the hardest part. This guy who forced himself on to this girl is me." He agreed to be found formally in violation of the campus sexual misconduct policy and have a formal "conduct reprimand" in his file. Since Sameer had no other conduct charges in the three years since this incident and as it was just weeks before their graduation, the administrator decided that Sameer was not a threat to others and would not need to be suspended or expelled.

Collaboratively, they developed a list of remedies that best met Anwen's needs and the concerns of the institution:

- Reading and responding to Anwen's extensive writing about the incident.
- Writing an article discussing the misconduct for a student magazine that focuses on issues of gender and sexuality.
- Teaching others about the incident. Both Anwen and Sameer agreed to present their story together at a campus bystander intervention workshop, focusing on how power, privilege, emotional manipulation, and coercion help facilitate and perpetuate campus sexual misconduct.

- Collaborating with gender violence programming on campus to advocate for mandatory bystander intervention and other prevention training for all student athletes and Greek Letter organizations as well as developing strategies to encourage sincere and engaged participation by these students.
- Reaching out to students who provide peer support for sexual assault survivors to identify ways in which student offenders could speak with them and learn from them.
- Developing sexual violence prevention education programming for local middle and high school students.

After the RJ dialogue, Anwen and Sameer met regularly to plan their presentation and worked together to create a video where they recounted the night of the incident, each sharing what happened from their perspective. Sameer, after he graduated, continued to work with the conduct administrator for six months in order to finalize the community service project focused on prevention education in the local schools. Two years later, Anwen observed, "One of the things I realized during and after the restorative justice process is that Sameer's honestly one of the people that knows me best and I him. We know each other's deepest horrible moment. There's not a lot that can't be said. I don't think I'll ever lose contact entirely with Sameer."

Tier III restorative interventions assist with the reintegration of students who have been suspended. Not only are these students anxious about how they will be received upon their return to campus, but the wider community needs reassurance that they will be responsible and committed to causing no further harm. Following the highly successful restorative justice model for sex offenders returning to the community after incarceration, Circles of Support and Accountability (CoSA) can be developed to support returning students (Karp et al., 2016). CoSAs meet frequently with the student to provide social support, but also monitor the student's behavior and intervene early if concerns arise. Concurrently, support circles for survivors can help reduce their anxiety during this transition period. They may be organized to specifically support the survivor of a returning student or be a reciprocally supportive circle of survivors.

REENTRY CIRCLE FOR A STUDENT SUSPENDED FOR SEXUAL MISCONDUCT

A reentry circle was convened for an undergraduate student's return to a U.S. university campus after a period of separation due to an incident of sexual misconduct (McMahon et al., 2018). The staff who participated in the circle included three representatives from the Dean of Students Office, one person from Academic Affairs, one person from the international study office, and a representative from the campus counseling center. In addition, there were three support people for the returning student who were members of the campus community: a male student leader and two faculty members.

The student of concern, "Ivan" (a pseudonym), was a junior when he was suspended for coercion for sexual activity. The reentry circle was included in the sanctioning process as a prerequisite to Ivan's request to study abroad for his academic return to campus. As a student of color at a predominantly White institution, Ivan was involved in significant social justice leadership roles on campus. At the time of the incident of sexual misconduct, Ivan was struggling with significant mental health issues and these were central to understanding the context in which he committed the harm, was separated from the institution, and his return to campus.

During the preparation process, the facilitators interviewed the circle participants, asking: 1) How could they serve as a resource to Ivan? 2) What concerns did they have about Ivan and his reentry process? and 3) What was their connection to this incident and to Ivan? When the facilitators spoke with Ivan, he expressed anger and a sense of isolation after interacting with the staff during the formal Title IX process. The facilitators listened and reflected back what they heard Ivan say, reiterating that the focus of the reentry circle was to provide support to Ivan *and* to address the needs of the community members with whom he would be studying abroad. Staff members expressed concerns about institutional racism, tokenism, and fears about possible racial revictimization of Ivan in the circle as a result of these dynamics on campus. There were also concerns about the timing of the circle, as Ivan would not be returning directly to the campus, but re-enrolling as a student and studying abroad first.

The reentry circle is structured by elements common to restorative circle practices (Boyes-Watson & Pranis, 2015). These include the use of a "talking piece" (a symbolic object that is passed from speaker to speaker); circular turn-taking as the talking piece is passed sequentially around the circle; and phases of the circle that begin with questions or activities that help to establish trust, progress to questions of concern, and then collective brainstorming to develop a plan for action—in this case a plan for reintegration support. The questions posed in this reentry circle included: 1) Can you describe a time in which you faced a difficult reintegration or community transition? 2) How are you connected to the issue at hand? 3) What happened from your perspective? 4) What concerns do we need to address? 5) What needs do we have to meet? 6) What plan will address those concerns and needs?

In their reflections on this circle, the facilitators observed that there was a great deal of sadness about this incident of sexual misconduct, as Ivan was a well-respected student leader on campus. The concerns expressed by participants included a variety of themes including mental health; lost student leadership opportunities; frustration with the formal adjudication process; social support while studying abroad; concerns about race and racism on campus; and how the campus climate could affect Ivan's overall well-being and his reintegration to the campus community.

To meet the needs of this student and the campus community, the group committed to regular check-ins with Ivan throughout his time abroad and upon his return to campus. For his part, Ivan agreed to participate in a facilitated conversation with the student leader who attended the circle in order to address peers' concerns about him upon his return to campus. Counseling center staff agreed to reinvigorate efforts to address the mental health needs of students of color. Administrators committed to reviewing the campus Title IX process for best practices, as well as ways to increase communication, transparency, and support for all parties involved in the process.

Conclusion

This chapter has drawn a distinction between the current regulatory framework for campus sexual assault and a restorative justice approach. Table 10.2 summarizes key distinctions. The current approach is challenged by a focus on determining violations when evidence in sexual assault cases is often weak. The RJ approach focuses less on the violation in favor of identifying and addressing harm. The current approach promotes denials of responsibility, while an RJ approach seeks to increase responsibility-taking. The current approach polarizes participants and campus communities, often leading to litigation, whereas RJ seeks collaborative solutions that avoid adversarialism. RJ is intended to be inclusive, particularly for people with little access to lawyers and other dimensions of social privilege. RJ is intended to offer resolution options that better meet the needs of the key stakeholders, increasing their likelihood of reporting misconduct and pursuing a resolution process. RJ seeks strategies, where possible, to reduce fear, offer social support, and make it possible for students to coexist safely on campus. RJ seeks to provide voice and empowerment to participants, treating them with respect and a belief that their active participation will yield better, more durable outcomes for all.

Despite the promise of RJ for campus sexual misconduct, several challenges and questions remain to be addressed.

The Opportunity and Pressure to Participate

One of the primary values of restorative justice is voluntary participation. It is easy for a university to write policy that states participation is voluntary and no institution is likely to require participation in an RJ process for an incident of sexual harm. But it is more difficult to protect against coercive pressure, which is much more subjective. An assault survivor may experience pressure to respond in various ways, and the anticipation of such external pressure may be one reason so many survivors choose not to report their victimization. They may experience pressure to report or not to report; to go forward with a restorative justice process or a formal hearing process; to go to the police; to speak publicly about their victimization; to join solidarity groups, and so on. Victim advocates, as representatives of the institution, may be torn between encouraging the survivor to avoid an adversarial process that may be retraumatizing and encouraging them to go forward because they want the institution to hold the offender accountable. Friends may want the survivor to proceed as a political act in support of the student movement against sexual assault. Or they may discourage the survivor from responding because they also share a friendship with the offender. Any institutional representative of an RJ process must present the option in a way that is informative without adding to the inevitable pressures that already exist.

TABLE 10.2 Distinguishing Regulatory Formalism and Responsive Regulation for Campus Sexual Assault

Regulatory Formalism under Title IX	Responsive Regulation/RJ
Focus on policy violation under uncertainty	Focus on harm
Denial of responsibility	Conditions for taking responsibility
Adversarial/backlash	Collaborative
Economic/racial disparities	Accessible
Low reporting/filing	Responsive to reporting needs
Separation (no contact, suspension)	Peaceful coexistence or reconciliation
Undermines agency	Empowerment/voice

For an accused student, the opportunity to participate may provide a path to meaningful accountability. But it may also put the student at risk for harsher consequences should the RJ process fail. Although survivors can always pursue a formal hearing or criminal case, using the RJ process to obtain evidence for them is problematic. It is essential to develop policy mechanisms to protect the confidentiality of the RJ process in order to prevent it from becoming a retributive mechanism for obtaining confessions (Coker, 2016). RJ conferences must be both voluntary and confidential.

Public Accountability

Restorative justice conferences are a private process and participants are often concerned with confidentiality. They are designed to be emotionally transformative for the participants as they gain a deeper understanding of each other's perspectives. Agreements are created that reflect this and are customized to meet the unique needs of those involved. Onlookers to the process, however, do not experience this transformation and can have a hard time understanding the outcome, especially when it deviates from standard retributive punishments. The wider community also needs "justice" and is looking for predictable, substantive outcomes. A private process with a limited number of participants cannot easily provide this broader, public accountability. The most likely candidates to be effective spokespersons on behalf of the RJ process are harmed parties, but again it is important not to impose further burdens. In a well-known application of RJ in response to campus sexual harassment at Dalhousie University (Llewellyn, Chapter 9 this volume), the harmed students were among the persuasive voices in favor of the RJ process (Llewellyn, Demsey, & Smith, 2015). In one conferencing script, participants are specifically asked if and how they would like to communicate the outcomes of their agreement with the larger community (Karp, 2015). Ideally, individual RJ cases not only explore private harms, but the broader factors that lead to and perpetuate sexual assault. They should inspire responsive actions that meet individual needs and address systemic issues that affect campus climate.

Informal vs. Formal Process

Often, RJ is categorized as an alternative dispute resolution process, like arbitration or mediation. It may be a diversion from formal adjudication. This can be a procedural advantage to avoid the effects of formal labeling, but unfortunately positions RJ as the informal, experimental, non-serious approach and, therefore, more easily dismissed. Braithwaite's sanctioning pyramid helps codify its location within a larger regulatory framework, adding to its legitimacy. A central question for campus policy is whether it is necessary for a student to agree to be formally found in violation of the sexual misconduct policy as an indication of their willingness to take responsibility. Or, can a purely informal, diversionary process be perceived as meeting the standards of institutional accountability that many are demanding?

Safety

Restorative justice emphasizes mutual understanding, which requires communication, often face to face. The standard campus response in the face of safety concerns is social distance, either through a no-contact order or a progressive separation (removal from co-enrolled classes, housing, suspension, expulsion). Restorative justice encourages the development of informal social control systems that enlist those who are closest to the key stakeholders, much like bystander intervention programs are designed for those most likely to be in proximity to a dangerous situation. Restorative justice calls for a paradigmatic shift away from the common belief that separation is the only means to achieve safety. Overcoming entrenched beliefs that separation is the only and best option for safety is a significant challenge.

Campus sexual assault has been a regulatory nightmare, but it does not have to remain that way. Restorative justice can provide a new approach that provides accountability for a deeply hurtful form of misconduct, but does so in a way that leverages social support and leads to healing for individuals and a safer campus climate for living and learning. RJ is a promising approach, though it will not be suitable for or chosen by everyone. Implementation will need to be slow and considered, but it is one of the few hopeful innovations available for this vexing social problem.

References

AAUP. (2016). *The history, uses, and abuses of Title IX*. Washington, DC: American Association of University Professors. Retrieved from www.aaup.org/report/history-uses-and-abuses-title-ix.

ABA. (2017). *ABA criminal justice section task force on college due process rights and victim protections: Recommendations for colleges and universities in resolving allegations of campus sexual assault*. Chicago, IL: American Bar Association. Retrieved from www.americanbar.org/content/dam/aba/publications/criminaljustice/2017/ABA-Due-Process-Task-Force-Recommendations-and-Report.authcheckdam.pdf.

ACPA. (2017). *ACPA-college student educators launches compliance U*. Washington, DC: ACPA. March 24. Retrieved from www.myacpa.org/article/acpa-college-student-educators-launches-compliance-u%E2%84%A2.

Affirmative Consent Laws. (2017). Retrieved from http://affirmativeconsent.com/affirmative-consent-laws-state-by-state/.

Alani, H. (2017). Judge drops rape case against U.S.C. student, citing video evidence. *New York Times*, August 5. Retrieved from www.nytimes.com/2017/08/05/us/usc-rape-case-dropped-video-evidence.html.

Assegued, V. (2017). Personal communication, May 2.

ATIXA. (2017). *ATIXA position statement on the equitable use of no-contact orders*. Berwyn, PA: Association of Title IX Administrators. Retrieved from https://atixa.org/wordpress/wp-content/uploads/2015/03/2017-POSITION-NCOs_FINAL.pdf.

Bartholet, E., Gertner, N., Halley, J., & Suk Gersen, J. (2017). Fairness for all students under Title IX. *Digital Access to Scholarship at Harvard*. Retrieved from https://dash.harvard.edu/handle/1/33789434.

Bogle, K. A. (2008). *Hooking up: Sex dating, and relationships on campus*. New York: New York University Press.

Boyes-Watson, C., & Pranis, K. (2015). *Circle forward: Building a restorative school community*. St. Paul, MN: Living Justice Press.

Braithwaite, J. (2002). *Restorative justice and responsive regulation*. New York: Oxford.

Braithwaite, J. (2017). *Responsive regulation*. Webpage. Retrieved from http://johnbraithwaite.com/responsive-regulation/.

Brown, S. (2017). An uncertain future for Title IX Compliance Consultants. *Chronicle of Higher Education*, January 24.

Brownmiller, S. (2000). *In our time: Memoir of a revolution*. New York: Dial.

Burford, G., & Adams, P. (2004). Restorative justice, responsive regulation and social work. *The Journal of Sociology & Social Welfare, 31*(1), 7–26.

Burnett, A., Mattern, J. L., Herakova, L. L., Kahl, D. J., Tobola, C., & Bornsen, S. E. (2009). Communicating/muting date rape: A co-cultural theoretical analysis of communication factors related to rape culture on a college campus. *Journal of Applied Communication Research, 37*(4), 465–485.

Busch-Armendariz, N. B., Wood, L., Kammer-Kerwick, M., Kellison, B., Sulley, C., Westbrook, L., . . . Hoefer, S. (2017). *Cultivating learning and safe environments: An empirical study of prevalence and perceptions of sexual harassment, stalking, dating/domestic abuse and violence, and unwanted sexual contact—The University of Texas System Academic Institutions*. Austin, TX: Institute on Domestic Violence & Sexual Assault, The University of Texas at Austin.

Campus Sexual Violence Elimination Act of 2013, 20 USC § 1092(f)(8)(B)(i)(I).

Carleton, A. (2018). Instead of protecting victims, Title IX changes would favor institutions and perpetrators. *WBUR Boston Public Radio*, September 12. Retrieved from https://www.wbur.org/cognoscenti/2018/09/12/campus-sexual-harassment-amy-carleton.

Chronicle of Higher Education. (2018). *Title IX: Tracking investigations.* Retrieved September 25, 2018, from https://projects.chronicle.com/titleix/.

Cirioni, F. (2016). Personal communication. July 11.

Coker, D. (2016). Crime logic, campus sexual assault, and restorative justice. *Texas Tech Law Review, 49,* 147–210.

Dick, K. (Director). (2015). *The hunting ground* [Documentary]. Los Angeles, CA: Chain Camera Pictures.

Ederly, S. R. (2014). A rape on campus: A brutal assault and struggle for justice at UVA. *Rolling stone,* November 19. Retrieved from www.rollingstone.com/culture/features/a-rape-on-campus-20141119.

Foderaro, L. W. (2011). At Yale, sharper look at treatment of women. *New York Times,* April 7. Retrieved from www.nytimes.com/2011/04/08/nyregion/08yale.html.

Gersen, J., & Suk, J. (2016). The sex bureaucracy. *California Law Review, 104,* 881–948.

Gray, E. (2014). The sexual assault crisis on American campuses. *Time,* May 15. Retrieved from http://time.com/100542/the-sexual-assault-crisis-on-american-campuses/.

Halley, J. (2015). Trading the megaphone for the gavel in Title IX enforcement. *Harvard Law Review, 123,* 103–117.

Harper, S., Maskaly, J., Kirkner, A., & Lorenz, K. (2017). Enhancing Title IX due process standards in campus sexual assault adjudication: Considering the roles of distributive, procedural, and restorative justice. *Journal of School Violence, 16,* 302–316.

Holland, K. J., & Cortina, L. M. (2017). "It happens to girls all the time": Examining sexual assault survivors' reasons for not using campus supports. *American Journal of Community Psychology, 59,* 50–64. doi: 10.1002/ajcp.12126.

Iverson, S. V. (2016). A policy discourse analysis of sexual assault policies in higher education. In R. Mitchell & S. C. Wooten (Eds.), *The crisis of campus sexual violence: Critical perspectives on prevention and response* (pp. 15–32). New York: Routledge.

Jeanne Clery Disclosure of Campus Security Policy and Campus Crime Statistics Act of 1990, 20 U.S.C. § 1092(f).

Kaplan, M. (2017). Restorative justice and campus sexual misconduct. *Temple Law Review, 89,* 701.

Karp, D. R. (2015). *The little book of restorative justice for colleges and universities* (2nd ed.). New York: Good Books.

Karp, D. R., & Schachter, M. (2018). Restorative justice in colleges and universities: What works when addressing student misconduct. In T. Gavrielides (Ed.), *The Routledge handbook of restorative justice* (pp. 247–263). New York: Routledge.

Karp, D. R., Shackford-Bradley, J., Wilson, R. J., & Williamsen, K. M. (2016). *Campus PRISM: A report on promoting restorative initiatives for sexual misconduct on college campuses.* Saratoga Springs, NY: Skidmore College Project on Restorative Justice. Retrieved from www.skidmore.edu/campusrj/documents/Campus_PRISM_Report_2016.pdf.

Khan, S. R., Hirsch, J. S., Wamboldt, A., & Mellins, C. A. (2018). "I didn't want to be 'that girl'": The social risks of labeling, telling, and reporting sexual assault. *Sociological Science, 5,* 432–460.

Kipnis, L. (2017). *Unwanted advances: Sexual paranoia comes to campus.* New York: Harper Collins.

Kirven, S. J. (2014). Isolation to empowerment: A review of the campus rape adjudication process. *Journal of International Criminal Justice Research, 2,* 1–15.

Koss, M. P., & Lopez, E. C. (2014). VAWA after the party: Implementing proposed guidelines on campus sexual assault resolution. *CUNY Law Review, 18,* 4–13.

Koss, M. P., Wilgus, J. K., & Williamsen, K. M. (2014). Campus sexual misconduct: Restorative justice approaches to enhance compliance with Title IX guidance. *Trauma, Violence & Abuse, 15,* 242–257.

Krakauer, J. (2015). *Missoula: Rape and the justice system in a college town.* New York: Doubleday.

Lepp, S. (Producer). (2018, December 3). A survivor and her perpetrator find justice [Audio podcast]. Retrieved from http://www.reckonings.show/episodes/21.

Lisak, D., & Miller, P. (2002). Repeat rape and multiple offending among undetected rapists. *Violence & Victims, 17*(1), 73–84.

Llewellyn, J. J., Demsey, A., & Smith, J. (2015). An unfamiliar justice story: Restorative justice and education. Reflections on Dalhousie's Facebook Incident 2015. *Our Schools/Our Selves, 25,* 43–56.

Lofgreen, A. M., Mattson, R. E., Wagner, S. A., Ortiz, E. G., & Johnson, M. D. (2017). Situational and dispositional determinants of college men's perception of women's sexual desire and consent to sex: A factorial vignette analysis. *Journal of Interpersonal Violence.* https://doi.org/10.1177/0886260517738777.

McCreary, G. (2015). The drunk sex problem. *Perspectives.* October, 10–14.

McMahon, S. M., Karp, D. R., & Mulhern, H. (2018). Addressing individual and community needs in the aftermath of campus sexual misconduct: Restorative justice as a way forward in the re-entry process. *Journal of Sexual Aggression.* doi: 10.1080/13552600.2018.1507488.

Mitchell, R., & Wooten, S. C. (Eds.). (2016). *The crisis of campus sexual violence: Critical perspectives on prevention and response.* New York: Routledge.

Morrison, B. (2007). *Restoring safe school communities: A whole school response to bullying, violence and alienation.* Sydney, Australia: Federation Books.

Morse, A., Sponsler, B. A., & Fulton, M. (2015). *State legislative development on campus sexual violence: Issues in the context of safety.* Washington, DC: NASPA. Retrieved from www.naspa.org/images/uploads/main/ECS_NASPA_BRIEF_DOWNLOAD3.pdf.

Murphy, C. (2015). Another challenge on campus sexual assault: Getting minority students to report it. *The Chronicle of Higher Education,* June 18. Retrieved from http://chronicle.com/article/Another-Challenge-on-Campus/230977.

Pavela, G. (2017). *Sexual misconduct litigation update.* Retrieved from https://docs.google.com/document/d/1NdB4k736siV6cdIWVNpIzntEizNAQOG5jR0pfCyGVR0/edit.

Pointer, L. (2018). *Restorative dialogue as a means to understand sexually harmful behavior. Diana Unwin Chair in Restorative Justice.* Wellington, NZ: Victoria University.

Rice Lave, T. (2016). Ready, fire, aim: How universities are failing the constitution in sexual assault cases. *Arizona State Law Journal, 48,* 637.

Sabina, C., & Ho, L. Y. (2014). Campus and college victim responses to sexual assault and dating violence: Disclosure, service utilization, and service provision. *Trauma, Violence, & Abuse, 15*(3), 201–226. doi: 10.1177/1524838014521322.

Samuels, A. (2015). Frat suspended over "freshman daughter drop off" signs. *USA Today,* August 25. Retrieved from www.usatoday.com/story/news/nation-now/2015/08/24/virginia-frat-suspended-old-dominion-university/32298193/.

SB-967 Student safety: Sexual assault. (2014). Retrieved from https://leginfo.legislature.ca.gov/faces/billNavClient.xhtml?bill_id=201320140SB967.

Sherman, L. W. (1993). Defiance, deterrence, and irrelevance: A theory of the criminal sanction. *Journal of Research in Crime and Delinquency, 30*(4), 445–473.

Silbaugh, K. (2015). Reactive to proactive: Title IX's unrealized capacity to prevent campus sexual assault. *Boston University Law Review, 95,* 1049–1076.

Smith, T. (2017). With an eye on healing, campuses try new way of handling campus assault cases. *NPR All Things Considered.* July 25. Retrieved from www.npr.org/2017/07/25/539334346/restorative-justice-an-alternative-to-the-process-campuses-use-for-sexual-assaul.

Sokolow, B. A., Lewis, W. S., Schuster, S. K., & Swinton, D. C. (2015). *ATIXA gender-based and sexual misconduct model policy.* Berwyn, PA: Association of Title IX Administrators. Retrieved from www.atixa.org/wordpress/wp-content/uploads/2012/01/ATIXA-Model-Policy-041715.pdf.

SUNY. (2017). *Sexual assault & violence response (SAVR) resources.* Albany, NY: State University of New York. Retrieved from www.suny.edu/violence-response/.

Swartout, K., Koss, M. P., White, J. W., Thompson, M. P., Abbey, A., & Bellis, A. L. (2015). Trajectory analysis of the campus serial rapist assumption. *JAMA Pediatrics, 169*(12), 1148–1154. doi: 10.1001/jamapediatrics.2015.0707.

Tewksbury, R. (2012). Stigmatization of sex offenders. *Deviant Behavior, 33*(8), 606–623. doi: 10.1080/01639625.2011.636690.

Title IX of the Education Amendments of 1972, 20 U.S.C. §1681.

Tyler, T. R. (2006). Restorative justice and procedural justice: Dealing with rule breaking. *Journal of Social Issues, 62*(2), 307–326. doi: 10.1111/j.1540-4560.2006.00452.x.

U.S. Department of Education, Office for Civil Rights. (2011, April 4). *Dear colleague letter: Sexual violence background, summary, and fast facts*. Retrieved from http://www2.ed.gov/about/offices/list/ocr/letters/colleague-201104. html.

U.S. Department of Education, Office for Civil Rights. (2017). *Q&A on campus sexual misconduct*. September. Retrieved from https://www2.ed.gov/about/offices/list/ocr/docs/qa-title-ix-201709.pdf.

Villasenor, J. (2016). A probabilistic framework for modelling false Title IX "convictions" under the preponderance of the evidence standard. *Law, Probability & Risk, 15*(4), 223–237. doi: 10.1093/lpr/mgw006.

Violence Against Women Act of 1994, 42 U.S.C. § 13701.

Wade, L. (2017). *American hookup: The new culture of sex on campus*. New York: W.W. Norton.

Wooten, S. C. (2016). Heterosexist discourses: How feminist theory shaped campus sexual violence policy. In R. Mitchell & S. C. Wooten (Eds.), *The crisis of campus sexual violence: Critical perspectives on prevention and response* (pp. 33–52). New York: Routledge.

Yoffe, E. (2017). The question of race in campus sexual-assault cases. *The Atlantic*. September 11.

11

RESPONSIVE ALTERNATIVES TO THE CRIMINAL LEGAL SYSTEM IN CASES OF INTIMATE PARTNER VIOLENCE

Leigh Goodmark

Introduction

In the United States, as in most nations of the Global North, the primary regulatory response to intimate partner violence is the criminal legal system. Since the late 1970s, the United States has stepped up enforcement of existing law, enacted new laws criminalizing intimate partner violence, increased penalties for particular acts of intimate partner violence, and funded intervention programs that rely primarily on law enforcement. As former Vice President Joe Biden recently stated, "Violence against women is a crime, pure and simple" (United State of Women Summit, 2016).

But intimate partner violence is not quite that simple, and the crime-based regulatory response to intimate partner violence is often ineffective and destructive. The concentrated attention to and funding of the United States' criminal legal system response to intimate partner violence for the last 40 years has had little if any impact on rates of domestic violence and has produced serious unintended consequences. Moreover, as John Braithwaite has argued, regulation should provide a space for healing when people violate their obligations towards one another (Braithwaite, 2002). For many people subjected to abuse, the criminal legal system fails to provide that healing space, or, put differently, fails to meet the justice needs of those who have been harmed. Criminalization of intimate partner violence, working alone, is not serving its regulatory function. Restorative justice could help. Supplementing the criminal legal response to intimate partner violence with restorative regulatory strategies could increase the justice options available to people who have been harmed and foster community accountability for intimate partner violence. Moreover, employing restorative justice in some cases of intimate partner violence could free up an overburdened criminal legal system to focus on habitual offenders. Anti-violence advocates have been leery of using restorative justice in cases involving intimate partner violence, citing important concerns about the safety of people who have been harmed, as well as the need for accountability both from those who do harm and from the state. But a violence informed, victim-centered restorative program running parallel to the criminal system could address their concerns and create alternatives to the state-based systems that many people subjected to abuse continue to avoid.

DOI: 10.4324/9780429398704-11

Rather than continuing to single-mindedly pursue criminalization, anti-violence advocates should look to restorative justice both to develop a new theoretical frame for the response to intimate partner violence and to implement concrete policies and practices that could prompt the kind of culture change needed to effectively regulate intimate partner violence and create the space for justice.

A Brief History of Criminalization

Criminalization has claimed the vast majority of the time and attention paid to intimate partner violence law and policy in the United States. The roots of criminalization are deep; the Massachusetts Bay Colony criminalized wife abuse as early as 1641. By 1920, every state in the United States had some law forbidding intimate partner violence. In fact, legal historian Carolyn Ramsey has argued, "The historical unwillingness of police and courts to intervene in intimate-partner violence [in the United States and Australia] has been overstated" (Ramsey, 2011, p. 199). Nonetheless, by the 1970s, police and prosecutors in the United States had become far more reluctant to intervene in what they saw as the private problems of intimate partners. Police officers were advised not to make arrests in cases involving intimate partner violence, and prosecutors were loath to pursue such cases if police did make an arrest, particularly if the complaining witness was not willing to appear. In response, the anti-domestic violence movement of the late 1970s and early 1980s advocated for treating intimate partner violence as a crime like any other, arguing that criminalization would hold abusive people accountable for their behavior, provide people subjected to abuse with safety, and change societal attitudes about intimate partner violence.

Turning first to the problem of police unwillingness to use their discretion to arrest those who abused their partners, anti-violence advocates championed mandatory arrest policies. These policies required police to make arrests in cases involving intimate partner violence whenever they had probable cause to do so. Mandatory arrest policies were bolstered by studies suggesting that arrest deterred further violence, research that proved difficult to replicate and more nuanced than first thought. Later studies suggested that mandatory arrest laws had deterrent effects in some places, no effect on recidivism in others, and contributed to increases in violence in other locations (Berk et al., 1992; Dunford, 1990; Dunford, Huizinga, & Elliott, 1990; Garner, Fagan, & Maxwell, 1995; Hirschel, Hutchison, & Dean, 1992; Pate & Hamilton, 1992). Nonetheless, as of 2011, at least 21 states had some form of mandatory arrest policy in place. Given concerns about the research and the unintended consequences of mandatory arrest (discussed below), some states have opted for preferred rather than mandatory arrest; preferred arrest policies encourage, but do not require, police to make arrests. The vast majority of the states have either mandatory or preferred arrest policies in place today.

Mandatory arrest laws led, unsurprisingly, to an increase in the number of arrests made in intimate partner violence cases. But prosecution and conviction rates did not initially rise, in large part because of prosecutorial reluctance to take cases forward, particularly when those who were harmed refused to testify against their partners (Daly & Bouhours, 2010). Anti-violence advocates suggested a number of policy fixes to this problem, including "no drop" prosecution. No drop policies required prosecutors to push their cases forward even in those instances when the person harmed did not wish to participate in or was actively opposed to prosecution. Soft no drop policies encourage people subjected to abuse to participate by offering resources that would make such participation viable. In hard no drop jurisdictions, however, prosecutors compel those who have been harmed to testify, if necessary through the use of subpoenas, arrest warrants and imprisonment. Feminist prosecutors and writers justified the implementation of hard no drop policies by arguing that such policies helped prosecutors promote equality for women, ensure public safety, and undermine male supremacy.

Criminalization is suffused throughout the United States' signature piece of legislation on intimate partner violence, the Violence Against Women Act (VAWA). Since its passage in 1994, VAWA has allocated hundreds of millions of dollars yearly to courts, police and prosecutors and created incentives for ratcheting up the criminal system's response to intimate partner violence. While VAWA funds other services for people subjected to abuse, including civil legal services and transitional housing, approximately 85% of VAWA funding goes to the criminal legal system (Messing et al., 2015). VAWA also championed mandatory and preferred arrest and no drop policies, providing incentives for police and prosecutors to adopt and implement such policies.

Criminalization has failed to realize a significant return on that investment of ideology, money, time and effort, however. Between 1994 (when VAWA monies were first appropriated) and 2000, rates of intimate partner violence fell significantly in the United States. So did the overall crime rate, for any number of reasons, including income growth, changes in alcohol consumption, an aging population, decreased unemployment and the number of police on the streets. Between 2000 and 2010, both rates of intimate partner violence and the overall crime rate continued to fall. Notwithstanding the continued infusion of federal monies into law enforcement efforts to address intimate partner violence, the overall crime rate fell more than rates of intimate partner violence over that same period. The sharp turn to criminalization over the last 40 years was intended to stem the tide of intimate partner violence in the United States. But that violence is again increasing. In 2015, the National Crime Victimization Survey recorded 806,050 incidents of intimate partner violence, 333,210 of them categorized as "serious"—an increase of over 100,000 incidents, and almost 70,000 serious incidents, from the previous year. In the last several years, a number of states, including Maryland, Wisconsin and Massachusetts, have noted increases in the number of intimate partner violence homicides. There is no social science evidence to suggest that criminalization is having a significant deterrent effect on the perpetration of intimate partner violence. Studies show that arrest has effects on recidivist intimate partner violence ranging from modest to nonexistent, and that arrest exacerbates violence in some groups (Felson, Ackerman, & Gallagher, 2005; Maxwell et al., 2001; Sherman et al., 1992; Ventura & Davis, 2005). The evidence on prosecution is similarly equivocal, with studies focused more on the impact of conviction (which may deter recidivism, but only when imprisonment and/or close monitoring are part of the sentence) than on prosecution itself (Gross et al., 2000; Sloan et al., 2013; Thistlewaite, Wooldredge, & Gibbs, 1998; Murphy, Musser, & Maton, 1998).

For those who do turn to the criminal legal system to find justice, the experience can be a frustrating one. While prosecution rates have increased in the last 40 years, they still vary considerably from jurisdiction to jurisdiction. Most acts of intimate partner violence are prosecuted as misdemeanors, regardless of their severity. Conviction rates vary significantly among jurisdictions, and incarceration is still relatively rare (Garner & Maxwell, 2009). To reach those results, people subjected to abuse must engage with the criminal system, which can be destructive for them. As witnesses in the criminal legal system, the stories that people subjected to abuse tell are constrained by the rules of evidence and the determinations of judges as to what is relevant and are tested through aggressive and hostile cross-examination. People's motives for coming forward are questioned; their testimony is viewed skeptically by judges and juries alike. Any opinion a person harmed has as to the just resolution of the case is secondary to the goals of prosecutors, who represent the state, the only party whose desires matter in a criminal proceeding. At the end of the process, the person who has done harm might be acquitted or, even if convicted, might receive a sentence that the person harmed deems insufficient or unresponsive to their needs. Participation in the criminal legal system can be a singularly disempowering experience for a person subjected to abuse.

The criminalization of intimate partner violence has also had profoundly problematic unintended consequences. Increased criminalization of intimate partner violence has contributed to the rise in arrest and incarceration rates in the United States, particularly among men of color. In Milwaukee County, Wisconsin, for example, researchers found that men of color make up 24% of the population, but accounted for 66% of the defendants in domestic violence cases. In 2014, inmates convicted of offenses related to intimate partner violence made up 20% of Vermont's incarcerated population. Changes to policing and prosecution policies have led to increases in arrests and incarceration not just among those who abuse, but among those subjected to abuse as well. Arrests of women increased significantly in jurisdictions that adopted mandatory arrest laws, and at least part of that increase, criminologist Alesha Durfee explains, "is directly attributable to the implementation of mandatory arrest policies and not simply an increased use of violence by women in intimate relationships" (Durfee, 2012, p. 75). Confronted at the scene of an incident with conflicting versions of events, police are more likely to make dual arrests, bringing both parties into custody rather than trying to determine who the primary aggressor might be. Prosecutors in hard no drop jurisdictions routinely ask judges to compel people to testify, if necessary by having them arrested and even held in custody until that testimony is given (Goodmark, 2012), although the arrest and incarceration of people subjected to abuse was surely not one of the intended outcomes of the drive to increase prosecution rates.

The criminal legal system will always have a role to play in cases of serious intimate partner violence. Some people who use violence are simply so dangerous that they must be incapacitated. But given the failure of the criminal legal system to meaningfully deter intimate partner violence or provide justice for some of those who choose to use it, and its many unintended consequences, anti-violence advocates have begun to seek alternate routes to justice for people subjected to abuse. One of those options is restorative justice.

Responding to Intimate Partner Violence With Restorative Justice

Reliance on criminalization is grounded in part in the belief that retribution is the most effective and appropriate way to respond to intimate partner violence. Retributive theorists see punishment as the only morally acceptable response to wrongdoing, so long as the punishment is proportionate to the harm inflicted. Punishment communicates the wrongfulness of the acts to the person who does harm and restores the moral balance that is upset by the harm. In cases of intimate partner violence, however, the punishment assessed, if any, by the criminal legal system often seems disproportionate to the harm inflicted. Given low rates of arrest (between 2006 and 2015, police made arrests in just 39% of intimate partner violence cases, Reaves, 2017), prosecution and conviction, as well as the overwhelming likelihood that even serious abuse will be prosecuted and punished as a misdemeanor, few people who abuse are being given punishment commensurate to the harm they cause. Some have argued that we cannot know whether criminalization of intimate partner violence is an effective strategy because it has never been fully implemented (Barata, 2007). Moreover, retribution fails to provide the justice that many people subjected to abuse seek. Studies show that many victims of crime are more interested in rehabilitation than retribution (Alliance for Safety and Justice, 2016). For people subjected to abuse particularly, justice may be more tied to the concepts of voice (the ability to tell one's story), validation (an acknowledgment that harm was done) and vindication (condemnation of the offense) than to punishment, and accountability may mean much more than being placed under state control. The criminal legal system provides some, albeit limited, opportunities for voice. But validation and vindication come only through convictions, and only to the extent that a judge or jury is willing to provide them. People who do harm need never accept responsibility for their actions, and, in fact, are discouraged from doing so by lawyers concerned about losing the presumption of innocence that protects the client and any possible grounds for appeal. Accountability in the criminal legal system is achieved through punishment, which is a passive form of accountability, requiring only that "people sustain the suffering imposed upon them for their transgression" (Sered, 2017, p. 17). Punishment does not require those who have done harm to work to remedy the harm they have caused.

Restorative justice is responsive to a broader array of people's justice needs. Restorative justice shifts the conversation by focusing on harms rather than crimes. A restorative conference, for example, is organized around three questions: What was the harm? What was the impact of the harm? What can be done to right the harm? That broader focus enables people subjected to abuse to address acts that may be destructive but not illegal, like most forms of emotional or psychological abuse. Restorative processes can require that people who do harm accept responsibility for the harms done prior to engaging in dialogue with the person harmed, a form of accountability unavailable through the criminal legal system. Restorative processes are free of the evidentiary constraints that restrict voice. Validation can come through a person's acceptance of responsibility for the harm and through the community's acknowledgment of the harm in the restorative process. The community's response—verbal, emotional and through more concrete manifestations, like reparations and accountability plans—can provide vindication to a person subjected to abuse. Moreover, accountability is an active process in restorative justice. Restorative justice requires that people who do harm take responsibility for their actions, meet with those they have harmed or with surrogates, listen to how the harm they caused affected the person harmed and their supporters, and work to repair the harm. Through that work, change in a person's behavior and attitudes can be observed and measured. Because they are not bound by the remedies available through the criminal legal system, restorative processes create space for more creative and meaningful ways of holding people who do harm accountable, measures that are often more responsive to the harmed person's justice needs than imprisonment would be. Justice can be anything that counteracts the loss of liberty some people subjected to abuse experience at the hands of their partners and that returns power to them. People who participate in restorative processes are more likely to believe that those who have harmed them have been held accountable (Karp et al., 2016). And in those situations where incarceration is necessary, restorative justice provides people subjected to abuse who are concerned about the impact of criminal legal interventions on their partners with the comfort of knowing that they have tried regulatory alternatives other than incarceration and those alternatives simply have not worked.

Restorative justice can be empowering for people subjected to abuse, offering them opportunities to exercise agency not available through the criminal legal system. People subjected to abuse decide whether and when restorative processes will be used, who should be involved and what role they choose to play in the proceedings, including whether to interact directly or through a surrogate with their former partners. People subjected to abuse can ask specifically and directly for the things they need to feel whole through restorative processes. Fully 80% of the participants in intimate partner violence victim/offender mediations in Austria reported feeling empowered by the process (Liebman & Wootton, 2010). After facing her former partner in a restorative process, one woman subjected to abuse "felt as if I could knock out Mike Tyson. I could have taken on anything or anyone. In the days and weeks afterwards, it was as if a massive weight had been lifted off my shoulders. I had been carrying it for so long that I did not even notice it anymore, so when it disappeared it was amazing. I felt completely empowered" (House of Commons Justice Committee, 2017, p. 15).

The benefits of restorative justice extend to the broader community as well. Using restorative processes could help to change community norms around intimate partner violence—something that anti-violence advocates have been working towards since the inception of the battered women's movement, with very little success. The early battered women's movement believed that passing laws declaring intimate partner violence a crime would begin to create this change; laws expressing the community's disapproval of such behavior, they believed, would help to curtail that behavior. But, as mentioned earlier, those laws have existed in most states for at least the last 30 years, and community norms (at least as measured by the prevalence of intimate partner violence) do not seem to have changed significantly. Community norms have remained static, in part, because communities are largely disengaged from the process of holding those who do harm accountable for intimate partner violence. As criminologist Nils Christie writes, "Modern criminal control systems represent one of the many cases of lost opportunities for involving citizens in tasks that are of immediate importance to them" (Christie, 1977, p. 7). This reliance on the state has created a vicious cycle that has made reinvigorating community responses to crime much more difficult. Once intimate partner violence is defined as a crime, communities come to believe that the state, and only the state, has the power to address that behavior. The state (and the private actors who benefit from assisting the state in incarcerating huge swaths of the population) encourages the carceral response and fails to provide support or incentives for sharing responsibility or developing alternatives. Communities become further disengaged from taking any regulatory role when incidents of intimate partner violence occur.

Integrating restorative practices into communities could help to shift community norms. Restorative justice expands the number of people in a community who are aware of abuse and who might view the issue differently when seen through the lens of family and friends than they do in the abstract. Community members' views of violence can be unearthed and confronted in restorative processes; if kept secret, such views go unchallenged. Although critics fear that providing restorative alternatives will re-privatize intimate partner violence, the opposite is in fact true: restorative processes make intimate partner violence more public, moving consideration of such cases out of courtrooms where few can bear witness and into the consciousness of the community.

Community serves a number of functions in restorative practice—as the location where restorative practices take place, the source of support for people who have been harmed and those who have done harm, the guarantors of accountability, and the bulwark against further harm. Communities monitor and support the self-regulation of those who do harm through restorative processes and agreements. This notion of community responsibility for harms, if married to justice strategies that rely upon, even require, community involvement, could reinvigorate community efforts to "police" intimate partner violence. Asking community members to identify intimate partner violence and to conceive of and implement appropriate responses could fundamentally transform how communities understand that violence, leading to the shifting of community norms that anti-violence advocates have long sought.

Moreover, restorative justice can remake community norms without using violence to do so. The carceral system models violence, overpowering and controlling those who have been accused and/or convicted of crimes. But, as John Braithwaite notes in *Restorative Justice and Responsive Regulation*, using nonviolent forms of justice inculcates community norms around nonviolence and sends the message that violence is unacceptable regardless of whether it comes from the individual or state. He writes,

"If we want a world with less violence and less dominating abuse of others, we need to take seriously rituals that encourage approval of caring behavior so that citizens will acquire pride in being caring and nondominating" (Braithwaite, 2002, p. 80).

Turning to restorative justice could help to expand how the community understands intimate partner violence. The law's conception of intimate partner violence is quite narrow, generally providing redress for physical harm and threats of physical harm and little else. But people subjected to abuse experience multiple forms of violence that the law does not reach—verbal, emotional and psychological, economic, reproductive and spiritual. Restorative processes could allow people subjected to abuse to address harms involving conduct that, while legal, is exceedingly harmful as well as conduct that is legally actionable. Communities could discuss the impact of these other forms of violence on the person subjected to abuse and the wider circle; restorative agreements could monitor and provide redress for a variety of forms of violence. These conversations would not only help to broaden the community's definition of intimate partner violence, but also to establish community opposition to the use of such tactics. The carceral system is admittedly ineffective as a backup mechanism in cases where criminal prosecution is not a viable course of action. But different forms of violence call for different responses. The peak of the regulatory pyramid in a case involving harmful but legal conduct might be severe community or civil legal sanctions, rather than arrest or incarceration, which would be the ultimate sanctions in a case involving illegal conduct. That type of resolution is preferable to what the criminal legal system would do—which would be nothing. And if initial restorative efforts to address these abusive but legal behaviors are successful, the violence will not escalate, and there would be no need for further action.

Restorative justice honors the humanity of both people subjected to abuse and their partners. The criminal legal system assumes the oppositional binary of victim and offender, cast in the roles of the good and blameless versus the evil and culpable. Those labels can have profound consequences for the people to whom they are affixed. Victims are often stereotyped as weak, meek and passive, which is not how many people subjected to abuse see themselves. Moreover, when people subjected to abuse act in ways that are inconsistent with those stereotypes—when they fight back against those who hurt them, for instance—they may be deprived of assistance meant only for "victims." For those who do harm, the perpetrator label can be debilitating and impede real change and growth. In their book, *South of Forgiveness: A True Story of Rape and Responsibility*, Thordis Elva and Tom Stranger discuss the impact of those labels. Stranger says, "The label of rapist stuck to me as if it were my profession, one that was right up there with my name, where I was born, and how old I was—the basic fundamental facts that I saw as defining me and the part I had to play in this world." Elva responds, "I suppose I could refer to you as a 'rapist,' at the very least 'my rapist.' But it wouldn't be true—hell, it wouldn't even cover a fraction of the truth about who you are. . . . I've been raped. That does not make me a 'victim.' People do good and bad things throughout their lives. My point is that I'm a person. Not a label. I cannot be reduced down to what happened that night. And neither can you" (Elva & Stranger, 2017, pp. 111–112).

The victim/offender binary also ignores how complicated the relationships between people subjected to abuse and their partners can be, failing to account for the affectional and family ties that may continue to exist between the two. Some people subjected to abuse are co-parenting with their former partners, requiring them to see their partners as something more than simply perpetrators. Some people subjected to abuse love their partners despite their violence and want to maintain their relationships (Suntag, 2014). In a study of the Bennington, Vermont Integrated Domestic Violence docket, researchers found that 70% of the litigants either were still in relationships or planned to continue their relationships. While these people subjected to abuse recognize their partners' actions as harmful and want the violence to stop, they do not want their partners demonized as they work to repair their families. The criminal system, focused as it is on separating people who have been harmed from those who have done harm, sometimes forces undesired distance upon people subjected to abuse, requiring their partners to stay away from them regardless of whether such orders are requested or welcome. Restorative justice creates space for consideration of the complexities of these continuing relationships in ways that the criminal system often cannot.

The criminal system uses shame, via labeling and criminal punishment, to express its condemnation of intimate partner violence. Feminist scholars have argued that, given the state's history of ignoring intimate partner violence, stigma is an important component of establishing community norms against violence. But shaming and stigmatizing may instead exacerbate criminality. Psychologist James Gilligan has argued that shame makes people more likely to use violence; through hurting and humiliating others, a person can prevent or subdue their feelings of shame (Gilligan, 2001). Restorative justice, by contrast, employs reintegrative shaming, a process that expresses clear disapproval of the violent act without condemning the actor. Such shaming enables those who do harm to "pay in a meaningful and dignified way for what they have done" without depriving them of the "opportunity to repair the harm that will allow them out of shame and its associated violence" (Sered, 2017, pp. 17–18). In the context of intimate partner violence, reintegrative shaming requires rejection of the stereotyping and demonization of people who abuse their partners, which creates unproductive shame. Individuals and communities can express their disapproval of a person's actions while simultaneously making clear that they will maintain hope and trust for the person who has committed those acts, unless and until that person proves unworthy of that hope and trust. Restorative justice engenders remorse rather than anger or shame; remorse, in turn, helps those who do harm to take meaningful responsibility for their actions.

Fostering remorse may also help those who do harm to transform the beliefs and emotions driving their violence. Criminalization creates incentives for people who abuse to curtail or abandon some behaviors to avoid further criminal involvement, but is unlikely to spur fundamental change in their attitudes and behaviors toward their partners. The research on intimate partner violence offender intervention programs illustrates this problem. While some participants in offender intervention programs decrease their use of physical violence, their verbal and psychological abuse of their partners tends to escalate. The programs (and the punishment) don't make those who abuse more empathetic; they simply teach them how to abuse without risking criminal liability. Shaming does not help people to develop empathy for their partners or to internalize nonviolent norms. Shame and stigma will not precipitate the kind of change in a person's beliefs that leads to decreases in violence.

Challenges to Using Restorative Justice to Address Intimate Partner Violence

Restorative justice advocates tout the many benefits of bringing a restorative lens to intimate partner violence. But significant opposition to the use of restorative justice in cases of intimate partner violence exists, particularly among anti-violence advocates and organizations (Busch, 2002; Stubbs, 2002; Zorza, 2011). Critics cite concerns about the safety of restorative practices for people subjected to abuse. Those fears involve both the proximity of people subjected to abuse to their former (or current) partners during restorative processes and the inability of facilitators and others involved in restorative processes to recognize and effectively address safety issues that arise during the process itself. Secondly, critics charge that those who do harm cannot be held meaningfully accountable outside of the criminal legal system, both because they may be unlikely to take accountability seriously outside of the criminal legal system and because restorative processes may be taking place within communities that have ignored, condoned or even facilitated, the violence. Finally, having fought for years to ensure that intimate partner violence would be treated like any other form of crime, some anti-violence advocates are loathe to relieve the state of its responsibility for handling those crimes.

Many of those fears can be allayed. Because restorative justice is a voluntary process, no person subjected to abuse should ever be compelled to participate. Studies show that people subjected to abuse are best placed to assess the danger they face from their partners. Those people who believe restorative processes are too unsafe for them could decide not to participate, and the process would go no further. If at any point during the preparation for a restorative intervention, or during the intervention itself, a person felt unsafe, they could also stop the process. People subjected to abuse could opt to have supporters attend a restorative process and express their thoughts in their stead, allowing them to take part in restorative practice without having to be physically present. Moreover, those facilitating restorative justice processes involving intimate partner violence could be required to have specialized training that sensitizes them to the issues of safety that could emerge during a conference or mediation.

Secondly, criminal prosecution is only one form of accountability (and only holds those who do harm accountable when prosecution leads to conviction, which is far from a certain outcome). Restorative processes offer a number of other options that are as likely, if not more likely, to hold those who do harm meaningfully accountable. Punishment, as noted earlier, is passive accountability, requiring nothing more of the offender than that they serve whatever sentence is meted out. The accountability required by restorative justice is an active accountability—those who do harm must accept responsibility for their behavior, engage in a restorative process with the person harmed or her proxy that requires the person who does harm to confront the person harmed, hear how his behavior affected others and agree to undertake tasks that restore the person harmed to wholeness, as she defines that term. Moreover, engaged communities can monitor accountability more closely than the criminal legal apparatus. Community members can have regular, even daily, contact with residents, supervise the enforcement of agreements made through the restorative process and provide concrete assistance (like housing or finances) to both those who are harmed and those who do harm.

Finally, expanding the options available to address intimate partner violence does not require abandonment of the criminal legal system. Making restorative justice available might actually increase the effectiveness of the criminal legal system by focusing that system's efforts on those whose behavior cannot be changed in any other way. When less intrusive approaches fail, the criminal legal system can serve as a last line of defense for ensuring the safety of both the individual person harmed and the community. Moreover, a substantial number of people subjected to abuse opt out of engagement with the criminal system and must find justice elsewhere. Notwithstanding 40 years of development of the criminal legal response to intimate partner violence, reporting rates for intimate partner violence are still relatively low. According to the U.S. Bureau of Justice Statistics, between 2006 and 2015, about 56% of nonfatal incidents of intimate partner violence were reported to law enforcement (Reaves, 2017). Significant numbers of people subjected to abuse, then, are not reporting that abuse to law enforcement, for various reasons. Some, as mentioned earlier, are not interested in having their justice needs met through retributive systems. Others fear exposing themselves to the state. As law professor Donna Coker has written, some people subjected to abuse, particularly low-income women, are afforded too little privacy from the state, rather than too much (Coker, 2002). For those whose housing, financial stability and parenting are subjected to state scrutiny, often with destructive results, community-based justice processes that do not involve the state might be preferable to state intervention.

Even the most ardent restorative justice advocates acknowledge, however, that there are a number of additional concerns that must be addressed. Restorative processes are both time- and resource-intensive. Preparing those who have been harmed, their supporters and those who have done harm for restorative processes takes a significant amount of effort in any context. In the context of intimate partner violence, that investment of time and energy is likely to be greater, particularly if people subjected to abuse are preparing to meet their partners face to face. Moreover, restorative practitioners handling cases of intimate partner violence will need specialized training and experience, which few are likely to have. Any attempt to completely replace the criminal legal system, which processes hundreds of thousands of cases of intimate partner violence per year, would require systematizing restorative practices in ways that create significant risks to the elements that make restorative justice unique. Insufficient preparation, reliance on facilitators without intimate partner violence expertise and the elimination of participation requirements that should be essential in this context (like acceptance of responsibility) would all undermine attempts to provide a meaningful justice alternative for people subjected to abuse. Embedding restorative practices within state systems carries significant risks as well. In parts of the United Kingdom, people subjected to abuse are being pressured to opt for "community resolution" or "restorative practices," enabling police to dispose of the cases without making an arrest, raising the specter of the "bad old days" of police nonintervention (House of Commons Justice Committee, 2016). Making restorative justice part of a state system of justice also runs the risk of importing all of the structural issues inherent in that state system—including systemic racism, homophobia and transphobia—into restorative processes.

Responsive Regulation of Intimate Partner Violence

Despite these cautions, there is significant interest in applying restorative theory and practice to intimate partner violence. What many anti-violence advocates lack, though, is a concrete sense of what a responsive approach to intimate partner violence might look like in practice. In 1994, in the Australian context, John Braithwaite and Kathleen Daly suggested a regulatory pyramid structure for responding to intimate partner violence (Braithwaite & Daly, 1994). That structure, which starts at its base with self-sanctioning and social disapproval, moves through various levels of community and state intervention and peaks with incarceration, is just as relevant for addressing some forms of violence today as it was when first conceived. As Braithwaite and Daly note, when self-sanctioning fails to preclude someone from using violence with a partner, families and communities should informally step in to sanction that behavior. If those informal checks on violence are unsuccessful, formal community intervention is warranted. In Braithwaite and Daly's pyramid, these informal social sanctions are followed by a first state intervention, with police issuing a warrant. In the United States context, this first state intervention might look slightly different. Police could be called, and, depending upon the severity of the allegations, could issue a warning of some sort, but are unlikely to seek an arrest warrant without the intention of acting upon that warrant, particularly in those jurisdictions with mandatory or preferred arrest policies. Because the goal at this level of the pyramid is to create disincentives to further violence without actually instituting criminal proceedings, a U.S. pyramid might instead include monitoring by the police. This sort of monitoring is being piloted in a number of jurisdictions, including High Point, North Carolina, using a strategy known as "focused deterrence." Focused deterrence classifies people based on the frequency and seriousness of the offenses they commit. D-class offenders in High Point—those who are not arrested—are informed that police will be monitoring their behavior and will be likely to intervene punitively if called to respond to violence again (Sechrist, Weil, & Shelton, 2016). With the harmed person's consent, heightened monitoring, including police dropping in or driving by the parties' home, could replace the issuance of a warrant in the regulatory pyramid. Knowing that police are carefully watching their behavior might serve the same "sword of Damocles" function as having a warrant issued but not executed.

The middle tiers of Braithwaite and Daly's pyramid rely on restorative conferences, bringing the person harmed, the person who has committed the harm, their supporters and other community members together to determine how the wrongdoer should be held accountable. Braithwaite and Daly call for three levels of community conferences, with escalating intervention if earlier conferences fail to curtail the abusive behavior. A first conference might require a promise from the harm doer to remain nonviolent, to seek counseling and to report nonviolence to family members. A conference agreement could also provide economic support to a person subjected to abuse, delineate parenting responsibilities, set spatial and temporal limits on interactions between the parties and respond to any other need affecting the safety and stability of the person subjected to abuse. Later agreements might establish more concrete boundaries or include terms that could be found in a civil protective order, including provisions forbidding the person who does harm from contacting his partner or requiring the abusive partner to move out of the family home. Braithwaite and Daly recognize that some might be reluctant to adopt a framework that allows for a cycle of failed conferences and further violence before incarceration is sought. But current criminal alternatives create the same sort of opportunities for failure, in that serial offenders receive little punishment for "minor" offenses (though some of those minor offenses are initially charged as felonies and bargained down), even when they come repeatedly before the court for the same behavior. For example, Kenneth Woodruff of Lacombe, Louisiana, was first arrested for domestic violence in 2005, convicted of a misdemeanor and sentenced to probation and community service. In 2006, he was convicted of a second misdemeanor and sentenced to probation. In 2008, Woodruff was convicted twice: once of misdemeanor domestic violence (pled down from a felony), the second time of a felony. In February 2009, he was convicted of another felony and sentenced to a year in jail. In October 2009, Woodruff was convicted for a sixth time and finally given a significant sentence—15 years' imprisonment, eight years suspended (Le Breton, 2010). Clearly, repeated criminal prosecutions failed to deter Woodruff from continuing his violence.

The apex of Braithwaite and Daly's regulatory pyramid is arrest and incarceration. Braithwaite and Daly recognize that in the most serious cases, immediately moving to the peak of the pyramid will be necessary. But in many cases, the hope is that community intervention will lead to greater accountability and behavior change than "routine perfunctory criminal justice processing" is currently achieving (Braithwaite & Daly, 1994). The criminal legal system is the stick that makes the carrot of community intervention more effective, and that stick can have a greater deterrent power when criminal intervention is viewed as a last resort carrying swift and certain sanction.

Braithwaite and Daly's pyramid works well when applied to cases in which the violence being addressed could ultimately be subject to criminal punishment. But in cases of emotional, psychological, reproductive, spiritual and economic abuse—cases where the abuse is harmful but legal—their pyramid is inapposite. Those cases would require a different pyramid. The lower levels of the pyramid would likely look very similar: self-sanctioning, informal expressions of family and community disapproval and restorative conferencing. Conference agreements would target the specific forms of abuse being practiced. In a case involving spiritual abuse, neighbors, friends and parishioners might commit to ensuring that a person is free to live out their religious beliefs without interference. If the issue is economic abuse, the harm doer could be tasked with providing economic support or reparation to the person being subjected to that abuse or could be prohibited from interfering with a partner's work or education. But without the threat of police intervention, advocates will have to be more creative in creating regulatory disincentives to violence at the apex of the pyramid. Depending on the law of the jurisdiction and the particular type of abuse, the apex of the pyramid might include seeking a civil protective order, filing for divorce, custody of children, or child support or taking other legal action to sever ties with the partner. For those in small religious, geographic or ethnic communities, more severe sanctions might also include being required to leave the community for a period of time in order to ensure safety for the person subjected to abuse.

Conclusion

Intimate partner violence is a multi-faceted problem, poorly suited to one-size-fits-all solutions. Myopic reliance on the criminal system has yielded little success in decreasing rates of intimate partner violence in the United States, has serious unintended consequences and fails to reach certain forms of abuse or meet the justice needs of some individuals subjected to abuse. Adding restorative justice to the menu of options available to regulate intimate partner violence expands the possibilities for meeting those needs, avoids inflicting harm on both those who do harm and those subjected to abuse and bolsters the effectiveness of criminal legal sanctions in situations where such sanctions are unavoidable or necessary to ensure safety. Precluding people subjected to abuse from opting into restorative justice ignores the evidence on people's satisfaction with restorative practices and denies them agency. While restorative processes will not be appropriate in every case, they have the potential to empower people subjected to abuse, help communities to reclaim their role in ensuring members' safety, and ultimately, to change community norms around intimate partner violence in ways that could significantly decrease that violence—one of the original goals of the anti-violence movement. And even if they fail to meet all of those hopes, the bar for assessing the success of restorative practices is fairly low. As Lawrence Sherman, co-author of the earliest studies on mandatory arrest has argued, "Since there is no evidence that standard justice is any more effective than doing nothing in response to an incident of domestic violence, the only challenge to restorative justice is to do better than doing nothing" (Sherman, 2000, p. 281). The research on restorative justice and intimate partner violence suggests that restorative practices have already surpassed that standard in other parts of the world. Only by piloting and evaluating such projects in the United States can we know if the promise of restorative justice can be realized here as well.

References

Alliance for Safety and Justice. (2016). *Crime survivors speak: The first-ever national survey of victims' views on safety and justice.* Retrieved from Alliance for Safety and Justice website https://allianceforsafetyandjustice.org/wp-content/uploads/documents/Crime%20Survivors%20Speak%20Report.pdf.

Barata, P. C. (2007). Abused women's perspectives on the criminal justice system's response to domestic violence. *Psychology of Women Quarterly, 31*(2), 202–215.

Berk, R. A., Campbell, A., Klap, R., & Western, B. (1992). A Bayesian analysis of the Colorado Springs spouse abuse experiment. *Journal of Criminal Law and Criminology, 83*(1), 170–200.

Braithwaite, J. (2002). *Restorative justice and responsive regulation.* New York: Oxford University Press.

Braithwaite, J., & Daly, K. (1994). Masculinities, violence and communitarian control. In T. Newburn & B. Stanko (Eds.), *Just boys doing business: Men, masculinities and crime*, (p. 189). London, UK/New York: Routledge.

Busch, R. (2002). Domestic violence and restorative justice initiatives: Who pays if we get it wrong? In H. Strang & J. Braithwaite (Eds.), *Restorative justice and family violence* (p. 223). Cambridge: Cambridge University Press.

Christie, N. (1977). Conflicts as property. *British Journal of Criminology, 17*(1), 1–15.

Coker, D. (2002). Transformative justice: Anti-subordination processes in cases of domestic violence. In H. Strang & J. Braithwaite (Eds.), *Restorative justice and family violence* (p. 128). Cambridge: Cambridge University Press.

Daly, K., & Bouhours, B. (2010). Rape and attrition in the legal process: A comparative analysis of five countries (for comparative international data in the context of rape and sexual assault). *Crime and Justice, 39*(1), 565–650.

Dunford, F. W. (1990). System-initiated warrants for suspects of misdemeanor domestic assault: A pilot study. *Justice Quarterly, 7*(4), 631–653.

Dunford, F. W., Huizinga, D., & Elliott, D. S. (1990). The role of arrest in domestic assault: The Omaha police experiment. *Criminology, 28*(2), 183–206.

Durfee, A. (2012). Situational ambiguity and gendered patterns of arrest for intimate partner violence. *Violence Against Women, 18*(1), 64–84.

Elva, T., & Stranger, T. (2017). *South of forgiveness: A true story of rape and responsibility*. New York: First Skyhorse Publishing.

Felson, R., Ackerman, J. M., & Gallagher, C. A. (2005). Police intervention and the repeat of domestic assault. *Criminology, 43*(3), 563–580.

Garner, J., Fagan, J., & Maxwell, C. (1995). Published findings from the spouse assault replication program: A critical review. *Journal of Quantitative Criminology, 11*(1), 3–28.

Garner, J. H., & Maxwell, C. D. (2009). Prosecution and conviction rates for intimate partner violence. *Criminal Justice Review, 34*(1), 44–79.

Gilligan, J. (2001). *Preventing violence (Prospects for Tomorrow)*. New York: Thames and Hudson.

Goodmark, L. (2012). *A troubled marriage: Domestic violence and the legal system*. New York: New York University Press.

Gross, M., Cramer, E. P., Forte, J., Gordon, J. A., Kunkel, T., & Moriarty, L. J. (2000). The impact of sentencing options on recidivism among domestic violence offenders. *American Journal of Criminal Justice, 24*(2), 301–312.

Hirschel, J. D., Hutchison III, I. W., & Dean, C. W. (1992). The failure of arrest to deter spouse abuse. *Journal of Research in Crime and Delinquency, 29*(1), 7–33.

House of Commons Justice Committee. (2017). *Restorative justice: Fourth report of session 2016–17*. London: House of Commons.

Karp, D. R., Shackford-Bradley, J., Wilson, R. J., & Williamsen, K. M. (2016). *A report on promoting restorative initiatives for sexual misconduct on college campuses*. Saratoga Springs: Skidmore College Project on Restorative Justice.

Le Breton, S. (2010). Man sentenced after fifth domestic violence conviction. *St. Tammany News*.

Liebmann, M., & Wootton, L. (2010). Restorative justice and domestic violence/abuse: A report commissioned by HMP Cardiff. Retrieved from https://restorativejustice.org.uk/sites/default/files/resources/files/Restorative%20Justice%20and%20Domestic%20Violence%20and%20Abuse.pdf.

Maxwell, C. D., Garner, J. H., Fagan, J. A., & National Institute of Justice. (2001). *The effects of arrest on intimate partner violence: New evidence from the spouse assault replication program*. Washington, DC: U.S. Department of Justice.

Messing, J. T., Ward-Lasher, A., Thaller, J., & Bagwell-Gray, M. E. (2015). The state of intimate partner violence intervention: Progress and continuing challenges. *Social Work, 60*(4), 305–313.

Murphy, C. M., Musser, P. H., & Maton, K. I. (1998). Coordinated community intervention for domestic abusers: Intervention system involvement, and criminal recidivism. *Journal of Family Violence, 13*(3), 263–284.

Pate, A. M., & Hamilton, E. E. (1992). Formal and informal deterrents to domestic violence: The Dade County spouse assault experiment. *American Sociological Review, 57*(5), 691–697.

Ramsey, C. B. (2011). Domestic violence and state intervention in the American west and Australia, 1860–1930, 86 Ind. L. J. 185, 199.

Reaves, B. A. (2017). Police response to domestic violence, 2006–2015.

Sechrist, S., Weil, J., & Shelton, T. (2016). *Evaluation of the offender focused domestic violence initiative (OFDVI) in High Point, NC & Replication in Lexington, NC*. Washington, DC: United States Department of Justice.

Sered, D. (2017). *Accounting for violence: How to increase safety and break our failed reliance on mass incarceration*. New York: Vera Institute of Justice.

Sherman, L. W. (2000). Domestic violence and restorative justice: Answering key questions. *Virginia Journal of Social Policy and the Law, 8*(1), 281.

Sherman, L. W., Schmidt, J. D., Rogan, D. P., Smith, D. A., Gartin, P. R., Cohn, E. G., . . . Bacich, A. R. (1992). The variable effects of arrest on criminal careers: The Milwaukee domestic violence experiment. *Journal of Criminal Law &Criminology, 83*(1), 137–169.

Sloan, F. A., Platt, A. C., Chepke, L. M., & Blevins, C. E. (2013). Deterring domestic violence: Do criminal sanctions reduce repeat offenders? *Journal of Risk and Uncertainty, 46*(1), 51–80.

Stubbs, J. (2002). Domestic violence and women's safety: Feminist challenges to restorative justice. In H. Strang & J. Braithwaite (Eds.), *Restorative justice and family violence* (p. 42). Cambridge: Cambridge University Press.

Suntag, D. V. (The Honorable). (2014, July). *DV and the traditional court model: Why we fail and what we can do about it. The Integrated Docket (IDV) alternative*. Powerpoint Presentation at Restorative Justice, Responsive Regulation and Complex Problems Conference, University of Vermont, Davis Center, July 16–18, 2014.

Thistlewaite, A., Wooldredge, J., & Gibbs, D. (1998). Severity of dispositions and domestic violence recidivism. *Crime and Delinquency, 44*(3), 388–398.

United State of Women Summit. (2016). Remarks of Vice President Joe Biden.

Ventura, L. A., & Davis, G. (2005). Domestic violence: Court case conviction and recidivism. *Violence Against Women, 11*(2), 255–277.

Zorza, J. (2011, April/May). Restorative justice: Does it work for DV victims? *Domestic Violence Report, 16*(4).

12

RESPONSIVE AND INCLUSIVE HEALTH GOVERNANCE THROUGH THE LENS OF RECOVERY CAPITAL

A Case Study Based on Gambling Treatment

David Best and Amy Musgrove

Introduction

Addiction to drugs is the most stigmatized health condition in the world according to the World Health Organisation (WHO, 2001), with alcohol rating fourth, and both significantly higher than major mental health problems. Addiction is seen as a loss of self-control and a personal failing whether this is alcohol, drugs or process addictions like gambling. Yet in spite of this, the estimated rates of sustained long-term recovery are high across the range of addictive behaviours with Sheedy and Whitter (2009) summing the existing evidence to estimate that 58% of those who experience a lifetime addiction will eventually achieve stable recovery (defined as five years or more free from addictive behaviours). Consensus attempts at defining recovery have largely focused on individual change factors with the Betty Ford Institute Consensus Panel (2007) defining recovery as a "voluntarily maintained lifestyle characterised by sobriety, personal health and citizenship" (2007, p. 222). This position is consistent with the UK Drug Policy Commission statement on recovery as "voluntarily sustained control over substance use which maximises health and wellbeing and participation in the rights, roles and responsibilities of society" (2008, p. 6).

Nonetheless there is a strong evidence base that would suggest there are a range of social determinants of recovery, as part of a growing research body assessing what the underlying mechanisms of change are in the recovery process (Kelly, 2017). Beattie and Longabaugh (1999) reported that whilst both general social support and abstinence-specific support predicted abstinence at three months post-treatment amongst formerly alcohol-dependent people, only social support for abstinence predicted longer-term abstinence (at 15 months post-treatment). Similarly, Longabaugh et al. (2010) found that greater opposition to a person's drinking from within their social network predicted more days without alcohol use both during and after treatment, and fewer heavy drinking days post-treatment. Positive social networks provide both social resources and support but also provide access to wider networks and communities and allow excluded individuals to leave behind their using or offending groups and replace them with prosocial activities and groups that offer reintegration opportunities. So, whilst there is a recognition that recovery is a process that takes place over

DOI: 10.4324/9780429398704-12

time and is both personal and unique to each individual, there is increasing awareness that effective reintegration and sustainable recovery requires acceptance from local communities and from a range of statutory bodies.

Excluded and marginalized populations, including those suffering from addiction problems, require not only specialist care and support, but effective pathways to reintegration into communities for recovery to be holistic and stable. This is a central component of what has been termed by Granfield and Cloud (1999) as 'recovery capital' and refers to the sum of resources available to support effective reintegration. Recovery capital is used as an organizing principle for governance and regulation in addiction treatment—including the partnerships of peers and helping professionals in building and sustaining recovery in communities. Recovery capital encompasses more personal and social capital. There is a third level to the process of growing recovery capital that goes beyond the personal and social change processes to focus on the contextual and societal. In their review of factors that contribute to recovery capital, Best and Laudet (2010) used data from the UK and the US to categorize recovery resources in terms of:

- Personal Recovery Capital: which refers to those internal factors such as resilience, coping skills, communication skills, self-esteem and self-efficacy, that will allow the individual to manage their own recovery pathway in time—what Dennis and Laudet (2014) have called 'self-sustaining recovery'.
- Social Recovery Capital: which relates to the human resources and networks that people can tap into and the resulting social identities and groups they belong to and are committed to. This is a reciprocal model of social support and the strength of the bind to that support.
- Community Recovery Capital: which refers to the resources that exist in communities that can support recovery pathways and journeys, including access to safe and respectable housing, to college courses, to employment opportunities and to memberships of desirable groups and associations.

In an operationalization of this model based on work with recovery residences in Florida, USA, Cano et al. (2017) found that the benefits of retention in residential services were mediated by meaningful activities and active engagement in the local community. What the analysis indicated was that retention in service enabled the space for engaging with the community which in turn led to improvements in personal and social capital and in wellbeing. The core lesson was that community capital precedes personal and social capital in that active engagement with community activities enabled the growth in positive networks and personal resources and strengths.

What is also important about the Florida project (Best et al., 2016) was that it provided evidence that recovery capital could be measured (using an indicator called the REC-CAP to assess recovery strengths) and that this could be used to develop recovery care plans that in turn directed active engagement with the local community. The paper also provides support for the idea that social and community capital (group memberships and through them access to resources that are available in the community) effectively create the scaffolding around the individual that affords them the space and the opportunity to develop the personal capital—self-esteem, self-efficacy, resilience—to support and sustain individual recovery efforts (Moos, 2007). It is in this arena that professional addiction treatment services have a role to play that goes beyond individual treatment or therapy to include care coordination and effective linkage to community groups and activities (Savic et al., 2017) and that this should be done early in the treatment process.

What this in turn links to is the idea that there are interventions at the service and systems level that can increase the opportunities for individual recovery, and that these are embedded within a social and community-focused model of intervention. This has been conceptualized as Recovery-Oriented Systems of Care (Kelly & White, 2010) and the principles for the implementation of a successful system have been outlined by the Substance Abuse and Mental Health Services Administration (SAMHSA) (Sheedy & Whitter, 2009). Its 17 elements of recovery-oriented systems of care and services are defined in the following way in this paper:

1. Person-centred;
2. Inclusive of family and other ally involvement;
3. Individualized and comprehensive services across the lifespan;
4. Systems anchored in the community;
5. Continuity of care;
6. Partnership-consultant relationships;
7. Strength-based;
8. Culturally responsive;
9. Responsiveness to personal belief systems;
10. Commitment to peer recovery support services;
11. Integrated services;
12. System-wide education and training;
13. Inclusion of the voices and experiences of recovering individuals and their families;
14. Ongoing monitoring and evaluation;
15. Evidence driven;
16. Research based;
17. Adequately and flexibly funded.

From our perspective, what is critical about this model is the notion that outcomes rely on a combination of professional inputs and processes integrated with a broader framework of community resources—and that the individual and their family and community are at the heart of the system. The SAMSHA model also challenges the assumption of ordering in which specialist interventions in specialist settings should precede (temporally) community engagement.

There is very little evidence around gambling and recovery, both because of the newness of gambling as an area for academic investigation and secondly because there have been almost no peer-driven recovery activities in the gambling area. In most countries, including the UK, structured treatment for gambling has been extremely localized until the last few years. Using the case study of gambling treatment services, primarily in the UK, the chapter will outline models for supporting and sustaining change involving models of regulation of service delivery. The resulting frameworks and models are used to support and ensure quality systems that enable the building of trust and confidence between stakeholders. Our particular focus is on the role of regulatory systems in creating strengths-based approaches to prevention and treatment, and on constructing models for building social and community capital as a core part of specialist delivery. In the UK, GambleAware (GA)—previously the Responsible Gambling Trust—has become the main commissioner of interventions and treatment for problem gamblers in the UK. In 2015/16, GA embarked on a programme of work to create a commissioned system of interventions and treatment in the UK. GA has embarked on a re-commissioning

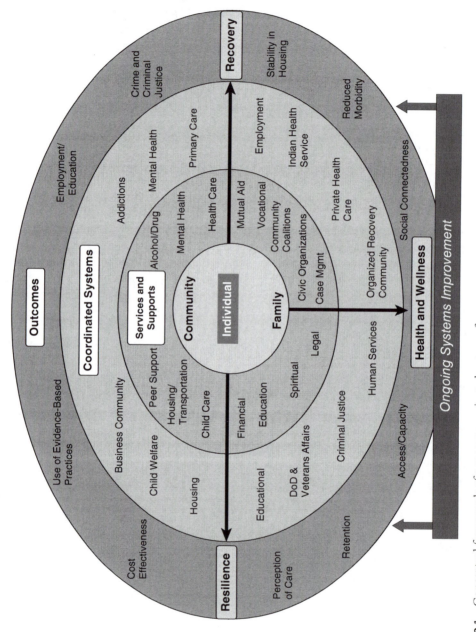

FIGURE 12.1 Conceptual framework of a recovery-oriented system of care

Source: Sheedy & Whitter (2009, p. 3).

of the problem gambling treatment system in the UK, from a small group of 'preferred providers' to enable the development of a more structured, tiered and efficient gambling treatment system in each area within the UK. This affords a significant opportunity for establishing a clear governance framework linked to quality assurance and effective systems management.

Strengths-Based Approaches to Managing Systems

This model, and the strengths-based approach that sits within it, assumes that people are active agents of their own care—with the underlying assumptions of choice and self-determination. This requires all of the key parties involved recognizing that treatment and intervention is a partnership process between equal stakeholders and not something done by experts to passive patients, and that strengths-based approaches apply to all of the relevant stakeholders, including specialist treatment staff, managers and members of the wider community that the client and agency are located within. This model poses a huge challenge to professional hegemonies and the related and underlying models of knowledge.

Crucially, what this also means is that the process of recovery as a journey of growth applies every bit as much to the staff as it does for people in recovery and their families. This is the first critical implication for a positive or strengths-based regulatory framework, which is the overall aim and model of the chapter and the aspiration for the gambling system in the UK. This is a nascent treatment system that is small and unified enough for those responsible for the commissioning of services and supporting the regulation of gambling treatment services to create a delivery system predicated on strengths-based regulation.

The quest for wellbeing and a process of dynamic and shared growth are critical components for all system participants, and so an overall ethos of collective efficacy and wellbeing is essential, predicated on social and community relationships that attempt to generate both trust and hope in all of the participants within the system. What the aim of a regulatory system for gambling treatment involves is a regulatory diamond based on social relationships between all parties which, as much as possible, are predicated on strengths and shared objectives. The aim with the new system is to create credibility to a range of external stakeholders including Government and the general public, to establish perceptions of fairness and consistency as outlined for charities by Braithwaite (2013).

In our previous work on worker wellbeing (Best et al., 2015), based on a sample of 208 addiction workers in Victoria, Australia, using an anonymous online survey to gather data, there was a clear association between greater worker wellbeing and higher levels of therapeutic optimism. Conversely, those workers who had lower wellbeing and quality of life were more pessimistic in their prognoses for their clients. Working within a strengths-based paradigm is both salutogenic, meaning that it focuses on factors that support human health and wellbeing, rather than on factors that cause disease, and contagious and these principles can be applied within a regulatory model which sees itself as embedded within a social system. The next section will outline in greater detail how a strengths-based approach to regulation can be embedded within a recovery-oriented model based on a sense of belonging (social identity) and commitment to the effectiveness of the system—in this case, high-quality recovery-oriented gambling treatment.

Characteristics of a Strengths-Based Approach at a Systems Level

The initial premise of a strengths-based and recovery-oriented system would be to start with the assumption of 'do no harm' and build from this to a space where growth is a positive sum game. Positive actions and the growth of prosocial inclusive networks generates new capital, in the same way that exclusion and the diminution of networks diminishes net social and community capital. There is some evidence of this from the application of health geography principles to recovery—which has been referred to as the creation of a 'therapeutic landscape for recovery' (Wilton & DeVerteuil, 2006).

A 'therapeutic landscape' is described as "changing places, settings, situations, locales and milieus that encompass the physical, psychological and social environments associated with treatment or healing" (Williams, 1999, p. 2). This has been applied to recovery from alcohol and drugs and the importance of context in recovery. Wilton and DeVerteuil (2006) describe a cluster of alcohol and drug treatment services in San Pedro, California, as a 'recovery landscape' as a foundation of spaces and activities that promote recovery. As with much of the addiction recovery research, this has primarily focused on alcohol and illicit drugs, but the lesson for gambling is that visible recovery in the community both breaks down stigma and increases the accessibility of pathways to community support. This is done through a social project that extends beyond the boundaries of the addiction services into the community through the emergence of an enduring recovery community, in which a sense of fellowship is developed in the wider community. The underlying idea here is that recovery is promoted through community celebration of success and in doing so creates greater visibility of recovery success so increasing the likelihood of a contagion of hope and change. As Braithwaite has argued, "the strongest predictors of willingness to act with the authority are the 'feel good' emotions of being part of a group, believing in the democracy, and trusting the institutions that are in place to administer the system" (Braithwaite, 2004b, p. 147). For the commissioning of a gambling system, this involves generating a sense of pride and positive social identity that becomes manifest through client and community acceptance and engagement of gambling treatment as efficacious and sustainable.

The idea that the community is a place that can nurture change has also been championed in community studies, primarily in the area of public health (Improvement and Development Agency, 2010) in a number of areas in the north of England where challenges of social isolation and issues of poor health protection and disease prevention were addressed in this way. This is part of a program of work that has been undertaken in the UK recently on the application of a US model of community engagement called Asset Based Community Development (Kretzmann & McKnight, 1993). In this model, resources are seen to exist in local communities and the task is to engage and mobilize those resources to support reintegration rather than rely too heavily on professionals to do this. Much of the work is done by 'community connectors' (McKnight & Block, 2010) who act as the bridges between vulnerable individuals or groups and the assets that have been identified in their local communities. Within a treatment paradigm for addictive behaviours, this offers an opportunity for services to have a formalized mechanism of supplementing the achievements they make with partnerships and assets in local communities that can be mobilized to support and sustain such changes. What this offers to addiction services is both a way of supplementing their meagre resources through community engagement and also crucially providing a continuity of care and support beyond what is possible with the scarce resources that are available in specialist treatment services.

Our own first attempt at deploying the ABCD model was undertaken in partnership with the Salvation Army Therapeutic Community on the Central Coast of Australia (Best et al., 2014), where the aim was to support residents' reintegration through identifying community assets that were suitable to provide positive networks and meaningful activities but also to give something back. Instead of treatment being seen as a standalone resource, it was seen as a part of the community in which it was located. For this reason, we branded this model 'Reciprocal Community Development' as the aim was to build recovery capital among residents and to use the residents to build capital in the community (Best et al.,

2014). This was based on a very clear agenda of asserting that the residents had something worth giving and that they, and the therapeutic community as a whole, should play an active role in community building and community wellbeing. There was also a second component which was the assumption that shared resources and assets between the Therapeutic Community (TC) and the community would add up to more than the sum of its parts. The project succeeded to the extent that staff in the TC used their own personal networks to engage the residents in community activities and also to engage graduates of the program in supporting the process. Neither the sustainability of the model nor its impact on the wider community were assessed because of funding limitations. Nonetheless, this model of a developing set of connectors creates a recovery coalition of staff, ex-residents and current residents in a shared enterprise around effective engagement in community activity. Thus, it defines the core 'third parties' in a regulatory model as the professionals and services, the community and the clients, and attempts to bring these groups together for a shared purpose, which we want to separate out into stakeholders within the system (families, clients) and those outside (the broader community and external groups and bodies). From a strengths-based approach, this creates multiple opportunities for social networks that overlap and that actively engage with each other for the benefit of the community and for the residents, through attempting to align and reconcile their needs and objectives. This creates a space for a strengths-based and solution-focused learning model that brings together stakeholders to support the needs of an excluded group (that would include problem gamblers) using an approach that is sensitive to the needs of the wider community, including families and treatment service staff.

The conclusion of this section is that the creation of a recovery-oriented system involves a transition from professionalized roles and rules based on governance and a clear distance between worker and client to more of a partnership model where at the heart of the approach is the assumption that wellbeing is a strengths-based outcome for all participants. This can be socially contagious and inspire connections, relationships, networks suffused with hope not only among clients, but among staff and into the communities in which the services are based. This has profound implications for how professional staff and managers of services come to see themselves and also for how the service is configured and structured and how it relates to its commissioners and partner agencies, as well as in its relationship to the community it serves and the physical community in which it is based. This is consistent with a strengths-based regulatory approach as described by Braithwaite in discussing rewards within a responsive regulation model for charities. She described "a pyramid to recognise strengths empowers regulated actors to devise their own improvements through the regulatory framework and be leaders in the reform process" (Braithwaite, 2013, p. 9).

This is not a simple task. Collective hope has conflicts with individual hope. Attempting to provide an environment where all the parties involved feel they are heard and understood can be a challenge, particularly in a new area with limited history and limited evidence of effectiveness, like the treatment delivery system for problem gambling. A regulatory framework which enables individuals' hopes to be heard and harmonized to complement each other and bring about change and work towards common and conflicting goals requires all parties to be encouraged to work collectively to create connectedness and empowerment. The concept of collective hope within society works in the same way in a recovery-oriented regulatory system as it provides for inclusion of all: commitment to shared goals, collective efficacy through active participation and a sense of ownership and group membership and trust in the regulator (Braithwaite, 2004a). Before examples of how a recovery-oriented approach to service systems and governance is presented, a brief overview will be given of regulatory models and responsive regulation.

Regulatory Mechanisms

Regulation and oversight offers a significant opportunity for system change, and so the implementation of a recovery-oriented system of care has implications for regulatory approaches. As Drahos and Krygier (2017) have argued "Law has to become part of a much larger regulatory world in which there are many defenders, guardians and protectors of public interests, all operating under conditions of full information, mutual transparency and accountability" (cited in Drahos and Krygier in Drahos, 2017, p. 6). This is consistent with Parker and Braithwaite's (2003) assertion that regulation is a fluid process of influencing the flow of events, in which legal rules and rights are only one component part of a relational process of regulation as an interpersonal dynamic embedded in a series of shifting systems and mechanisms. Within this fluid approach, responsive regulation is consistent with the recovery paradigm, and for a new treatment system, like gambling in the UK, it offers the option of creating a strengths-based regulatory model predicated on relationship building and the equality of multiple stakeholders.

It has also been argued that regulation is about 'tripartism' where each cornerstone must play a part in the regulation of the industry for it to work effectively. Much regulation is transactional involving only the State and the business industry in a two-way interaction between these two parties. For responsive regulation to work effectively you need to bring along third parties, in the form of a series of public interest groups, and the suggestion from a recovery-oriented systems approach is that there will potentially be a fourth party in the form of both service users and service employees. Thus, the model presented in Figure 12.2 needs to be extended to enhance the role of a broader domain of stakeholders, and with the assumption of much more fluidity and movement between the stakeholders.

This model deliberately attempts to separate out third parties within the system from those external stakeholders who have contact with the system—in this case, gambling treatment, as they are likely to have different needs and their perceptions of success are different. However, the critical difference is around identity—all of the internal partners should perceive themselves as having a sense of belonging to the system that is not the case for external stakeholders.

From the perspective of a recovery-oriented system, the aim would be to embed recovery-oriented system of care (ROSC) principles of strengths-based, inclusive, community-anchored and

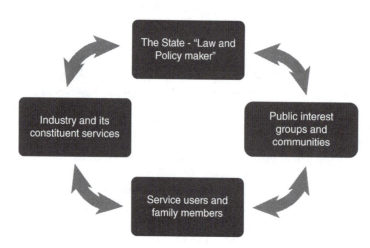

FIGURE 12.2 The Regulatory Diamond

evidence-based; and that these are recognized and accepted by both internal and external stakeholders. The aim of this model is to move the service user and their families into the system and make them a focal point with a clear identity and role in the regulatory process. Regulation will work within all these cornerstones and at different levels but it is essential that their needs are addressed separately from other third parties (public interest groups and communities). By developing an additional focus on the regulation of vulnerable populations (not only individuals with addictions but those with mental health problems, homeless people and so on) there is potential for the development of a 'regulatory capital' to be conceptualized both as a way of generating resources within the regulatory system, but also as a potential mechanism for increasing the transparency, ethics and effectiveness of delivery systems. Promoting partnership and cooperation across the points of the diamond will enhance stakeholder wellbeing but also will augment the status and reputation of the system as a whole.

Creating a strengths-based approach in which responsive regulation can be reconciled with the promotion of values and goals for the individuals who interact with the system. This would include not only the internal stakeholders but the clients or customers of gambling treatment services, but their family members, the staff who work in services and, externally, the communities that will interact with services and their representatives. The value of a strengths-based approach means that all four cornerstones become empowered within the system, meaning that any risks associated with a two-way transaction between the State and the industry, for example, corruption and profit-driven objectives, are reduced. By empowering all cornerstones the opportunities for growth are richer and regulatory capital has the potential to spread. This takes the system beyond the original bipartite regulatory framework and towards a holistic approach which benefits many more stakeholders within the system.

Regulatory capital will only ever have a superficial impact if the regulatory diamond does not enable listening and cooperation with multiple stakeholders and decisions that are inclusive. This means that the internal configuration of stakeholders cooperate and demonstrate the value and impact of their decisions on external partners and the general public, with the aim and outcome of strengthening the overall system. This is about making regulation part of a quality system which is responsive to the needs of all stakeholders, all of whose satisfaction is essential for a recovery-oriented approach that fulfils the requirement of reciprocal development (Best et al., 2014). Based on a responsive regulation model (Ayers & Braithwaite, 1992), this means that restorative solutions are seen as a learning and developmental opportunity for individual services and the whole sector, whereas punitive approaches would be regarded as evidence of 'negative regulatory capital', as they reduce the strength of the ties and the commitment to the principles of partnership and shared ownership. Overly punitive or overly permissive regulation weakens the whole regulatory system and reduces regulatory capital as it breaches the principles of partnership and so diminishes the strength of the social networks. This requires the growth of trust as a dynamic in a process of both internal stakeholder relations and relationships with a diverse range of external groups and bodies. Thus, in the case of gambling treatment, these external bodies will include healthcare organizations, the Citizens Advice Bureau, debt agencies, as well as a range of local community groups and associations.

Regulatory capital is predicated on social relationships that are trusting, transparent, enduring and reliable. If this process is adhered to the system becomes stronger and generative for all the stakeholders and creates a sense of belonging and ownership. If this process fails, on a consistent basis, to create regulatory capital, appropriate sanctions for non-compliance are required and responsive regulation switches to more punitive measures which are placed on the industry or specific providers. By creating a system which merges responsive regulation, strengths-based approaches and regulatory capital it affords for the system to be driven by the satisfaction of all the stakeholders but also, and arguably most importantly, the positive connection and transparency of the links and nodes across the networks in the regulatory diamond. However, as Braithwaite (2013) has suggested with the depiction of a pyramid of rewards, the core of a strengths-based model lies in the emphasis on the pyramid of rewards as relationship and partnership building not on the utilization of sanctions as the determinant of system effectiveness.

Strong, positive relationships are a recognized as a marker for success. Conversely, if the relationship between any two stakeholders becomes too strong or too exclusionary, then the overall levels of engagement, satisfaction and network development fails across the diamond. In the context of gambling, the greatest concern in the UK is that there is too strong a bind between the industry and the regulator, GambleAware. GambleAware is also the commissioner and de facto quality assurer of the gambling treatment system in the UK, and so the other key stakeholders, gamblers, their families, possibly the staff in gambling agencies and the broader community, suffer as a consequence of this strong and exclusive relationship. For GambleAware, this exclusivity cannot be addressed simply by hosting a few public consultation events, rather it necessitates a fundamental change in systems approaches. The change must embed all of the stakeholders in the regulatory process and drive the growth of nodes and links across the regulatory diamond both as a treatment delivery system for problem gambling and as part of the wider communities that it engages. Recovery-oriented and strengths-based systems would progress this further in that the aim would be to make the regulatory process participatory and empowering for the less powerful stakeholders across the cornerstones. This would mean also bringing clients, families and frontline workers into the heart of the system. This is a process that will take place in inter-personal spaces over elongated periods of time.

In this way, positive outcomes of all forms of dispute resolution would include 'learning the lessons' and contributions to evidence-based practice, but also contribute to strengthening the ties in the network. Thus, every effective resolution that actively engages all of the stakeholders in both process and outcome acts as a means of legitimating the diamond and as strengthening the ties across social networks. Where there are agreed, transparent and consensual processes and outcomes, the system itself grows regulatory capital and its status and reputation grows as a consequence. In areas as contentious as gambling, this is critical to not only the perceived credibility of the regulator, but also to the self-respect and professional credibility of all those working within the system.

Data and reporting compliance is one domain of regulation that can contribute to a learning community and that can generate models for the sector. It can also offer a degree of transparency, depending on the timeliness with which data becomes available. For gambling treatment in the UK, the quest for a viable, cost-effective and transparent data system is a core component of the development of a tool for commissioners and regulators to be able to judge effectiveness and to monitor and measure the impact of interventions. For the regulatory system to have viable regulatory capital it needs to achieve the ROSC principle of being evidence-driven, but also to have a data system sufficiently specific and sensitive that it can be seen by all parties as a useful and accurate mechanism for testing the effectiveness of interventions, including but not restricted to, those required by regulators. For gambling, that means that intervention by the regulators is not only seen to be inclusive and evidence-driven but that its impacts can be monitored and measured to be effective, meeting stated needs and the ongoing needs of all stakeholders. Such actions create regulatory capital and increase the social ties across the regulatory diamond. However, with an inclusive system, transparency is not enough on its own and there need to be ways that the data can be made useful and accessible to all of the stakeholders.

Nonetheless, and irrespective of the domain of compliance, the system goal is the generation of positive 'regulatory capital' that enhances all of the stakeholders and that results in improved practice, improved wellbeing and outcomes for clients and workers and results in system contributions to community wellbeing. The basic assumptions underpinning this model are that the effectiveness of regulatory models are based on the evolution of long-term trust and cooperation between the multiple stakeholders involved in the process, and that the emerging regulatory social capital is the basic premise of moving away from punitive regulation. In the gambling example, this requires GambleAware to ensure that its dealings with the gambling industry are both transparent and at a distance, and that all disputes about delivery are based on equivalent participation from each point of the diamond with the challenge of supporting poorly resourced groups such as families and problem gamblers to be able to be active participants. As Braithwaite (2017) has argued, this is also an issue of identity and pride—for addiction and its treatment, there is an inevitable concern about stigma (for families and workers this is secondary stigma) (Braithwaite cited in Drahos, 2017). So, generating a system that has credibility and transparency in its governance is necessary for it to truly be effective. In order for effective governance oversight is central to third (and fourth) party participation in the regulatory process. In an emerging field like gambling treatment, where there are clear power and resource imbalances between stakeholder groups, one of the core challenges for the regulatory body is to ensure each cornerstone is supported and trained to grow and develop into its own viable group with a voice that is heard, and respected. This applies not only to external bodies like user and recovery groups, and family support groups, but also to staff representative organizations to ensure that gambling staff have that sense of network engagement and belonging.

Regulatory Capital and the Use of Sanctions

In a system like the gambling treatment services delivery model, the basic question is around ensuring inclusive, effective and evidence-based care that is consistent with a holistic model of recovery. Providers are therefore expected to offer a safe space and professional and competent staff who will deliver both care coordination and evidence-based interventions to support change. For GambleAware, as the commissioning and regulatory body for the system, its role is to ensure that there is consistency and that all providers are held to account but this can often be counterproductive for the quality of outcomes. Striving for consistency should not be at the cost of innovation or quality. The underpinning principle of this accountability is a model of responsive regulation that is consistent with the model of a recovery-oriented system of care as outlined above. As commissioners as well as the overseers of health governance, that means regulation focuses on patient safety, engagement, retention and client outcomes (including satisfaction) and impact of intervention on re-uptake of gambling and the resulting harms.

The additional component to this approach is that the longer-term aim should be the generation of regulatory capital that is driven by strong ties across all four stakeholder groups in the Regulatory Diamond, and that builds hope, trust, credibility and capacity both within the gambling treatment system and in its dealings with a wider group of community stakeholders. As Braithwaite (2017) has argued "Cooperation does not guarantee regulatory success, but it helps. Cooperation and willingness to comply are most likely to occur if those being regulated see benefits, believe the regulation is fair and feel a sense of obligation to defer to a regulatory authority's wishes" (Braithwaite 2017, p. 28).

As shown in the regulatory pyramid developed by Braithwaite (2016) in developing better strategies for problem-solving, there has to be a hierarchy of coerciveness starting off at that point of less corrosive solutions first (shown at the bottom of Figure 12.3) and moving up the hierarchy until one of them is successful, but alongside this there also should be sanctions for non-compliance (the tip of the pyramid). Thus, a regulatory capital model must rest on social relationships and a 'middle strip' within a pyramid of regulation that affords space for responsive regulation, as shown in Figure 12.3. The zone of punishment is explicitly part of responsive regulation (with gambling, for example, revoking or suspending the licence of providers or revoking or suspending the right of gamblers to enter casinos). Indeed, it is an integral part of the responsive regulation explanatory framework that the existence of sanctions at the peak of pyramid paradoxically allows most of the regulatory action to occur lower in the pyramid.

Within our model, the primary relationships between regulator and the treatment provider have broken down if there is too little intervention (the bottom of the pyramid) or too frequent intervention, or, as Murphy (2017) has argued, there is seen to be a failure of procedural fairness about the process of who is punished and when. Murphy highlights that there has been a "plethora of studies published and demonstrate how procedural justice can build legitimacy and promote a voluntary compliance" and that "many of these studies found a direct link between procedural justice evaluations and subsequent self-reported compliance behaviours" (Murphy, 2017, p. 47). Procedural justice can enhance willingness to cooperate but it tends to be top-down in approach. If stakeholders involved feel that they have received fair and just treatment from the regulators it creates a sense of respect among the different stakeholders and individuals involved. The perception of fairness, transparency and timeliness in regulation of gambling treatment services can also be a catalyst for driving forward evidence-based practice and the commitment of all of the stakeholders to a participatory and recovery-oriented treatment system for gambling. In a nascent system, the establishment of trust and hope-based partnerships (that recovery is possible and that treatment services can support that process) is possible when governance and regulation are linked to commissioning of services, as is the case with gambling treatment in the UK.

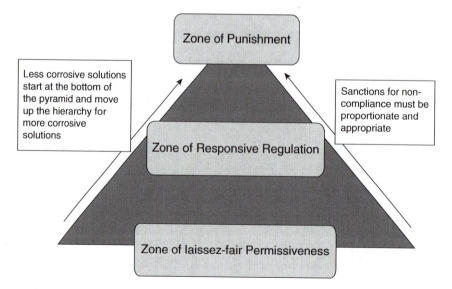

FIGURE 12.3 Regulatory processes and responsive regulation

However, in an emerging industry, with a limited evidence base and limited resources, such as the treatment of gambling problems, the central zone in Figure 12.3 has to be large enough for the development of a quality system that allows training, growth and innovation as part of the regulatory process and that does not result in the small pool of treatment providers exiting the system because they feel that regulation is too exacting or unreasonable.

As alluded to above, there is also the need for the development of a data system that does not place too intensive a resource demand on the providers but allows sufficient depth, rigour and transparency to generate confidence within the system. This is key to the dynamic component of the regulatory model in its role as a quality assurance mechanism. The importance of social ties—and underlying issues of social identity (e.g. Jetten, Haslam, & Haslam, 2012)—are critical here within a recovery-oriented system of care that generates trust and pride. In other words, for clients or families to engage with gambling treatment services, they must believe that the services they offer are effective and that core professionalism issues of confidentiality, respect and so on will be respected and managed appropriately. For the regulator to support and enable those beliefs, failures must be addressed in such a way that capacity in the system grows and the strength of the relationship with providers of services, users of services and their family members and broader groups of community stakeholders, are networked and linked together in such a way as to generate hope and trust. Thus, the responsive component has at its core a systems capacity component predicated on lasting relationships between all four points of the diamond that are predicated on trust.

Regulation of this nature is not bipartite nor is the system sufficient if it were only to consider the third component in the diamond, as the issue of capacity and delivery will require a broader set of community engagements, so that people can be referred for case management to appropriate external bodies, and external bodies will take gambling treatment seriously and engage with it as a fair and effective system. Having regulation that is responsive creates a meta-strategy by empowering the stakeholders to solve a particular problem, predicated on the idea of longevity in the relationship and the need for trust to exist both with other parties and in the process and model.

This means that if you gain voluntary agreement from the different stakeholders and the right programmes for enhancement and development are in place, then the engagement with the system is likely to improve, leading to stronger ties. In the addictions field, this is critically important as there is a strong relationship between worker wellbeing, therapeutic optimism and client outcomes, as Best et al. (2016) have shown with drug and alcohol treatment services. When this is applied in the area of gambling, it will lead to a stronger system that generates treatment effectiveness through positive regulatory capital where 'bonding' capital improves among the three internal stakeholders in the diamond (regulators, regulated treatment providers and patients, their families and staff) and 'bridging' capital to external bodies and the general public augments the status and viability of the model. This is very much about motivating stakeholders to implement what works, starting off with strategies that are less coercive before seeking more punitive actions as a last resort, where improvements do not occur as a result of non-compliance or poor attempts at participative and engaging mechanisms of addressing the needs of the multiple stakeholders.

Burford and Pennell (1998) have discussed how to redesign restorative justice so that it improves the quality of choices and empowers individuals to respond—this fits with both recovery capital and with the ideas of the Regulatory Diamond and of regulatory capital in that the notion of systems growth is both socially driven and positively valenced to create hope and trust within the stakeholder network and increase credibility and acceptability in the larger communities that the gambling treatment system will interact with. However, this is a long-term goal that is reliant upon a commitment to evidence-based processes, to shared learning and to a monitoring and measurement model that will provide both the robustness and the sensitivity to identify and detect changes.

Conclusion: Human Services that CHIME

In their review of the effective components of recovery interventions in the mental health field, Leamy et al. (2011) concluded that there were five core components of all successful recovery interventions and models, summarized in the acronym CHIME: Connectedness; Hope; Identity; Meaning; and Empowerment. These are core principles that fit with the idea of a recovery-oriented system of care (ROSC, Sheedy & Whitter, 2009). Within the gambling treatment system in the UK, there is an emerging model of continuity of care that is based on recovery principles that are shared across treatment providers who are attempting to offer holistic interventions that lead to stable recovery. Overseeing this process and providing the regulatory framework is GambleAware, who also have the role of commissioning treatment for gambling in the UK. The gambling system is new and is based on a diverse workforce and a limited treatment effectiveness literature. This means it is essential that the regulatory model is inclusive and participative, and, as with any addiction treatment system can deal with both stigma and scepticism. Our contribution to the broader field of regulatory theory is around the idea of regulatory capital and a regulatory capital that is based on the concept of a system of tripartite stakeholders—regulator/commissioner, service provider and service users in the broadest sense (patients, family members and staff in treatment services). Here the model is about identity and social networks as the basis for a strengths-based and inclusive foundation for regulation. However, there is a fourth point in a Regulatory Diamond that is about external stakeholders—both the big institutions of community, media and government; and secondly the partner organizations that will influence the effectiveness of the gambling treatment system—mental health, criminal justice and so on.

The model for regulation provided here is based on the idea of regulatory capital and a Regulatory Diamond in which GambleAware is the regulator, there is a series of regulatees in the form of treatment providers, the users of services (and their families) are accorded an equal status as stakeholders as is the lived community and the diverse range of external groups with which the system interacts. Regulatory capital is seen as the sum of resources available to ensure a responsive and dynamic system that is built on trust and hope to ensure the best treatment outcomes for gamblers while supporting and promoting the needs and wellbeing of gambling treatment staff, users' families and external groups affected by gambling.

For trust and hope to be instigated within this framework and then for it to be developed and embedded within a Regulatory Diamond all the key agencies and groups have to enable and accommodate these principles for them to flourish, both within the system and in its relationships to external stakeholders. Trust cannot be imposed on any of the four corners of the Diamond; it must be a shared experience and once shared, the hope will develop between the cornerstones of the Diamond to create a strong and well-balanced system which supports the individuals in recovery, here the gamblers, but also their families, the wider communities and the staff working in treatment services. The development of this is key but continuing to allow this to mature "brings capacity to self-scaffold, individuals retain the capacity to draw on the strengths and hopes of others to rekindle their own sense of agency and to realign their hopes when things become difficult" (Braithwaite, 2004a, p. 12). Providing such opportunities for growth and benefit across all of the cornerstones is fundamental to thinking beyond the original bipartite regulatory framework and towards one of regulatory capital.

References

Ayers, I., & Braithwaite, J. (1992). *Responsive regulation: Transcending the deregulation debate.* Oxford: Oxford University Press.

Beattie, M., & Longabaugh, R. (1999). General and alcohol-specific support following treatment. *Addictive Behaviours, 24,* 593–606.

Best, D., Byrne, G., Pullen, D., Kelly, J., Elliot, K., & Savic, M. (2014). Therapeutic communities and the local community: Isolation or integration. *Therapeutic Communities Journal, 35*(4), 150–158. Retrieved from https://salvos.org.au/scribe/sites/auesalvos/files/Recovery_in_community.pdf.

Best, D., Edwards, M., Cano, I., Mama-Rudd, A., Durrance, J., Lehman, J., & White, W. (2016). Measuring an individual's recovery barriers and strengths. *Addiction Professional,* 1–5.

Best, D., McKitterick, T., Beswick, T., & Savic, M. (2015). Recovery capital and social networks among people in treatment and among those in recovery in York, England. *Alcoholism Treatment Quarterly, 33*(3), 270–282.

Best and Laudet. (2010). *The potential of recovery capital.* Retrieved from www.thersa.org/globalassets/pdfs/blogs/a4-recovery-capital-230710-v5.pdf.

Best, D., Savic, M., & Daley, P. (2016). The wellbeing of alcohol and other drug counsellors in Australia: Strengths, risks and implications. *Alcoholism Treatment Quarterly, 34*(2), 223–232.

Betty Ford Institute Consensus Panel. (2007). What is recovery? A working definition from the Betty Ford Institute. *Journal of Substance Abuse Treatment, 33,* 221–228.

Braithwaite, J. (2016). *Restorative justice and responsive regulation: The question of evidence* (Working paper). School of Regulation and Global Governance (RegNet). Australia: Australian National University.

Braithwaite, V. (2004a). Collective hope. *The Annals of the American Academy of Political and Social Science Journal, 592,* 6–15.

Braithwaite, V. (2004b). The hope process and social inclusion. *The Annals of the American Academy of Political and Social Science Journal, 592,* 128–151.

Braithwaite, V. (2013). *A regulatory approach for the Australian charities and not-for-profit commission: A discussion paper* (Regulatory Institutions Network Occasional Paper 19). Canberra: Australian National University.

Braithwaite, V. in Drahos, P. (Eds.). (2017). *Regulatory theory: Foundations and applications.* Acton, Australia: ANU Press. 25–41.

Burford, G., & Pennell, J. (1998). *Family group decision making project. Outcome report* (Vol. 1). St. John's, NF: Memorial University of Newfoundland, Institute for Social and Economic Research.

Cano, I., Best. D., Edwards, M., & Lehman, J. (2017). Recovery capital pathways: Modelling the components of recovery wellbeing. *Drug & Alcohol Dependence, 181,* 11–19. doi: http://dx.doi.org/10.1016/j.drugalcdep.2017.09.002.

Dennis, M., Scott, C., & Laudet, A. (2014). Beyond bricks and mortar: Recent research on substance abuse disorder recovery management. *Current Psychiatry Report, 16*(4), 1–7.

Drahos, P., & Krygier, M., in Drahos, P. (Eds.). (2017). *Regulatory theory: Foundations and applications.* Acton, Australia: ANU Press. 1–22.

Granfield, R., & Cloud, W. (1999). *Coming clean: Overcoming addiction without treatment.* New York: New York University Press.

Improvement and Development Agency. (2010). *A glass half-full: How an asset approach can improve community health and wellbeing.* London, UK: Local Government Association.

Jetten, J., Haslam, C., & Haslam, S. A. (2012). *The social cure: Identity, health and well-being.* New York: Psychology Press.

Kelly, J. (2017). Is alcoholics anonymous religious, spiritual, neither? Findings from 25 years of mechanisms of behavior change research. *Addiction Journal, 112*(6), 929–936.

Kelly, J., & White, W. (Eds.). (2010). *Addiction recovery management.* New York: Springer.

Kretzmann, J., & McKnight, J. (1993). *Building communities from the inside out: A path toward finding and mobilising a community's assets*. Skokie, IL: ACTA Publications.

Leamy, M., Bird, V., Le Boutillier, C., Williams, J., & Slade, M. (2011). A conceptual framework for personal recovery in mental health: Systematic review and narrative synthesis. *British Journal of Psychiatry, 199*, 445–452.

Longabaugh, R., Wirtz, P. W., Zywiak, W. H., & O'Malley, S. S. (2010). Network support as a prognostic indicator of drinking outcomes: The COMBINE study. *Journal of Studies on Alcohol and Drugs, 71*(6), 837.

McKnight, J., & Block, P. (2010). *The abundant community: Awakening the power of families and neighbourhoods*. San Francisco: Berrett-Koehler Publishers Inc.

Moos, R. (2007). Theory-based processes that promote remission of substance use disorders, *Clinical Psychology Review, 27*, 537–551.

Murphy, K. in Drahos, P. (Eds.). (2017). *Regulatory theory: Foundations and applications*. Acton, Australia: ANU Press. 43–58.

Parker, C., & Braithwaite, J. (2003). Regulation. In P. Cane & M. Tushnet (Eds.), *The Oxford handbook of legal studies* (pp. 119–145). Oxford: Oxford University Press.

Savic, M., Best, D., Manning, V., & Lubman, D. I. (2017). Strategies to facilitate integrated care for people with alcohol and other drug problems: A systematic review. *Substance Abuse Treatment, Prevention, and Policy, 12*, 19.

Sheedy, C. K., & Whitter, M. (2009). *Guiding principles and elements of recovery-oriented systems of care: What do we know from the research?* (HHS Publication No. (SMA) 09–4439). Rockville, MD: Center for Substance Abuse Treatment, Substance Abuse and Mental Health Services Administration.

UK Drug Policy Commission. (2008). *The UK drug policy commission recovery consensus group: A vision of recovery*. London, UK: UK Drug Policy Commission. Retrieved from www.ukdpc.org.uk/wp-content/uploads/Policy%20 report%20-%20A%20vision%20of%20recovery_%20UKDPC%20recovery%20consensus%20group.pdf.

Williams, A. (1999). Introduction. In A. Williams (Ed.), *Therapeutic landscapes: The dynamics between place and wellness* (pp. 1–11). Lanham, MA: University Press of America.

Wilton, R., & DeVerteuil, G. (2006). Spaces of sobriety/sites of power: Examining social model alcohol recovery programs as therapeutic landscapes. *Social Science and Medicine, 63*, 649–661.

World Health Organization. (2001). *The World Health Report. Mental health: New understandings, new hope*. Geneva: World Health Organization. Retrieved from www.who.int/whr/2001/en/.

13

WHY DO WE EXCLUDE THE COMMUNITY IN "COMMUNITY SAFETY"?

Robin J. Wilson and Kathryn J. Fox

Introduction

Sexual violence continues to dominate headlines around the world. In the recent past, it has come out of the basements, playgrounds, and back alleys into the spotlight shone by movements such as #MeToo and Time's Up. However, no matter how much popular attention sexual violence commands, there are still far too few suggestions for what to do about it. Over the past 30 or so years, forensic and correctional practitioners have been quietly making gains in establishing effective methods of assessing, treating, and managing the risk posed by individuals known to have engaged in sexually abusive conduct (see Wilson & Sandler, 2018), but these advancements are all but unknown outside of the professional community that developed them. As Wilson and Sandler note, this is due in part to the tendency for research or scholarly commentary to be published in obscure scientific journals or books, which often amounts to "preaching to the choir." Unfortunately, little has been done to share these encouraging results with ordinary citizens, begging the question: Why do we exclude the community when discussing community safety?

Efforts to address sexual violence have been varied over time, but have tended to focus on containment of identified persons who have offended through largely retributive measures (e.g., mandatory minimum sentences, sex offender registries, and residency restrictions, among others). Although few, if any, of these measures have been demonstrated to reduce sexual recidivism (see review in Wilson & Sandler, 2018), there is a general perspective that anything that makes life difficult for someone who has sexually offended is something worth implementing. Some of this perspective is likely rooted in historical distaste and disregard for "ex-cons" generally, but it would be our submission that these strongly emotional responses are heightened when that released individual has a history of sexual offending. In turn, this has often led to a process of ignoring best practice suggestions because there is a belief that they somehow do not or cannot apply to persons who have sexually offended. For example, the Risk-Need-Responsivity model (RNR; see Bonta & Andrews, 2016, and explained in detail below) underpins much of modern, western correctional practices. There is little reason to believe that the RNR principles would not apply to persons committing sexual crimes as much as they do for those committing non-sexual crimes, yet Hanson and colleagues (Hanson et al., 2009) believed it was necessary

DOI: 10.4324/9780429398704-13

to conduct a meta-analysis proving this point and leading them to recommend incorporation of RNR principles in treatment for sexual offending.

Broadly, professional approaches to management of sexual violence have included ongoing research in supervision practices and treatment methods. Focus here has been on development of new technologies and implementation of evidence-based practices; however, demonstrating that these new technologies actually accomplish the intended goal has been difficult. Further, ensuring general adherence to best practices has been equally difficult in a culture that has emphasized containment of risk to the community, almost to the exclusion of provision of reintegration opportunities for individuals returning to the community after criminal sanction. In the next section, we outline some of the history of program development and evaluation, both in regard to correctional interventions broadly and approaches to sexual violence specifically.

'Nothing Works' and the Rise of Effective Interventions

In 1974, Martinson published an influential evaluation of correctional programming, decreeing that individuals participating in prison-based interventions were just as likely to reoffend as their counterparts who did not participate. This finding formed the basis of the Nothing Works perspective that persists in many correctional management circles even today, in spite of the fact that Martinson eventually retracted his declaration (Martinson, 1979). Further, several very large-scale meta-analytic reviews have subsequently concluded that programming meeting certain basic rules is significantly more likely to reduce recidivism than sanction alone (see Aos, Miller, & Drake, 2006; Lipsey & Cullen, 2007; Smith, Goggin, & Gendreau, 2002).

> We are confident that, no matter how many studies are subsequently found, sanction studies will not produce results indicative of even modest suppression effects or results remotely approximating outcomes reported for certain types of treatment programs.
>
> *(Smith et al., 2002, p. 19)*

Demonstration of treatment effectiveness in sexual violence prevention has also proven difficult and controversial. An early review (Furby, Weinrott, & Blackshaw, 1989) concluded that there was insufficient evidence to suggest that treatment for persons engaging in sexual offending was having any meaningful effect on recidivism. However, somewhat different to Martinson's claims, Furby et al. asserted that the state of the research base was too inconsistent and mired by poorly contrived studies to allow for any real conclusions to be drawn. Nearly 30 years later, sexual violence researchers continue to have difficulty deciding what is the best way to demonstrate treatment efficacy, with many suggesting that randomized controlled trials (RCT) are the only *real* way to know for sure (e.g., Långström et al., 2013; Seto, Marques, et al., 2008). Others, however, have suggested that RCT methods are difficult to use in assessing treatment for persons engaging in sexual violence and that there may be ethical considerations (see Levenson & Prescott, 2014; Marshall & Marshall, 2007, 2008).

In spite of seemingly dire representations of the (f)utility of treatment for persons who have sexually offended, meta-analytic reviews have typically shown significant differences in rates of reoffending between those who complete treatment and those who do not (e.g., Hanson et al., 2002, 2009; Schmucker & Lösel, 2015). However, it is fair to say that while those differences may be significant, they are relatively small and methodological issues remain in the sexual violence treatment efficacy literature.

The Principles of Effective Interventions

In response to the Nothing Works doctrine, forensic-correctional researchers in many jurisdictions sought to counter Martinson's proclamations and the unfortunate groundswell of administrators who chose to cancel or defund programming they now believed would not have any effect on outcome (i.e., reduced recidivism). Two of the most prominent of those researchers were Canadians Donald Andrews and James Bonta, whose seminal text *The Psychology of Criminal Conduct* (Bonta & Andrews, 2016; originally Andrews & Bonta, 1994) has essentially become a how-to guide for practitioners who want to get the most out of treatment for clients who have engaged in criminal acts (as noted above, including persons who have sexually offended—see Hanson et al., 2009).

Although the Andrews and Bonta book includes a wealth of information about the factors that predict reoffending and how to craft interventions that are most likely to promote desistance, it is their Risk-Need-Responsivity model that has been most revolutionary to the field of correctional treatment. These three principles, when appropriately considered and followed, assist in the creation of a therapeutic framework that leads to considerable reductions in reoffending. The first principle—*Risk*—is essentially a dosage principle. Those individuals posing the greatest likelihood of recidivism are those who should be provided with the most intensive interventions. Similarly, clients at lower levels of risk should receive less intensive programming, if they need any at all—many lower-risk individuals are likely to desist receiving very little in the way of either supervision or treatment (see Hanson et al., 2009, 2017). Indeed, mismatching of risk and treatment intensity can lead to negative outcomes, and that it is not just a problem to under-intervene with higher-risk individuals, it is also problematic when we over-intervene with lower-risk individuals (i.e., if it ain't broke, don't fix it).

The *Need* principle is equally simple in stating that targets of treatment and supervision must be implicated in potential reoffending. That is, those personality traits (e.g., antisociality, narcissism) and lifestyle management variables (substance abuse, interpersonal violence, impulsivity) that are linked to engagement in criminal activities are those that should be the principal focus of intervention. One potential reason for early findings (e.g., Martinson, 1974) that programming had no effect on recidivism was that interventions of that era (e.g., Rogerian group experiences, insight-oriented psychotherapy) tended to focus on self-esteem and other poor predictors of future engagement in criminal conduct. This is not to say that those methods are of no merit; they just did not appropriately address criminogenic need.

The last component of the RNR model is *Responsivity*, which has proven to be the most difficult of the three constructs to ensure compliance to its prescriptions. The responsivity principle requires that interventions be crafted in such a way as to ensure that clients are *able to respond* to them. Considerations must include learning styles, motivation, and client abilities. Modifications must be made when clients have special needs (e.g., mental health problems, learning and intellectual disabilities, etc.); however, it is surprising how many programs claim to have RNR as their underlying, guiding principles, yet they fail to ensure that important aspects of their clientele are considered in building, implementing, and revising programmatic options. Indeed, this lackadaisical approach to responsivity has become one of the major criticisms of the RNR model, with some theorists (e.g., Ward, Melser, & Yates, 2007) claiming that risk and need have focused the correctional world on the assessment of risk and provision of treatment services without appropriate consideration of what involvement in those services might actually mean for clients. Accordingly, strength-based approaches like the Self-Regulation and Good Lives models have sought to include greater focus on holistic methods and therapeutic engagement (Marshall et al.,

2011; Yates, Prescott, & Ward, 2010). Others have highlighted the complementary aspects of the RNR and Good Lives models (see Wilson & Yates, 2009). Similarly, Braithwaite (2011) emphasizes the ways in which authorities can become agents of change by embedding a positive, strength-based approach within a collaborative relationship.

In defence of their model, RNR researchers have highlighted that RNR is not a treatment approach, *per se*. Rather, it is an evidence-based framework in which good treatment can occur (Andrews, Bonta, & Wormith, 2011), and those researchers assert that risk and need were never intended to be implemented without attendant consideration of responsivity. Indeed, we would argue that responsivity may well be the most important consideration of the three RNR principles. At present, poor understanding and general overestimation of the risk posed by individuals who have sexually offended has led to sometimes draconian practices in sentencing and post-correctional civil commitment. The latter practice—seen largely in the United States, but with analogs developing in other countries—involves the indefinite, involuntary civil commitment of certain persons deemed to be "sexually violent predators" (or persons—SVP; see Brandt, Wilson, & Prescott, 2015). Twenty US states and the US federal government have implemented SVP programs, some of which have released very few individuals over their histories, in spite of evidence that most civilly committed persons would not likely sexually reoffend if released to the community (see Carr, Schlank, & Parker, 2013; Duwe, 2013).

There are also difficulties in regard to the implementation of the need principle. The risk principle focuses mainly on global risk to reoffend based on largely historical or static variables and ultimately assists in determining the location (correctional, inpatient, outpatient, etc.) and intensity of intervention. In contrast, the need principle seeks to define the individual in the present according to personality and behavioural elements. This allows for development of lifestyle management considerations aimed at providing clients with the resources and guidance necessary to ensure optimal balance and self-determination in the community. However, some jurisdictions have imposed community risk management plans on clients without consideration of what those plans might mean in terms of real opportunities for reintegration. For instance, social isolation has long been known as a detrimental factor in most aspects of the human condition, yet many components of risk management plans either create or exacerbate social isolation (e.g., residency restrictions, prohibitions regarding with whom they can associate, and public notification practices).

Ultimately, it is our position that risk and need, without reasonable consideration of responsivity, amounts to bad practice that will ultimately fail to address our goals of no more victims and increased client reintegration potential. The originators of the RNR model have long asserted that sanction without application of human service is ultimately destined to fail in reducing reoffending. Similarly, we argue that failing to ensure true adherence to the responsivity principle is equivalent to removing the humanity from human service. Addressing responsivity involves a community-based approach because reintegration is an essential dimension of successful reentry, as we have already noted that isolation often serves to increase risk (Willis & Grace, 2008, 2009).

Further, an emerging literature has highlighted a nexus between need and responsivity. Specifically, there is a growing appreciation of the role of adverse childhood experiences (ACE) in the life trajectories of those who ultimately become involved in crime; particularly sexual crimes (see Levenson, Willis, & Prescott, 2016; Reavis et al., 2013). More than anything, these findings have illuminated the often complex clinical and social profiles of individuals identified as high-risk and/or high-need. In order to effectively address the sometimes myriad difficulties experienced by these individuals, interventions well-steeped in the responsivity principle are required.

In the next section, we turn our attention to perspectives and approaches that seek to ensure opportunities for people who have offended to regain membership in community while maintaining public safety. Focal to our thesis is the necessary consideration of restorative practices, transformative approaches, and the critical role to be played in these endeavours by members of the community.

Restorative Justice and Transformative Processes

Desistance

In recent years, the criminological literature about the persistence of criminal offending has turned its attention to the question of why some people succeed in desisting from a life of crime. This field of study, often referred to as the "desistance literature," examines successful desisters to assess what they have in common. There are roughly two sets of answers to this question: ones that focus on external stabilizers, such as marriage and employment (Laub & Sampson, 2001) and those that highlight internal stabilizers, such as shifts in identity and in others' perceptions of the individual who offended (Maruna, 2001; McNeill, 2006; Shover, 1983, 1996). Best and Musgrove (Chapter 12 this volume) also discusses the mutually reinforcing and steadying effect of inclusive communities. Although external stabilizers, such as jobs and housing, are helpful in the process of participating in a prosocial life, some argue that a change in one's sense of self is crucial for genuine commitment to non-offending. Organizations devoted to assisting formerly incarcerated individuals in the process to desistance have tried various approaches, some which focus on concrete supports such as employment help, while less often some address the social-psychological aspect of identity.

Maruna (2001, 2012) explains the many ways that desistance is a social process. In addition to the ways that would-be desisters "signal" to the outside world their efforts to desist, perhaps more significant are the ways that community members validate those attempts and reinforce them (Fox, 2015a, 2016a). Restorative justice is conceived in various ways, some narrow and others expansive. However, in considering reintegration process as a mechanism for promoting safety, the communal aspects take on a restorative character. Over the past decade or more, reentry programs have blossomed in huge varieties, most of which are conducted by paid professionals. As such, they are similar to other human services. Maruna (2016) explains the ways in which restorative justice and desistance share similar concerns, with particular relevance seen in a "belief in redeemability" (p. 295). With this belief as the fulcrum, community integration, narrative and identity transformation, and citizen restoration make community safety more possible.

Maruna (2004) argues in several places that notions such as reciprocity and mutual obligation are key to transformation from a persistent criminal identity to a desistant (non-criminal) one. Petrich (2016) emphasizes the importance of a "catalyst" (p. 395) for this transformation. In considering the very social concepts of reciprocity, obligation, and a desire to make positive commitments to the future, the catalysts come from relationships. As Fox (2016a) has argued, stabilizing factors, such as housing and employment, may be crucial but not sufficient. Similarly, Ward and Maruna (2007) assert that such transformation does not easily occur within a risk-based (i.e., deficit-based) rehabilitation space. Rather, creating pathways to social capital (Fox, 2015b) formation and recovery capital formation (Best and Musgrove, Chapter 12 this volume) via positive, ordinary, reciprocal relationships can provide the fertile ground for identity transformation.

Governments around the globe have realized the detrimental effects of incarceration and have created reentry programs to help ease the transition back to communities after prison release (interestingly, sometimes for all types of individuals who have offended except those who engaged in sexual offences). In the US, most of these programs involved the collaboration of federal agencies and their funding to address issues such as housing, employment, health, substance abuse, and education. Most of the programs have used federal funding sources to augment capacities within correctional departments to assist with these sorts of external stabilizers. Moreover, to the extent that they are part of a criminal justice apparatus—one that actively regulates the movement and behaviour of its subjects—housing reentry programs within such a system is by design a different project than a community-driven model. While it is not essential that a top-down governmental reentry program would be inattentive to recreating a prosocial identity, our assertion is that a community-based approach may address issues around identity change more fruitfully than a government-generated initiative.

Fox (2015a) argues that the role of the community in reentry programming has been underused and undertheorized. Maruna (2001) asserts the importance of "generativity" as a dimension in successful desistance. Generativity, according to Maruna (drawing on McAdam's, 2006 research), is a concern for the future of the next generation or, in other words, a commitment to making the world a bit better. This notion can also be configured as a type of optimism. Broadly speaking, this stream of research flows from a social-psychological perspective on the impact of labelling, which has a long history within sociology. Rather than assuming personal pathology within those who break the law, labelling theory asserts that the process of negative labelling has impacts on self-identity that exacerbate criminal behaviours. Likewise, de-labeling is an important component of creating a prosocial identity (Maruna, 2004, 2011). Maruna (2001) and others (Willis, 2018) have found that significant others, including probation officers, can assist in the de-labeling process, by creating opportunities for narrative reconstruction. In other words, the "criminal" can reframe their story and, thus, their self-understanding to one in which they are essentially prosocial and their criminal history was a diversion from their true nature. To demonstrate our commitment to de-labeling, we have used person-first language throughout this chapter.

The desistance research that emphasizes the critical dimension of shifting self-identity addresses the importance of others in assisting a transformative narrative. However, the shift is internal and therefore reliant upon the ability to catalyze the power of such a prosocial identity. In other words, if one succeeds in constructing a prosocial self-understanding, how does that translate to her or his ability to function positively in the community?

Some recent research highlights the role of community reintegration in the process of desistance (Fox, 2015a). An improved self-identity as a law-abider is, perhaps, necessary but not sufficient for true desistance (or what McNeill refers to as secondary desistance). In addition to a new view of self—what Maruna calls redemption scripts—one needs relationships to draw upon in the community. This is particularly important given that parole conditions often limit the social relations an individual under supervision can have and that the formation of "social capital" and "recovery capital" (Best and Musgrove, Chapter 12 this volume) are important features of successful reintegration. Farrall (2004) points to the role of the community in establishing links to ordinary citizens.

Restorative Processes in Sexual Violence Prevention

A good many restorative justice (RJ) theorists and practitioners would likely opine that RJ is not really well suited to situations of interpersonal violence, including sexual violence (Marsh & Wager, 2015). The difficulty regarding the latter is ensuring safe opportunities for the voices of persons who have been sexually victimized. This is a fair criticism. However, does that mean that restorative justice principles cannot inform efforts to address the effects of sexual violence on the many stakeholders impacted? Specifically regarding restorative and transformational processes in sexual violence prevention, Yantzi (1998) published an early book expounding on how RJ could be used to address and begin to heal the many wounds inherent in that domain. Indeed, Yantzi was an early participant in the birth of restorative justice in Canada and was also an influential figure in the operationalization of a unique approach to restoration in sexual violence prevention that we describe in detail below.

An example of a community-based approach to utilizing ordinary citizens in reentry is the Circles of Support and Accountability (CoSA) model (see Wilson et al., 2007a; Wilson, McWhinnie, & Wilson, 2008). Drawing upon the authors' research in Canada, the United Kingdom, and Vermont, the CoSA model is an approach that emanated from a grassroots, community level and has ultimately been incorporated into the structure of "correctional service" as policy, with the model varying to a degree by jurisdiction. Braithwaite's (2011) concept of "responsive regulation" refers to a regulatory mechanism that is strength-based and supportive, internally and externally. As such, the Vermont Department of Corrections' experience with CoSA is a prime example of internally responsive regulation, and an example of the development of a model that shares power with key stakeholders.

Origins of the Circles of Support and Accountability Model

In the spring of 1994, a prison psychologist with the Correctional Service of Canada (CSC) had a dilemma. One of the high-risk/high-need clients on his caseload—a man convicted of many sexual offences against children—was slated for release to the community in the upcoming summer. Prudently, the psychologist contacted his community counterparts in South-Central Ontario (essentially, the Greater Toronto Area) in an attempt to ascertain what types of services would be available to the client when he was released. Unfortunately, due to a glitch in Canadian law certain persons who had offended could be detained in prison until the very last day of their sentences (known as detention). This provision was instituted to allow the National Parole Board to deny the usual statutory release on supervision at the two-thirds point in order to delay community release for those individuals deemed high-risk to engage in further personal injury offences during the last third of the sentence. An unintended side-effect of detention, however, was that it negated access to aftercare services reserved for those still under warrant on parole. This was the scenario at hand in the case described here.

Upon learning that the client would be released on the expiry of his warrant (equivalent to "maxing out" in the USA), community officials rightly determined that no aftercare services would be available—the client would no longer be under the umbrella of the Correctional Service of Canada and, as such, he would have to fend for services like any other citizen. But, of course, he was not just any other citizen; this fellow posed significant risk to the community or, at least, that was the actuarial and clinical projection. And, in spite of the parole board's efforts to keep him in, he was going to be released in June. This scenario put in motion a problem solving effort not previously seen regarding the release of a person of this man's risk and need status. Because services provided by CSC would not be available, alternative services had to be identified; however, all of the usual providers were reluctant to take this man on.

Ultimately, a decision was taken to solicit advice from the faith community, given that one of the CSC community staff problem-solving the referral was the District Chaplain. Upon discussing the situation with his colleagues, the pastor of a local urban Mennonite congregation stepped forward and said something akin to, "Send him to me." The elders of the church agreed that this would be a good thing to do—provide community support to a high-risk/high-need individual with no other services available to him—and they collectively established the first of what has since become known as Circles of Support and Accountability (Hannem, 2013). Although the local community was not initially supportive of the Mennonite group's attempts to assist in this man's community repatriation, with time they recognized that he was no longer engaging in the same dangerous behaviours as before.

Following this initial grassroots, outside-the-box solution to an issue of community safety and personal reintegration in South-Central Ontario, more circles projects were started in Canada and numbers eventually approached those required to engage in research. An ongoing research thread in CoSA has developed in Canada, with several evaluations of both recidivism rates and circle processes (i.e., qualitative findings). It was on the strength of these initial findings (Wilson, Cortoni, & McWhinnie, 2009; Wilson et al., 2007a, 2007b, 2007c) that the model attracted attention in other jurisdictions.

The Roots of CoSA

In asking the question, "Who is responsible for safety in the community?" many are likely tempted to point to police and other government agencies as accountable for the maintenance of public safety. However, with a little coaxing most people would ultimately agree that community safety cannot be achieved without some degree of involvement of the community (Wilson & McWhinnie, 2013).

In the early 19th century, Sir Robert Peel was twice Prime Minister of the United Kingdom. Generally regarded as the "father" of modern policing, Sir Robert has been variously quoted as having said, "The police are the public and the public are the police." Implicit in this statement is an understanding that communities are safer when they work together with statutory authorities. In a similar vein, the late Norwegian sociologist Nils Christie (as quoted by Cayley, 1998, p. 168; see also Christie, 1977) called for citizens to embrace the "conflict" raised by criminal justice difficulties:

> community is made from conflict as much as from cooperation; the capacity to solve conflict is what gives social relations their sinew. Professionalizing justice "steals the conflicts," robbing the community of its ability to face trouble and restore peace. Communities lose their confidence, their capacity, and, finally, their inclination to preserve their own order. They instead become consumers of police and court "services" with the consequence that they largely cease to be communities.

For additional insight regarding the need for partnership between citizens and statutory agencies (police, government risk management services), surprisingly, we look to the field of urban planning. In her book *The Death and Life of Great American Cities*, Jane Jacobs (1961, pp. 31–32) shared her views on the key responsibilities of community members in maintaining the "public peace":

> The first thing to understand is that the public peace—the sidewalk and street peace—is not kept primarily by the police, necessary as police are. It is kept primarily by an intricate, almost unconscious, network of voluntary controls and standards among the people themselves and enforced by the people themselves. No amount of police can enforce civilization where the normal causal enforcement of it has broken down.

In consideration of these thoughts from somewhat disparate fields, it is clear to us that the community has as much of a role to play in its own safety as does any person or agency with an "official" role. However, it is likely that many citizens are unsure what their role should be, and their thoughts about sexual violence prevention are likely consumed more by fear and intolerance than by support and restoration. Indeed, the strong emotions experienced by many in the community have been expressed as overt forms of community unrest, including picketing and vigilantism (Silverman & Wilson, 2002), some of which was observed during the early days of the release of the fellow we described above.

In the professional domain, the criminal justice approach to persons convicted of sexual offences has become increasingly punitive and controlling, to the extent that such persons are likely the most closely managed criminal justice population. Measures such as registration, residency restrictions, electronic and global position satellite (GPS) monitoring, and strict community management policies have been implemented in an effort to contain the risk posed by individuals who have engaged in sexual violence. However, research has not clearly demonstrated the efficacy of such measures (see summary in Wilson & Sandler, 2018), suggesting that other, more creative approaches to increasing public safety may be required.[1] It is against this backdrop that we promote the use of Circles of Support and Accountability.

Mechanics of the CoSA Model

The CoSA model has evolved, but is now generally understood as concentric circles—the inner of which comprises a core member (the released individual) and three to five community members who have had training in volunteering with people who have sexually offended.[2] These individuals meet as a group and individually with the core member, generally on a weekly basis, to assist him (and, sometimes, her) with tasks associated with community reintegration (or "integration" as is often the case for many core members who were likely never integrated in the community prior to CoSA). This inner circle in encapsulated within an outer circle of sexual violence professionals (e.g., psychologists, probation/parole officers, law enforcement, victim advocacy representatives, etc.) who are available to provide support to the inner circle when they encounter issues or scenarios beyond the scope of their roles as volunteers. As such, the core member receives support from the inner circle, which is in turn supported by the outer circle. Additionally, most CoSA projects also have a paid project coordinator who manages the macro aspects of the project and liaises with a steering committee or management board that guides the project as a whole (see Wilson & McWhinnie, 2017).

As a model, CoSA has three guiding principles: 1.) no more victims, 2.) no one is disposable, and 3.) nobody does this alone. Embodied in these principles is an understanding that sexual and other interpersonal violence must stop, but that accomplishing that goal includes ensuring that those who have engaged in violence have opportunities to reclaim their lives and an understanding that this can-not be accomplished without assistance. However, for those who have been labelled "sexually violent predators," or some facsimile thereof, there is no welcome wagon of neighbours delivering cookies and lemonade when they arrive in the community. There is fear, anger and, often, hatred. Worse still, for many persons convicted of sexual offences, there are no family members or friends left who would provide them with post-release assistance. This underscores the critical importance of the volunteers who populate the inner circle in the CoSA model.

In the first few weeks of circle meetings, there are often many things core members need. Maslow's (1943) well-known "hierarchy of needs" is often a good place to start, beginning with the basics—food, water, clothing, warmth, rest, and basic safety and security. Translating these simple constructs into CoSA work includes ensuring that core members have adequate clothing, food, and a place to stay that fits inside the restrictions often imposed by community supervision frameworks. Over and above these concerns are transportation needs, such as getting to the probation office, checking in with police, meeting registry requirements, and so forth. All of these issues need to be addressed before the restora-tive and transformative goals of CoSA can begin to emerge. "Higher-order" emotional and psychologi-cal needs (e.g., friendship, intimacy, building trust, etc.) are important to all people, but they cannot be met until basic needs are being consistently and reliably met. As such, the first few weeks of any core member's life in the community will be absorbed in meeting those basic needs, sometimes against a backdrop of community upheaval (picketing) and mini-crises.

Accountability is an important feature in CoSA. Occasionally, we see a scenario in which volunteers and staff believe their role is, besides supporting a core member, to "hold him" or "make him" account-able. As in all things within a healthy CoSA, the behaviour we want to see our core members exhibit is behaviour we must also model. We, too, must not just be accountable, but demonstrate through our own behaviour what accountable behaviour looks like and what real "accountability" is. Moreover, accountability evolves organically out of a supportive relationship.

Vermont's Commitment to Restorative Justice

Vermont has a history of restorative practices that is three decades long. The story goes that in response to market research conducted to determine how well the Department of Corrections (DOC) was doing, the DOC decided to create a structure at the community level (i.e., towns and cities) to address low-level crime. The market research suggested that citizens wanted more involvement and voice in decisions about crime in their communities. Hence, the community justice system was born in Ver-mont. The DOC funded municipalities to create citizen boards to decide upon sanctions for low-level offences, such as retail theft and first-time "driving under the influence" charges. The idea was for citizens to represent the community, which is the third angle in the restorative justice triangle. Also, in keeping with restorative principles, the sanction would be mutually agreed upon and non-punitive; rather, the sanction would be restorative. There are now more than 20 justice centres in the state cur-rently engaged in various restorative justice activities, including CoSA.

In the early 2000s, the federal government became engaged in addressing the problems associated with community reintegration for the vast numbers of individuals released from US prisons, through such initiatives as the Second Chance Act. Each state received funding to develop programs designed to assist formerly incarcerated individuals in their states to find housing and employment, and to access education and mental health services. While most states used these funds to augment correctional services in the community, Vermont DOC opted to divest the funds to the justice centres, premised on the idea that communities know best what programs might work for them. Although DOC eventually settled on CoSA as the state-wide model for reentry programming, the idea to explore CoSA interestingly came from the directors of a few community justice centres. During the planning stage, they asked DOC for funding to visit the CoSA program in Canada, and returned enthusiastic to try it in Vermont. The remarkable note is that the model emerged as a sort of grassroots effort rather than as an edict from government officials.

This community-driven, "bottom-up" approach to CoSA project development in Vermont is quite similar to that observed in Canada and is somewhat different from CoSA analogs in such locations as Minnesota, where the MnCoSA endeavour (see Duwe, 2013, 2018) has been ensconced within the Minnesota Department of Corrections as a programmatic option. Although the bulk of the "CoSA work" in Minnesota remains the purview of community volunteers, this "top-down" approach to project development is likely meaningfully different from the Canadian and Vermont experiences.

Proliferation of the CoSA Model

CoSA projects now exist internationally throughout Canada, the United States, the United Kingdom, Europe, and Australia and New Zealand. Six evaluation studies focusing on differential reoffense rates have been undertaken, with largely similar results achieved on matched or randomly assigned comparison groups of individuals who either got a CoSA or who did not. Two studies from Canada (Wilson et al., 2007c, 2009), three studies from the US (Duwe, 2013, 2018; Wilson, Fox, & Kurmin, 2017), and one from the UK (Bates et al., 2013) have each shown varying, but largely statistically significant reductions in post-release offensive conduct (sexual, violent, and otherwise) for those individuals who were involved in CoSA.

It is important to note that CoSA evaluation studies have, to date, been generally hampered by small sample sizes, short follow-up times, and methodological issues; however, the results have been generally consistent internationally. Clarke, Brown, and Völlm (2017); Duwe's (2018) most recent publication using an RCT design with 50 participants in each group has shown a statistically significant difference in rates of sexual recidivism (an 88% reduction by comparison), as well as a return on investment of $3.73 for every dollar spent on CoSA. At this point, the consistency of the quantitative results suggests that the CoSA research endeavour should now turn its focus to the processes in CoSA; as in, what is it that is occurring in these restorative-justice-informed volunteer-led initiatives that is having such an important effect on recidivism?

Fox (2015a, 2016a) examined the interpersonal and human aspects of a CoSA experience, for community volunteers and core members. She argued (2015a, p. 85) that to the extent that a CoSA can contribute to desistance, the relationships demonstrate that participants share the same "moral and normative space." The power stems from the voluntary nature of the relationships; core members report feeling moved by the fact that volunteers choose to spend time with them. Ordinary, prosocial activities, such as playing a sport or sharing a meal, can be instrumental in fostering a sense of belonging, forging a new identity, and creating a sense of reciprocity. In many cases, the core member has felt like a pariah in the community, and the welcoming by ordinary citizens is impactful. In addition to the concrete, practical supports supplied by a CoSA, the model represents a blueprint for civic engagement, and provides space for formerly incarcerated individuals in "a community." CoSA teams model normative relationships, but also communicate "the values of inclusion, citizenship, fundamental human rights, and forgiveness," which reflects a form of restorative justice and responsive regulation (Fox, 2015a, p. 86).

Closing Remarks

Throughout this chapter it has been our position that the community must play a greater role in the establishment of true community safety. Such an argument can be made from a rehabilitation perspective, through a restorative justice lens, and from a desistance standpoint. These three notions are discrete yet overlapping. What they share is a premise that processes of healing, transformation, and reformation are fundamentally social in nature. Fox (2015a) argues that integration precedes desistance from crime. As such, the leap of faith that is community inclusion can have positive effects for community well-being, and extending citizenship to formerly incarcerated individuals is a critical component. Rather than the deficit-based traditions of criminal justice, community-based inclusion represents a strength-based approach that is restorative for communities.

In our introductory paragraphs, we highlighted some of the difficulties inherent in both demonstrating and underscoring the need for evidence-based practices, using sexual violence prevention as an example. While the broader community continues to view "sex offenders" with revulsion and distrust, it is clear that some members of the community have come to a different conclusion—no one is disposable. Although CoSA may have started as a "faith-based" initiative, it is clear that the good work done by volunteers in these projects transcends the traditional faith in a spiritual higher power to include faith in their fellow citizens, even those who have engaged in sexual violence. CoSA is fully RNR compliant and is approaching designation as "evidence based." And, most importantly, as these CoSA core members have sought to develop balanced, self-determined lifestyles in the community with the assistance of their courageous volunteers, the "no more victims" mantra has also been honoured.

Notes

1. Additionally, most of these measures are applied wholesale to a majority of persons convicted of sexual offences, with little consideration of the risk and need principles, the result being that any effects are perhaps obscured by inappropriate implementation (Wilson & Sandler, 2018).
2. Training for volunteers is intensive and wide-ranging in topics related to sexual violence prevention; however, it is not of the sort that would render volunteers experts or professionals. This underscores the importance of the outer circle.

References

Andrews, D. A., & Bonta, J. (1994). *The psychology of criminal conduct* (1st ed.). Cincinnati, OH: Anderson.

Andrews, D. A., Bonta, J., & Wormith, S. (2011). The risk-need-responsivity (RNR) model: Does adding the good lives model contribute to effective crime prevention? *Criminal Justice and Behavior, 38*, 735–755.

Aos, S., Miller, M., & Drake, E. (2006). *Evidence-based adult corrections programs: What works and what does not.* Olympia, WA: Washington State Institute for Public Policy.

Bates, A., Williams, D., Wilson, C., & Wilson, R. J. (2013). Circles South-East: The first ten years 2002–2012. *International Journal of Offender Therapy and Comparative Criminology, 58*, 861–885.

Bonta, J., & Andrews, D. A. (2016). *The psychology of criminal conduct* (6th ed.). Cincinnati, OH: Anderson.

Braithwaite, J. (2011). The essence of responsive regulation. *UBC Law Review, 44*, 475–520.

Brandt, J., Wilson, R. J., & Prescott, D. S. (2015). Doubts about SVP programs: A critical review of sexual offender civil commitment in the U.S. In B. Schwartz (Ed.), *The sex offender* (Vol. 8) (pp. 5.1–5.29). Kingston, NJ: Civic Research Institute.

Carr, C., Schlank, A., & Parker, K. (2013, September). *Review of Florida's sexually violent predator program.* Tallahassee, FL: Department of Children and Families, Substance Abuse and Mental Health Program Office.

Cayley, D. (1998). *The expanding prison: The crisis in crime and punishment and the search for alternatives.* Toronto: Anansi.

Christie, N. (1977). Conflict as property. *The British Journal of Criminology, 17,* 1–15.

Clarke, M., Brown, S., & Völlm, B. (2017). Circles of Support and Accountability for sex offenders: A systematic review of outcomes. *Sexual Abuse, 29,* 446–478.

Duwe, G. (2013). Can circles of support and accountability work in the United States? Preliminary results from a randomized experiment in Minnesota. *Sexual Abuse, 25,* 143–165.

Duwe, G. (2018). Can circles of support and accountability (CoSA) significantly reduce sexual recidivism? Results from a randomized controlled trial in Minnesota. *Journal of Experimental Criminology, 14,* 463–484. Published online first.

Farrall, S. (2004). Social capital and offender reintegration: Making probation desistance focused. In S. Maruna & R. Immarigeon (Eds.), *After crime and punishment: Pathways to offender reintegration* (pp. 57–82). London, UK: Routledge.

Fox, K. J. (2015a). Theorizing community integration as desistance-promotion. *Criminal Justice & Behavior, 42*(1), 82–94.

Fox, K. J. (2015b). Trying to restore justice: Bureaucracies, risk management and disciplinary boundaries in New Zealand criminal justice. *International Journal of Offender Therapy and Comparative Criminology,* 519–538.

Fox, K. J. (2016a). Civic commitment: Promoting desistance through community integration. *Punishment & Society, 18,* 68–94.

Furby, L., Weinrott, M. R., & Blackshaw, L. (1989). Sex offender recidivism: A review. *Psychological Bulletin, 105,* 3–30.

Hannem, S. (2013). Experiences in reconciling risk management and restorative justice: How circles of support and accountability work restoratively in the risk society. *International Journal of Offender Therapy and Comparative Criminology, 57,* 269–288.

Hanson, R. K., Bourgon, G., Helmus, L., & Hodgson, S. (2009). The principles of effective correctional treatment also apply to sexual offenders: A meta-analysis. *Criminal Justice and Behavior, 36,* 865–891.

Hanson, R. K., Bourgon, G., McGrath, R. J., Kroner, D., D'Amora, D. A., & Thomas, S. S. (2017). *A five-level risk and needs system: Maximizing assessment results in corrections through the development of a common language.* New York: Justice Centre.

Hanson, R. K., Gordon, A., Harris, A. J. R., Marques, J. K., Murphy, W., Quinsey, V. L., & Seto, M. C. (2002). First report of the collaborative outcome data project on the effectiveness of treatment for sex offenders. *Sexual Abuse, 14,* 169–194.

Jacobs, J. (1961). *The death and life of great American cities.* New York: Random House.

Långström, N., Enebrink, P., Laurén, E.-M., Lindblom, J., Werkö, S., & Hanson, R. K. (2013). Preventing sexual abusers of children from reoffending: Systematic review of medical and psychological interventions. *BMJ: British Medical Journal,* 347–358.

Laub, J. H., & Sampson, R. J. (2001). Understanding desistance from crime. *Crime and Justice, 28,* 1–69.

Levenson, J. S., & Prescott, D. (2014). Déjà vu: From Furby to Långström and the evaluation of sex offender treatment effectiveness. *Journal of Sexual Aggression, 20.*

Levenson, J. S., Willis, G. M., & Prescott, D. (2016). Adverse childhood experiences in the lives of male sex offenders and implications for trauma-informed care. *Sexual Abuse, 28,* 340–359.

Lipsey, M. W., & Cullen, F. T. (2007). The effectiveness of correctional rehabilitation: A review of systematic reviews. *Annual Review of Law and Social Science, 3,* 297–320.

Marsh, F., & Wager, N. M. (2015). Restorative justice in cases of sexual violence: Exploring the views of the public and victims. *Probation Journal, 6,* 336–356.

Marshall, W. L., & Marshall, L. E. (2007). The utility of the random controlled trial for evaluating sexual offender treatment: The gold standard or an inappropriate strategy? *Sexual Abuse, 19*, 175–191.

Marshall, W. L., & Marshall, L. E. (2008). Good clinical practice and the evaluation of treatment: A response to Seto et al. *Sexual Abuse, 20*, 256–260.

Marshall, W. L., Marshall, L. E., Serran, G. A., & O'Brien. (2011). *Rehabilitating sexual offenders: A strength-based approach*. Washington, DC: American Psychological Association.

Martinson, R. (1974). Nothing works: Questions and answers about prison reform. *The Public Interest, 35*, 22–54.

Martinson, R. (1979). New findings, new views: A note of caution regarding sentencing reform. *Hofstra Law Review, 7*, 242–258.

Maruna, S. (2001). *Making good: How ex-convicts reform and rebuild their lives*. Washington, DC: American Psychological Association.

Maruna, S. (2004). Desistance from crime and explanatory style: A new direction in the psychology of reform. *Journal of Contemporary Criminal Justice, 20*, 184–200.

Maruna, S. (2011). Reentry as a rite of passage. *Punishment & Society, 13*, 3–28.

Maruna, S. (2012). Elements of successful desistance signaling. *Criminology & Public Policy, 11*, 73–86.

Maruna, S. (2016). Desistance and restorative justice: It's now or never. *Restorative Justice, 4*, 289–301.

Maslow, A. H. (1943). A theory of human motivation. *Psychological Review, 50*, 370–396.

McAdams, D. P. (2006). The redemptive self: Generativity and the stories Americans live by. *Research in Human Development, 3*, 81–100.

McNeill, F. (2006). A desistance paradigm for offender management. *Criminology & Criminal Justice, 6*, 39–62.

Petrich, D. M. (2016). Theorising desistance-promotion in circle processes: The role of community in identity transformation. *Restorative Justice, 4*.

Reavis, J., Looman, J., Franco, K., & Rojas, B. (2013). Adverse childhood experiences and adult criminality: How long must we live before we possess our own lives? *The Permanente Journal, 17*, 44–48.

Schmucker, M., & Lösel, F. (2015). The effects of sexual offender treatment on recidivism: An international meta-analysis of sound quality evaluations. *Journal of Experimental Criminology, 11*, 597–630.

Seto, M. C., Marques, J. K., Harris, G. T., Chaffin, M., Lalumière, M. L., Miner, M. H., . . . Quinsey, V. L. (2008). Good science and progress in sex offender treatment are intertwined: A response to Marshall and Marshall (2007). *Sexual Abuse, 20*, 247–255.

Shover, N. (1983). The later stages of ordinary property offender careers. *Social Problems, 31*, 208–218.

Shover, N. (1996). *Great pretenders*. Boulder, CO: Westview.

Silverman, J., & Wilson, D. (2002). *Innocence betrayed: Paedophilia, the media and society*. Cambridge: Polity Press.

Smith, P., Goggin, C., & Gendreau, P. (2002). *The effects of prison sentences and intermediate sanctions on recidivism: General effects and individual differences* (Research Report 2002–01). Ottawa: Solicitor General Canada.

Ward, T., & Maruna, S. (2007). *Rehabilitation: Beyond the risk assessment paradigm*. London, UK: Routledge.

Ward, T., Melser, J., & Yates, P. M. (2007). Reconstructing the risk need responsivity model: A theoretical elaboration and evaluation. *Aggression and Violent Behavior, 12*, 208–228.

Willis, G. M. (2018). Why call someone by what we don't want them to be? The ethics of labeling in forensic/correctional psychology. *Psychology, Crime & Law, 24*, 727–743. Published online first.

Wilson, R. J., Cortoni, F., & McWhinnie, A. J. (2009). Circles of support & accountability: A Canadian national replication of outcome findings. *Sexual Abuse, 21*, 412–430.

Wilson, R. J., Fox, K. J., & Kurmin, M. (2017, November). *CoSA in Vermont: Quantitative outcomes and qualitative understandings*. Presentation made at the 36th Annual Research and Treatment Conference of the Association for the Treatment of Sexual Abusers, Kansas City, MO.

Willis, G. M., & Grace, R. C. (2008). The quality of community reintegration planning for child molesters: Effects on sexual recidivism. *Sexual Abuse, 20*, 218–240.

Willis, G. M., & Grace, R. C. (2009). Assessment of community reintegration planning for sex offenders: Poor planning predicts recidivism. *Criminal Justice and Behavior, 36*, 494–512.

Wilson, R. J., & McWhinnie, A. J. (2013). Putting the "community" back in community risk management. *International Journal of Behavioral Consultation and Therapy, 8*, 3–4.

Wilson, R. J., & McWhinnie, A. J. (2017). *Circles of support & accountability: A "how to" guide for establishing CoSA in your location*. Report compiled under contract to Counseling and Psychotherapy Center, Inc. for the United States Department of Justice, Office of Justice Programs, Office of Sex Offender Sentencing, Monitoring, Apprehending, Registration, and Tracking. Washington, DC: US Department of Justice.

Wilson, R. J., McWhinnie, A. J., Picheca, J. E., Prinzo, M., & Cortoni, F. (2007a). Circles of support & accountability: Engaging community volunteers in the management of high-risk sexual offenders. *Howard Journal of Criminal Justice, 46*, 1–15.

Wilson, R. J., McWhinnie, A. J., & Wilson, C. (2008). Circles of support & accountability: An international partnership in reducing sexual offender recidivism. *Prison Service Journal, 138*, 26–36.

Wilson, R. J., Picheca, J. E., & Prinzo, M. (2007b). Evaluating the effectiveness of professionally-facilitated volunteerism in the community-based management of high risk sexual offenders: Part one—Effects on participants and stakeholders. *Howard Journal of Criminal Justice, 46*, 289–302.

Wilson, R. J., Picheca, J. E., & Prinzo, M. (2007c). Evaluating the effectiveness of professionally facilitated volunteerism in the community-based management of high risk sexual offenders: Part two—A comparison of recidivism rates. *Howard Journal of Criminal Justice, 46*, 327–337.

Wilson, R. J., & Sandler, J. C. (2018). What works (or does not) in community risk management for persons convicted of sexual offenses? A contemporary perspective. *International Journal of Offender Therapy and Comparative Criminology*. Published online first.

Wilson, R. J., & Yates, P. M. (2009). Effective interventions and the good lives model: Maximizing treatment gains for sexual offenders. *Aggression & Violent Behavior, 14*, 157–161.

Yantzi, M. (1998). *Sexual offending and restoration*. Waterloo, ON: Herald Press.

Yates, P. M., Prescott, D. S., & Ward, T. (2010). *Applying the good lives and self-regulation models to sex offender treatment: A practical guide for clinicians*. Brandon, VT: Safer Society Press.

14

LEARNING FROM THE HUMAN SERVICES

How to Build Better Restorative Justice and Responsive Regulation

John Braithwaite, Gale Burford and Valerie Braithwaite

Why Restorative Justice and Responsive Regulation?

A theme of this book has been that restorative justice has little chance of resilience and scale of transformative potential when it stands alone. Either as an alternative to or an add-on to criminal justice, marginalization remains its fate. We have seen that when it does scale up inside the criminal justice system, its empowerment and relational values tend to wither. While we support making restorative justice values more mainstream inside the justice system, the battle for its core strengths will be lost unless we also have a strategy for putting families, parenting and other primary group relationships as its core and at its front door across justice, health, education and other social welfare and social service settings. If the only time families encounter restorative justice is when they collide with the criminal or youth justice systems, then the family will never become a cohering locus that brings together all the institutions, specialties and sub-specialties they run into as a family with education, health, social services, car accidents and beyond. In this concluding chapter we argue that a degree of institutional forcing of a New Zealand kind is required to make families nodally powerful (Shearing, 2001; Drahos, Shearing, & Burris, 2005; Wood & Shearing, 2013). We must empower individual families (legislatively) to provide the glue to connect up the constellations of complex systems that circle around families.

States and corporations must be regulated by a restorative social movement politics that demands that scaling up. Restorative justice practice must be regulated by peer review and professional standards that bubble up from within that same social movement when practice fails to remain relational and empowering in the process of scaling up. Prospects for accomplishing this are dim without a tripartism in which the social movement for restorative justice is a third party that balances and invigorates contests between the state and regulated actors (be they individuals or corporations) (Ayres & Braithwaite, 1992: Chapter 3). States, corporate executives and professionals always take over in our version of Michels (1915) iron law of oligarchy unless third parties responsively regulate them to disrupt their takeover manoeuvers (Voss & Sherman, 2000).

One of our remedies is to set out Restorative Justice and Responsive Regulation as one path to freedom as non-domination that decenters individualized casework approaches in favor of centering

DOI: 10.4324/9780429398704-14

group, family and community meetings as ongoing ways of doing business. This book has argued that a relational regulatory approach is needed to reconcile human rights and social justice at the human services coal face. It is needed to shed light on the relational complexities of people impacted by life crises and crises of heavy-handed state or corporate intervention in their lives. Multiple-loop-learning among state and non-state actors and policy makers is needed (Parker, 2002). More than that, societies can and must learn how to ripple empathy, trust and hope out from families and other primary groups across civil society and up to the state (Job & Reinhart, 2003). Then our human services might CHIME with Connectedness, Hope, Identity, Meaning and Empowerment (as in the work of David Best and Amy Musgrave, Chapter 12). This book reveals that there are places in the hearts and communities of our dear planet where this happens, and happens in ways that connect up from micro problems that are the daily toil of social workers to macro-structural struggles for justice. The beauty of a strategy of struggle for social justice that centers families (and other primary groups like peer groups in schools and primary work groups in workplaces) is that it gives even the most disadvantaged individuals a starting point for collective engagement with the big political struggles that matter most.

Freedom as non-domination (Pettit, 1997) starts with a strategy for turning personal troubles into political issues (Mills, 2000), the theme of the next section. Chapter 1 articulated a macro ambition for combining Restorative Justice and Responsive Regulation to become a hedge against destructive processes of capitalism that include markets in vices from abuse of tobacco, sugar, fat, waste, carbon, to abuse of physical and chemical restraint in aged, mental health and disability care. In response, Restorative Justice and Responsive Regulation must go holistic and structural, seeking seats at many tables of deliberation for ordinary survivors of corporate harms and state harms to repair them relationally and accomplish structural transformation through maximally relational means.

Making the Personal Political in Struggles for Human Services

Valerie Braithwaite's Chapter 3 explains that trial and error learning naturally teaches families and schools to be restorative and responsive, at least to some considerable degree. This means the policy challenge can be conceived as how to encourage that natural evolution of relational practices in civil societies to grow. This is a central issue addressed in this chapter.

Several chapters show that extended families of kin and kith naturally do rally to provide relational and concrete supports when parents cannot cope or when they fail to meet community standards in caring for children. This is a core justification for the New Zealand policy in its child, family and youth justice systems of mandating and supporting the opportunity for extended family members to discuss the situation in a family group conference before the state takes any drastic action like removing a child. In most cases, it will become natural for grandparents, uncles, aunties and other family and friends to rally to provide extra support. Usually this makes it unnecessary to resort to alternative enforcement-oriented paths such as removal of a child or young person.

On the restorative analysis, the challenge for the welfare state is understood as emanating from both crises of under-funding and from the collapse of confidence in certain dedicated, unresponsive and often costly top-down policies and practices. The state takes it upon itself to remove more children than it should, to put more children, young persons and adults in foster and congregate care and prisons than it should, to expel more students from schools than it should, and to underwrite or, as is discussed later, collude with large-scale profiteering that contributes to bad health outcomes for the most marginalized (e.g., mass incarceration, over-regulation through psychotropic pharmaceuticals). This has the effect of excessively commandeering and focusing enforcement resources in areas such as child protection investigation and police enforcement of the criminal law that dominates the helping, care, educational and other lower-tier ways to encourage self-efficacy and regulation (Featherstone et al., 2018; Braithwaite, 2015; Waldfogel, 2001). This downloads burdens for front-line workers to find some other place for the child to get care and an education, for case managers to find health care for people with no insurance, for community corrections workers to find housing and employment for people reentering communities, for police to engage with situations that erupt from mental-health and relational challenges, and for families and communities to absorb their members along with the impacts that the over-use of enforcement interventions have created. The status quo directs attention and resources away from in-depth analysis and responsive strategy development and over-invests in punitive responses for extreme cases. Concerns that ought to invoke de-escalation and inquiry get ramped up to investigation or even armed attack.

Policies and practices of separation leave people with the closest ties to their family members and friends excluded from knowing what is happening while their relatives are separated from them. In the example of aged and disability care, policy makers took a long time to learn that they were incarcerating and tying up more old and disabled people in institutions than they needed to (Chapter 2), when so many of these aged and disabled folk who did not want to go there could have been much more cheaply supported in the community by giving more home and community care support from the state to families. Business bleats about the unreasonable regulatory burden of generous paid maternity and paternity leave as a right in labor law, but in fact this right creates stronger families that ripple out social capital from families to workgroups back to the state itself to build richer economies (Paul Adams, Chapter 6; Valerie Braithwaite, Chapter 3; Job & Reinhart, 2003). Deinstitutionalization also has its risks, of course, as we saw when most states, including New Zealand, failed to manage the closure of mental health institutions in the 1970s with sufficient home and community care support to prevent adult prisons from being transmogrified into the largest mental health institutions in western societies. Likewise in New Zealand, as in all western societies, rich restorative practice reforms are not complemented by rich enough support for family plans from restorative conferences to help the wider family of caregivers who have taken on the care of children. Nor would it seem, again with the partial exception of New Zealand in its children and young persons' services, is restorative justice well enough understood among the general public to help people exercise informed choice as indicated by Gavrielides's (2018) recent study.

Steering toward a more developed, responsively regulated, welfare state is needed to provide the supports for families to engage on more egalitarian terms with health, social services, legal and education service providers. In other words, we have argued that good regulatory settings create the conditions for restorative and responsive care, and these in turn create the conditions for stronger societies and economies in turn inviting and supporting families to take up roles as architects of civil society.

Here in our view *Aotearoa* New Zealand is the only state that has taken one of the necessary steps to defend its welfare state from wasteful and harmful child removals and incarceration of children. As we write this chapter its inspiring Prime Minister, Jacinta Ardern, is on paid maternity leave. We take from this an important message about support for pre- and post-natal care as good for children but also having exponential benefits for families, work and beyond.

New Zealand provides lessons for the world in the process of restorative reforms and formal push-back, and the ongoing contest between the two at the political level. When New Zealand introduced the Children, Young Persons and Their Families Act in 1989 it quickly halved the number of children who were incarcerated in state-funded institutions and in subsequent years youth incarceration rates reduced further (Braithwaite, 2002). Likewise New Zealand has more than halved removals of children from families. It achieved this by mandating the universality of restorative family group decision-making conferences (as a human right as Joan Pennell and her colleagues persuasively put it in Chapter 7). Pennell et al. point out that protests by Māori against Eurocentric approaches motivated the underlying philosophy that children belong with their families and that government must respect cultural traditions and partner with communities. Māori are mandated as active leaders, *whanau* (extended families) are empowered as decision makers in designing practice and *iwi* (tribes) are engaged in partnership with government to plan how services are shared and delivered locally to their people. At the same time there is contestation of whether this has been genuinely realized by indigenous critics such as Moyle and Tauri (2016, p. 87) whose empirical research found that Māori often see social work practice around family group conferences as subordinating indigenous culture and people 'within a Eurocentric, formulaic, and standardized process'. Imported Northern assessment tools operating alongside the family group conference reforms are seen to undermine Māori voice and empowerment (Moyle & Tauri, 2016). This is a colonized iron law of oligarchy that corrodes reforms that at first attracted considerable Māori leadership from the likes of Māori Chief Youth Court Judge of the early 1990s Mick Brown. The drift of the state is to claw back control in matters of child welfare but the FGC model in New Zealand does give some protection from this creep; protection that has been in need of renewal from time to time. We should not lose sight that these assessment tools are being exported from the same colonizing sources against which the 1989 Act was designed to push back. Nor that they lend themselves to increased regulatory formalism, especially when coupled with prescriptive systems of performance management and case reporting (Parton, 2017) in their countries of origin, serving to further distance state actors from the children and families (Featherstone et al., 2018; Morris & Burford, 2017; Shlonsky & Mildon, 2017).

All other states that we know have instituted programs for such restorative conferences that are non-mandatory for alleged child offenders, or for neglected and allegedly abused children. Many child welfare jurisdictions have enabling legislation such as the Province of New Brunswick in Canada (New Brunswick Family Services Act, SNB 1980) where a family group conference may be held at the discretion of the social worker. Experience tells a sad story in places like the State of Vermont (where statute requires that social workers engage with families in a process of case planning that will "actively engage families, and solicit and integrate into the case plan the input of the child, the child's family, relatives, and other persons with a significant relationship to the child" (State of Vermont 3 V.S.A § 5121 effective Jan. 1, 2009)). The sad story is that key decisions are left entirely at the discretion of state workers (Burford & Gallagher, 2015; Gallagher & Burford, 2015). This is not good enough. The New Zealanders were wise to see that families, beyond just the parents, must be guaranteed a right to be heard in conversation with the key decision makers about any drastic action that might be taken against their child. This mission to universalize *familiness* as both a right and a proactive hedge against erosion and over-reach of the state and professional interests is taken up by Elisabetta Carrà in Chapter 5. In particular, children and young people themselves must be guaranteed by the state a more profound right to be heard in family group decision making (Burford, 2013, 2018b) and other restorative and statutory interventions about their futures (Gal, 2015) in the way only New Zealand law currently seeks to guarantee.

Chapter 1 argued that there is a lot of evidence that community-based restorative programs that are richly restorative are at risk of becoming less relational when state or other narrow interests dominate and scale them up to national programs, or even city-wide programs. Usually they fail to build in crucial principles with inclusive and responsive oversight from the beginning. A response to this dilemma is to avoid the trap of relying primarily on either state or private programs. Most of the restorative and responsive energy is best to come bottom-up rather than top-down from the state. Most of the accountability pressure on universal state programs that lose their relational edge should also come from that bottom-up source. Likewise, most of the entrepreneurial energy to move restorative and responsive principles into completely new domains of the human services is best to come bottom-up from restorative communities. So how can that be accomplished?

RSVP: Restorative Spaces, Vistas, Places and the Role of Social Movements

An encouraging development towards accomplishing this is the Restorative City idea across the social movement for restorative justice that has expanded to states, provinces, organizations, virtual learning communities and even to "re-membered" preferred configurations of community used to mobilize just relations. Of course there are other social movements that aim to help cities and communities rebuild and flourish, but the Restorative City idea brought forward the added-value of holding restorative justice at the forefront. It started to our knowledge with the RJ City project of the Centre for Justice and Reconciliation of Prison Fellowship International. Dan Van Ness first tossed the idea around with Kay Pranis and many others in the late 1990s at KU Leuven in Belgium, long a key node of research-based restorative justice, and in other locales. A number of those involved in that Leuven conversation ended up on the RJ City Project Advisory Board. In 2006 Van Ness was the author of the first report of a five-year research project to design what a restorative city might look like (subsequently updated in 2010: Van Ness, 2010). The RJ City project imaginary was international, with Van Ness conducting project focus groups in the US, Canada, the UK and New Zealand. These were the countries where the Restorative Community vision first took off, particularly the UK.

Hull took the lead as a restorative city in the UK, followed by Leeds, where comprehensive implementation across a diverse range of agencies in each city has been attributed to the considerable capabilities of leadership embracing restorative standards and the use of a framework of results or outcome-based accountability to enlist purposeful collaboration (Hull Centre for Restorative Practice, n.d.). Following Hull and Leeds, initiatives were also underway in Bristol, County Durham, Norfolk, Wokingham, Stockport, Swansea and Cardiff (Liebmann, 2016), and with Southampton launching a Restorative City Charter in 2017 and Belfast (long a restorative justice leader) starting a Restorative City conversation in 2018. In *Aotearoa* New Zealand Wanganui is an important lead city. The Province of Nova Scotia in Canada has demonstrated high levels of achievement within the province and in collaboration with restorative networks in Leeds and Hull (United Kingdom), Wanganui (New Zealand), Canberra and Newcastle (Australia), and the state of Vermont (USA) has worked to adapt the restorative community idea into a glocal (local-global) 'learning community' ideal whereby restorative community networks consolidate iterated conversations about relational justice.

A mega city devastated by crime and marginalization in the US that has seen recent building of a Restorative City network is Detroit which is diffusing a 'whole of neighborhood approach' to expanding out and connecting up local inkspots of restorative justice in collaboration with the International Institute for Restorative Practices (Clynes, 2013). The vision of the original RJ City project was one of rather nodal governance (Shearing, 2001; Shearing & Wood, 2003; Drahos et al., 2005; Wood & Shearing, 2013) with a Hub that 'is the Network's coordination center and guardian of restorative justice principles, values and goals' (Van Ness, 2010, p. 16). The Hub facilitates restorative innovations into new justice challenges across many spheres of the life of the city. More recently the Limerick, Ireland, Restorative City has transformed the nodal idea of a Restorative Hub by re-designating it as a 'Restorative Heart', thereby linking the nodal idea to a relational ethic of care that eschews discourses of command and control (Le Chéile, 2014; see also Quigley, Martynowicz, & Gardner, 2015).

Some Australian states (the Australian Capital Territory and Victoria) and New Zealand have restorative networks where lively conversations and research collaborations are underway to invigorate the marriage of green restorative visions with restorative justice visions. In Vermont, USA a loosely knit, voluntary consortium of agencies and practitioners that began informal meetings in 1999–2000 has recently received support from state agencies and the Vermont Law School, a national leader in environmental law that is launching graduate education in restorative justice, to support its role in the development of RJ in the state. Oakland, California, has explicitly invoked a green restorative city vision (Kaplan, 1995; Louv, 2012; World Future Council, 2010; Kuo & Sullivan, 2001; Sullivan, Kuo, & Depooter, 2004; Kim & Kaplan, 2004; Dobbs, 2007; Kweon, Sullivan, & Wiley, 1998; Toronto Public Health, 2015; Roe, 2016; Baggs, 2018; University of Minnesota, 2018), this green vision programmatically married to a restorative justice vision of the city. In Oakland, this in turn connects to the Black Lives Matter campaign, a resolve to 'restorganize', a term coined by Fania Davis, to move away from imprisonment of the marginalized, and much more (Bankhead, George, & Poretz, 2018).

Hybridity of State/Community/Market Provision

A bottom-up community-based model of relational justice is a beautiful ideal. It is one, however, that ultimately can burn people out, leaving behind disappointment and the usual "we tried that; it doesn't work", often reflecting too little appreciation of the relational complexity involved in responsively engaging with change. As has often been the case in human service sector reform efforts, we see examples of this at a more micro level with restorative justice in schools. An entrepreneurial member of a school community who might be a teacher, a counsellor, a parent or even a student shows the leadership to establish a restorative justice program in a particular school. It flourishes for a number of years, reducing suspensions, improving learning and grapples with bullying and other behavior problems. Then that key entrepreneurial leader moves on to another school or another phase in their life. Many other members of the school community say they want the restorative program to continue but they are flat out with their teaching and family obligations and do not have the capacity to step up to volunteer the energy the departing entrepreneur contributed. So the restorative program begins to wither away. After a number of restorative schools wither, critics enter the fray with the counternarrative that restorative circles in schools gave troublemakers too much voice to give teachers a hard time (Roberts, 2018).

An important research agenda is to study the exceptional communities where this has not happened. One may be Nova Scotia, where Jennifer Llewellyn has reported that, at the time of this writing, 106 schools persist in providing restorative programming. Our hypothesis on why this seeming sustainability has been accomplished in Halifax is that compared to most cities it has an unusually vibrant bottom-up quality to its restorative network. This means when one entrepreneur moves to another job or place, there are many other relational entrepreneurs, and critics with their own ambitions, waiting to step into the breach. This is consistent with the experience in Hull, UK. Leadership has been persistent, present and visible with considerable investment in relationship building. Restorative standards have been infused in all aspects of the life of the school and with the community. This has generated high levels of recognition and prompted investment in moving the approach out to other schools and involving new partners.

Another reality check for school programs is the imperative for advocates who enjoy relational rituals to listen to teachers and students who enjoy it less, who might say they want restorative justice, but that they want to reduce the frequency and duration of disruption to teaching time from the convening of circles. In the interests of sustainability, advocates must be self-critical about whether each ritual element, each form of protracted talk that they favor, is a good use of time in the interests of the education of the students.

Our conclusory remedy to the limits of the beautiful ideal of purely a bottom-up community-based model of relational justice is that explicit commitment to a hybrid of state/community/market provision is needed to generate practice, policy and research insights across disciplines, methodologies, organizational and funding silos (on the hybridity ideal see Wallis et al., 2018). Halifax as a city, and the Province of Nova Scotia, manifest this hybridity because it is also a place where solid bases of restorative programming and training have been forged in a variety of state institutions, even if they are not as universalistic as *Aotearoa* New Zealand youth justice and child protection, or as driven and centrally supported as is Leeds where leadership and commitment of resources come from the child and family services, and Hull where the leadership has emanated from schools. In Nova Scotia, a state-funded university, Dalhousie, has also been critical to the solidification of restorative community in that Canadian province in part from the leadership and support of the Dalhousie Law School and the Nova Scotia Restorative Justice Community University Research Alliance under the directorship of Jennifer Llewellyn (Chapter 9) but also from willing and committed government, cultural and service user groups and coalitions. So we resist putting all the weight on a restorative community network to drive everything. This is why we are attracted to a hybrid of a vibrant bottom-up restorative community network and a New Zealand–style universal state program that provides a solid base for restorative justice training and reinvigoration when the restorative community loses energy or falls on hard times as a result of internal divisions or any number of other normal stresses of civil society mobilization. At the same time, the state efforts are more likely to stay on course and be responsive to families, community and culture, if they are held to account from strong engagement with those groups.

For the same reason, market provision of restorative and responsive human services can be embraced rather than spurned. Restorative activists sometimes disparage those who establish businesses to sell restorative services or restorative training. John Braithwaite witnessed an extreme version of this on a committee considering a draft mediation and traditional justice law for Afghanistan in 2014 that would empower, authorize and mandate standards for mediation and restorative justice, particularly in the form of traditional jirgas and shuras. More than a few around the table argued that acceptance of money for providing mediation services was corrupt and should be banned by the law the committee was drafting. One can't help but admire the superiority of Afghan society in terms of its commitment to an ethicality of the volunteerism of 'whitebeards and whitehairs' and younger helpers who volunteer and even put their own money into providing food and transport to convene mediations. But the group ultimately rejected a recommendation to the justice minister that the law make it a crime to accept payment for mediating a dispute.

This debate in Kabul was one that kept coming back to remind us of the virtues of restorative mediation as something that has its greatest power when it is a gift of love for a community of friends, and when seen as such. Neoliberal restorative justice and responsive regulation is certainly a risk that we do well to see through Afghan eyes. Yet the sustainability of relational giving is something that can at times be preserved by a bit of help from markets in mediation and training services, just as it can be preserved at critical junctures by help from state provision. How could these three writers think otherwise when they have spent their lives in universities that operate in the market for training and in state-funded universities. Yes, we can guard against universities slipping more deeply under the spell of a neoliberal market mentality, but that does not mean that we think university teaching should be something always volunteered without payment. We need strong gift economies in the human services; but gift economies can be brittle; reliance on them must be hedged by state and market supports so they become even stronger gift economies.

The dangers of excess in neoliberal market provision of human services are mainly posed by under-investment in tax collection and in public spending on the human services. While many human services have improved and have attracted increased funding over time, most have not. Best et al. (2016) have pointed out that a precondition for many of the recovery capital programs discussed in Chapter 12 (Best and Musgrove) is secure housing. Secure public housing is expensive, so most western states have retreated from it. This issue is also discussed in Wilson and Fox's Chapter 13. For a person with a substance abuse problem, for example, only if they have that publicly funded base of secure housing when they do not have the resources to pay for it in the private market for housing will recovery grow. Nearly all economies have grown much wealthier year by year during the past 70 years. This has made it easier and easier for them to fund human services with the decency required for human flourishing. Instead, we have seen the super-rich capture most of these fruits of greater affluence at the expense of the poor. Improved restorative and responsive support for the poor awaits more effective restorative and responsive regulation of the taxpaying of rich individuals and corporations (Braithwaite, 2005). In the above fundamental senses, effective restorative and responsive regulation of business is inextricably linked to viable restorative and responsive regulation of human services, and vice versa.

Limits of Law Reform Ritualism

While that is the essence of the positive message of this book about how to build human services that deliver freedom from want and freedom from violence and domination, a conclusion about our negative message is also in order. This book has shown through varied examples that the state rarely delivers high-quality human services by simply enacting a law that says something should be done. Laws do not of themselves mobilize relational energy and commitments. We have seen, for example in Leigh Goodmark's Chapter 11, that laws that mandate reporting of child abuse, mandatory arrest and no-drop laws for domestic violence prosecutions are examples of rituals of comfort (Power, 1997) that have equivocal evidence of effectiveness and create complex and conflicted choices for the most disadvantaged people. They are laws designed to seduce critics of failed state responses to domination that something tough is being enacted. No-drop laws for domestic violence and mandatory reporting of abuse have arisen along a trajectory of commitment to maximally punitive criminal enforcement against serious violence, followed by evidence of failure of these policies. The response has been to dig the system deeper into that hole of failure by measures that limit discretion against being non-punitive (Burford, 2018a) but allow discretion to double-down on punitive measures.

To make things even worse, new laws typically do not foresee the way police, statutory front-line actors of enforcement at the street, school-hallway or client interface will make them work. Because police could get into trouble for failure to arrest, when both partners at a scene of domestic violence accused the other of initiating the violence, frequently, especially in minority families, the police take the safe path of arresting both (Burford, 2018a; Roberts, Chapter 8; Goodmark, Chapter 11). This has driven the unexpected result that the campaign for more aggressive criminal enforcement against domestic violence has resulted in increasing numbers of minority women, the most marginalized of people, being charged. Dorothy Roberts in Chapter 8 reports that black children in the United States are nearly nine times more likely to have an incarcerated parent than white children.

Sherman and Harris (2015) followed up the Milwaukee domestic violence experiments by counting how many victims had died by 2012–13 in cases randomly assigned to mandatory arrest (or away from it) in 1987–88. They found that victims were 64 per cent more likely to have died from all causes when their abuser was arrested and jailed compared to cases randomly assigned to a warning and being allowed to stay at home (normally with minimal social support). For African-American survivors, this elevated risk from their perpetrator being randomly assigned to arrest was particularly high: 98 per cent higher risk of early death when their offender was arrested and went to prison, as opposed to receiving a warning. Calling the police for help for a woman can be a risk factor for losing housing, having child protection enter your life, being further abused or worse (Goodmark, 2012, 2018).

Webs of regulatory action and nodes of human activism are also required to bring laws to life. Mandatory reporting laws can be undermined by 'don't ask, don't tell' realities of ritualistic response to them. No-drop laws can be undermined by no-pick-up realities. Particularly ritualistic are laws that mandate tough criminal enforcement as the one and only response to a specified wrongdoing. The criminal justice system has long faced a system capacity crisis (Pontell, 1978) which means that when new laws are written to mandate more criminal prosecutions, criminal prosecutions must be reduced somewhere else where other laws mandate a criminal enforcement response. The way this mostly works is that if we mandate more criminal enforcement against blue-collar criminals, the effect is that the impunity white-collar criminals already enjoy becomes even more certain as a more total impunity. This occurs not only because wealthy criminals have more political power to plead for impunity, but because their crimes are more complex and resource-intensive to prove than, for example, the crimes of a teacher or child care worker who fails to report bruises on a child.

Besides, responsive regulatory theory argues that criminal law has more power when it is held in reserve near the peak of a regulatory pyramid, when many other lower-cost, less-punitive remedies have been tried first (Leigh Goodmark, Chapter 11). This book has discussed the many reasons for this. If persuasion has been tried before punishment, when the punishment does come it can be accepted as more legitimate. This is especially so when agents of law enforcement say 'I am giving you a warning and some support to come into compliance this time, but you must realize that I will be in trouble with my boss if you break this law again and I do not refer your case for prosecution' (or for some other drastic state action like child removal).

David Karp's analysis in Chapter 10 of the failure of the criminal legal system and regulatory formalism to make criminal enforcement effective against the epidemic of campus rape, sexual harassment, rape chants and rape culture on campus illustrates the policy failure well. Legal formalism seems to heighten defiance and denial by perpetrators and fails to embrace remedies that teach others the lesson the perpetrator has learned. Those of us who live among university students know well that they are overwhelmingly reluctant to disrupt their studies and their lives by reporting campus date rape to the police. Karp documents this empirically. Hence Karp makes the case that universities have a responsibility to fill the vacuum with an evidence-based response that replaces inaction with something effective, which he argues includes campus restorative justice (prevention circles, restorative conferences and reintegration circles for re-entry support), restorative enquiries (Llewellyn, Chapter 9) and a campus sexual assault regulatory pyramid. Moreover, structural change was required of 'the Faculty, the university and the profession' and the higher education ecosystem, its regulation and self-regulation. 'Regulatory formalism as the systemic or ideological backdrop makes working responsively and restoratively difficult if not, sometimes, impossible' is Llewellyn's important structural conclusion (Chapter 9).

Jennifer Llewellyn focuses on one particularly wide and notorious sexual harassment incident at one university, Dalhousie, to explore broader learnings about the untapped 'potential of restorative justice as a theory of justice to affect our understanding of justice itself and the structures, systems and institutions through which it is pursued'. At the heart of her analysis is the relational complexity required for responsiveness. Restorative and responsive justice requires 'more than a one-off intervention (no matter how restorative)'. It can also require a multidimensional enquiry or even a multidimensional UN peace operation that restores and transforms the human services of a society, and much more.

The more promising line of empirical enquiry is to come to an understanding of when and how horizontal moves to enforcement of norms against violence in civil society work. This is because, as Mimi Kim (n.d.) put it in our discussion of her work in Chapter 1, first responders to violent situations are usually friends, family, community members and clergy, so why are we not doing more to equip them with the knowledge and skills for responsive interventions. Or as Leigh Goodmark put it in Chapter 11:

> The notion of community responsibility for harms, if married to justice strategies that rely upon, even require, community involvement, could reinvigorate community efforts to "police" intimate partner violence. Asking community members to identify intimate partner violence and to conceive of and implement appropriate responses could fundamentally transform how communities understand that violence, leading to the shifting of community norms that anti-violence advocates have long sought.
>
> *(Chapter 11)*

Joan Pennell and Gale Burford's (1995) Newfoundland and Labrador research on family group decision making concerning violent abuse of children and women was one example of a program designed to strengthen horizontal response and extended family empowerment to enforce anti-violence norms relationally. The initial sampling was of violent abuse, but it turned out that families with a lot of that very often also had a lot of other challenges, including some families where there was sexual abuse, that also had to be addressed in the intervention. This necessitated offering every family member in the circle, including those who had abused others, the opportunity to have a designated support person lest their behavior or emotions, including shame, violent or sexual victimization required help to manage, and to ensure that abused persons had someone with them who could support them. It was a practice influenced by Paul Adams and his characterization of the virtue 'of accepting that one is not and should not be in control of a family' (as discussed in Chapter 6). The approach and implementation results have been described in detail (Burford, Pennell, & MacLeod, 1995; Pennell & Burford, 1995) with protocols field tested and adapted for use particularly in situations of intersecting child abuse and domestic violence (Family Group Decision Making, Pennell et al., Chapter 7; Nixon et al., 2005; Sen et al., 2018).

The empirical evaluation of outcomes of the Newfoundland and Labrador program (Burford & Pennell, 1998; Pennell & Burford, 2000) found a marked reduction in both child abuse and neglect and abuse of mothers and wives and several other relevant measures after the restorative intervention.

Briefly, of note is the way holism made the intervention into more than a child protection innovation; it was a generalized human services intervention for the whole family that prioritized the needs of children but also set the needs of the children in the context of the need for safety for all family members. Programs like this one and others that have built off similar assumptions about the capacities of families and communities including Hollow Water, Ma Mawi and many others (Burford & Pennell, 1998; Pennell & Burford, 1995; Government of Canada Department of Justice, n.d.; Couture et al., 2001; Daly & Barrett, 2014; Daybreak, 2018; Government of Canada Public Safety Canada, n.d.; Sawatsky, 2009; Ma Mawi Wi Chi Itata, n.d.; Mi'kmaw Family and Children's Services of Nova Scotia, 2018; George Hull Centre for Children and Families, n.d.; Pennell et al., Chapter 7; Schmid & Morgenshtern, 2017; Sen et al., 2018) show that assumptions that restorative family violence programs necessarily threaten domination rather that assumptions that restorative family violence programs will dominate rather than liberate women must be questioned. We see this questioning in the Royal Commission of senior feminist judge, Marcia Neave (State of Victoria Royal Commission into Family Violence, 2016) and in the work of many scholars and leaders in North America (discussed in Goodmark, Chapter 11 and in Roberts, Chapter 8) and others (c.f. Coker In Press; Coker & Ahjané, 2015; Goodmark, 2018; Pennell & Kim, 2010).

Joan Pennell, Kara Allen-Eckard, Marianne Latz and Cameron Tomlinson build on this contribution in Chapter 7 by discussing how family empowerment restorative processes run well can build 'collective hope'. They discuss the mistake of shielding children too much from participation because of the friction that arises in conflicts between the state and the family. Lost hope means that families are likely then to react through motivational postures of resistance, disengagement or game playing to undermine agency rules. Special opportunities for building the self-efficacy of children are then lost. These child engagement issues were viewed through the empirical prism of data from the North Carolina Community Child Protection Team (CCPT) (Pennell et al., Chapter 7). Chapter 13 by Wilson and Fox likewise has this kind of emphasis on engagement with the creation of a politics of health.

Pennell and Burford's research is just one part of a wider body of research that has found women's voices tend to get more air time in restorative conferences than in other processes like court cases. Gabrielle Maxwell (1993, p. 292) concluded that restorative conferences are 'places where women's voices are heard'. Rigby (1996, p. 143) showed with data from 8,500 students that at all ages girls are more interested than boys in talking through school bullying problems. Kathy Daly (1996) found that while a minority (15 per cent) of youth justice conferencing offenders were female, women could still be a majority in the room (with 54 per cent of victims, 58 per cent of victim supporters and 52 per cent of offender supporters being women). In the Canberra RISE experiments offenders were more likely to feel that they were disadvantaged due to 'age, income, sex, race or some other reason' when they were randomly assigned to court than when they were randomized to a restorative justice conference (Barnes, 1999; Sherman & Barnes, 1997; Sherman et al., 1998). Joe Hudson (1998) likewise found in Canada that 80 per cent of restorative conference participants were 'very satisfied' that all participants were treated as equals, a result that could not be achieved without most women being satisfied on this score. In Pennell et al.'s Chapter 7 in this book, mother and child participation was reported as high in North Carolina Community Child Protection Team (CCPT) meetings. The challenge as they see it is to build what Tali Gal (2015) calls a culture of child participation. Leigh Goodmark makes the point in Chapter 11 with respect to gendered violence that 'Restorative processes are free of the evidentiary constraints that restrict voice'. In contrast, David Karp argues in Chapter 10, legal formalism can undermine women's agency in the case of university sexual assault and harassment. So can informalism of course. The challenge of restorative and responsive justice is a formalism that both checks and enables informalism; and an informalism that checks and enables formalism.

We have seen more generally in this book that improved human services never inexorably follow from a law that simply mandates them. Nor does it follow from empowerment alone, as Paul Adams argues: empowerment, good processes and values must be complemented by habits, dispositions, qualities of character, virtues, required for and developed by such practice. Democracy as the art of association and social justice count among these virtues on the Adams analysis (Chapter 6). The accomplishments of indigenous justice in *Aotearoa* New Zealand have been significantly enabled by the way the Treaty of Waitangi allowed the flourishing of indigenous versions of these virtues. 'The practice of the virtue of social justice consists in learning new skills, both of leadership and of cooperation and association with others, to accomplish ends that no one individual can achieve on his own' (Adams, Chapter 6).

The Treaty was the worst kind of ritualism for Māori after 1877, however, when *Wi Parata v Bishop of Wellington* ruled the Treaty a nullity for the racist reason that Māori were not capable of signing a treaty (Evans, 2018). It was only during the Māori Renaissance when Māori civil society responsively escalated their demands, their protest marches, their occupations of land, that a nullified law was brought to life by renewed contestation through the Waitangi Tribunal from the mid-1980s. This was the virtue that Paul Adams (Chapter 6) described in Edward R. Murrow's 1960 documentary, *Harvest of Shame* (Friendly & Murrow, 1960), when the film exposed the appalling conditions of agricultural migrant labor in the United States, and when the laborers themselves rose up to organize and demand social justice. The Waitangi Tribunal institutionalized an incipiently restorative practice of justice in the way it conceived Māori as survivors and the Crown as the 'offender' (Evans, 2018; O'Sullivan, 2007). Tribunal settlements include historical accounts of Treaty breaches acknowledged by the Crown, cultural redress in forms such as changing place names, transferring land to claimant groups or national parks, co-governance of rivers and lakes formerly dominated by *Aqua Nullius* (Marshall, 2017, 2018) and commercial redress. For all the limits of restorative practice in New Zealand through Māori eyes (Moyle & Tauri, 2016), the Treaty at least provides a structurally restorative and responsive foundation for justice as a better future (Froestad & Shearing, 2007).

In conversations within the Canberra Restorative Community (Tito Wheatland, 2018), one topic of conversation is the signing of Treaties between the Australian Capital Territory (ACT) government and the elders of the Ngunnawal and Ngambri peoples. One hope for such treaties could be that they would mandate a reduction in child removals from Aboriginal families. It is the same problem here that Dorothy Roberts (Chapter 8) documented for the United States that 'prison and foster care systems work together to monitor, regulate, and punish black mothers in ways that help to extend an unjust carceral state'. Sadly in the decade after the Australian Apology by Prime Minister Rudd for the Stolen Generations of Aboriginal children, the Australian Capital Territory became the jurisdiction with the highest rate of indigenous child removal of any jurisdiction in Australia.

The ACT Law Reform Advisory Council has pointed out that Canberra has since 2008 had *Aotearoa* New Zealand style laws to enable family group conferences before child removal in which families are empowered to decide what the process will be for deciding what to do about the neglect or abuse of a child. The key difference from the New Zealand law is that it is not mandatory to empower families in this way. The consequence of that difference, in turn, has been that ACT child protection authorities have opted consistently to keep the power over families in professional hands. Responsive escalation of civil society enforcement against the state is needed to bring a non-punitive law to life, whether through demands for mandatory empowerment of Aboriginal families in an ACT Treaty or just by protests against government inaction to use this law. Inspiringly organized indigenous 'GMARs' (Grandmothers Against Removals) featured in Larissa Behrendt's (2017) documentary, *After the Apology*, agitating for political change. Canberra Restorative Community aligned with some of the GMARs to advocate a meaningful dialogue on state child removals. GMAR, filmmaker, restorative community, then Treaty activism on this issue illustrates one possible healing edge of civil society regulation of state domination of indigenous families. The alliance of GMAR, filmmaker, restorative community, then Treaty activism on this issue illustrates one possible healing edge of civil society regulation of state domination of indigenous families.

Another part of the Canberra Restorative Community conversation on the desirability of ACT Treaties with indigenous peoples has picked up on some of David Best and Amy Musgrove's recovery capital work (Chapter 12). Best and Musgrove point out that programs to foster recovery from addictions and other challenges faced in the human services rarely work without the client enjoying secure housing. The lack of secure housing, particularly for indigenous Australians, is a blight on Australian society. There is almost non-existent shame in white Canberra society about comfortable suburban landholders living on, claiming to own, stolen land. By-passed shame and denial are rife.[1] A practical process of shame acknowledgement and apology for the theft of Canberra's land is needed. It would not be a practical outcome to gift back all of Canberra to Aboriginal Elders because this would cause business disinvestment that would hurt Aboriginal people along with everyone else. One pathway beginning to be discussed in the Canberra Restorative Community is giving all Ngunnawal and Ngambri a right of return to their traditional lands and fully publicly funded housing on that land in a form chosen by the indigenous people themselves. Likely they would choose some sort of mix of cooperative housing in a space where indigenous justice and indigenous rule could be given some special sway, and some privately owned houses for those who choose to eschew cooperatives. To achieve this politically, however, greatly escalated pressure would be required on white society and its political leaders to acknowledge shame for the harm of the theft of the land, and acquit that shame by negotiated reparative action. In the USA this would include both acknowledgment of harm and theft with indigenous and enslaved peoples' groups but also to address continuing harms.

Virtues of Restorative Justice

With intimate partner violence, Leigh Goodmark in Chapter 11 sees accountability as a central issue and argues that forward-looking active responsibility enabled by restorative justice is superior to backward-looking passive justice in the legal system. She sees the criminal legal system as undermining safety for women and children by stigmatizing the violence of men, making the label 'rapist' the whole story of who they are, for example, instead of reintegratively shaming rape culture and the practices of rape they perpetrated. It is community members who 'have regular, even daily, contact with residents' that are in the best position to provide workable supervision to enforce agreements or court orders and restorative justice, Goodmark argues. Community members demanding community rights to stakeholder decision making are in the best position to catalyze this community ownership of active responsibility. Dorothy Roberts in Chapter 8 argues that 'restorative justice breaks away from the retributive paradigm that punishes past wrongdoing to focus instead on "making the future safer" by reconciling offending and victimized individuals to each other and/or to their communities'. Roberts contends that dominant conceptions of restorative justice fail to meet this potential because they do not account for institutionalized discrimination, surveillance and violence perpetrated by the very state systems relied on for restorative processes. Family group decision making and feminist anti-carceral approaches to domestic violence, according to Roberts, can be the light on the hill for how we might develop a restorative justice framework that contributes to dismantling unjust carceral systems and creating an equitable and humane society.

See also Wilson and Fox's Chapter 13, which contends that a "risk/need/responsivity" model (Bonta & Andrews, 2016) that empowers community members using the Circles of Support and Accountability model is an example of communities as responsive regulators. Circles of Support and Accountability are found by Wilson and Fox to enjoy growing evidence of cost-effectiveness, as in Duwe's (2018) randomized controlled trial showing a statistically significant difference in rates of sexual recidivism (an 88% reduction), as well as a return on investment of $3.73 for every dollar spent. The responsivity principle means in Wilson and Fox's account that clients are able to respond to interventions in terms of client capacities, motivation and learning cycles, for example. Under this restorative model, ordinary citizens can contribute to public safety by integrating and supporting persons who have sexually offended upon release from prison.

Virtues of Responsive Regulation

Brenda Morrison and Tania Arvanitidis in Chapter 4 concluded that nine heuristics of a regulatory framework would have helped the response to the 2011 Vancouver Stanley Cup riots. They brought together an evocative illustration of what is required for these nine principles of responsive regulation to work: attend to context; listen actively; engage resisters with fairness; praise committed innovation; achieve outcomes through support and innovation; signal a range of sanctions; engage wider networks; elicit active responsibility; evaluate and communicate lessons learnt. This is the chapter that goes to these critical step-by-step processual demands that are the essence of responsive regulation. In both restorative justice and responsive regulation, the strong evidence base that motivational interviewing works (Lundahl et al., 2010) informs the practical edge of how to listen actively, the first of the nine principles. If desistance from alcohol abuse is agreed in a restorative and responsive process as an aim, the motivational interviewer asks the drinker why this aim matters to them and their family, and then later what strategies might follow from this shared reason for wanting to desist, to which the family could commit to support them. The same motivational interviewing strategy can be applied to a restorative and responsive approach to reducing the use of restraints in a facility for the disabled. Like Jennifer Llewellyn (Chapter 9), Morrison and Arvanitidis found a formalistic and prescriptive system that consistently emphasized deterrence made a restorative and responsive response difficult. Learning and growth through norm clarification is difficult when instead of a collective response to a collective cultural phenomenon, the response is a long line of individual prosecutions. 'Collective commitment to listen and learn' is the starting point for that more contextually subtle response sought by Morrison and Arvanitidis. This is complemented in their analysis by a redundancy of strategies that cover weaknesses of one response with strengths of another as the society commits to stick with talking through and responding to the problems (which included trauma) until they were resolved. Morrison and Arvanitidis explain how social support and educative responses are so much more important than formal legal responses to moral panics of the kind they studied. What seems like an issue for the legal justice system then becomes an issue for the heart and soul of the democracy.

Carrà conceived the familiness of relational sociology as a fundamental building block of responsive human services in Chapter 5. The ideals identified by Carrà here include family-focused policies, empowerment of family associations, whole family and thick family approaches, family systems theory, family impact analysis as an alternative to individual impacts and good practices in services to the family.

This was embedded in the pluralism of her lively evidence-based defense of Mediterranean virtues against Northern liberalism. This is the chapter on why families must be at the front door of a human services that transcend individual casework.

David Best and Amy Musgrove (Chapter 12) conceive the building of recovery capital as fundamental to the strengths-building of a restorative and responsive project for human services. They developed the responsive pyramid into a 'regulatory diamond' whereby regulatory capital becomes fundamental to recovery capital. This can happen when bonding capital adheres across the elements of the diamond. Then we can have human services that CHIME with the Connectedness; Hope; Identity; Meaning; and, Empowerment that the evidence suggests works with recovery from addictions to drugs, alcohol, gambling and more (see also Wilson and Fox in Chapter 13).

The Ugly Side of Responsive Regulation

It is possible for a restorative justice person to be a pacifist, an abolitionist on criminalization, who eschews institutionalized state politics. We deeply respect the positions of many of our restorative friends who defend those standpoints. But it is not possible for a responsive regulatory thinker to be like that. It is possible, as Jennifer Llewellyn argues in Chapter 9, to adopt a 'restorative approach to responsive regulation', to refuse to conceive restorative justice and responsive regulation as merely process ideals, but to see them also as infused with distinctive values such as environmental restoration, relational justice, listening, empowerment and non-domination. We can do our best to preserve these and other restorative values as we escalate up responsive regulatory pyramids, as Llewellyn argues in Chapter 9. Responsive regulation must have, as Llewellyn and Chapter 2 argue, explicit strategies for relational de-escalation such as GRIT (Graduated Reciprocation in Tension Reduction) (Osgood, 1962) and for horizontal scanning to forestall escalation, as it does have (Ayres & Braithwaite, 1992; Braithwaite, 2008).

We can do our best to honor restorative values as we escalate up a responsive regulatory pyramid to putting a person in prison while listening to prisoners, empowering prisoners with voice and choice, setting up restorative justice units in correctional administrations, abandoning criminal law's proportionality principle by releasing prisoners as soon as they no longer pose a severe danger and similar measures that deliver on restorative values. What we cannot do is describe escalation to imprisoning a person as a restorative justice measure because to imprison is to dominate a person, to strip them of freedom, to wrench them from their children, partners, parents and dearest friends, to uproot indigenous people from the sacred spaces of their land that forges who they are, their CHIME in the words of Best and Musgrove (Chapter 12). Dorothy Roberts in Chapter 8 dramatically illustrates how more than half of all mothers in US prisons receive no visits at all from their children. To describe imprisonment near the peak of a responsive regulatory enforcement pyramid as anything less than an anti-restorative measure would tear the heart out of what it means to be restorative, as Jennifer Llewellyn argues in Chapter 9. Yet sadly, we point out that of course it is sometimes necessary to imprison serial killers to long sentences and sometimes it is necessary to do worse to school shooters and suicide bombers. Responsive regulation has a pointy end to its enforcement pyramid. The responsive regulatory theorist must not be timid in saying that it is a good thing that the state has the power to remove children from families, even as these authors believe, because of their restorative values, that the overwhelming majority of children that are being removed from families by the state in our societies should not be so removed.

In political campaigns to change this reality it is occasionally necessary to get our hands dirty with the ugly politics of ending the political careers or the civil service careers of those defending the barricades that keep children under state and professional control. These people believe in what they are doing; they have families to care for and bills to pay; and we know politicians often suffer mental health problems when we drive them from office, stripping them of their identity as a leader. Politics is ugly this way. Getting our hands dirty with the business of ridding ourselves of them is not a very relational practice, though the best politicians do their best to make our politics more relational. Responsive regulatory theorists believe that sometimes it is necessary to get ugly, as in the actions that created the Waitangi Treaty, to get into the streets, occupy buildings and yell. Yet restorative and responsive activists also believe that civil society activism should mostly be transacted collaboratively in a soft register.

The responsive regulatory thinker believes it is a good idea to have prisons that take freedom away from some rapists. Yet they also believe that the overwhelming majority of people who are currently sent to prison, even as rapists and murderers and even in societies with low imprisonment rates, can be regulated at lower levels of the enforcement pyramid in more relational ways without dragging offenders away from their families. Responsive regulatory theorists believe it is a good idea to have institutions dedicated to killing people in large numbers called defense departments. They see the empirical record of history that states without armies are taken over internally by armies without states, or externally by armies with a state (Braithwaite & D'Costa, 2018, pp. 125–127). Yet they think our objective should be to always prefer relational diplomacy and never to deploy an army to a war at the peak of this pyramid except for defense against attack. It should never be used preemptively. Our human services would have far fewer challenges if in the past we had been more successful in keeping our soldiers at home taking care of their families. Even in war, to the extent possible, we can seek to focus on 'achievement of the conditions of just relationship—of mutual respect, care/concern and dignity' (Jennifer Llewellyn, Chapter 9). The responsive regulatory thinker is not reluctant to say that the state should have the power for extra-judicial assassination. Yet it should only use that power in extreme situations such as a police sniper taking out a school shooter or a terrorist about to ignite a suicide vest.

As Valerie Braithwaite explained in Chapter 3, a responsive regulatory theorist does not wish to abolish school suspensions of students, even as they believe the overwhelming majority of students who currently get suspended should be dealt with lower in an enforcement pyramid. Optimum harm minimization in schools requires that we move down the U-curve of harm of Figure 2.3 (Chapter 2) by reducing over-regulation. The responsive regulation theorist certainly agrees with more purist restorativists that societies are too judgmental—and that restorative justice activists can be too judgmental about one another. Yet responsive theorists cannot totally embrace 'no-blame' approaches. Productive shifts toward less blaming cultures of regulation tend to encourage regulated actors, be they parents or pilots, to learn from their near misses by being open about them. Yet this can only be secured by blaming and sometimes punishing quite severely those who cover up their near misses. One way the Catholic Church might have learnt from the indigenous wisdom employed in places like the First Nation community of Hollow Water in Manitoba (Couture et al., 2001; Sawatsky, 2009) is that a matter as serious as sexual abuse of children can be responded to non-punitively, but only if those who cover up abuse after they were given the opportunity of a restorative resolution are targeted and prosecuted. Again, as Chapter 3 argues, while it is imperative for parents to be less judgmental of their children as we encourage them to learn from their own mistakes, it is our mistake when we fail to confront our children with love about their cover-ups of bad behavior.

We cannot fail to blame Canberra homeowners in denial who feel there is no shame involved in living on land stolen from people much poorer than themselves. When men who indulge in domestic violence refuse to engage with relational justice to effectively regulate their violence, we can be left with no choice but to lock them up. The balancing of restorative justice with responsive regulation does therefore involve some contingent brutalizing of the relationality of mainstream restorative discourse. More importantly, of course, it relationalizes the institutionalized brutality of the punitive discourse of the mainstream of the wider state and society. The argument of this book is that without both kinds of balancing we fail to be the activists we could be for societies with less domination. Integrity requires that we speak plainly and clearly about the dark side of some of the things the responsive regulatory theorist intentionally supports. We must not pretend that we have a philosophy, a theory and a political practice that is all light, freedom and peace in its restorative virtue. The contestatory core (Pettit, 1997) of republican political theory that is the normative heart of responsive regulation also mandates that we put our dark side on the table, and what we propose to limit its damage, so this can be contested across the democracy.

From Naïveté to Getting Results by Averting Capture

Why is it important to labor this point with such a long list of nasty practices that responsive regulatory theorists openly endorse? It is important because this responds to the main criticisms of restorative and responsive theorists that they are naïve. Restorativists reject Hobbesian prescriptions to design institutions with the presumption that people will be knaves. Yet as they design institutions on the presumption that most people can be coaxed and caressed against being knaves most of the time, they must have safety nets for the cases where people persist in acting as knaves, especially when they are powerful people. Many readers will be familiar with this criticism with respect to domestic violence. Feminist critics rightly point out that the empirical record is that many batterers repeatedly apologize and commit to changing their ways to their partners, only to willfully batter again (Busch, 2002; Stubbs, 2010). Their contrition can be part of a conscious tactic of manipulation of naïve partners (and naïve restorative advocates) who wish to place trust in their shallow promises. Of course, we respond that this is why restorative justice must be complemented by many layers of escalated regulatory practices up to incarceration that we stick with until abuse stops.

The need to be on guard against naïveté is even more profound with corporate criminals because many corporations have skyscrapers full of highly paid lawyers and accountants whose job is to find new ways of getting around laws after they are nailed for their breach. So too are state authorities. They have legal departments using an arsenal of legal and regulatory tactics to defend against charges of human rights abuse and calls for transparency and accountability. Justice departments outsource incarceration, defense departments conduct and outsource torture, child protection outsources careless and uncaring out-of-home care, immigration departments outsource detention centers. Europe today even outsources the turning back of boats to slave traders, and quite recently the USA outsourced the detention of migrant children to private contractors (Fernandez & Benner, 2018).

Politically progressive people are repeatedly dissuaded from supporting restorative and responsive business regulation because they think that those who advocate this approach are a coalition of naïve nice guys duped by a larger pro-business group of supporters who see responsive regulation as a politically sophisticated path to business capture of the regulatory state. The problem they point to is real. Many regulators do embrace responsive regulation because they want to be loved by business, they want to get their pro-business political bosses off their back, they want to get a job in business after they leave government service, to stop the constant harassment by powerful business lobbyists making their daily work life a misery, or they are hegemonically seduced by the belief that what is good for

General Motors is good for America. This is why we need active citizens in the social movement sector to regularly call for the replacement of captured regulators. Capture in domains well beyond financial regulation takes the more nuanced form of regulators wanting to be comfortable doing desk audits of paperwork, systems analyses and risk analyses when to become more effective most regulators need to kick more tires and kick more corporate heads than they currently kick so they can be taken more seriously. Human rights agencies and ombudsmen that regulate child protection agencies likewise need to transcend state capture by getting out to talk to families who have been ignored, and sometimes they need to recommend shake-ups to the management structure of the child protection agency.

These various forms of capture by the powerful are why we need prosecution units in business regulatory agencies that counter the ruthlessness of the corporate lawyers with their own brand of determination to be very tough and cynical in a rather anti-restorative way, even as front-line regulatory staff are more faithfully following restorative values. It is why restorative and responsive activists were on Wall Street with the Occupy movement, willing to break laws about legal assembly, even if they had to travel from Australia, after the great crash of 2008. This regulatory politics is a human services issue. The behavior of Wall Street up to 2008 caused 34 million people to lose their jobs worldwide (ILO, 2010); it threw a greater number of people out of their homes. It goes without saying that if human services social work is just a professional practice that mops up after such catastrophes rather than getting active with the brutal politics of confronting political capture by Wall Street as a preventive practice, it is hardly a profession that takes its values seriously. It is a marginal profession for nice people who do nice stuff sometimes. At the end of the day, nice people who wanted to be nice to their first black president allowed the Obama Administration to give handouts to Wall Street to bail them out without demanding a share of the ownership of these companies on the stock market proportionate to the quantum of the bailouts in the way Gordon Brown's administration did demand in the UK. In Britain these shares were sold for the benefit of taxpayers when bailed-out banks returned to profitability. The Obama Administration insisted on some Green New Deal reforms in 2008, for example, insisting that General Motors reciprocate its bailout by building greener cars, but China and Korea went much further with such demands toward a Green New Deal after the Global Financial Crisis (Tienhaara, 2018, pp. 12–13).

Two kinds of politics were needed in 2008 to bring restorative values of voice, healing and forgiveness together with political acuity in contesting power. One was for active citizens to confront the police lines, disrupt the traffic, call the Obama Administration out. Active citizens should have been arguing for a publicly owned ratings agency to compete in the market with the corrupted practices of Moodys and Standard and Poors. The second kind of politics was to give dramatic examples of restorative response to the most horrible of business crimes when corporate contrition is given a chance to prove it is genuine, and monitored. Our favorite example is that when Michael Milken (of Michael Douglas 'Greed is Good' on Wall Street fame) was convicted after the 1987 Wall Street crash, he offered in plea negotiations a billion-dollar fine payment, certain measures to help victims and a number of years of community service commitment to helping developing countries extricate themselves from the debt crises that were afflicting them in that period. Ralph Nader excoriated the offer; no one who mattered in the United States thought it good idea to take Milkin's offer seriously. He went to prison for his terrible crimes of the 1987 crash.

John Braithwaite argued at the time for the benefits of taking up Milkin's offer to repair financial harm because Michael Milkin was the most brilliant mind in the world financial system of that era. It was an idea spurned as being soft, restorative and naïve. But the story evolved to have a restorative rather than the feared exploitative turn. In 2017, John was in Myanmar talking to the senior economic advisor of Aung Sun Suu Kyi on the considerable problem of insolvent banks that posed a deep risk to the fragile future of that struggling country. The advisor had his files in a bag marked 'Milkin Family Foundation Workshop on Bank Regulation in Myanmar'. Yes, even though Michael Milkin did go to prison after his offer was spurned, he honored the offer to repair the harm regardless. After anecdotes of this kind, the restorative and responsive activist can move on to point out that the restorative city movement started as an idea hatched by Prison Fellowship International, an organization founded by Watergate criminal Charles Colson after his release from prison.

To put all of this another way, a kind of shock politics is needed to take on wicked challenges like these and like climate change. One of the best ways of preventing climate change is to shift the shape of economies through tax and other regulatory policies that shift spending away from the consumption of consumer durables and toward the consumption of human services. Spending on social workers, teachers and other care workers causes little pollution compared with spending on material consumption. On the one hand, paradigm shifts can be coaxed by confronting cynics with shocking examples of why it might have made the world a safer place to have worked restoratively with a Michael Milkin, with China on climate change, with the Taliban leadership after the September 11 attack on New York, with Saddam Hussein as he planned and executed the invasion of Kuwait, with Muammar Gadaffi during the Arab Spring (Braithwaite & D'Costa, 2018, Part I). On the other hand, responsive regulatory paradigm shifts can be coaxed by confronting the weakness of calls simply to put bad individuals in prison when what was needed was strategic socialism to temporarily put corporations that had behaved badly into public ownership. The point of this is that part of the power of restorative and responsive regulation comes from its advocacy of more brutal stuff than politics as usual. The theoretical reason for this is the paradox of the pyramid that by being able to escalate to very tough stuff, more of the regulatory action that matters can be driven down to collaborative trust, just relations and relational justice with verification at the base of the pyramid. It is the politics of walking softly without being a soft touch. It is the power of re-narrating history both through stories of wading through the corpses of political and corporate careers we killed off and stories of flipping great evil to a politics of care.

Conclusion: Learning from the Human Services and The Regulatory Imagination

Some change is afoot. Contemporary English regulation of aged, disability and all residential social care of adults has taken a relational turn, emphasizing the imperative to 'do with' rather than 'do to' or 'do for' aged care and disability residents (Trigg, 2018). While the US and Australian regulatory systems have not made this shift, individual nursing homes have. The English regulatory shift has been dramatic, bringing all quality regulation decisions under the umbrella of one relational principle: 'the Mum test'. Chief Inspector of Social Care, Andrea Sutcliffe, explained the Mum test as follows:

> [I]nspection teams [are asked] to consider whether these are services that they would be happy for someone they love and care for to use. If they are, then we will celebrate this through our ratings. If they are not, we will take tough action so improvements are made.
>
> *(Trigg, 2018, p. 126)*

The Mum test is a version of the Platinum Golden Rule. It motivates just five questions about fundamental standards (that sit under each question): Is it safe? Is it effective? Is it caring? Is it responsive? Is it well-led? For example, standards under the 'Caring' question include: 'How are positive caring relationships developed with people using the service'? Standards under the 'Responsive' standard include: 'How do people receive personalized care that is responsive to their needs?; 'How does the service routinely listen and learn from people's experiences, concerns and complaints'? (Care Quality Commission, 2015). This is a promising approach aimed at averting the danger of gaming and ritualism that 'hits the target but misses the point' (Bevan & Hood, 2006, p. 521; Trigg, 2018).

The human services take the kind of virtues that Paul Adams discussed in Chapter 6 and Jennifer Llewellyn in Chapter 9 more seriously than other domains of governance. These are virtues and arts of association and non-domination. Such virtues are important to all corners of state and society. Welfare states are transparently involved in governance by providing, distributing and steering. This is perhaps not so obviously true for those parts of state and society that fight wars and run stock markets. Part of our argument is that war and markets can likewise only be governed by judicious mixes of providing, distributing and steering. The literature on regulatory capitalism is about the discovery that the steering part of governance has become more pivotal in contemporary conditions of complexity (Levi-Faur & Jordana, 2005; Braithwaite, 2008).

The human services are a key to preventing capitalism from descending into horrific future economic catastrophes, future fascisms and future wars. Yet this promise of the human services can only be realized if societies sharpen their steering capabilities. What we are particularly thinking of here is the uncertainty over whether Artificial Intelligence ultimately will cause massive unemployment when, for example, all the truck drivers, delivery drivers, taxi drivers, Uber drivers, bus, train, light rail drivers and postal workers are replaced by driverless vehicles or decentralized drone deliveries. And this is just one example of a much more generalized risk of massive unemployment when the next financial crash occurs. These authors are not competent to answer when and whether this risk will be fully realized. The remedy to the risk, if and when it is realized, however, seems clear to us. It is to steer the economy so that more tax is collected from the corporations and individuals who garner the benefits of these improved efficiencies so that a good slice of those economic windfalls are redistributed to public provision of jobs that are desperately undersupplied in domains like health, education, aged care, disability care and services for children and parents. Accomplishing this is not beyond the wit of our regulatory imaginations. It will certainly need aggressive regulation by social movement activists for a politicized human services, regulation of those who happen to be in the right jobs and the right industries to collect these windfalls, so the growing riches can be redistributed for the benefit of all.

Nuanced hybridity has been shown to be important for responsive engagement with the complexity of the challenges of diverse human services considered in this book. This nuanced hybridity is equally relevant, however, to the complexity of the challenges of war, peace and business (Forsyth et al., 2017; Wallis et al., 2018). Wherever domination arises, regulatory theory questions that go to how to regulate for non-domination are likely to be worth asking. At the same time, this book has argued that regulatory theory is insufficiently engaged in the human services. This is because regulation of others inevitably has its ugly side even when the regulation is explicitly designed to reduce the amount of domination in the world. We hope for a future of human services scholarship that is less squeamish about regulatory theory. And we hope for moving beyond the considerable literatures showing both promise and limitations of restorative justice and of responsive regulation (Braithwaite, 2002, 2016) to empirical evaluations of innovative regulatory mixes that are restorative and responsive.

Note

1. At least in other parts of Australia landowners can say they bought their land from someone who did not steal it, as in turn did their vendor, and that it was a long time ago that the land was stolen. This particular politics of denial is denied to Canberrans because of a peculiarity of its history. When the new national capital was planned more than a century ago it was decided that all land would be owned by the Crown and made available on 99-year leases. People buy and sell homes as elsewhere, but legally in Canberra our homes are leased from the very Crown that stole the land from the traditional owners after frontier wars and other genocidal practices were directed against them to our benefit.

References

Ayres, I., & Braithwaite, J. (1992). *Responsive regulation: Transcending the deregulation debate.* New York: Oxford University Press.

Baggs, D. (2018). *Lean cities—low carb materials & the role of restorative sustainability.* Retrieved from www.ecospecifier.com.au/knowledge-green/articles/lean-cities-low-carb-materials/.

Bankhead, T., George, A., & Poretz, J. (2018, June). *Growing roses in concrete: Our journey towards a restorative Oakland.* Keynote presentation presented at the Newcastle as a Restorative City symposium, Newcastle, NSW.

Barnes, G. (1999). *Procedural justice in two contexts: Testing the fairness of diversionary conferencing for intoxicated drivers.* Unpublished PhD Dissertation, College Park, MD: Institute of Criminal Justice and Criminology, University of Maryland.

Behrendt, L. (Director). (2017). *After the apology* [Motion picture]. Sydney: Screen Australia.

Best, D., Beswick, T., Hodgkins, S., & Idle, M. (2016). Recovery, ambitions, and aspirations: An exploratory project to build a recovery community by generating a skilled recovery workforce. *Journal of Alcoholism Treatment Quarterly, 34*(1), 3–14.

Bevan, G., & Hood, C. (2006). What's measured and what matters: Targets and gaming in the English public health care system. *Public Administration, 87*, 514–538.

Bonta, J., & Andrews, D. A. (2016). *The psychology of criminal conduct.* New York: Routledge.

Braithwaite, J. (2002). *Restorative justice and responsive regulation.* Oxford: Oxford University Press.

Braithwaite, J. (2005). *Market in vice, markets in virtue.* Oxford: Oxford University Press.

Braithwaite, J. (2008). *Regulatory capitalism: How it works, ideas for making it work better.* Cheltenham, UK: Edward Elgar.

Braithwaite, J. (2016). *Restorative and responsive regulation: The question of evidence* (RegNet Working Paper No. 51). Retrieved from RegNet website: http://regnet.anu.edu.au/sites/default/files/uploads/2016-10/SSRN_2016_updated_Braithwaite%20J.pdf.

Braithwaite, J., & D'Costa, B. (2018). *Cascades of violence: Crime, war and peacebuilding across South Asia.* Canberra: ANU Press.

Braithwaite, V. (2015). *Overcoming oppression in child protection: Restorative justice, responsive regulation and political courage* (RegNet Research Paper No. 95). Retrieved from SSRN website: https://papers.ssrn.com/sol3/papers.cfm?abstract_id=2685453

Burford, G. (2013). Family group conferences in youth justice and child welfare in Vermont. In K. S. van Wormer & L. Walker (Eds.), *Restorative justice today: Practical applications* (pp. 81–92). Thousand Oaks, CA: Sage Publications.

Burford, G. (2018a, June). *Domestic violence and the use of restorative approaches.* Keynote presentation presented at the Newcastle as a Restorative City symposium, Newcastle, NSW.

Burford, G. (2018b). Family engagement and social work in statutory settings. In T. Maschi & G. Leibowitz (Eds.), *Forensic social work: Psychosocial and legal issues across diverse populations and settings* (2nd ed., pp. 389–410). New York: Springer.

Burford, G., & Gallagher, S. (2015). Teen experiences of exclusion, inclusion and engagement in child protection and youth justice in Vermont. In T. Gal & B. F. Duramy (Eds.), *International perspectives and empirical findings on child participation: From social exclusion to child-inclusive policies* (pp. 227–255). New York: Oxford University Press.

Burford, G., & Pennell, J. (1998). *Family group decision making: After the conference—progress in resolving violence and promoting well-being: Outcome report* (Vols. 1 & 2). St. John's, NF: Memorial University of Newfoundland.

Burford, G., Pennell, J., & MacLeod, S. (1995, August). *Manual for coordinators and communities: The organization and practice of family group decision making* (revised). St. John's, NF: Memorial University of Newfoundland, School of Social Work. (In English, French, and Inuktitut). Retrieved from http://social.chass.ncsu.edu/jpennell/fgdm/manual/.

Busch, R. (2002). Domestic violence and restorative justice initiatives: Who pays if we get it wrong? In H. Strang & J. Braithwaite (Eds.), *Restorative justice and family violence* (pp. 223–248). Cambridge: Cambridge University Press.

Care Quality Commission. (2015). *How CQC regulates: Residential adult social care services.* London, UK: Care Quality Commission.

Clynes, M. (2013). *Repairing Detroit through restorative practices.* Retrieved from www.michigannightlight.com/features/repairingdetroitthroughrestorativepractices.aspx.

Coker, D. (In Press). Restorative responses to intimate partner violence. (forthcoming 2019) In M. Moscati, M. Palmer, & M. Roberts (Eds.), *Comparative dispute resolution: A research handbook* (Research Handbooks in Comparative Law Series [eds] Francesco Parisi & Tom Ginsburg). Cheltenham, UK/Northampton, MA: Edward Elgar.

Coker, D., & Ahjané, M. (2015). Alternative U.S. responses to intimate partner violence. In R. Goel & L. Goodmark (Eds.), *Comparative perspectives on gender violence: Lessons from efforts worldwide* (pp. 169–181). Oxford, UK: Oxford University Press.

Couture, J., Parker, T., Couture, R., & Laboucane, P. (2001). *A cost-benefit analysis of hollow water's community holistic circle healing process.* Retrieved from Public Safety Canada website: www.publicsafety.gc.ca/cnt/rsrcs/pblctns/cst-bnft-hllw-wtr/cst-bnft-hllw-wtr-eng.pdf.

Daly, K. (1996). *Diversionary conferences in Australia: A reply to the optimists and skeptics.* Paper prepared for presentation at the American Society of Criminology Annual Meeting, 1996, Chicago. Retrieved from www.ncjrs.gov/App/Publications/abstract.aspx?ID=183519.

Daly, A., & Barrett, G. (2014). *Independent cost benefit analysis of the Yuendumu Mediation and Justice Committee.* Retrieved from Central Desert Regional Council website: www.centraldesert.nt.gov.au/sites/centraldesert.nt.gov.au/files/attachments/yuendumu_cba_0.pdf.

Daybreak. (2018). *Information for families.* Retrieved from www.daybreakfgc.org.uk/about-fgcs.

Dobbs, D. (2007, November 13). *The green space cure: The psychological value of biodiversity* [Web news blog]. Retrieved from https://blogs.scientificamerican.com/news-blog/the-green-space-cure-the-psychologi/.

Drahos, P., Shearing, C. D., & Burris, S. (2005). Nodal governance. *Australian Journal of Legal Philosophy, 30,* 30–58.

Duwe, G. (2018). Can circles of support and accountability (CoSA) significantly reduce sexual recidivism? Results from a randomized controlled trial in Minnesota. *Journal of Experimental Criminology, 14,* 463–484. doi: 10.1007/s11292-018-9325-7.

Evans, D. (2018, June). *Building strong communities—Righting the wrongs of history—A restorative approach to justice.* Presentation presented at the Newcastle as a Restorative City symposium, Newcastle, NSW.

Featherstone, B., Gupta, A., Morris, K., & Warner, J. (2018). Let's stop feeding the risk monster: Towards a social model of "child protection". *Families, Relationships and Societies, 7*(1), 7–22.

Fernandez, M., & Benner, K. (2018, June 21). The billion-dollar business of operating shelters for migrant children. *The New York Times.* Retrieved from www.nytimes.com/2018/06/21/us/migrant-shelters-border-crossing.html.

Forsyth, M., Kent, L., Dinnen, S., Wallis, J., & Bose, S. (2017). Hybridity in peacebuilding and development: A critical approach. *Third World Thematics, 2*(4), 407–421. https://doi.org/10.1080/23802014.2017.1448717.

Friendly, F. W. (Director), & Murrow, E. R. (Presenter). (1960). *Harvest of shame* [Television documentary]. United States: CBS Television.

Froestad, J., & Shearing, C. (2007). Beyond restorative justice—Zwelethemba, a future-focused model of local capacity conflict resolution. In R. Mackay, M. Bošnjak, J. Deklerck, C. Pelikan, B. van Stokkom, & M. Wright (Eds.), *Images of restorative justice theory* (pp. 16–34). Frankfurt, Germany: Verlag für Polizeiwissenschaft.

Gal, T. (2015). Conclusion—From social exclusion to child-inclusive policies: Toward an ecological model of child participation. In T. Gal & B. F. Duramy (Eds.), *International perspectives and empirical findings on child participation: From social exclusion to child-inclusive policies* (pp. 451–463). Oxford: Oxford University Press.

Gallagher, S., & Burford, G. (2015). Finding our way back home after being a child of the state. In T. Garfat & L. Fulcher (Eds.), *Child and youth care practice with families* (pp. 169–188). Cape Town, South Africa: CYC-Net Press.

Gavrielides, T. (2018). Victims and the restorative justice ambition: A London case study of potentials, assumptions and realities. *Contemporary Justice Review, 21*(3). doi: 10.1080/10282580.2018.1488129.

George Hull Centre for Children and Families. (n.d.). *Family group conferencing Toronto.* Retrieved from www.georgehullcentre.on.ca/family-group-conferencing-toronto.

Goodmark, L. (2012). *A troubled marriage: Domestic violence and the legal system.* New York: New York University Press.

Goodmark, L. (2018). *Decriminalizing domestic violence: A balanced policy approach to intimate partner violence.* Oakland, CA: University of California Press.

Government of Canada Department of Justice. (n.d.). *Family violence initiative: Compendium of promising practices to reduce violence and increase safety of aboriginal women in Canada—Compendium annex: Detailed practice descriptions.* Retrieved from www.justice.gc.ca/eng/rp-pr/cj-jp/fv-vf/annex-annexe/p132.html.

Government of Canada. Public Safety Canada (n.d.). The Four Circles of Hollow Water. Retrieved from www.publicsafety.gc.ca/cnt/rsrcs/pblctns/fr-crcls-hllw-wtr/index-en.aspx.

Hudson, J. (1998). Conducting the family group conference process: An overview. In T. Wachtel (Ed.), *Conferencing: A new response to wrongdoing.* Pipersville, PA: Real Justice.

Hull Centre for Restorative Practices. (n.d.). Retrieved from www.hullcentreforrestorativepractice.co.uk/?page_id=326.

ILO. (2010). *Global employment trends* (January 2010). Retrieved from www.ilo.org/wcmsp5/groups/public/—ed_emp/—emp_elm/—trends/documents/publication/wcms_120471.pdf.

Job, J., & Reinhart, M. (2003). Trusting the tax office: Does Putnam's thesis relate to tax? *Australian Journal of Social Issues, 38,* 299–332.

Kaplan, S. (1995). The restorative benefits of nature: Toward an integrative framework. *Journal of Environmental Psychology, 15,* 169–182.

Kim, J., & Kaplan, R. (2004). Physical and psychological factors in sense of community: New urbanist Kentlands and nearby orchard village. *Environment Behavior, 36,* 313–334.

Kim, M. (n.d.). *Reimagining the movement to end gender violence.* Retrieved from http://mediaforchange.org/reimagine.

Kuo, F. E., & Sullivan, W. C. (2001). Environment and crime in the inner city: Effects of environment via mental fatigue. *Environment and Behavior, 33,* 343–367.

Kweon, B. S., Sullivan, W. C., & Wiley, A. (1998). Green common spaces and the social integration of inner-city older adults. *Environment and Behavior, 30,* 832–858.

Le Chéile. (2014). *A new home for Limerick's restorative heart.* Retrieved from www.lecheile.ie/a-new-home-for-limericks-restorative-heart/.

Levi-Faur, D., & Jordana, J. (2005). The rise of regulatory capitalism: The global diffusion of a new order. *The Annals of the American Academy of Political and Social Science, 598*(1), 200–217.

Liebmann, M. (2016, June). *Building the restorative city.* Powerpoints presented at the European Forum for Restorative Justice, Leiden. Retrieved from www.euforumrj.org/wp-content/uploads/2016/07/A028-Liebmann.pdf.

Louv, R. (2012). *The nature principle: Human restoration and the end of nature-deficit disorder.* Chapel Hill, NC: Algonquin Books.

Lundahl, B. W., Kunz, C., Brownell, C., Tollefson, D., & Burke, B. L. (2010). A meta-analysis of motivational interviewing: Twenty-five years of empirical studies. *Research on Social Work Practice, 20*(2), 137–160.

Ma Mawi. (n.d.). *Wi Chi Itata. Family group conferencing.* Retrieved from www.mamawi.com/family-group-conferencing/.

Marshall, V. (2017). *Overturning aqua nullius: Securing aboriginal water rights.* Canberra: Aboriginal Studies Press.

Marshall, V. (2018). *Overturning aqua nullius—An Aboriginal perspective on personhood.* Retrieved from www.global waterforum.org/2018/04/10/overturning-aqua-nullius-an-aboriginal-perspective-on-personhood/.

Maxwell, G. M. (1993). Arrangements for children after separation? Problems and possibilities. In *Women's law conference papers: 1993 New Zealand suffrage centennial* (pp. 289–296). Wellington, NZ: Victoria University of Wellington.

Michels, R. (1915). *Political parties: A sociological study of the oligarchical tendencies of modern democracy* (E. & C. Paul, Trans.). Kitchener, Ontario: Batoche Books.

Mi'kmaw Family and Children's Services of Nova Scotia. (2018). *Family group conferencing.* Retrieved from http://mfcsns.ca/index.php/our-services/family-group-conferencing.

Mills, C. W. (2000). *The sociological imagination.* New York: Oxford University Press.

Morris, K., & Burford, G. (2017). Engaging families in managing risk in practice. In M. Connolly (Ed.), *Beyond the risk paradigm in child protection* (pp. 91–108). London, UK: Palgrave Macmillan.

Moyle, P., & Tauri, J. M. (2016). Māori, family group conferencing and the mystifications of restorative justice. *Victims & Offenders, 11,* 87–106.

New Brunswick Family Services Act, SNB 1980, c F-2.2, s 31.1(1–6). Retrieved from http://canlii.ca/t/534bf.

Nixon, P., Burford, G., Quinn, A., with Edelbaum, J. (2005, May). *A survey of international practices, policy & research on family group conferencing and related practices.* Retrieved from www.academia.edu/891986/A_survey_of_international_practices_policy_and_research_on_family_group_conferencing_and_related_practices.

O'Sullivan, D. (2017). *Beyond biculturalism: The politics of an indigenous minority.* Wellington, NZ: Huia Publications.

Osgood, C. E. (1962). *An alternative to war or surrender.* Oxford: Oxford University Press.

Parker, C. (2002). *The open corporation: Effective self-regulation and democracy.* Cambridge: Cambridge University Press.

Parton, N. (2017). Concerns about risk as a major driver of professional practice. In M. Connolly (Ed.), *Beyond the risk paradigm in child protection* (pp. 3–14). London, UK: Palgrave Macmillan.

Pennell, J., & Burford, G. (1995). *Family group decision making: New roles for 'old' partners in resolving family violence: Implementation report* (Vols. 1 & 2). St. John's, NF: Memorial University of Newfoundland, School of Social Work.

Pennell, J., & Burford, G. (2000). Family group decision making: Protecting children and women. *Child Welfare, 79*(2), 131–158.

Pennell, J., & Kim, M. (2010). Opening conversations across cultural, gender, and generational divides: Family and community engagement to stop violence against women and children. In J. Ptacek (Ed.), *Restorative justice and violence against women* (pp. 177–192). New York: Oxford University Press.

Pettit, P. (1997). *Republicanism: A theory of freedom and government.* Oxford: Oxford University Press.

Pontell, H. N. (1978). Deterrence theory versus practice. *Criminology, 16*(1), 3–22.

Power, M. (1997). *The audit society: Rituals of verification.* Oxford: Oxford University Press.

Quigley, M., Martynowicz, A., & Gardner, C. (2015). Building bridges: An independent evaluation of Le Chéile's restorative justice project. Research Findings. *Irish Probation Journal, 12,* 241–272.

Rigby, K. (1996). *Bullying in schools—and what to do about it.* Melbourne: ACER.

Rigby, K. (1997). *Bullying in schools—and what to do about it* (British ed.). London, UK: Jessica Kingsley Publishers.

Roberts, J. (2018, June 7). Restorative justice "undermining teachers". *TES.* Retrieved from www.tes.com/news/restorative-justice-undermining-teachers.

Roe, J. (2016). Cities, green space and mental wellbeing. *Environmental Science.* doi: 10.1093/acrefore/9780199389414.013.9.

Sawatsky, J. (2009). *The ethic of traditional communities and the spirit of healing justice: Studies from hollow water, the iona community, and plum village.* London, UK: Jessica Kingsley Publishers.

Schmid, J., & Morgenshtern, M. (2017). Successful, sustainable? Facilitating the growth of family group conferencing in Canada. *Journal of Family Social Work, 20*(4), 322–339.

Sen, R. N., Morris, K., Burford, G., Featherstone, B., & Webb, C. (2018). 'When you're sitting in the room with two people one of whom . . . has bashed the hell out of the other': Possibilities and challenges in the use of

FGCs and restorative practice following domestic violence. *Children and Youth Services Review, 88*, 441–449. ISSN 0190–7409.

Shearing, C. (2001). A nodal conception of governance: Thoughts on a police commission. *Policing and Society, 11*(3–4), 259–272. doi: 10.1080/10439463.2001.9964866.

Shearing, C., & Wood, J. (2003). Nodal governance, democracy and the new 'denizens'. *Journal of Law and Society, 30*(3), 400–419.

Sherman, L. W., & Barnes, G. (1997). *Restorative justice and offenders' respect for the law* (Paper 3, RISE Working Paper, Law Program, RSSS). Canberra: Australian National University.

Sherman, L. W., & Harris, H. M. (2015). Increased death rates of domestic violence victims from arresting vs. warning suspects in the Milwaukee Domestic Violence Experiment (MilDVE). *Journal of Experimental Criminology, 11*(1), 1–20.

Sherman, L. W., Strang, H., Barnes, G. C., Braithwaite, J., Inkpen, N., & the, M. M. (1998). *Experiments in restorative policing: A progress report.* Canberra: Law Program, RSSS, Australian National University.

Shlonsky, A., & Mildon, R. (2017). Assessment and decision making to improve outcomes in child protection. In M. Connolly (Ed.), *Beyond the risk paradigm in child protection* (pp. 111–129). London, UK: Palgrave Macmillan.

State of Victoria Royal Commission into Family Violence. (2016). *Summary and recommendations* (Parl Paper No. 132). Retrieved from http://files.rcfv.com.au/Reports/Final/RCFV-All-Volumes.pdf

Stubbs, J. (2010). Restorative justice, gendered violence, and Indigenous women. In J. Ptacek (Ed.), *Restorative justice and violence against women* (pp. 103–122). New York: Oxford University Press.

Sullivan, W. C., Kuo, F. E., & Depooter, S. F. (2004). The fruit of urban nature: Vital neighborhood spaces. *Environment and Behavior, 36*, 678–700.

Tienhaara, K. (2018). *Green Keynesianism and the global financial crisis.* London, UK: Routledge.

Tito Wheatland, F. (2018). Bright Ideas–from people, places and research Canberra on the journey to become a restorative city. ACT Law Reform Advisory Council (LRAC) Reference 5. LRAC, Canberra.

Toronto Public Health. (2015). *Green City: Why nature matters to health—An evidence review.* Retrieved from www. ecohealth-ontario.ca/files/Green_City_Why_Nature_Matters_to_Health_An_Evidence_Review.pdf.

Trigg, L. (2018). *Improving the quality of residential care for older people: A study of government approaches in Australia and England.* Doctoral dissertation, London School of Economics, London, UK.

University of Minnesota. (2018). *The dog commons on-leash dog trails.* Retrieved from www.arboretum.umn.edu/ DogTrails.aspx.

Van Ness, D. (2010). *RJ city: Phase 1 final report.* Washington, DC: Prison Fellowship International. Retrieved from http://restorativejustice.org/am-site/media/rj-city-final-report.pdf.

Vermont Department for Children and Families Engaging families in case planning 3 V.S.A § 5121. Retrieved from http://dcf.vermont.gov/sites/dcf/files/FSD/Policies/122.pdf.

Voss, K., & Sherman, R. (2000). Breaking the iron law of oligarchy: Union revitalization in the American labor movement. *American Journal of Sociology, 106*(2), 303–349.

Waldfogel, J. (2001). *The future of child protection: How to break the cycle of abuse and neglect.* Cambridge: Harvard University Press.

Wallis, J., Kent, L., Forsyth, M., Dinnen, S., & Bose, S. (2018). *Hybridity on the ground in peacebuilding and development.* Canberra: ANU Press.

Wood, J., & Shearing, C. (2013). *Imagining security.* London, UK: Routledge.

World Future Council. (2010). *Regenerative cities.* Retrieved from www.worldfuturecouncil.org/regenerative-cities/.

INDEX

Note: Page numbers in *italics* indicate figures and in **bold** indicate tables on the corresponding pages.

Aboriginal peoples of Australia, Ngunnawal and Ngambri 221–222
access to restorative justice 4–5
active listening 60–61
active responsibility, elicitation of 65–66
ACT Law Reform Advisory Council 221–222
Adams, P. 13, 94, 219, 221, 229
Adichie, C. N. 5
adverse childhood experiences (ACE) 198
Afghan society 216–217
After the Apology 222
AGIL scheme 80–82
agricultural migrant labor 95–99
Ahmed, E. 42–43, 44, 45
Allen, R. I. 76
Allen-Eckard, K. 220
American Academy of Social Work and Social Welfare 11
Am Not a Tractor: How Florida Farmworkers Took on the Fast Food Giants and Won 97
AMP (Awareness, Motivation and a Pathway) 21
Andrews, D. 197
anti-carceral feminists 122–123
Aotearoa New Zealand 102, 112, 212, 214, 216, 221
Arab Spring 228
Archer, M. 78–79
Aristotelian happiness 75
Army Therapeutic Community on the Central Coast of Australia 184
Arvanitidis, T. 62, 223
Asbed, G. 95
Asseserued, V. 154

Asset Based Community Development 184
Association of Title IX Administrators (ATIXA) 147, 148, 149, 150
assumptions about regulated actors and strategies 28–30, *29*
ATIXA Gender-Based and Sexual Misconduct Model Policy 147
Aung Sun Suu Kyi 228
Australian Apology 221
Australian Capital Territory (ACT) government 221–222
Authoritarianism 2; "creep" of 7, 12; family group decision making and 122; parenting style 38–39, 43, 48, 51–52
Ayres, I. 24

Bakker, I. 11–12
Banfield, E. C. 78
Baumrind, D. 39
Beattie, M. 179
Behrendt, L. 222
Best, D. 180, 191, 199, 217, 222, 224
Betty Ford Institute Consensus Panel 179
black mothers: applying restorative justice to 120–121; family group decision making (FGDM) and 121–122; feminist anti-carceral approach to domestic violence and 122–123; involved in prison 117–118; in the prison and foster care systems 117; punitive functions of foster care 119; system intersection and 119–120; transforming restorative justice for 121
Bonta, J. 197

Boyes-Watson, C. 12

Braithwaite, J. 6, 20, 21, 24, 35, 58, 66, 91, 128, 144, 170–171, 186, 201, 216; on campus sexual assault regulation 151, *151*, 151–152; on charities 183; on deterrence theory 60; on FGC as democracy-building, community-enhancing practice 94; on importance history 61; intimate partner violence and deterrence-based strategy proposed by 174–175; on Michael Milkin 227–228; recovery capital model and 188, 189; rejection of retribution and punishment by 130–131; on willingness to act with authority 184

Braithwaite, V. 9, 13, 20, 35, 120, 211

Brown, M. 213

Brown, S. 205

bullying: community support for interventions for 50; conclusions on 52–53; emotional architecture that sustains 43–45; flushing action of responsive regulation for 49–50; institutional impediments in addressing 51–52; managing institutional resistance with 46–47; phenomenon of the bully-victim and 42–43; public campaigns against 41–42; soft 45–46; using responsive regulation with 47–48; what we know about 41–42

Burchard, J. 119

Burchard, S. 119

Burford, G. 76, 92, 97, 191, 219, 220

Campaign for Fair Food 97

Campus PRISM Project 143, 151

Campus SaVE Act (Campus Sexual Violence Elimination Act of 2013) 145

Canberra Restorative Community 222

Cano, I. 180

capacity development 29, *29*; engaging networks for 66–67; sanctions for 61–64; through innovation 63–64

carceral control of citizens 117, 170–171

carceral creep 12

carceral "dance" of criminal justice xiv

carceral feminism 122–123, 222–223

carceral regulation 117

carceral state 116–117, 120, 140, 170, 221

carceral systems of prison and foster care 116–117, 120–122

care giver and care taker relationship 79

Carrà, E. 223

Center for the Study of Social Policy Racial Equity Review 119

Child Abuse Prevention and Treatment Act (CAPTA) 103

child and family team meetings (CFTs) 101–102; structure of 103–105

children: in child and family teams in North Carolina 103–105 (*See also* Community Child Protection Team (CCPT)); in foster care 118–119; hopes of, within converging family and state networks of regulation 100–102; included in family meetings 102–103, 110–113; of mothers in prison 118, 120

Children, Young Persons and Their Families Act (New Zealand) 212–213

CHIME (Connectedness, Hope, Identity, Meaning, and Empowerment) human services 192–193, 211, 224

Christie, N. 170, 202

Chu, J. 57

Circles of Support and Accountability (CoSA) 157; closing remarks on 206; mechanics of 203–204; origins of 201–202; proliferation of 205–206; roots of 202–203; in Vermont 204–205

Citizens Advice Bureau 187

civil penalties *24*, 25

Clarke, M. 205

Clery Act (Jeanne Clery Disclosure of Campus Security Policy and Campus Crime Statistics Act of 1990) 145

Cloud, W. 180

Coalition of Immokalee Workers (CIW) 95–98

Coker, D. 12, 148, 173

Coleman, J. S. 78

collective commitment to listen and learn 60–61

collectivism 78

Colson, C. 228

Community Child Protection Team (CCPT) 101–102, 103–105, 220; discussion of 110–113; research results 106–110, **107**, **108**, **109**; research surveys 105–106

community recovery capital 180

community support for bullying interventions 50

Conditional Sentence Orders (CSO) 64–65

conservative welfare regimes 77–78

Convention on the Rights of the Child 112

co-production 75

Correctional Service of Canada (CSC) 201–202

Cortina, L. M. 176

creep of crime and commodification 12

crime logic xiv, 31, 59–60

Criminal Code 61

criminal penalties *24*, 25

criminalization 28, 224; brief history of 166–168; of intimate partner violence 165–166, 168, 172

crowdsourced policing 67, 69

culture of child inclusion 111–113

Daily, K. 174–175

Dalhousie Dentistry case: Academic Standards Class Committee (ASCC) 137–138; concluding reflections on 139–141; introduction to 127; relational understanding of the issues in 132–134; relational understanding of the parties and their roles in 134–136; responding to relational complexity in 127–132; responses to 132–141; responsive regulation for restorative justice in 136–139; restorative justice in 132–136

Daly, K. 220

"Danger of the Single Story, The" 5

Davis, A. 120

Death and Life of Great American Cities, The 203

defamilization 77–78

deinstitutionalization 212

democratic parenting 39–40

Department of Education Office of Civil Rights (OCR) 145, 155

desistance from sexual violence 199

deterrence-based strategy 29, *29*, 60, 174–175

DeVerteuil, G. 184

Dixon, R. 45

domestic violence 122–123; mandatory arrest laws for 166–167; *see also* intimate partner violence, criminalization of

Donati, P. 78–79, 80

Dorosh case 62

Drahos, P. 1, 9, 186

Durfee, A. 168

Duwe, G. 205, 223

elicitation of active responsibility 65–66

Elva, T. 171

emotional architecture that sustains bullying 43–45

empowerment 91, 92–93

enforcement pyramid *32*, 32–33

Esping-Andersen, G. 11, 74

Espinoza, L. 98

explorative model for analyzing familiness 80–83, *82*, **83**

Fair Food Program (FFP) 96, 97

Fair Food Standards Council (FFSC) 96–97

fairness, perception of 190

families and schools: benefits of responsive regulation for society, 40–41; bullying and 41–46; community support for interventions for 50; conclusions on 52–53; culture of child inclusion in 111–113; family group decision making (FGDM) and 121–122; flushing action of responsive regulation for 49–50; formal education and 41; institutional impediments in addressing bullying for 51–52; managing institutional resistance for 46–47; normalising responsive regulation and restorative practices for 38–41; using responsive regulation with difficult behavior in 47–48

familiness: defamilization, welfare regimes and family social capital in 77–78; evidence-based supports to 76–77; explorative model for analyzing 80–83, *82*, **83**; moving towards responsive regulatory pyramid for 83–85, *84*; relational sociology and 74–75

family centeredness 76

Family Group Conferencing (FGC) *82*, 82–83, **83**, 92; inclusion of children in 102–103; *see also* child and family team meetings (CFTs)

family group decision making (FGDM) 121–122

family impact 77

family relationships, importance of 79–80

family social capital 77–78

farmworkers 95–99

Farrall, S. 200

Farrington, D. P. 44, 46

feminist anti-carceral approach to domestic violence 122–123

flushing action of responsive regulation 49–50

focused deterrence 174–175

forbearance as principle of just practice and policy 6

formalism, regulatory *see* regulatory formalism

formal schooling: bullying in 41–46; managing institutional resistance in 46–47

foster care system *See* prison and foster care systems

Fox, K. J. 199, 200, 205, 206

Freire, P. 98

Funderburg, R. 3

Furlong, J. 63

Gadaffi, M. 228

Gal, T. 102–103, 113, 220

GambleAware (GA) 181, 183, 188–189, 192

Gavrielides, T. 62

Gersen, J. 146

Ghai, D. 11, 13

Gill, S. 11–12

Global Financial Crisis 227

Golden Rule, the 7

Good Lives model 197–198

Goodmark, L. 217, 219, 222

Grabosky, P. 8

GMAR (Grandmothers Against Removal) 222

GRIT (Graduated Reciprocation in Tenison Reudction) 224

Granfield, R. 180

Green New Deal 227

Growing Up in Australia: the Longitudinal Study of Australian Children (LSAC) 42–43

Gunningham, N. 8

Hackett, C. 12

Halperin, R. 120

Hanan, E. M. 3

Hanson, R. K. 195

harm minimization 27, *27*, 27–28

harmony values 46

Harris, H. M. 218

Harris, J. L. 120

Harris, N. 68, 120

Harvest of Shame 95, 221
Hayek, F. 93
Heiner, B. 12
Hitov, S. 95, 98
Holland, K. J. 176
Hollow Water 220, 225
Hong, S. H. 10
ho'oponopono 92
hope, collective *vs.* individual 185
Hopkins, B. 41
Hudson, J. 92, 97, 220
Hull, UK 214–216, 220
human services: CHIME (Connectedness, Hope, Identity, Meaning, and Empowerment) 192–193, 211, 224; in justice reform context 11–13; learning from regulatory imagination and 228–229; making the personal political in struggles for 211–214; re-centering justice in 13–14; relational sociology approach in (*see* relational sociology)
Hunting Ground, The 144
Hussein, S. 228
hybridity of state/community/market provision 215–217, 229
hybridization of governance 14

incapacitation 29, *29*
indigenous justice approaches 7–8, 92–93
individualization 75, 77–78
innovation, capacity building through 63–64
institutional impediments in addressing bullying 51–52
institutional resistance, management of 46–47
International Institute for Restorative Practices (IIRP) 6
intimate partner violence, criminalization of: brief history of 166–168; challenges to using restorative justice in 172–174; conclusions on 176; introduction to 165–166; responsive regulation in 174–176; restorative justice and 168–174; victim/offender binary and 171–172
Ivec, M. 120
Iverson, S. V. 150

Jacobs, J. 203
Job, J. 50
just law 131

Karp, D. 218, 220
Karstedt, S. 64
Keefe, D. J. 63
Kim, M. 10, 12, 219
Kipnis, L. 150
"Know Your IX" 144
Krygier, M. 186

Latz, M. 220
Laudet, A. 180

law reform 23
law reform ritualism, limits of 217–222
Leamy, M. 192
Leeds, UK 214, 216
Lejano, R. P. 3
Levi-Faur, D. 14
liberal welfare regimes 77–78
license revocation *24*, 25
license suspension *24*, 25
Life at School Survey 50
Lisak, D. 148
listening, active 60–61
Llewellyn, J. 215, 216, 219, 224, 229
Lofgreen 148
Longabaugh, R. 179
Lovitt, F. 2

Mabbett, D. 12
MacIntyre, A. 93
Ma Mawi 220
mandatory arrest laws for domestic violence 166–167
mandatory reporting for child sexual assault 217, 218
Māori Renaissance Tribunal 221
Marquis, S. L. 97, 98
Martinson, R. 196
Maruna, S. 199, 200
Maslow, A. 204
Maxwell, G. 220
May, E. 61
McCold, P. 6
Medicaid 21
Medicare 21
#MeToo 195
Michels, R. 210
Milkin, M. 227–228
Miller, P. 148
Missoula 144
morphogenetic theory 78–79
Morris, K. 76
Morrison, B. 46, 51, 223
Moyle, P. 213
Mugford, S. 27
multiple selves 30–31
MUM test 228–229
Murphy 63, 190
Murrow, E. R. 95, 221
Musgrove, A. 199, 222, 224

Nader, R. 227
"naming-and-shaming" 68
National Citizens Coalition for Nursing Home Reform 21, 22
National Observatory of the Family 76
Neave, M. 220
Nelson, K. 13

neoliberalism 12, 14, 117; austerity and 5; commodification and 216–217; neoliberal response to caregiving 119; noncarceral responses to violence and 140; social inequality and 116–117; as state regulation 117; welfare restructuring and 119
Neustadt, R. 61
Newfoundland and Labrador, Canada 219
New Brunswick, Canada 213
Night the City Became a Stadium, The 57
Nixon, P. 111
no-drop laws 11, 166–168, 217–218; non-compliance 40
normalising of responsive regulation and restorative practices 38–41
North Carolina Collaborative for Children, Youth, and Families 112
Nothing Works doctrine 196–199
Novak, M. 94
Nova Scotia, CA; Nova Scotia Restorative Justice Community University Research Alliance 127, 215–216; Halifax restorative city 127, 214, 216
nuclear option, being wary of the 34
nursing home industry, regulation of 23

Obama, B. 144, 227
Occupy movement 227
Olweus, D. 46
optimum harm minimization *27*, 27–28
oral traditions 7
origin stories 7, 8
Orlandini, M. 75
out-groups 68

parenting, democratic 39–40
Parker, C. 186
Pavela, G. 149
Peel, R. 202
Peepre case 62
Pellegrino, E. D. 93
Pennell, J. 191, 213, 219, 220, 220219
personalization 75
personal recovery capital 180
persuasion *24, 25*
Petr, G. C. 76
Petrich, D. M. 199
Pettit, P. 2
PEW Research Center 9
Platinum Golden Rule 228–229
Postmes, T. 62
Prandini, R. 75
Pranis, K. 214
Pride: healthy 6, 171, 184, 189, 191; management of 6, 60; professional 22; unhealthy 6
prison and foster care systems: applying restorative justice to black mothers in 120–123; black mothers in the 117–119; family group decision making (FGDM) and 121–122; feminist anti-carceral approach to domestic violence and 122–123; introduction to 116–117; system intersection 119–120; women as fastest growing group in 117–118
Prison Fellowship International 214, 228
procedural justice 35, 48, 190; anti-bullying policies and 47–48; in child protection 103–104, 120; failures of 190; restorative justice with 63; sexual assault and 143, 144, 147–148, 160
Psychology of Criminal Conduct, The 197
public health interventionists 11
Purposes and Principles of Sentencing 61
Putnam, R. D. 78
pyramids, regulatory *24*, 24–25, 130; familiness and 83–85, *84*; optimum harm minimization in *27*, 27–28; redundancy in 25–27, *26*; regulatory capital and 189–190; strengths-based pyramid 31–34, *32*

Ramsey, C. 166
RAND Corporation 97
Rankist prizes, rankism 33, 35n1
Reason, J. 26
re-centering justice in human services 13–14
Recovery capital model 80; categories of recovery resources in 180; characteristics of strengths-based approach at systems level in 183–185; human services that CHIME in 192–193; introduction to 179–183, *182*; Recovery-Oriented Systems of Care in 181, *182*, 186–187; regulatory capital and use of sanctions in 189–192, *190*; regulatory mechanisms in *186*, 186–192, *190*; strength-based approaches to managing systems in 183; therapeutic landscape for recovery in 184
Recovery-Oriented Systems of Care (ROSC) 181, *182*, 186–187
redundancy in pyramid design 25–27, *26*
reentry circles for students accused of sexual misconduct 157–158
Rees, J. 34
regulatory capital and use of sanctions 189–192, *190*
regulatory capture: averting 226–228; corruption 5, 10, 25, 187
Regulatory Diamond 192–193
regulatory formalism 60; higher education sexual assault adjudication and 145–147, *146*; unanticipated consequences of 147–151; undermining female agency 150–151
regulatory hotspots 3
regulatory mechanisms in recovery capital model *186*, 186–192, *190*
regulatory overreach 9
regulatory pyramid *see* pyramids, regulatory
Reicher, S. 63

Reinhart, M. 50

relational complexity 3, 13; hybridity of state/community/market provision and 215; nuanced hybridity and 229; regulatory capitalism and 229; relational understanding of issues and 132–134; relational understanding of parties and their roles and 134–136; as required for responsiveness 219; responding to 127–141; responsive regulation for restorative justice and 60, 136–139; in sexual encounters 150–151

relational good 79

relational-restorative contexts 5–7

relational sociology: defamilization, welfare regimes and family social capital in 77–78; evidence-based supports to familiness in 76–77; explorative model for analyzing familiness in 80–83, *82*, **83**; familiness and responsiveness in approach of 74–75; as theoretical framework for evidence-based family-centered pratices 78–80; *see also* Dalhousie Dentistry case

religion 7

republican democracy 2–4; freedom as non-domination 2, 129, 210–211

responsive regulation 1, 2–4, 9–11; assumptions about regulated actors and strategies in 28–30, *29*; be wary of nuclear option in 34; beyond regulatory formalism in 60; challenge of understanding 22–24; collective commitment to listen and learn in 60–61; conclusion on 35; in Dalhousie case 136–139; Dalhousie case and importance of 139–141; flushing action of 49–50; of intimate partner violence 174–175; learning, evaluating and communicating in 69–70; learning from human services and 228–229; naïveity in 226–228; normalising of 38–41; opportunity to hear from victims and 64–65; reasons for 210–211; regulatory pyramids in *24*, 24–25 (*see also* pyramids, regulatory); responding to relational complexity with 127–132; restorative justice as, in campus sexual assault cases *151*, 151–158, *153*; riots and 58; sanctions that build capacity in 61–63; signaling a range of sanctions in 66; supports and sanctions in 31–34, *32*; types of 20–22; ugly side of 224–226; understanding multiple selves and 30–31; used with difficult behavior 47–48; virtues of 223–224; without the state 95–99

Responsive Regulation 24

Restorative City model and restorative networks 214–215; Belfast, Ireland 214; Bristol, England 214; Detroit, US 214; Halifax, Nova Scotia, Canada 127, 215–216; Hull, UK 214–216, 220; Leeds, UK 214, 216; Nova Scotia, Canada 127, 214, 216, 220; Wanganui, New Zealand

restorative journey 7–8

restorative justice 1; access to 4–5; applied to black mothers 120–123; attending to relational-restorative contexts 5–7; elicitation of active responsibility in 65–66; empowerment in 91, 92–93; feminist anti-carceral approach to domestic violence and 122–123; as forward-thinking 3; hybridity of state/community/market provision in 215–217; indigenous practices in 92–93; for intimate partner violence 168–174; learning, evaluating and communicating in 69–70; limits of law reform ritualism in 217–222; normalising of 38–41; praxis, process, social movement and law in 4–7; reasons for 210–211; as regulatory strategy 29, *29*; responding to relational complexity with 127–132; responsive regulation, republican democracy and 2–4; as responsive regulation for campus sexual assault *151*, 151–158, *153*; Restorative City model in 214–215; riots and 58; for sexual violence 199–206; signaling a range of sanctions in 66; in Vermont 204–205; virtues in 93, 222–223, 232; without the state 95–99

Restorative Justice and Responsive Regulation 170

restorative practices continuum 6

restorative processes in sexual violence prevention 201–204

restraint in aged care 20–22

Review, The 66

Riestenberg, N. 51

Rigby, K. 43, 220

Riley, K. 122

riots, Vancouver: active engagement in prosecution and conviction of participants in 58–60; beyond regulatory formalism in 60; capacity building through innovation after 63–64; collective commitment to listen and learn from 60–61; direct, secondary, and tertiary impacts of 67; elicitation of active responsibility after 65–66; engaging networks that develop capacities and benefits for 66–67; learning, evaluating and communicating after 69–70; opportunity to hear from victims of 64–65; responsive regulation and restorative justice and 58; ritual of formalized criminal justice and 56–58; sanctions that build capacity after 61–63; signaling a range of sanctions after 66; signaling support and education to participants in 68–69

RISE experiments Canberra 220

Risk-Need-Responsivity model (RNR) 195, 197–198, 223

risk prevention, "Swiss Cheese" model of 26

Roberts, D. 218, 222

Rolling Stone 144

RSVP Restorative Spaces Vistas and Places 214–215

R v Loewen 56, 58–59, 64

Saito, N. T. 12

sanctions, capacity-building: innovation in 63–64; regulatory capital and use of 189–192, *190*; signaling denunciation with restraint 61–63

sanctions, signaling a range of 66
sanctions pyramid 49–50
Sandler, J. C. 195
Schiff, M. 47, 51
Schneider, C. 69
Schorr, L. 13
school culture 46–47
school-to-prison pipeline 47
secondary desistance 200
security values 46–47
self-regulation 23–24, 40, 91–92, 197
Selznick, P. 10
sexual assault policies, campus: accused students
    believing the process is illegitimate and filing more
    lawsuits with 149; accused students expressing
    greater denials of responsibility with 149; adversarial
    adjudication exaggerating biased decision-
    making with 148–149; campus communities
    becoming polarized and anxiety growing with
    148; conclusions on **159**, 159–161; defining the
    problem of sexual and gender-based misconduct
    and 144, **144**; disparities growing between
    rich and poor, white and black with 149–150;
    informal *vs.* formal process in 160; introduction
    to 143–144; not increasing reporting by survivors
    147–148; opportunity and pressure to participate
    in restorative justice programs for **159**, 159–160;
    public accountability in 160; regulatory formalism
    undermining female agency in 150–151; safety
    and 160–161; Title IX guidance and regulatory
    formalism and 145–147, *146*; unintended
    consequences of regulatory formalism in 147–151
sexual harassment case, Dalhousie *see* Dalhousie
    Dentistry case
sexual violence: desistance and 199; introduction to
    195–196; 'nothing works' and the rise of effective
    interventions for 196–199; proliferation of
    CoSA model for 205–206; restorative justice and
    transformative processes for 199–206; restorative
    processes in prevention of 201–204; Vermont's
    commitment to restorative justice for 204–205
shame and stigmatization 6–7; in bullying 44, 45;
    healthy shame 6; shame management 6–7, 44–45;
    stereotypes of black maternal unfitness 119
Sharpe, S. 60
Sherman, L. W. 149, 218
Shin, H. 42–43, 44
Sinclair, D. 8
Smith, P. 45
Smith, P. K. 43, 48
social capital, family 77–78
socialist welfare regimes 77–78
social justice 79, 93–94; responsive and restorative
    practices in 95–99
social recovery capital 180

societal perceptions of justice 66
soft bullying 45–46
*South of Forgiveness: A True Story of Rape and
    Responsibility* 171
Spears, R. 62
Stanley Cup riot *see* riots, Vancouver
state, responsive and restorative practices without the
    95–99
state laws on campus sexual assault 145–146
Strang, H. 65
Stranger, T. 171
strengths-based approaches to managing systems 183;
    characteristics of 183–185
strengths-based pyramid 31–34, *32*
student misconduct case *see* Dalhousie Dentistry case
subsidiarity as principle of just practice and policy:
    multiple selves and 30–31; optimum harm
    minimization and 27–28; redundancy and 25–26;
    regulated actors in 28–29; regulatory pyramid and
    24–25, 31–34
Substance Abuse and Mental Health Services
    Administration (SAMHSA) 181
Suk, J. 146
Sutcliffe, A. 228
Swartout, K. 148
"Swiss Cheese" model of risk prevention 26

Tauri, J. M. 213
technocratic regulation 51–52
Therapeutic Community (TC) 185
therapeutic landscape for recovery 184
*Think Family: A Literature Review of Whole Family
    Approaches* 76
Thomasma, D. C. 93
Three-Mile Island disaster 34
Time 144
Time's Up 195
Title IX legislation 143, 145–147, *146*, 155
Tocqueville, A. de 94
Tomlinson, C. 220
Treaty of Waitangi 221, 225
tripartitism 5–6, 10, 70, 186
Trottier, D. 69
Trump, D. 144
Ttofi, M. M. 44, 46
Tyler, T. 63
Tyson, S. 12

UK Drug Policy Commission 179
Untie the Elderly Campaign 21, 30
Unwanted Advances: Sexual Paranoia Comes to Campus 144
US Children's Bureau 113

Vancouver Province 69
Vancouver riot *see* riots, Vancouver

Van Ness, D. 214
VAWA (Violence Against Women Act of 1994) 145, 167
Vermont, restorative justice in 204–205
Vermont Law School 4
victims, hearing from 64–65
virtues 93; responsive regulation 223–224; restorative justice 222–223; social justice 79, 93–94
virtuous actor 91
Völlm, B. 205

Ward, T. 199
warning letters *24*, 25
welfare regimes, familiness in 74–75, 77–78
Welfare States in Transition 11
Whalley, E. 12

whānau hui 92
whole-family approaches in relational sociology 76
Williams case 62
Wilson, R. J. 195
Wilson and fox 223
Wilton, R. 184
Wi Parata v Bishop of Wellington 221
Wong, D. S. W. 46
Woodruff, K. 175
World Health Organisation (WHO) 179

Yantzi, M. 201
You, J. S. 10

Zehr, H. 127
Zellerer, E. 57